Lynching in America

Lynching in America

A History in Documents

EDITED BY

Christopher Waldrep

New York University Press

NEW YORK AND LONDON

NEW YORK UNIVERSITY PRESS
New York and London
www.nyupress.org

Library of Congress Cataloging-in-Publication Data
Lynching in America : a history in documents / edited by Christopher Waldrep.
p. cm.
Includes bibliographical references and index.
ISBN–13: 978–0–8147–9398–5 (cloth : alk. paper)
ISBN–10: 0–8147–9398–3 (cloth : alk. paper)
ISBN–13: 978–0–8147–9399–2 (pbk. : alk. paper)
ISBN–10: 0–8147–9399–1 (pbk. : alk. paper)
1. Lynching—United States—History.   I. Waldrep, Christopher, 1951–
HV6457.L95   2005
364.1'34—dc22   2005015600

New York University Press books are printed on acid-free paper,
and their binding materials are chosen for strength and durability.

For Pamela, Janelle, and Andrea

Contents

Acknowledgments

Deborah Gershenowitz conceived of this project before I did and remained enthusiastic as I worked through it. Martha Hunt Huie once again provided not just permission but encouragement. Rachel Van, Michael Mott, and Ann Wilson all took time from their own work to track down documents for this volume. The most essential support came from my family—Pamela, Janelle, and Andrea.

Prologue

Early in 2000 journalists began to report the news: the Atlanta antiques dealer James Allen had opened an exhibit of sixty-eight lynching photographs in a tiny New York art gallery, the Roth Horowitz. For decades writers had used text and narrative to document the same horrors that Allen's photographs depicted; nevertheless, no text could match the visual impact of these horrifying pictures. People lined up to get in, Stevie Wonder wanted a personal tour, and the *New York Times* assessed the exhibit first in a lengthy review and then in an article on its editorial page. The editorial writer reported he could hardly stand to look at the pictures. "There is," he said, "an unbearable measure of horror here that I have no interest in learning to endure." Allen's images prompted the *New York Times* to compare white America's war on African Americans to the Nazi Holocaust.[1]

The Allen exhibit crested a scholarly wave. Writers like Ida B. Wells, James E. Cutler, Arthur Raper, and Walter White had documented the horrors of lynching early in the twentieth century, but in 1951 C. Vann Woodward could still dismiss lynching with a single paragraph in *Origins of the New South, 1877–1913*.[2] In the 1960s American civil rights and antiwar protest kindled academic sympathy for "crowds"—they should not be called "mobs," we were cautioned. As is so often the case, American academics followed a European example. George Rudé had already rehabilitated European mobs as more purposeful and less violent than previously thought.[3] They had a "moral economy," E. P. Thompson asserted, becoming almost indignant that anyone would dare think a mob or crowd "spasmodic." Common people deserved more respect than that, he wrote.[4] The American Revolution proved a fruitful vineyard for making the same kind of findings in America. Leading American historians wrote that revolutionaries enforced their public virtue only after their colonial governments failed them.[5] Even brawling sailors, we learned, really fought for freedom and liberty.[6] Other researchers looked askance at Victorians' facile and class-based hostility toward crowd behavior.[7] Paul Gilje quoted Gouverneur Morris as saying, "The mob begin to think and reason." Gilje observed that this summed up the scholarship; historians had found the rationality in mob violence.[8]

We now know that those scholars had a gigantic blind spot, one Joel Williamson confessed in 1997. Williamson wrote after Clarence Thomas had battled the U.S. Senate for a seat on the Supreme Court. Confronted with allegations of sexual impropriety, Thomas had charged that the white senators raising the questions actually wanted to *lynch* him. This powerful language, visibly stunning the liberal Democrats arrayed against him, helped turn public opinion to Thomas's side. Thomas's language caught academics off guard. They had done little or no work on the meaning of lynching, the power of the word as rhetoric. Six years after Clarence Thomas, Joel Williamson still struggled to understand what had happened.

As a young white southerner, Williamson confessed, he had only vague ideas about lynching. The 1940 movie *The Ox-Bow Incident* connected mob law to westerners and cattle rustling in his mind. Williamson discovered the "horrendous wave of lynching" only some time after his 1965 book. "To my mind, this was something new on the land. Nothing in my living experience as a southerner and an American, nothing in my training and practice as a historian and professor, had prepared me for this." Jacquelyn Dowd Hall did not publish *Revolt against Chivalry,* with its powerfully influential chapter on lynching, until 1979. Historians, she wrote, "paid remarkably little attention to the phenomenon."[9]

Leonard Dinnerstein's book on the Leo Frank lynching preceded *Revolt against Chivalry,*[10] but the real rush came after Hall's monograph, in the 1980s. Not just academics but journalists, too, joined a small stampede of writers rushing to look at lynching.[11] Important scholars, authors of major books that did not touch lynching, now took up the subject, following Joel Williamson.[12] Scholars of all stripes examined single incidents and published broader surveys.[13] Lynching also began to appear more prominently in broader history works, books that once might have overlooked the topic.[14]

Through all this I had been collecting not pictures but words about lynching, newspaper articles, government documents, and manuscripts. James Allen's photographs, ranging from 1870 to 1960, with most falling between 1880 and 1940, make a kind of metaphor for scholars' lynching studies. Most follow the same time period and most served a similar purpose, revealing racist mob law for its shockingly savage barbarism. I sought a wider picture, from the first American to utter the word to the present. I was interested in how ordinary people connected with their Constitution and I realized that people formed mobs when they lost confidence in the abilities of their courts and government to protect them from crime. While American history textbooks tended to celebrate the nation's commitment to constitutionalism, I found the darker side of American history. Americans have always had only a tenuous hold on law and a faltering commitment to due process. Political expediency and talent for organizing and mobilizing crowds has always powerfully appealed to Americans.

The result is a history of lynching, albeit one that differs a bit from the usual story focused only on exposing lynchers' malevolence. Most writing about lynching, like Allen's photographs, teaches us only the evils of racial violence, not how that evil took root and metastasized. Images of lynchings capture a reality about lynching scholarship, presenting Judge Lynch's victims poignantly but also silently.[15] Images do not engage the process by which most Americans learned about lynching—through printed narratives, stories told and repeated and distributed for sale. One historian has written that even the lynchers learned their rituals by reading of other lynchings. Most important, circulation of lynching stories became a strategy for the reformers opposed to mob law. Reformers learned that the white newspaper readers indifferent to the plight of black Americans could be won over with blood curdling accounts of cruelty, violence, and anarchic disorder. African American voices—not only Ida B.

Wells and W. E. B. Du Bois, but ordinary men and women as well—spoke powerfully against lynching. The relationship between journalism and mob violence remains one of the most understudied aspects of lynching.

As I have said elsewhere, the word "lynching" cannot be defined. That is its most important characteristic: it is a rhetorical dagger ready to be picked up and deployed by a host of actors in a variety of circumstances. For the purposes of this book it may be helpful to remember a common nineteenth-century understanding of the word's meaning. Nineteenth-century people defined lynching as violence sanctioned, endorsed, or carried out by a neighborhood or community acting outside the law. They did not bother to define "community" but probably understood the term to mean people living near one another and sharing a common ethic.[16] Often the chief lyncher, or lynch mob leader, is called "Judge Lynch." Sometimes "Judge Lynch" takes on mythical proportions to become the symbol of all violent mobbing. Thus, when a newspaper reports that "Judge Lynch" has acted, the paper means that a mob has struck. Similarly "Lynch law" is not law at all but rather its opposite: violent "justice" administered by a mob outside the law. The very terms we associate with mob violence mock the normal workings of courts and lawyers.

Through the twentieth century journalists created a dominant narrative and circulated it to ever expanding audiences. Some credit the political process with allowing and even encouraging the growth of media power that made mass media criticism of lynching possible. But public opinion organized against mob law in defiance of the formal political process. No political decision or government practice brought down mob law. Better technology—high-speed printing presses, telephones, radio, the telegraph—exposed the violence of isolated communities to national scrutiny at the same time politicians tried and failed to move against mob law. The ugly truth is that American political leaders almost never made or successfully enforced laws against lynching when confronted with mob violence. And yet mob violence eventually fell into disrepute anyway.

The introduction to this book reviews Americans' conversation about lynching from Ida B. Wells through the twentieth century. In essence, the introduction surveys modern explanations of lynching. It is intended as a kind of guide for the rest of the book. Or, perhaps, we should think of the rest of the book as an opportunity to test the lynching explanations proposed by modern writers. Particular explanations for lynching turn up over and over again, in a variety of guises, but essentially repeat the same fundamental points.

Chapter 1 documents the stories Americans tell about the origins of lynch law. Of course, the behavior of mobbing is timeless; the earliest humans must have formed violent crowds and targeted individuals that violated some social norm. Nonetheless, Americans have ceaselessly sought the "first" lyncher. The word "lynching" has always involved storytelling, narrative, efforts to mythologize its origins. These stories do not represent objective quests for truth. People tell particular stories about the origins of lynching to condemn or justify the practice.

Chapter 2 examines lynching in Jacksonian America. Andrew Jackson served as president from 1829 until 1837, but his promotion of democracy for white men has grafted his name onto a larger era. A whole series of political decisions entrenched lynch law in American life. A particularly critical moment came when President Jackson seemingly endorsed a localized version of popular sovereignty that made violent punishment of crime outside the law feel legitimate, just, and necessary to many ordinary Americans.

Chapter 3 shows how slavery promoted extralegal violence. Whites felt empowered by the laws and customs associated with slavery to punish black people outside the law. Chapter 4 tracks how western migration promoted lynching. Moving into supposedly lawless frontier regions led migrants to make their own law. The nation's press largely approved. White southerners pointed to western lynching as justifying their own extralegal violence. Across the country lynching won new legitimacy.

Chapter 5 looks at the impact of the Civil War and Reconstruction on American lynching culture. Abraham Lincoln and the Republicans proclaimed themselves defenders of the Constitution, and champions of law and order against anarchy. They sought to increase federal power and proposed policing heretofore autonomous neighborhoods. They took on the Ku Klux Klan, a vigilante force determined to defend neighborhood extralegal policing. The white South did not back down. Chapter 6 shows the rise of racialized lynching. In the last decades of the nineteenth century whites sought to exclude blacks from voting or any other political office. They more openly relied on violence to maintain their racist regime. At the same time more African Americans boldly protested; black newspapers flourished as never before. At the end of the nineteenth century powerful media giants marshaled their forces. The number of periodicals with a circulation of one hundred thousand quadrupled between 1885 and 1900. In the first years of the twentieth century magazines began to achieve circulations of one million and more.[17] In this era African Americans found they could effectively denounce whites' racial violence because cheap newspaper technology and a subsidized postal service gave them the means to do so.

It is a measure of just how committed most Americans were to mob law that even when state officials tried to stop mobbing, they failed, as becomes clear in chapter 7. While white southern governors shared the same racist ideology promoted by lynchers, they still feared disorder and anarchy. These governors regularly called out state militia units to fight mobs. Their efforts failed largely because they could not overcome the prevailing gender dynamic. White men posed as defenders of their women. Lynchers could always accuse law enforcement of breaching that ethos when state officers stood between a mob and a black man accused of any crime, not just rape.

Chapter 8 returns to the West, this time looking at westerners' mob violence in an age of industrialization. The growth of cities, the spread of railway transportation, and industrialization generally sentimentalized the "Old West" and provided fresh incentives for men to prove their manhood outside the law. On a per capita basis, western lynching outstripped the southern variety during this period. Lynching in the late nineteenth and early twentieth centuries coincided with the growth of powerful new magazines and newspapers. Investigative reporters exposed social evils to eager audiences. But these investigators did little with lynching. Chapter 9 charts the limits of progressive reform.

Chapter 10 tracks the minimal and halting efforts by the federal government to attack lynching early in the twentieth century. The same Republican Party that had once fought vigorously for civil rights measures now stalled, apparently more interested in reconciliation with the South than in equal rights for all American citizens.

Chapter 11 shows early federal efforts to attack lynching. When the federal government finally did begin to act, it moved tentatively, timidly, and then not at all. This changed after 1939. Contrary to the claims of some authors, President Franklin D. Roosevelt's Federal Bureau of Investigation energetically investigated lynchings, as is shown in chapter 12. Under President Roosevelt, the federal government vigorously investigated and prosecuted lynchers. Although often thwarted by local juries and a recalcitrant Supreme Court, the DOJ pledged to investigate every reported lynching in the country and, for a decade, did so. But while the Justice Department genuinely tried to prosecute the lynchers, this intervention faltered, to such an extent that historians sometimes still deny it ever happened or downplay its significance.[18]

The final chapter looks at lynching after federal efforts stumbled. The famous lynchings of the mid-twentieth century are well known not because government investigators brought them to the attention of the American people or because some politician denounced them in soaring rhetoric, but because market-based journalists used their increasingly sophisticated technology to break into isolated communities and expose once local practices to a national audience and national condemnation. Under President Dwight D. Eisenhower, the Department of Justice called off its efforts to prosecute lynchers. But news media interest in mob violence accelerated. Even so, scholars emerged in the late 1960s to defend mob violence, when carried out by the "good" people of a community for the purpose of achieving positive good. In this intellectually confused environment, Clarence Thomas could plausibly claim to have been "lynched" by a Senate committee investigating his alleged sexual improprieties.

American lynching is a story of private enterprise—journalism—exposing lynching to national audiences. Governmental efforts to control lynching failed. Political process failed. The federal government refused to outlaw lynching. According to a leading scholar of civil rights law, mob law prevented Supreme Court justices from fully implementing their decisions, rendering toothless one judicial command after another on behalf of racial justice. After *Moore v. Dempsey* (1923), white southerners continued to subject black defendants to kangaroo courts. After *Powell v. Alabama* (1932), white southerners continued to deny black defendants meaningful counsel. After *Norris v. Alabama* (1935), white southerners kept blacks off juries. After *Brown v. Mississippi* (1936), white sheriffs tortured black suspects. Publicity campaigns by the National Association for the Advancement of Colored People and other groups pressured the Court to render these decisions. Mob law rendered them meaningless. Because they feared localized violence would prevent vigorous enforcement, the justices did not dare push too hard for real change.[19] The civil rights revolution came only after lynching lost its legitimacy.

It was once said that only Americans lynch. But Americans did not invent the behavior of lynching. The urge to join a crowd against a scapegoat is too elemental, instinctive, for that. Instead, Americans invented the word and the rhetoric used to condemn the practice and created the media that would carry that condemnation across a continent and around the world, making possible a great movement for freedom.

. . .

A note on the editorial method: These documents are drawn from a wide variety of sources, including edited volumes of primary sources as well as handwritten original documents. This means that inconsistencies in editorial method cannot be avoided. My guiding principle has been to avoid my own editorial interventions as much as possible so that the texts are printed in a form as much like the originals as possible. I have kept notes to a minimum. In the case of academic writing by other scholars, I have removed the original notation. In the case of documents transcribed from handwritten originals, I have retained the author's false starts and corrections by retaining ~~strikeouts~~, where legible, and interlineations within <angled brackets>. Anything inserted by me appears in [square brackets]. Documents originally in Spanish have been translated.

NOTES

1. *New York Times*, January 13, 2000, April 9, 2000; *Toronto Star*, October 29, 2000. James Allen et al., *Without Sanctuary: Lynching Photography in America* (Santa Fe, N.M.: Twin Palms, 2000).

2. James E. Cutler, *Lynch-Law: An Investigation into the History of Lynching in the United States* (1905; reprint ed., Montclair: Patterson Smith, 1969); Arthur F. Raper, *The Tragedy of Lynching* (Chapel Hill: University of North Carolina Press, 1933); Walter White, *A Man Called White: The Autobiography of Walter White* (New York: Viking, 1948); Alfreda M. Duster, ed., *Crusade for Justice: The Autobiography of Ida B. Wells* (Chicago: University of Chicago Press, 1970; C. Vann Woodward, *Origins of the New South, 1877–1913* (Baton Rouge: Louisiana State University Press, 1951), 351–352.

3. George Rudé, *The Crowd in the French Revolution* (Oxford: Clarendon, 1959).

4. E. P. Thompson, "The Moral Economy of the English Crowd in the Eighteenth Century," *Past and Present* 50 (February 1971): 76–136.

5. Gordon Wood, "A Note on Mobs in the American Revolution," *William and Mary Quarterly*, 3rd series, 23 (1966): 635–642; Pauline Maier, *From Resistance to Revolution: Colonial Radicals and the Development of American Opposition to Britain, 1765–1776* (New York: Knopf, 1972); Richard D. Brown, *Revolutionary Politics in Massachusetts: The Boston Committee of Correspondence and the Towns, 1772–1774* (Cambridge, Mass.: Harvard University Press, 1970); Patricia U. Bonomi, *A Factious People: Politics and Society in Colonial New York* (New York: Columbia University Press, 1971).

6. Jesse Lemisch, "Jack Tar in the Streets: Merchant Seaman in the Politics of Revolutionary America," *William and Mary Quarterly*, 3rd series, 25 (1968): 371–407.

7. Gregory W. Bush, "Heroes and the 'Dead Line' against Riots: The Romantic Nationalist Conception of Crowd Behavior, 1840–1914," *Hayes Historical Journal* 8 (summer 1989): 34–57.

8. Paul A. Gilje, "'The Mob Begin to Think and Reason': Recent Trends in Studies of American Popular Disorder, 1700–1850," *Maryland Historian* 12 (1981): 25. For Gilje's own important work, see Paul A. Gilje, *The Road to Mobocracy: Popular Disorder in New York City, 1763–1834* (Chapel Hill: University of North Carolina Press, 1987); Paul A. Gilje, *Rioting in America* (Bloomington: Indiana University Press, 1996).

9. Joel Williamson, "Wounds, Not Scars: Lynching, the National Conscience, and the American Historian," *Journal of American History* 83 (March 1997): 1221–1253.

10. Leonard Dinnerstein, *The Leo Frank Case* (1968; reprint ed., Athens: University of Georgia Press, 1987).

11. Michael Fedo, *The Lynchings in Duluth* (1979; reprint ed., St. Paul: Minnesota Historical Society Press, 2000); Seth Cagin and Philip Dray, *We Are Not Afraid: The Story of Goodman, Schwerner, and Chaney and the Civil Rights Campaign for Mississippi* (New York: Macmillan, 1988); Harry Farrell, *Swift Justice: Murder and Vengeance in a California Town* (New York: St. Martin's, 1992); Ben Green, *Before His Time: The Untold Story of Harry T. Moore, America's First Civil Rights Martyr* (New York: Free Press, 1999); Mark Curriden and Leroy Phillips Jr., *Contempt of Court: The Turn-of-the-Century Lynching That Launched a Hundred Years of Federalism* (New York: Anchor Books, 1999); Laura Wexler, *Fire in a Canebrake: The Last Mass Lynching in America* (New York: Scribner, 2003); Steve Oney, *And the Dead Shall Rise: The Murder of Mary Phagan and the Lynching of Leo Frank* (New York: Pantheon, 2003).

12. Joel Williamson, *The Crucible of Race: Black-White Relations in the American South since Emancipation* (New York: Oxford University Press, 1984); Winthrop D. Jordan, *Tumult and Silence at Second Creek: An Inquiry into a Civil War Slave Conspiracy* (Baton Rouge: Louisiana State University Press, 1993); Leon Litwack, *Trouble in Mind: Black Southerners in the Age of Jim Crow* (New York: Knopf, 1998); Suzanne Lebsock, *A Murder in Virginia: Southern Justice on Trial* (New York: Norton, 2003).

13. Many scholars have taken the case study approach: see James R. McGovern, *Anatomy of a Lynching: The Killing of Claude Neal* (Baton Rouge; Louisiana State University Press, 1982); Howard Smead, *Blood Justice: The Lynching of Mack Charles Parker* (New York: Oxford University Press, 1986); Stephen J. Whitfield, *A Death in the Delta: The Story of Emmett Till* (New York: Free Press, 1988); Dennis B. Downey and Raymond M. Hyser, *No Crooked Death: Coatesville, Pennsylvania, and the Lynching of Zachariah Walker* (Urbana: University of Illinois Press, 1991); Richard B. McCaslin, *Tainted Breese: The Great Hanging at Gainesville, Texas, 1862* (Baton Rouge: Louisiana State University Press, 1994); Dominic J. Capeci Jr., *The Lynching of Cleo Wright* (Lexington: University Press of Kentucky, 1998); and James H. Madison, *A Lynching in the Heartland: Race and Memory in America* (New York: Palgrave, 2001). There have also been several surveys; see W. Fitzhugh Brundage, *Lynchings in the New South: Georgia and Virginia, 1880–1930* (Urbana: University of Illinois Press, 1993); Stewart E. Tolnay and E. M. Beck, *A Festival of Violence: An Analysis of Southern Lynchings, 1882–1930* (Urbana: University of Illinois Press, 1995); and Michael J. Pfeifer, *Rough Justice: Lynching and American Society, 1874–1947* (Urbana: University of Illinois Press, 2004). Scholars have also published state surveys; see George C. Wright, *Racial Violence in Kentucky, 1865–1940: Lynchings, Mob Rule, and "Legal Lynchings"* (Baton Rouge: Louisiana State University Press, 1990); Stephen J. Leonard, *Lynching in Colorado, 1859–1919* (Boulder: University Press of Colorado, 2002); Benjamin Heber Johnson, *Revolution in Texas: How a Forgotten Rebellion and Its Bloody Suppression Turned Mexicans into Americans* (New Haven: Yale University Press, 2003).

14. Gail Bederman, *Manliness and Civilization: A Cultural History of Gender and Race in the United States, 1880–1917* (Chicago: University of Chicago Press, 1995); Martha Hodes, *White Women, Black Men: Illicit Sex in the Nineteenth-Century South* (New Haven: Yale University Press, 1997); J. Douglas Smith, *Managing White Supremacy: Race, Politics, and Citizenship in Jim Crow Virginia* (Chapel Hill: University of North Carolina Press, 2002).

15. One recent popular survey of lynching leaves out important black voices. See Philip Dray, *At the Hands of Persons Unknown: The Lynching of Black America* (New York: Random House, 2002).

16. Christopher Waldrep, *The Many Faces of Judge Lynch: Extralegal Violence and Punishment in America* (New York: Palgrave Macmillan, 2002), 12.

17. Paul Starr, *The Creation of the Media: Political Origins of Modern Communications* (New York: Basic Books, 2004), 262.

18. Michael J. Klarman, *From Jim Crow to Civil Rights: The Supreme Court and the Struggle for Racial Equality* (New York: Oxford University Press, 2004), 270.

19. Klarman, *From Jim Crow to Civil Rights*, passim, but see, esp., 117–135, 225–232, 263–294.

Introduction
Explanations

Untold thousands of Americans have perished at the hands of their fellow citizens organized into mobs. Often the lynchers made a clean getaway, leaving only a brief newspaper notice to memorialize their victims. For example, in 1874 newspapers reported that "a silent, well-organized mob of several hundred mounted men" hanged a black man known only as "Soliver" in Martinsburg, West Virginia. The murder and reported rape of a thirteen-year-old child had excited the populace. "A large representative church element" joined the mob, which had been "winked at" by law enforcement officers.[1] Three days later, on August 16, a thousand Mississippians took Dick Cooper, Anthony Grant, and Silas Grant from the Brookhaven jail and hanged them. Whites alleged that Cooper and the Grants had "violated" "Mrs. Burnley."[2]

Through the nineteenth century newspapers carried such stories in a kind of sickeningly regular rhythm. On the same day that the *New York Times* reported Soliver's death, it published a Georgia lynching. The next day it carried news that a Tennessee mob had taken from jail and might have killed as many as sixteen African Americans.[3] These lynchings, and many others, occurred before 1882, when the *Chicago Tribune* began publishing its annual lynching tally. For this reason, these lynchers came in under the radar of virtually every lynching scholar, a whole cohort of victims off the academic grid, so to speak. A better date—not the best date, but better—might be 1835. After 1835 a new kind of newspapering, aimed at larger audiences, made a better effort than previous generations at reporting mob killings. But while lynching reports appeared only rarely before 1835, only the breathtakingly naïve can believe that the actual mob violence occurred so infrequently.

Lynching reports finished out the nineteenth century on a not-quite-daily basis and then marched into the twentieth. No wonder Americans have long seen themselves as uniquely violent, *peculiarly* addicted to mob violence. In 1905 the sociologist James Elbert Cutler described lynching as "a criminal practice which is peculiar to the United States." In the 1930s anti-lynching activist Jessie Daniel Ames denounced "this peculiarly American custom." Thereafter, reports of "lynchings" surfaced in England,[4] Germany,[5] Kenya,[6] on the West Bank,[7] in Israel,[8] South Africa,[9] and Mexico.[10] Nonetheless, remnants of Americans' dogged faith in their old peculiarity remain. "Lynchings are by no means an exclusive American practice," the *Washington Post* conceded in 2001, but "they are a form of ritualized execution that some Americans have pursued with peculiar enthusiasm during various states in our history."[11] Explaining Americans' alleged "peculiarity" is a central part of the history of lynching.

Serious academic efforts to understand why Americans lynched began in the 1890s, establishing patterns of explanations that both reflected the Gilded Age and remain with us today. Some thought American lynching revealed a tragic flaw in the American constitutional system.

Americans lynch, a Maryland lawyer named Omer Hershey wrote in 1900, because they barely believe in law and due process. Ordinary citizens feel that since they made the law, they can form crowds and enforce it on the street, outside legal institutions.[12] According to Hershey, popular sovereignty is an American trait and lynching is its logical extension, popular sovereignty run amok. James E. Cutler subscribed to this theory, arguing that Americans understand law only as a device to secure freedom. "Where the people . . . make the law," Cutler explained, "it is inevitable that the legal machinery will prove powerless to control popular excitements."[13]

Given that efforts to explain lynching began in the 1890s, it is no surprise that several writers attributed lynching to Americans' supposed frontier mentality, an argument that recalled Frederick Jackson Turner's claim that the frontier experience crafted Americans' collective character. More surprising is the persistence of this theory. Writing fifty years apart, in 1941 and 1992, the journalist W. J. Cash and the historian Edward Ayers agreed that lynchings most often occurred on thinly settled landscapes where institutionalized law enforcement had yet to win widespread acceptance. This frontier theory does not necessarily contradict the popular sovereignty argument. Both insisted that weak law enforcement mechanisms explain lynching. At the end of the nineteenth century, and early in the twentieth, this idea had garnered widespread acceptance. The Supreme Court justice David Brewer, the Harvard legal intellectual Roscoe Pound, as well as various governors and other politicians, all believed that weak or inept law enforcement explained mob law.[14] Paul Walton Black, a University of Iowa graduate student, documented this idea in 1910. Black wrote numerous letters to aged Iowans, asking about their experiences with lynching. The letters that came back squarely identified popular attitudes toward law as the central factor motivating mobs. Some old lynchers explained that "a want of faith in courts" caused mobbing. One lawyer said his area had no lynchings because "there has been no complaint of dilatory criminal procedure."[15]

Some proponents of this nonracial, constitutional view of lynching, held heinous racial beliefs. James Cutler thought the law "utterly unsuited" for "negro criminals," members of "a race of inferior civilization."[16] Such racism no doubt works to discredit the constitutional argument. This view that the fundamental problem was not racial seems counterintuitive, to say the least. Lynching now seems almost exclusively racial, white mobs torturing black bodies. But if Hershey and Cutler are right, Americans would have had a problem with mob violence even if the country had entirely solved its racial problems. Race fanned the flames, but the underbrush of American society would have smoldered anyway.[17]

Some time around World War II it became increasingly harder to criticize lynching on such nonracial grounds. Leading scholars began to see lynching as a tool that elite classes used to control their subordinates. The social psychologist John Dollard wrote that white southerners maintained their caste privileges through mob violence. Gunnar Myrdal, the Swedish social scientist often credited with knocking the intellectual props out from under segregation, thought lynching resulted from white southerners' culture, an idea that presaged historian Bertram Wyatt-Brown's work on southern honor. Myrdal offered an explanation almost entirely sectional. Sexually repressed narrow-minded evangelicals turned to mob violence out of boredom with small-town dullness, he charged. The white South, Myrdal said, "has an obsession with sex which helps to make this region quite irrational in dealing with Negroes generally." In such an "emotional puritanical region," young women tended to overreact to innocent incidents. Narrow-minded evangelical religion exacerbated both this tendency and the response to it. Myrdal's thinking on this point recalled a 1929 book written by Walter White (1893–1955), Acting Secretary of the National Association for the Advancement of Colored People (NAACP), *Rope and Faggot: A Biography of Judge Lynch.*[18] In 1948 Oliver Cromwell Cox (1901–1974), a sociologist born in Trinidad and educated at the University of Chicago, defined lynching as "a special form of mobbing—mobbing directed against a whole people or political class." Lynchers, Cox wrote, intended to suppress a people trying to better themselves.[19] By limiting his study to "a special kind of mobbing," Cox explicitly abstracted racial violence from its larger constitutional context, which he ignored. In 1967 the sociologist Hubert Blalock thought that inadequate data prevented the study of "symbolic or ritualistic forms of violence, such as lynching" but argued anyway that such violence flowed from a "power contest" between the two groups. Subsequent scholars tried to test Blalock's theory.[20] Robyn Wiegman, Martha Hodes, and Joel Williamson[21] all saw lynching as a tool white men used after emancipation when they needed to reestablish patriarchal control over women.

By the end of the twentieth century historians had become conscious of the gap between reality and representation. In no way did Grace Elizabeth Hale discount the gruesome grammar of lynching; she recognized that mob violence put real bodies on real trees, real fire scorched very human flesh. But Hale also demonstrated that lynching reached most consumers as spectacle. Influenced by Jacquelyn Dowd Hall's insight that stories that lynching represented a kind of folk pornography, Hale observed that most people experienced lynching secondhand, through newspapers, radio, photography, and conversation. Mass representations of racial violence told and retold stories to generate a metanarrative so powerful that actual lynchers even fashioned their lynchings to meet public expectations. "My goal," Hale wrote, "has been to illuminate who white southerners imagined they were and the stories and images that enabled them to make their collectiveness powerful and persuasive and true."[22] Industrialized consumer culture allowed them to use lynching violence to define themselves.

Although largely forgotten after her death in 1931 until the publication of her autobiography in 1970, the journalist Ida B. Wells's writings seem powerfully prescient today, anticipating the work of virtually every major writer on lynching. Wells, born in 1862, dated the origins of lynching to emancipation. Her case study approach, investigating particular lynchings, the same procedure followed by Robert C. O. Benjamin (1855–1900), the African American lawyer, poet, and journalist, formed a template picked up by the NAACP leader Walter White, the sociologist Arthur Raper, the reformer and activist Howard Kester, and the historians Leonard Dinnerstein, James McGovern, Howard Smead, and many others.[23] She based her argument on statistical evidence, a procedure that dominates not just historical inquiry but lynching consciousness to this day.[24] Unlike subsequent writers, however, Wells saw lynching rhetoric in historical terms. White racial violence evolved, changing forms and justifications across time. Before emancipation, Wells wrote (incorrectly, as we will see in this book) that whites rarely lynched their slaves. In 1866 major riots erupted in Memphis and New Orleans. In both cities whites attacked blacks. Whites apparently felt threatened by the waves of African Americans migrating into cities after the fall of slavery. Trouble in New Orleans started after Republicans organized a constitutional convention to enfranchise blacks and prohibit ex-Confederate whites from voting.[25] Wells explained Reconstruction rioting as resulting from black voting and political activity. Finally, she said, whites manufactured a new justification: an alleged black tendency to rape white women. But, in fact, this supposed historical progression suggested no real change over time. In an argument that characterizes lynching scholarship to this day, Wells held that whites' timeless propensity to racist violence actually changed little beneath the rhetoric. Whites scrambled to find one justification after another, but, according to Wells, white lust for violence changed not at all. Unchanging racism, disguised by a series of pretexts, explained all the violence. Wells's apparent historicism, then, is no contradiction after all. In every way she ultimately defined late-twentieth-century understandings of lynching. Racial violence ultimately represented a problem more sociological than historical.

1. Ida B. Wells, "The Case Stated," 1895

The student of American sociology will find the year 1894 marked by a pronounced awakening of the public conscience to a system of anarchy and outlawry which had grown during a series of ten years to be so common, that scenes of unusual brutality failed to have any visible effect upon the humane sentiments of the people of our land.

Beginning with the emancipation of the Negro, the inevitable result of unbridled power exercised for two and a half centuries, by the white man over the Negro, began to show itself in acts of conscienceless outlawry. During the slave regime, the Southern white man owned the Negro body and soul. It was to his interest to dwarf the soul and preserve the body. Vested with unlimited power over his slave, to subject him to any and all kinds of physical punishment, the white man was still restrained from such punishment as tended to injure the slave by abating his physical powers and thereby reducing his financial worth. While slaves were scourged mercilessly, and in countless cases inhumanly treated in other respects, still the white owner rarely permitted his anger to go so far as to take a life, which would entail upon him a loss of several hundred dollars. The slave was rarely killed, he was too valuable; it was easier and quite as effective, for discipline or revenge, to sell him "Down South."

But Emancipation came and the vested interests of the white man in the Negro's body were lost. The white man had no right to scourge the emancipated Negro, still less has he a right to kill him. But the Southern white people had been educated so long in that school of practice, in which might makes right, that they disdained to draw strict lines of action in dealing with the Negro. In slave times the Negro was kept subservient and submissive by the frequency and severity of scourging, but, with freedom, a new system of intimidation came into vogue; the Negro was not only whipped and scourged; he was killed.

Not all nor nearly all of the murders done by white men, during the past thirty years in the South, have come to light, but the statistics as gathered and preserved by white men, and which have not been questioned, show that during these years more than ten thousand Negroes have been killed in cold blood, without the formality of judicial trial and legal execution. And yet, as evidence of the absolute impunity with which the white man dares to kill a Negro, the same record shows that during all these years, and for all these murders only three white men have been tried, convicted, and executed. As no white man has been lynched for the murder of colored people, these three executions are the only instances of the death penalty being visited upon white men for murdering Negroes.

Naturally enough the commission of these crimes began to tell upon the public conscience, and the Southern white man, as a tribute to the nineteenth century civilization, was in a manner compelled to give excuses for his barbarism. His excuses have adapted themselves to the emergency, and are aptly outlined by that greatest of all Negroes, Frederick Douglass, in an article of recent date, in which he shows that there have been three distinct eras of Southern barbarism, to account for which three distinct excuses have been made.

The first excuse given to the civilized world for the murder of unoffending Negroes was the necessity of the white man to repress and stamp out alleged "race riots." For years immediately succeeding the war there was an appalling slaughter of colored people, and the wires usually conveyed to northern people and the world the intelligence, first, that an insurrection was being planned by Negroes, which, a few hours later, would prove to have been vigorously resisted by white men, and controlled with a resulting loss of several killed and wounded. It was always a remarkable feature in these insurrections and riots that only Negroes were killed during the rioting, and that all the white men escaped unharmed.

From 1865 to 1872, hundreds of colored men and women were mercilessly murdered and the almost invariable reason assigned was that they met their death by being alleged participants in an insurrection or riot. But this story at last wore itself out. No insurrection ever materialized; no Negro rioter was ever apprehended and proven guilty, and no dynamite ever recorded the black man's protest against oppression and wrong. It was too much to ask thoughtful people to believe this transparent story, and the southern white people at last made up their minds that some other excuse must be had.

Then came the second excuse, which had its birth during the turbulent times of reconstruction. By an amendment to the Constitution the Negro was given the right of franchise, and, theoretically at least, his ballot became his invaluable emblem of citizenship. In a government "of the people, for the people, and by the people," the Negro's vote became an important factor in all matters of state and national politics. But this did not last long. The southern white man would not consider that the Negro had any right which a white man was bound to respect, and the idea of a republican form of government in the southern states grew into general contempt. It was maintained that "This is a white man's government," and regardless of numbers the white man should rule. "No Negro domination" became the new legend on the sanguinary banner of the sunny South, and under it rode the Ku Klux Klan, the Regulators, and the lawless mobs, which for any cause chose to murder one man or a dozen as suited their purpose best. It was a long, gory campaign; the blood chills and the heart almost loses faith in Christianity when one thinks of Yazoo, Hamburg, Edgefield, Copiah, and the countless massacres of defenseless Negroes, whose only crime was the attempt to exercise their right to vote.

But it was a bootless strife for colored people. The government which had made the Negro a citizen found itself unable to protect him. It gave him the right to vote, but denied him the protection which should have maintained that right. Scourged from his home; hunted through the swamps; hung by midnight raiders, and openly murdered in the light of day, the Negro clung to his right of franchise with a heroism which would have wrung admiration from the hearts of savages. He believed that in that small white ballot there was a subtle something which stood for manhood as well as citizenship, and thousands of brave black men went to their graves, exemplifying the one by dying for the other.

The white man's victory soon became complete by fraud, violence, intimidation and murder. The franchise vouchsafed to the Negro grew to be a "barren ideality," and regardless of numbers, the colored people found themselves voiceless in the councils of those whose duty it was to rule. With no longer the fear of "Negro Domination" before their eyes, the white man's second excuse became valueless. With the Southern governments all subverted and the Negro actually eliminated from all participation in state and national elections, there could be no longer an excuse for killing Negroes to prevent "Negro Domination."

Brutality still continued; Negroes were whipped, scourged, exiled, shot and hung whenever and wherever it pleased the white man so to treat them, and as the civilized world with increasing persistency held the white people of the South to account for its outlawry, the murderers invented the third excuse—that Negroes had to be killed to avenge their assaults upon women. There could be framed no possible excuse more harmful to the Negro and more unanswerable if true in its sufficiency for the white man.

SOURCE: Ida B. Wells, *A Red Record: Tabulated Statistics and Alleged Causes of Lynchings in the United States, 1892–1893–1894* (Chicago: Donohue and Henneberry, 1895).

Despite Ida B. Wells's statistical evidence, many white Americans continued to explain lynching as resulting from black criminality. In 1897 an anonymous white man, writing as "Georgia," excused lynching in a letter to the *New York Times*. The virulent racism, with its assumptions about supposed black criminality, show the limits of Wells's campaign against lynching.

2. "Georgia," 1897

Many persons, from reading the accounts of our own dailies, and especially as those statements of theirs are reproduced with comments in the Northern press, would draw a conclusion that in Georgia we were a race of lawless savages; and, naturally, the law-abiding will avoid our State in seeking for homes.

It is useless to deny much that is said to be true, but there is so much that is true that is not told that I think perhaps there might be a different verdict if these untold facts were known.

I am free to admit that any man of any race who assaults a woman with vile intent will likely be hanged by the mob without bringing him into court or giving him a legal trial.

I admit as candidly that the men who do this lynching are never arrested nor is their act considered by the people generally as criminal.

It is useless for our papers to say that public sentiment is against lynching for rape. The lawyers are opposed to it, the daily press opposes it, and the preachers condemn it, but the masses of the people approve it, and say, "When brutes cease to rape helpless women men will cease to hang the brutes. Till then, not."

It is also true that it is a rare thing for a white man or a mulatto to be lynched. The victims are generally black negroes of the lowest order.

For other crimes than rape there is not often any lynching. Dr. Ryder, a white man, whose case has excited great attention, who had shot and killed a beautiful and accomplished young lady in a fit of jealous rage, and who had been found guilty by a jury, and a negro who shot at his wife and killed another woman, and then killed in cold blood a prominent merchant are the only cases I now recall.

For other crimes than rape the law takes its tedious way.

Tom Woolfolk murdered his whole family, to get the estate. No man doubted his guilt, the jury convicted him before leaving the box, but it took two years and two jury trials and an expenditure of $20,000 to get him to the gallows.

A negro killed an old man near Macon in cold blood for a few dollars worth of supplies, and after a long delay was hanged by the Sheriff.

A negro killed his wife cooly and brutally. It took two years and two trials to hang him and then he was hanged by the Sheriff, but a negro assaulted a few weeks ago a little girl of six years, and nearly killed the child. He was hung by the mob. A negro assaulted a fair young lady of one of our best families, and she barely escaped with her life. He was hanged by the mob.

A white man assaulted a young woman who was afterward found to be a woman of doubtful reputation. The jail was broken open by the mob and he was hanged.

I merely mention these cases because they came almost under my own eye, and were in one section of the State.

The reason the negroes are generally the victims of lynch law is because the negro is generally the criminal. It is not hostility to the race, else he would be lynched for other crimes, but it is because he seems particularly given to this odious crime. Nearly all our thieves and burglars and house-burners are negroes, but for these crimes they are never punished save by regular legal process, and as we said above, lynching is generally done for one crime alone, and is rarely done, for that crime is not common. It is almost always committed by negroes, and negroes of the lowest order. Among the hundreds of thousands of this race in Georgia, there are but few who have been charged with this crime. When it is committed the utmost care is taken to identify the criminal and only when his identity is beyond question is the execution ordered. It is done in a quiet, decided way as a general thing, although in cases of great atrocity sometimes the criminal is shot as well as hanged.

I am not defending this extra judicial process of punishing crime, but it is not more cruel than a long confinement in a close dungeon, and a halter in a jail yard at the end of it. The only ground of objection to this mode of dealing with these criminals is the fear that the innocent might suffer. As the most careful precautions are taken against this result it is not a likely thing lest the wrong man is executed.

Before the law, all are equal; juries have no respect to color in making their verdicts. A rich planter left $400,000 to a negro woman, said to be his child. The kinspeople tried to break the will, but it was sustained in every court; but, while all this is true, a man who assaults a woman, black or white, will be hanged.

. . . Our people say: We would like to have the good opinion of our Northern friends, but we can get along without it if it is to be secured by falsehood. The Northern people are not here. If they were, the first time one of their daughters was assaulted they would head the mob. The Northern people could help to remedy this evil. If those who have given the negroes so much money and so great sympathy would simply say, "This thing must stop; if your people commit these crimes they ought to die, and you need not expect sympathy from us," then the preachers and teachers who are their beneficiaries would speak out, and there would be a change of sentiment, which would be a great blessing to those who make it.

Our daily press denounces lynching, our Governor denounces it, our preachers denounce it, but it is simply falsehood to say that the people are with them. It may be a sad truth, but I am sure that the people are fixed as destiny and there is, as far as I can see, only one remedy for it and that is to stop the crime. It was almost unknown before the negro was freed. It is now always committed by young negroes who have been born in freedom. They are not ignorant, they are simply vile, and they must know the inexorableness of the doom.

I do not think the people who condone the offense of the lynchers like lynch law no more than those who resisted the fugitive slave law liked the rebellion against the United States Government, nor those who managed the underground railroad were glad to be habitual law breakers. They simply recognize the fact that these are extraordinary occasions.

The number of those who commit these crimes are not many, and the dread of those who have never lived in the South of violence to their families is not well founded.

The daily papers make the most of every case, and seem to delight in magnifying the evil. One would suppose, who was not well informed, that his family would be in peril because of the presence of these savages and judging from the fact that so many negroes are criminals he might come to the conclusion that the whole race was debauched. The fact is, we are not a law-breaking people, in the main, neither white men nor negroes—but the fact is that while we have a great many law-abiding negroes, a great many good citizens among them, nearly all of our criminals come from that class. The people who compose your criminal classes do not come this way and our white people are generally law-abiding, and so the robberies, burglaries, assaults, in our land come generally from the negroes. They do not often murder white men, for difficulties between these two races are rare. They murder each other. They have their own dives kept by people of their own color, and this is where the gambling and drinking goes on, and where the blood is generally shed.

It may seem strange to those who think this is a land of cutthroats to say that in no land is there a morality more Puritanical than in Georgia. A glass of soda would not be sold on Sunday. A fruit stand may not be opened. A freight train is not permitted to turn a wheel; in 100 counties no whisky is sold; $1,000,000 a year is spent on the common schools.

A Republican is as highly esteemed as a Democrat. If our individual States are not competent to manage these local troubles, they cannot be managed, and it is not the wisest course for those who are far removed from the scene of the danger to decide positively what ought or ought not to be done.

I have not attempted to defend the lynchers, no more than to defend the Vigilance Committee or committees of safety, but simply to state the case as I am sure it really is.

SOURCE: *New York Times*, September 16, 1897.

Americans have long seen lynching as sectional. John Carlisle Kilgo saw mob violence as resulting from the unique history of the South, a legacy of Spanish and French colonizers' feudal influence. In 1902, when he wrote this essay, Kilgo, a Methodist minister and native of South Carolina, served as president of Trinity College, now Duke University. In 1910 Kilgo became a Methodist bishop. Kilgo's cultural arguments, anticipating Walter White and then Gunnar Myrdal, put gender at the center of white southerners' lynching impulse.[26]

3. *John Carlisle Kilgo, "An Inquiry concerning Lynchings,"* 1902

[T]he real cause of lynching lies in the peculiar ideals and influences that make up the social order of the South, especially that order found in the States lying south of North Carolina. The immediate crime which excites a community to such speedy revenge is not the cause, but the occasion of lynching. Similar crimes are not revenged after this manner in other sections of this country and in other countries. Crimes produce different effects in different sections, according to the characteristics of their social organization and growth. The likelihood that the assassin of President McKinley would have been lynched had the assassination taken place in New Orleans or Atlanta instead of in Buffalo indicates a distinct difference between the social spirits of the two sections. Lynching is the outgrowth of peculiar social development. It will be scarcely possible to explain all the features of lynching from any other point of view.

There is a distinct historical basis of the social feelings and ideals in that section of the South including South Carolina, Georgia, Alabama, Florida, Mississippi, Louisiana, Arkansas, and Texas. The original social feelings and ideals of these States were largely influenced by France and Spain. Besides the Spanish possessions in Florida and Mexico, and the French ownership of the Mississippi Valley, the English who settled in South Carolina generally came from the West Indies, bringing with them the influences of Spanish life and social order. The colonists who settled Virginia and the New England States came directly from the British Islands, and the basal principles of their social growth were radically distinct from those in the extreme South. It will not be difficult to understand Southern life and its peculiar social dispositions if proper consideration is given to the sources of them.

French and Spanish society was strongly feudal. It was a social order in which were emphasized the degradation of the servant, the extreme dignity of the baron, and the independence of the land owner. Out of feudalism sprang chivalry, the growth of a spirit of social refinement, seeking to infuse into warfare a nobler feeling. Feudalism and chivalry were the basal ideas of the social development of these two nations and by them were introduced into the South, not so much in forms as in their spirit. The distinct features of these ideas and ideals were a sensitive distinction between servant and master, the high social position of the landlord, domestic luxury and ease, extreme sanctity of the family circle, independence of the individual in matters of personal protection, the subordinate relation of civil orders to the will of the citizen, a jealous regard of personal honor, and a deification of woman as a social being. Such a social organization must be marked by a highly nervous temperament and an intense sensitiveness. It cannot, in the nature of things, be otherwise. . . .

This sensitiveness of Southern society has reached the height of its intensity in its ideals of woman and of the home. To the outside world there may appear something of a poetic glamor about these ideals, and there may seem to be certain contradictions in them, but the fact that there is a severity in the sensitive feelings for them cannot be disregarded. For their defense there are unwritten laws, laws that belong to social sympathies, which take precedence of statuatory enactments, and courts are powerless to convict for an act of violence in the defense of the home and of women of good birth when the twelve jurors follow their sympathies rather than the logic of facts. The family feeling in South Carolina, and this is the State from which social ideals originally emanated in the far South, is so strong that only one divorce has been granted by its courts during its entire history, and that was in the reconstruction period. Nor is this social jealousy for the protection of women and the home a sensuous feeling. It bestows upon woman the most delicate attentions, always providing for her, whether it be a sitting in a church or a seat in a railway car. In England woman is a laborer, in Italy she is nearly a slave, in France she is an ornament, in the South she is a social deity upon whom men are expected to bestow high honor and all possible luxuries.

These facts indicate in the most general way the psychical nature of southern society, as well as show the historical growth of it. They also explain the causes that have made lynchings, not only possible, but rather peculiar to the South. Lynchings are the acts of a temporary social insanity. They are not the deeds of an insane element in a community, nor is the insanity of a full and permanent sort. But organized as is Southern society, with intensest feelings regarding certain ideals, it is liable to be outraged suddenly to an uncontrollable point, and thus crazed in its social emotions takes speedy revenge upon the violator of its laws and standards. Lynchers do not feel that they are violators of law, simply because they have reached such a degree of feeling as to make moral consciousness and judgment impossible. One who has never experienced the wild rush of feeling that sweeps a Southern community in which certain crimes have been committed can know nothing of the real conditions that surround a lynching. . . .

The condition, the psychical condition, of the social mind could not be made to hear arguments on dangers of mob law. The home, the woman, not the State, were outraged and men were wild. They followed their wild impulses. . . .

These distinctions and corresponding feelings were peculiar to feudalism and enter into Southern society. But when a man of high standing has accessibility to a home of like standing, and persuades the wife into infidelity to her husband or takes advantage of the confidences and esteem of the daughter and ruins her, the husband, the father, or the brother shoots him down in the streets, and the act is called a homicide. Between this act and a lynching are these differences; In one instance the single man acts, in the other the community acts; and the method of the first is less horrible as an execution than the usual methods of the second. But both acts spring from the same social sensitiveness, both are done in a state of social insanity, both are acts of revenge, and both have the approval of social ideals. They are essentially the same class of executions. It would be astonishing to know how many homicides are committed annually in the South, the occasion being some indignity perpetrated on the home. Perhaps the number is greater than the lynchings. There is a consistency in revenging the outraged sensitiveness of the social ideals that enter home life in the South, and it cannot be charged to racial prejudices.

SOURCE: John Carlisle Kilgo, "An Inquiry concerning Lynchings," *South Atlantic Quarterly* 1 (January 1902): 4–9.

Few academic writers can match the achievement of James Elbert Cutler, still cited as an authority one hundred years after publication of his original work.[27] Cutler made a constitutional argument: He thought ordinary American's peculiar ideas about sovereignty, more than racial prejudice, explained mob law. Cutler's argument was hardly original. The idea that Americans believed that popular sovereignty authorized mob law had circulated widely for years before 1905. Omer F. Hershey, for example, a Maryland lawyer and speaker on legal and scientific subjects, made the same argument five years before.[28]

4. James Elbert Cutler, "Lynch Law," 1905

The question naturally arises, what is the peculiarity about American society which fosters and tolerates lynching? Why is lynching a peculiarly American institution? It has been suggested that the explanation lies along racial lines. Some have said that the Scotch-Irish are responsible for the introduction into this country of the practice of illegally punishing public offenders. Others say that it is race prejudice, a result of the coming together of many races in one country, and particularly that it is the racial antagonism between the white race and the negro race, which explains the matter. Looking at the history of the practice in the United States from colonial times down to the present day, one can scarcely regard such an explanation as either adequate or conclusive. The real explanation lies along a somewhat different line, and it can be pointed out best by drawing some contrasts between the administration of the law in the United States and its administration in the older countries of Europe.

The American people are not any more disposed toward lawlessness—they are not less law-abiding—than European peoples; it is rather that they maintain a wholly different attitude toward the law. Social and political conditions are different, and the law, instead of being something in itself to reverence and respect, is little more than a device for securing freedom. The value of laws as rules of conduct is not minimized but there is no sense of sanctity pertaining to them. To outwit, avoid, defy, or forget the laws is not a serious offense so long as an appeal can be made to the individual sense of justice in support of such courses of action.

In Europe, where the statutes have grown up from tradition and ancient custom, the law is regarded as a more sacred institution; in a very real sense it is the product of a superior authority. Law in its institutional sense is as much a predetermined factor in daily affairs as is one of the laws of nature. Social and political conditions are fixed. Politics do not enter into the enforcement of law. Civilization is distributed in a more nearly equal measure and the law is enforced with equal vigor over the whole country. The judicial and administrative officers are persons socially and politically distinct from the masses, and their individuality is so completely subordinated to their representative capacity that the law thus comes to have a majesty and dignity which can be given it in no other way.

In the United States, on the contrary, the body of the law lacks the support of long tradition and ancient practice. The early immigrants brought with them the European conception of law, but in the midst of new conditions, with no strong government to enforce it with an impartial and an iron hand, along with the growth of the democratic spirit, a new *esprit des lois,* as Montesquieu would call it, has been developed. Where the people, either directly or through their representatives, make the laws and then elect the officers who are to enforce them, it is inevitable that the legal machinery will prove powerless to control popular excitements. Politics also enter very largely into the whole question. In remote districts, too, the people seldom have occasion to meet any other officers of the law than their own neighbors and friends whom they have elected to minor civil offices. It is for this reason that the execution of the law varies so greatly in different parts of the United States, being either vigorous or lax, in accordance with the moral sentiment of the community.

In a monarchy or a highly centralized form of government, the law is made for the people and enforced against them by officials who are in no sense responsible to them.

In a democracy with a republican form of government, like the United States, such is not the case. The people consider themselves a law unto themselves. They make the laws; therefore they can unmake them. Since they say what a judge can do, they entertain the idea that they may do this thing themselves. To execute a criminal deserving of death is to act merely in their sovereign capacity, temporarily dispensing with their agents, the legal administrators of the law. While not always expressed in language so unmistakable in meaning, yet this is the spirit exhibited, the vague and perhaps unconscious attitude toward the law, which seems particularly to pervade the United States.

The tendency toward public disorder has existed in this country from its earliest settlement, and as the line of the frontier has slowly moved westward there has always been a region on the border where the forces of law were unorganized. There has thus been a constant opportunity for a plea of necessity in certain cases for resorting to the popular execution of justice. In recent years the customary explanations of lynchings attribute them to mob rule, emotional insanity of the crowd, race prejudice, contempt for the "niggers," intense community feeling, vivid hatred of crime, *lex talionis* and the like. It is often asserted that lynchings occur because the courts are slow, uncertain, and unduly sympathetic with the rights of the accused, because corrupt jurymen, shrewd lawyers, the technicalities of the law or the undue sympathies of the pardoning powers frequently prolong and save a guilty person's life. While it is true on psychological grounds that punishment to be effective must be prompt and certain, and while such explanations have validity in particular cases, the fundamental explanation lies deeper. It is to be found in the peculiar and distinctively American attitude toward those institutions connoted by the term "the law." There is a readiness on the part of the people in the United States to take the law into their own hands which is not found in other countries, and the consequent immunity from punishment which is generally accorded to lynchers renders an American mob exceedingly open to the suggestion of lynching.

Source: James Elbert Cutler, *Lynch-Law: An Investigation into the History of Lynchings in the United States* (New York: Longmans, Green, 1905), 267–270.

The psychologist John Dollard, influenced by Sigmund Freud, rejected cultural explanations. He thought lynching resulted from white efforts to maintain their racial caste system. Born in Wisconsin, educated at the University of Chicago and Berlin Psychoanalytic Institute, Dollard lived in Indianola, Mississippi (which he called "Southerntown"), for five months in 1935 and 1936 while conducting his study.

5. *John Dollard, "Caste and Class," 1937*

White aggression against Negroes and the social patterns which permit it are forms of social control; they are instrumentalities for keeping the Negro in his place and maintaining the supraordinate position of the white caste. We know now from our study that the whites did not fight for social superiority just for fun; on the contrary, they are attempting to minimize or eliminate Negro competition in the spheres of economics, sex, and prestige. . . .

I remember a conversation with a naive Negro who had been thinking about this point. He stated that in his belief the white people actually hated the Negroes. . . .

In the end it seems a better statement to say that white people fear Negroes. They fear them, of course, in a special context, that is, when the Negro attempts to claim any of the white prerogatives or gains. Since the wider American social pattern, however, offers to the Negro the hope of personal advancement and so directs his striving that he is in continuous actual or potential opposition to the caste system, the whites must constantly fear him. Negro opposition to white gains can only be manifested in aggressive action; and this is the source of white fear. This fear, of course, has a long history, fear of revolt, fear of Negroes running away, and fear of isolated assault or terrorism. Before the Civil War efficient policing institutions and the isolation of plantation life reduced these fears, although even then the white owner and overseer apparently watched Negro behavior very carefully for signs of recalcitrance. It is urged that, when the North interfered with existing social and property relationships in the South, this fear became much more intense and continuous. It is so to the present day, especially in rural black-belt areas of the type in which Southerntown is located. White people fear that Negroes actually will demand equal status, equal economic opportunity, and equal sexual chances, including under the latter the right to protect their homes and women from sexual aggression. By a series of hostile acts and social limitations the white caste maintains a continuous threatening atmosphere against the possibility of such demands by Negroes; when successful, as these threats are now, the effect is to keep the social order intact. Minor caste taboos are here viewed as indirect forms of aggression exercised against the actual or potential claims for advancement on the part of the Negro, claims which would disrupt the existing caste and class relationships. Many minor taboos will seem senseless unless this principle is constantly kept in mind. The Negro is allowed only the feeblest of efforts to realize the American ideal of vertical social mobility; efforts that would be considered normal in others are experienced by white men as fabulously aggressive when they are made by Negroes.

There are two important considerations to raise in the matter of white fear of Negroes. There is a reality element in this fear, viz., that our major American institutions encourage the Negro to leave his "place" as defined by southern regional culture. If debarred, as he is, he is likely to express his legitimate resentment in some drastic way. The cases of shooting from the bush and rape . . . are sources of real fear on the part of real people. Such acts are constantly alleged to be the sole inciting source of white aggression and intimidation of Negroes.

There is, however, another form of fear which must be discussed. This is not based on real acts of aggression by Negroes or the expectation of them; it is rather the unconscious expectation of retaliation for the hostile acts of whites on Negroes. The justification for this assumption is the fact that white people seem to be much more afraid of Negroes than there is any real reason to be. The Negroes seem, in fact, to be rather well adjusted to the situation and to have, by and large, renounced aggression and organization as means of changing their status. The fright shown by white caste members seems disproportionate to the threat from the Negro's side; in such a case we may invariably postulate that unconscious mechanisms are functioning, in this case a fear of retaliation for the gains aggressively acquired by the white caste at the expense of the Negroes. Only on such a basis may the unreasonable, often panicky, fears which the whites have toward the rather helpless Negroes be accounted for. The lesson that hatred may be expected from those attacked is learned early in life and is one of the most enduring attitudes planted in the individual by our society. Wherever it is possible, and not too dangerous, the best defense against a feared aggression from others is an aggression on one's own part which keeps the others from going into action. Real fear and neurotic fear are compounded to build up a permanent necessity for severe measures against Negroes on the part of the white caste.

SOURCE: John Dollard, *Caste and Class in a Southern Town* (New Haven: Yale University Press, 1937), 314–319.

The prize-winning author of *Simple Justice: Brown vs. Board of Education*, Richard Kluger, called Gunnar Myrdal "a nervy Swedish economist," willing to write what no white man had written before, "two-fisted investigative reporting" combined with sociology. Myrdal's *An American Dilemma* caused a sensation in American intellectual circles, offering a scientific examination of American race relations that squarely placed responsibility on the white population, refuting claims that blacks were to blame for their own oppression. It is not entirely clear just why Myrdal wielded such influence. Perhaps it was because his sprawling two-volume work appeared so comprehensive. It may have helped that he also seemed objective, all the more so for his foreign birth. Or, perhaps, after decades of protest by the National Association for the Advancement of Colored People and other groups, the time was just right.

Myrdal may not have been at his best when analyzing lynching. His work seems derivative: his great contribution was that he repeated Ida B. Wells's statistics and Walter White's cultural argument, making both more legitimate for coming from "a nervy Swedish economist."[29]

6. Gunnar Myrdal, "An America Dilemma," 1944

The danger of Negroes' desire to rape white women has acquired a special and strategic position in the defense of the lynching practice. Actually, only 23 per cent of the victims were accused of raping or attempting to rape. There is much reason to believe that this figure has been inflated by the fact that a mob which makes the accusation of rape is secure against any further investigation; by the broad Southern definition of rape to include all sex relations, between Negro men and white women; and by the psychopathic fears of white women in their contacts with Negro men. The causes of lynching must, therefore, be sought outside the Southern rationalization of "protecting white womanhood."

This does not mean that sex, in a subtler sense, is not a background factor in lynching. The South has an obsession with sex which helps to make this region quite irrational in dealing with Negroes generally. In a special sense, too, as William Archer, Thomas P. Bailey, and Sir Harry Johnston early pointed out, lynching is a way of punishing Negroes for the white Southerners' own guilt feelings in violating Negro women, or for presumed Negro sexual superiority. The dullness and insecurity of rural Southern life, as well as the eminence of emotional puritanical religion, also create an emphasis upon sex in the South which especially affects adolescent, unmarried, and climacteric women, who are inclined to give significance to innocent incidents. The atmosphere around lynching is astonishingly like that of the tragic phenomenon of "witch hunting" which disgraced early Protestantism in so many countries. The sadistic elements in most lynchings also point to a close relation between lynching and thwarted sexual urges.

Lynching is a local community affair. The state authorities usually do not side with the lynchers. They often try to prevent lynchings but seldom take active steps to punish the guilty. This is explainable in view of the tight hold on the courts by local public opinion. The lynchers are seldom indicted by a grand jury. Even more seldom are they sentenced, since the judge, the prosecutor, the jurors, and the witnesses are either in sympathy with the lynchers or, in any case, do not want to press the case. If sentenced, they are usually pardoned. While the state police can be used to prevent lynching, the local police often support the lynching. From his study of 100 lynchings since 1929, Raper[30] estimates that "at least one half of the lynchings are carried out with police officers participating, and that in nine-tenths of the others the officers either condone or wink at the mob action."

The actual participants in the lynching mobs usually belong to the frustrated lower strata of Southern whites. Occasionally, however, the people of the middle and upper classes take part, and generally they condone the deed, and nearly always they find it advisable to let the incident pass without assisting in bringing the guilty before the court. Women and children are not absent from lynching mobs; indeed, women sometimes incite the mobs, into action.

The Psychopathology of Lynching

The psychopathology of the lynching mob has been discussed intensively in recent years. Poverty and economic fear have been stressed as background factors. It is generally held that the rise of lynchings and race riots during and immediately after the First World War had much to do with the increased mobility of, and competition from, Negroes during this period. A substantial correlation from year to year between low cotton prices and high lynchings is demonstrated.

Economic fear is mixed with social fear: a feeling that the Negro is "getting out of his place," and the white man's social status is being threatened and is in need of defense. "lynching is much more an expression of Southern fear of Negro progress than of Negro crime," writes Walter White. Tannenbaum[31] observed that:

> The South gives indications of being afraid of the Negro. I do not mean physical fear. It is not a matter of cowardice or bravery; it is something deeper and more fundamental. It is a fear of losing grip upon the world. It is an unconscious fear of changing status.

It is this feeling which is behind the common saying which a visitor to the South will hear even today from lower class whites that "a lynching now and then" is expedient or necessary in keeping the Negroes from becoming "uppity." It is commonly observed that after the First World War many lynchings of Negro soldiers—sometimes in uniform—were openly motivated by the fear that they had gotten "wrong ideas" about their social status while serving in France.

The low level of education and general culture in the white South is another important background factor. Allied with it is the prevalence of a narrow-minded and intolerant "fundamentalist" type of Protestant evangelical religion. Occasional violently emotional revival services, and regular appeals in ordinary preaching to fear and passion rather than to calm reasoning, on the one hand, and denunciations of modern thought, scientific progress, and all kinds of nonconformism, on the other hand, help to create a state of mind which makes a lynching less extraordinary. Methodist and Baptist preachers were active in reviving the Ku Klux Klan after the First World War. With but rare exceptions preachers and local religious leaders have not come out against lynchers.

Another important background factor in the causation of lynching and other major forms of violence is the isolation, the dullness of everyday life and the general boredom of rural and small town life in the South. There is a lack of wholesome recreation or even variation, which gives a real and sinister meaning to H. L. Mencken's statement that "lynching often takes the place of the merry-go-round, the theatre, the symphony orchestra, and other diversions common to larger communities."[32]

Thus far we have considered the background factors and underlying causes of lynching. The causation is such that, when the time is ripe, almost any incident may touch it off. The incident is usually some crime, real or suspected, by a Negro against a white, or merely a "racial insult," such as when a Negro buys an automobile or steps beyond the etiquette of race relations in any way. Rumors will often start or accelerate a lynching. The lynching itself may take one or two main forms: in a *mob lynching* the whole community will participate with a high degree of frenzy; in a *vigilante lynching* a restricted number of men, often disguised, will perform the deed with much ceremony.

The effects of lynchings are far-reaching. In the locality where it has happened and in a wide region surrounding it, the relations between the two groups deteriorate. The Negroes are terror-stricken and sullen. The whites are anxious and are likely to show the assertiveness and suspicion of persons with bad, but hardened, consciences. Some whites are afraid of Negro retaliation or emigration. Every visitor to such a community must notice the antagonism and mutual lack of confidence between the two groups.

The long-run effects of lynching also are bad: As students of the Negro problem have long recognized, crime will not be hampered but rather stimulated by violence. Far outside the locality where the lynching has occurred, in fact, all over the nation, it brutalizes feelings. Even in the North, some people have ceased to be concerned when another lynching occurs; and they jest about going South to see a lynching. It must have a particularly bad influence upon interracial attitudes of young people in the two groups. Thus lynching has a psychological importance out of all proportion to its small frequency.

In every locality where there has been a lynching there are a great many people—sometimes a clear majority—who, when they think calmly, consider the incident most unfortunate. The nation-wide publicity created around a lynching community is, for one thing, commonly recognized to be damaging. The present writer has met few whites of the middle and upper classes in the South who have expressed themselves as in favor of lynch justice. But equally few have pretended that they would take any personal risks to hinder a lynching, and they make no effort to punish the lynchers. The ordinary Southerner apparently thinks that neither the upholding of the majesty of the law nor the life of even an innocent Negro is worth such a sacrifice. And, above all, Negroes must not have the satisfaction of seeing the whites divided or their assailants punished.

SOURCE: Gunnar Myrdal, *An American Dilemma: The Negro Problem and Modern Democracy*, 2 vols. (New York: Harper and Brothers, 1944), 1:561–564. Copyright © 1944, 1962 by Harper & Row Publishers, Inc. Reprinted by permission of HarperCollins Publishers, Inc.

The journalist Wilbur Joseph Cash (1900–1941) wrote only one book, but *The Mind of the South* proved one of the most influential examinations of the South ever published, a volume that instantly made him the national expert on the South and things southern. Like Kilgo, Cash described southern culture as almost feudal; like Hershey and Cutler, he believed a disdain for law animated lynchers. Unlike Kilgo and Hershey, however, Cash traced the roots of white Southerners' feudalism and "rudimentary" attachment to law to a persisting frontier ethos that captured the southern imagination.

7. *Wilbur Joseph Cash, "The Mind of the South,"* 1941

Whatever his original derivations, the frontier had loosened his bonds as completely as it is possible to imagine them being loosed for man in a social state. The thin distribution of the population over vast reaches of country, the virtual absence of distinctions, and of law and government save in their most rudimentary stages, the fact that at every turn a man was thrown back wholly upon his own resources—all these combined to give his native individualism the widest scope and to spur it on to headlong growth.

SOURCE: W. J. Cash, *The Mind of the South* (New York: Knopf, 1941), 29, 31–34, 42–43.

Cash believed that plantation culture continued the frontier mentality. A plantation, an "independent social unit, a self-contained and largely self-sufficient little world of its own," encouraged its owner to imagine himself so much in control of his own life as to have little need for law or courts. This individualism fed a willfulness that demanded immediate satisfaction when confronted with crime, Cash thought. In this culture, lynching flourished.

The historian Edward Ayers continued Cash's frontier thesis. Mob law occurred most often on thinly settled landscapes populated with many black newcomers, Ayers argued. Like Cash, Ayers attributes racial violence in part to the failure of white southerners to establish adequate institutional controls on their behavior. Ayers converted Cash's generalizations into a geographic argument, based on lynching rates by subregion.

8. *Edward Ayers, "In Black and White,"* 1992

Lynchings were far more likely to occur in some regions of the South than in others, and those patterns call into question easy assumptions about the forces behind lynching. No simple political argument will work. Although North Carolina witnessed the greatest amount of racial conflict in the political realm of any Southern state, including the brutal white supremacy campaign and Wilmington riot of 1898, the heavily black part of the state registered a remarkably low rate of lynching. Although white South Carolina under race-baiting Governor Ben Tillman was given every permission to hate, his state fell far below the regional average in the number of black men lynched. Although white Virginia felt compelled to hold a disfranchisement convention, it recorded one of the lowest lynching rates in the South. Kentucky, on the other hand, largely outside the maelstrom of Populism and disfranchisement, near the border of the North, and with a relatively diversified economy, saw a remarkably high rate of lynching. Even West Virginia, dominated by Republicans, reached the regional average in black lynching. Clearly, something other than the political environment triggered the bloodshed.

Two subregions witnessed especially high rates of lynchings: the Gulf Plain stretching from Florida to Texas, and the cotton uplands of Mississippi, Louisiana, Arkansas, and Texas. While both of these subregions had a high proportion of blacks in their populations, they were by no means the regions with the highest black proportion.

Neither did they register a particularly high level of voting against the Democratic regime.

What they did share was a particular demography. These subregions had an extremely low rural population density, often only half that of states in the east. In the last two decades of the nineteenth century they experienced tremendous rates of black population increase. While the average county in the South saw its black population grow by 48 percent between 1880 and 1910, counties in Florida's Gulf Plain grew by 131 percent, Alabama's grew by 119 percent, Mississippi's by 91 percent, and Texas's by 71 percent. The only state whose Gulf Plain area had a relatively low lynching rate, close to that of the region as a whole, was Louisiana's, which did not see great black population change. The subregions with the second and third highest rates of lynching—the cotton uplands and, surprisingly, the mountains of Appalachia—also combined a relatively low population density and high rates of black population growth.

The counties most likely to witness lynchings had scattered farms where many black newcomers and strangers lived and worked. Those counties were also likely to have few towns, weak law enforcement, poor communication with the outside, and high levels of transiency among both races. Such a setting fostered the fear and insecurity that fed lynching at the same time it removed the few checks that helped dissuade would-be lynchers elsewhere. Lynching served as a method of law enforcement in sparsely populated places where white people felt especially insecure. Whites dreaded the idea that black criminals could get away with harming a white person without being punished, worried that the lack of retribution would encourage others to raise their hand against isolated whites on remote plantations, farms, or roads.

The sporadic violence of lynching was a way for white people to reconcile weak governments with a demand for an impossibly high level of racial mastery, a way to terrorize blacks into acquiescence by brutally killing those who intentionally or accidentally stepped over some invisible and shifting line of permissible behavior. The brutality was not generated by crowding and friction; places such as the Black Belt and the Piedmont, with high population densities, saw relatively low rates of lynching. In such places, black people were more likely to know at least a few whites as neighbors or employers. They were also able to turn to black friends and allies should they be pursued by a lynch mob.

Lynchings tended to flourish where whites were surrounded by what they called "strange niggers," blacks with no white to vouch for them, blacks with no reputation in the neighborhood, blacks without even other blacks to aid them. Lynching seemed both more necessary and more feasible in places such as the Gulf Plain, the cotton uplands, and the mountains. In those places most blacks and whites did not know one another, much less share ties of several generations. The black population often moved from one year to the next in search of jobs at lumber camps and large plantations.

SOURCE: Edward L. Ayers, *The Promise of the New South: Life after Reconstruction* (New York: Oxford University Press, 1992), 156–157. Used by permission of Edward L. Ayers.

Sex has long been recognized as a critical part of the explanation for mob law. After Ida B. Wells and after white voices claiming a black propensity for rape fell silent, or at least retreated from respectable print venues, the historian Joel Williamson explained lynchers' motivations as essentially sexual. But while Williamson saw "the lynching phenomenon" as appearing suddenly, in 1889[33] other scholars, including Robyn Wiegman, thought lynching originated with the fall of slavery.[34] When one system of patriarchal organization collapsed, white men needed another to take its place.

9. Robyn Wiegman, "The Anatomy of a Lynching," 1993

[W]hy the charge of rape as the consolidating moment of lynching's justification? Why this sexualization of blackness as the precondition not only for mob action, but for lynching's broad cultural acceptance and appeal? The answer to this, like any accounting of the historical, is less apparent than the many contexts in which the evidence of lynching's sexualization appears. But if we begin where I have suggested, with the narrative of rape (and its culmination in lynching) translating the crisis of Emancipation from economic to sexual and gendered terms, we encounter a very powerful means through which not only black men but the entire black community could be psychologically and physically contained. Most important, we witness the way the rape narrative simultaneously recognizes and subverts the African American male's theoretical equality in the sexual as well as political and economic spheres. On a level less abstract, the rape mythos, as an overwhelmingly southern response to enfranchisement, also challenges the work of the Freedman's Bureau, where the patriarchal logic of the dominant culture became the defining mechanism for organizing the newly freed slave: not only did the bureau appoint the husband as head of the household, assigning to him sole power to enter into contractual labor agreements for the entire family, but it fought for the allotment of land for every freed "male," while granting only unmarried women access to this domain.

In these pronouncements—as in the routine gender segregation attending voting, jury duty, the holding of political and Republican party office—the official program of Reconstruction understood the freedom of black men to entail a "natural" judicial and social superiority over African American women. The nineteenth century's determination of public and private along strict gender lines thus provided a definitional structure through which social space and familial roles were shaped for a population no longer denied the right (and privilege) of maintaining family bonds. But while the patriarchalization of the black family served to institutionalize it within the gender codes prevalent in white bourgeois ideology, thereby securing the black family to the formal dimensions of white social behavior, many whites were decidedly threatened by the definitional sameness accorded former slaves. The loss of one patriarchal organization of social life—that of slavery—and its replacement by the seeming egalitarianism of a male-dominated black family, then, has the effect of broadening the competitive dimensions of interracial masculine relations, especially as the black male's new property governance of black women threatens to extend to women of the dominant group as well.

It is in this climate that the mythology of the black male as rapist emerges, working the fault line of the slave's newly institutionalized masculinization by framing this masculinity as the bestial excess of an overly phallicized primitivity. In the contours of

Western racial discourse, of course, the primitive sexual appetite associated with blackness is not a new articulation at the end of the nineteenth century, but its crafting in the highly stylized and overdetermined narrative structure of the rape mythos —along with the sheer frequency of its deployment—marks a particular historical configuration of the sexual and gendered in their relation to issues of race and nation. For while the slavery period in the United States often envisioned the Uncle Tom figure as the signification of the "positive good" of a system that protected and cared for its black "children," once emancipated, these children became virile men who wanted for themselves the ultimate symbol of white civilization: the white woman. The transformation of the image of the black man from simple, docile Uncle Tom to violent sex offender characterizes the oppositional logic underwriting the representational structure of black male images in nineteenth- and twentieth-century United States culture, a logic in which the discourse of sexual difference—from feminized docility to hypermasculinized phallicity—comes to play a primary significatory role.

South Carolina Senator Ben Tillman demonstrates this logic in his 1907 speech before Congress, when he argues for the abandonment of due process for blacks accused of sex crimes against white women:

> The white women of the South are in a state of siege. . . . Some lurking demon who has watched for the opportunity seizes her; she is choked or beaten into insensibility and ravished, her body prostituted, her purity destroyed, her chastity taken from her. . . . Shall men . . . demand for [the demon] the right to have a fair trial and be punished in the regular course of justice? So far as I am concerned he has put himself outside the pale of the law, human and divine. . . . Civilization peels off us . . . and we revert to the . . . impulses . . . to "kill! kill! kill!"

In proposing mob retaliation against the defilers of white womanhood, Tillman assures his listeners that he does not hate blacks by recalling "the negroes of the old slave days . . . the negroes who knew they were inferior and who never presumed to assert equality." These blacks, with minds like "those of children," posed no sexual threat, as was witnessed, according to Tillman, by the fact that during the Civil War, with white men away fighting, "there is not of record a solitary instance of one white woman having been wronged" by the nearly 800,000 black men left on plantation land. Only with Emancipation and the "return to barbarism" does rape follow; "the negro becomes a fiend in human form."

As Tillman's rhetoric indicates, the white woman serves, in the ethos of nineteenth-century racialism, as a pivotal rhetorical figure for shaping the mythology of the black rapist. Using her emblem as the keeper of the purity of the race, white men cast themselves as protectors of civilization, reaffirming not only their role as social and familial "heads," but their paternal property rights as well. In this way, as Trudier Harris observes, the white male maintains a position of "superiority not only in assigning a place to his women, but especially in keeping black people, particularly black men, in the place he had assigned for them." In this dual role, the mythology of the black male rapist simultaneously engineers race and gender hierarchies, masking the white male's own historical participation in "miscegenating" sexual activities and ensuring his dis-

ciplinary control over potential sexual—and, one must add, political—liaisons between black men and white women. Within the context of nineteenth-century abolitionist and feminist movements, the necessity for disrupting such potential bonds
seems important indeed.

SOURCE: Robyn Wiegman, "The Anatomy of a Lynching," *Journal of the History of Sexuality* 3
(January 1993): 456–462. Copyright © 1993 by the University of Texas Press. All rights reserved.

Grace Elizabeth Hale saw "spectacle lynching" as a product of modernization. Before 1893, she
writes, lynching had been merely "spontaneous" and "loosely organized." Thereafter whites
mobilized the attributes of a modern industrialized society to assemble mobs and publicize
their work.

10. *Grace Elizabeth Hale, "Spectacle Lynching," 1998*

Newspaper reporters and men around the stove at the crossroads store, telegraph operators and women at the local meeting of the United Daughters of the Confederacy,
law "enforcement" officials and trainmen who jumped from the car to tell the news at
each stop—all helped shape the stories of specific events into a dominant narrative of
southern spectacle lynchings that evolved in the decades between 1890 and 1940. But
widely circulated newspaper stories . . . were central to the power of these new
"amusements." While thousands of white southerners witnessed and participated in
lynchings as the twentieth century unfolded, the majority of Americans—white and
black, northern and southern—learned about these events from newspapers and to a
lesser extent books, pamphlets, and radio announcements. In many cases these accounts were written by reporters who personally witnessed the spectacle, but the experience for their readers or listeners was mediated, a representation at least once removed from actual involvement. And even those spectators who attended the lynching or later viewed the body or examined a display of "souvenirs" were affected as well
by the narratives constructed by reporters to describe and explain these events. Beginning in the 1890s, no matter the specific characteristics, representations of spectacle
lynchings increasingly fell into a ritualistic pattern as the narratives constructed by
witnesses, participants, and journalists assumed a standardized form. Spectacle lynchings, then, became more powerful even as they occurred less frequently because the
rapidly multiplying stories of these public tortures became virtually interchangeable.

Thus the modernization of the practice—the incorporation of cars and trains, ra-
dios, phones, and cameras—matched the standardization of the representations. As a
dominant narrative evolved and circulated more widely, innovations added in a particular lynching were easily spotted and picked up by subsequent mobs. The grisly di-
alectic began in the 1890s as newspaper coverage grew, crowds increased, and lynch
mobs adapted the rituals of public executions to the needs of vigilantism and racial
control. . . . before 1890 magazines ignored the subject entirely while local newspapers
printed small, sparse accounts. Three events in the early 1890s, however, initiated the
early development of spectacle lynchings as practice and as narrative. First, the lynching on March 14, 1891, of eleven Italian immigrants accused of aiding in the murder of

the New Orleans police chief brought international attention to mob murder in the South as the Italian government condemned the action and demanded indemnities. Before the fervor over these murders had faded, another public lynching in Louisiana occurred: a large crowd of whites tortured and burned an African American named Tump Hampton in St. Tammany Parish on May 30 of the same year. Significantly, publicity generated by the Italians' murder spilled over in this case onto the lynching of a black southerner. The founding event in the history of spectacle lynchings, however, was the final murder in the gruesome triad, the 1893 lynching of Henry Smith in Paris, Texas, for the alleged rape and murder of three-year-old Myrtle Vance.

The 1893 murder of Smith was the first blatantly public, actively promoted lynching of a southern black by a large crowd of southern whites. Adding three key features —the specially chartered excursion train, the publicly sold photograph, and the widely circulated, unabashed retelling of the event by one of the lynchers—the killing of Smith modernized and made more powerful the loosely organized, more spontaneous practice of lynching that had previously prevailed. In what one commentator aptly termed a "neglected feature of railroading," from 1893 on railroad companies could be counted on to arrange special trains to transport spectators and lynchers to previously announced lynching sites. On some occasions these trains were actually advertised in local papers; with railroad passenger service, even small towns could turn out large crowds. Even after automobiles cut into the railroads' "lynch carnival" business, a 1938 commentator found that "modern trainmen, schooled in the doctrine of service," helped "in an informative way" by relaying news of upcoming lynchings to train passengers and townspeople "all along the rail lines."

As crucial as the innovation in transportation, however, was the publication, after Henry Smith's lynching, of the first full account, from the discovery of the alleged crime to the frenzied souvenir gathering at the end: *The Facts in the Case of the Horrible Murder of Little Myrtle Vance, and Its Fearful Expiation, at Paris, Texas, February 1, 1893*. This widely distributed pamphlet is perhaps the most detailed account of a lynching ever written from a lyncher's point of view. It included a photograph of Smith's torture, probably also sold separately. This pamphlet initiated a new genre of lynching narrative, the author as eyewitness and in this case also participant.

SOURCE: Grace Elizabeth Hale, *Making Whiteness: The Culture of Segregation in the South, 1890–1940* (New York: Pantheon Books, 1998), 206–207. Used by permission of Grace Elizabeth Hale.

NOTES

1. *New York Times*, August 26, 1874.
2. Ibid., August 23, 1874.
3. Ibid., August 26, 27, 1874.
4. *London Independent*, May 16, 2000.
5. Ibid., November 26, 2000.
6. Ibid.
7. *London Daily Telegraph*, February 6, 2001.
8. *Toronto Star*, April 30, 2001; *Jerusalem Post*, May 6, 2001.

9. *London Guardian,* April 7, 2001.

10. *San Francisco Chronicle,* August 1, 2001.

11. *Washington Post,* October 16, 2001.

12. O. F. Hershey, "Lynch Law," *The Green Bag* 12 (1900): 466–469.

13. James Elbert Cutler, *Lynch-Law: An Investigation into the History of Lynching in the United States* (New York: Longmans, Green, 1905), 267–268.

14. David J. Brewer, "Plain Words on the Crime of Lynching," *Leslie's Weekly* 97 (August 20, 1903): 182; Roscoe Pound, "The Causes of Popular Dissatisfaction with the Administration of Justice," *Report of the Twenty-Ninth Annual Meeting of the American Bar Association* (Philadelphia: Dando Printing, 1906): 395–417; Richard Maxwell Brown, *Strain of Violence: Historical Studies of American Violence and Vigilantism* (New York: Oxford University Press, 1975), 145–179.

15. Michael J. Pfeifer, *Rough Justice: Lynching and American Society, 1874–1947* (Urbana: University of Illinois Press, 2004), 25.

16. Cutler, *Lynch-Law,* 224–225.

17. Pfeifer, *Rough Justice,* attempts to revive this argument but does not rigorously test the hypothesis.

18. Gunnar Myrdal, *An American Dilemma: The Negro Problem and Modern Democracy,* 2 vols. (New York: Harper and Brothers, 1944), 1:560–564; Bertram Wyatt-Brown, *Southern Honor: Ethics and Behavior in the Old South* (New York: Oxford University Press, 1982); Walter White, *Rope and Faggot: A Biography of Judge Lynch* (1929; reprint ed., Notre Dame: University of Notre Dame Press, 2001), 40–81. White became secretary in 1931. Walter White, *A Man Called White: The Autobiography of Walter White* (1948; reprint ed., Bloomington: Indiana University Press, 1970), 103, 115; Kenneth Robert Janken, *White: The Biography of Walter White, Mr. NAACP* (New York: New Press, 2003), 137–138, 161.

19. Oliver Cromwell Cox, *Caste, Class, and Race: A Study in Social Dynamics* (New York: Doubleday, 1948), 549.

20. Hubert M. Blalock Jr., *Toward a Theory of Minority-Group Relations* (New York: Wiley, 1967), 109, 148, 160–161; John S. Reed, "Percent Black and Lynching: A Test of Blalock's Theory," *Social Forces* 50 (1972): 356–360; J. Corzine et al., "Black Concentration and Lynchings in the South: Testing Blalock's Power-Threat Hypothesis," *Social Forces* 61 (1983): 774–796.

21. Joel Williamson, *The Crucible of Race: Black-White Relations in the American South since Emancipation* (New York: Oxford University Press, 1984), 180–223; Robyn Wiegman, "The Anatomy of Lynching," *Journal of the History of Sexuality* 3 (January 1993): 454–462; Martha Hodes, *White Women, Black Men: Illicit Sex in the Nineteenth-Century South* (New Haven: Yale University Press, 1997), 176–208.

22. Grace Elizabeth Hale, *Making Whiteness: The Culture of Segregation in the South, 1890–1940* (New York: Vintage, 1998), xi, 199–239; Jacquelyn Dowd Hall, *Revolt against Chivalry: Jessie Daniel Ames and the Women's Campaign against Lynching,* rev. ed. (New York: Columbia University Press, 1993), 129–157.

23. White, *A Man Called White;* Arthur Raper, *The Tragedy of Lynching* (Chapel Hill: University of North Carolina Press, 1933); Leonard Dinnerstein, *The Leo Frank Case* (1966; reprint ed., Athens: University of Georgia Press, 1987); James R. McGovern, *Anatomy of a Lynching: The Killing of Claude Neal* (Baton Rogue: Louisiana State University Press, 1982); Howard Smead, *Blood Justice: The Lynching of Mack Charles Parker* (New York: Oxford University Press, 1986).

24. Arguments similar to Wells are made by Robert C. O. Benjamin in *Southern Outrages: A Statistical Record of Lawless Doings* (n.p.: 1894). Most recently, see W. Fitzhugh Brundage, *Lynching in the New South: Georgia and Virginia, 1880–1930* (Urbana: University of Illinois,

1993); Stewart E. Tolnay and E. M. Beck, *A Festival of Violence: An Analysis of Southern Lynchings, 1882–1930* (Urbana: University of Illinois Press, 1995); Jesse Jackson, *Legal Lynching: Racism, Injustice, and the Death Penalty* (New York: Marlow, 1996); Stephen J. Leonard, *Lynching in Colorado, 1859–1919* (Boulder: University Press of Colorado, 2002).

25. Eric Foner, *Reconstruction: America's Unfinished Revolution, 1863–1877* (New York: Harper and Row, 1988), 262–263.

26. Later Bertram Wyatt-Brown and other scholars would revive the cultural explanations for things southern under the honor rubric. See Wyatt-Brown, *Southern Honor*; Edward L. Ayers, *Vengeance and Justice: Crime and Punishment in the Nineteenth-Century American South* (New York: Oxford University Press, 1984).

27. See, for example, Brundage, *Lynchings in the New South*, 1.

28. O. F. Hershey, "Lynch Law," *Green Bag* 12 (1900): 466–469.

29. Richard Kluger, *Simple Justice: The History of Brown v. Board of Education and Black America's Struggle for Equality* (New York: Knopf, 1976), 256.

30. Arthur F. Raper is the author of an influential book documenting every recorded lynching in 1930. See Arthur F. Raper, *The Tragedy of Lynching* (Chapel Hill: University of North Carolina Press, 1933).

31. Frank Tannenbaum (1893–1969), educated at Columbia University and the Robert Brookings Graduate School in economic and political science, published numerous books, including *Darker Phases of the South* (1924), Myrdal's source for this quote.

32. For this Mencken quotation, Myrdal cites Walter White, *Rope and Faggot: A Biography of Judge Lynch* (New York: Knopf, 1929), 9–10. White provides no source for the quotation.

33. Williamson, *Crucible of Race*, 117.

34. Martha Hodes, "The Sexualization of Reconstruction Politics: White Women and Black Men in the South after the Civil War," *Journal of the History of Sexuality* 3 (1993): 402–417.

1

The First Lynchers

The first lyncher must have been Paleolithic. No archaeologist will ever identify his remains or track his steps. The impulse to kill in a crowd and imagine community approval is too elemental for that. When Americans tell their stories about the origins of lynching, they almost always do so to excuse or condemn the practice. Writing in 1887, Hubert Howe Bancroft justified "illegal administration of justice by the people" by tracing its origins to the Enlightenment. In feudal times governments operated systems of secret tribunals, he explained. The Enlightenment illuminated this feudal darkness when people took the law in their own hands. "Law is the voice of the people," Bancroft said, it is "the will of the community as a whole." Bancroft recognized that opinions differed on the origins of lynch law. The mayor of Galway, Ireland, was a candidate for the original Judge Lynch. A Virginia farmer was another possibility; a Judge Lynch who suppressed piracy might have been the first lyncher.

While Bancroft sought to justify "popular tribunals," James Cutler condemned mob law. For that reason, he wielded his scholarly skepticism like a sword, demolishing the ancient stories Bancroft had sallied. Cutler demolished the "Galway story" by observing that the Galway mayor's action failed to meet anyone's definition of a lynching. Cutler also made short work of the "pirate story." Whatever the facts might be about a man named Lynch who punished pirates without trial, "there is no evidence to show that they were ever known as Lynch's law."[1]

Story telling about the beginnings of lynching began long before Bancroft or Cutler. In 1820 James Hardiman published his version of the origins of the Lynch Law, conceding that "most of the minor incidents contained in this narrative are the offspring of fancy." Hardiman relied on "traditional accounts" and, "independently of the general voice of tradition," "several ancient manuscripts, many of which have passed through the hands of the author." He insisted, however, that he had captured accurately "the principal occurrence." Writers like Hubert Howe Bancroft, seeking to justify lynching, seek solace in Hardiman's account, suggesting as it does that extralegal violence has an ancient lineage. And Hardiman presents the first lyncher as upright, incorruptible, and morally steadfast. Any lyncher could be proud of such an antecedent.

11. *James Hardiman, "The Mayor of Galway,"* 1820

James Lynch Fitz-Stephen, an opulent merchant, and one of the principal inhabitants of Galway, was elected mayor in 1493, at which time a regular and friendly intercourse subsisted between the town and several parts of Spain. This mayor . . . went on a voyage to Spain, and was received, when at Cadiz, at the house of a rich and respectable merchant, of the name of Gomez, with the utmost hospitality. . . . Upon his departure for his own country, out of a wish to make some grateful return for the numerous civilities he had received from the Spaniard, he requested of him, as a particular favor, to allow his son, a youth of nineteen, to accompany him to Ireland, promising to take parental care of him during his stay, and to provide for his being safely restored to his friends whenever he desired to return. Young Gomez, who was the pride of his parents and relations, was rejoiced at this agreeable opportunity of seeing the world; and the merchant's request was gratefully complied with by his father. They embarked accordingly, and, after an easy passage, arrived in the bay of Galway. Lynch introduced the young stranger to his family, by whom he was received with that openness of heart and hospitality which has ever characterized the Irish, under any circumstances; and he also recommended him, in a particular manner, as a companion to his only son, who was but a year or two older than Gomez. . . . The young men lived together in perfect harmony, and frequent entertainments were given at the mayor's house, as well in honor of the stranger, as for the sake of advancing the suit of his son Walter to the beautiful Agnes. At one of these festivals, which, as usual, she adorned with her presence, it happened that her lover either saw, or which, with lovers, is the same, imagined that he saw, the eyes of the lovely maid beam with rapture on the young Spaniard. Wild with astonishment, the fairy spell was broken; his ardent and unruly passions took fire at the thought, and he seized an opportunity, not of asking his mistress if his suspicions were founded in fancy or reality, but of upbraiding her for her infidelity in terms of haughty anger. . . .

Urged by his rage, the lover pursued his imagined rival, who, being alarmed by a voice which he did not recognize, fled before him. From ignorance of the streets, he directed his steps towards a solitary quarter of the town, close to the shore; but, before he had quite reached the water's edge, his mad and cruel pursuer overtook him, darted a poniard into his heart, and plunged him, bleeding, into the sea. In the night the tide threw the body of this innocent victim of insanity back upon the beach, where it was found and soon recognized. The rash and wretched murderer (from himself the particulars were obtained) had scarcely committed the sanguinary deed than he repented it. . . .

Within the short compass of a few days, a small town in the west of Ireland, with a population, at the time, of little more than three thousand persons, beheld a sight of which but one or two similar examples occur in the entire history of mankind—a father sitting in judgment, like another Lucius Junius Brutus, on his only son, and, like him, too, condemning that son to die, as a sacrifice to public justice. . . . No sooner was his sentence known to the populace, than they surrounded the place of the criminal's confinement: at first they were content with expressing their dissatisfaction by murmurs of regret and expostulations with the guards; but, by degrees, they became tumultuous, and were prevented only by the military force from attacking the prison, and pulling down the magistrate's house; and their disorders were increased by understanding that the prisoner was now desirous of being rescued; which in some measure was true, for, as his madness subsided, his love returned. The thought of forever parting from the object of his affections was intolerable, and he began to see of what value the gift of existence was, by which his remorseless hand had deprived an unoffending stranger . . . the mayor . . . descended, at night, to the dungeon where his son lay, for the double and direful purpose of announcing to him, that his sentence was to be executed on the following morning. . . . It was scarcely day, when the expected summons to prepare was given to the guards without. The father rose, and assisted the executioner to remove the irons which still bound his unfortunate son; then, unlocking the door, he ordered him to stand between the priest and himself, and lean upon the arm of each. In this manner they ascended a flight of steps, lined with soldiers, and were passing on to gain the street, where a strong escort had been appointed to receive and go along with them to the usual place of punishment, at the eastern extremity of the town. . . . Prodigious crowds had gathered, and were loud in their outcries for mercy, threatening instant destruction to the magistrate, if not complied with. In vain did he exhort them to preserve tranquility, and suffer the law to take its course. The soldiers themselves were melted by the circumstances of this most pitiable case, and, no longer able or willing to do their duty, permitted the populace to approach the house, and to continued their well-meant, but unlawful, opposition. To attempt to pass through them was hopeless. . . . It is probable he was prepared for this extremity; for, turning back, and still keeping hold of his son, he mounted by a winding stairs within the building, which led to an arched window that overlooked the street in which the populace was assembled: he there presented himself and his victim, about whose neck he had previously fastened the rope with which he had been bound, and, securing the other end in an iron projecting from the wall, "You have little time to live, my son," said he; "let the care of your soul employ these few moments —take the last embrace of your unhappy father:"—he embraced his unfortunate son, and launched him into eternity! A few moments put an end to his existence. Expecting instant death from the fury of the rabble, this extraordinary man retained his station, satisfied with the silent approval of a good conscience, perfectly regardless of the applause or censure of the multitude, conscious of having fulfilled his duty to God, to man, and his country: but this act of greatness awed them; they stood motionless with amazement; a sentiment of admiration and sorrow united along prevailed; and, when all was over, they slowly and peaceably retired—so wondrous is the influence of an exalted and daring mind, when actuated by the principles of virtue.

SOURCE: James Hardiman, *The History of the Town and County of the Town of Galway, From the Earliest Period to the Present Time* (Dublin: W. Folds, 1820), 70–76. Thanks to Kevin Mullen for leading me to this text.

In the summer of 1835, after a mob executed five gamblers in Vicksburg, Mississippi, journalists scrambled to find the origins of "lynching." Several newspapers claimed to find the first lynching in Pennsylvania. Unfortunately their accounts lack specificity, claiming, for example, that the original lynching occurred "many years ago." This version appeared in the Portland, Maine, *Daily Evening Advertiser,* August 4, 1835.

12. "A Farmer Named Lynch," 1835

In Washington county, Pa., many years ago, there lived a poaching vagabond, who, it was believed, maintained himself and family by pilfering from the farmers around him. Though universally suspected, yet he managed so adroitly as always to avoid detection. At length a Mr. Van Swearingen laid the following trap for him, in which he was caught. Having a newly-born calf, he concealed it from his neighbors for several days—then rode over to the poacher's, and told him that a young calf had recently strayed to his farm, which he had penned, and was anxious to find the owner. The poacher asked him how long he had had it, its size and color, and being told, said it was his, and that it had gone off just at the time spoken of. Being thus detected in a lie with a design to defraud, Van Swearingen reproached him with it, and told him he would give him twenty-four hours to leave the neighborhood, adding that if he remained longer he would prosecute him.

The poacher only laughed at his threats, while the latter went to consult with his neighbor as to what was to be done. At the expiration of the twenty-four hours, five or six of them repaired to the poacher's whom they found perfectly unintimidated. The party, however, proceded to try him in due form, choosing one of their number, a farmer named *Lynch,* to be judge. Van Swearingen related the offence, which the poacher of course denied. The case was submitted to the judge, who decided that the poacher should be tied up and receive three hundred lashes, "well laid on," and then be given twenty-four hours to leave the place, under a penalty of receiving three hundred more if found after that time. The first part of the sentence was inflicted on the spot, with much *good intent* as to render its repetition unnecessary. The culprit made off as fast as his lacerated limbs would permit him.

SOURCE: Portland, Maine, *Daily Evening Advertiser,* August 4, 1835.

Often the origins of lynch law are traced to the American Revolution. Tories complained that "the useful arts of agriculture and commerce are neglected for cabaling, mobbing this or the other man." Mobs, the Tories charged, "were a necessary ingredient" in the Revolutionaries' "system of opposition."[2] A Virginia farmer named William Lynch lived in Pittsylvania County, Virginia, at a time when Tories plotted insurrection. Years after the Revolution, William Lynch moved to South Carolina and there encountered the diarist Andrew Ellicott. Lynch's tales of leading "Lynch-men" against Tories disgusted Ellicott, who expressed his feelings in his diary.

13. *Andrew Ellicott, "Captain William Lynch,"* 1811

October 25th the diary notes that the party after toilsomely traversing the wooded mountain ridges, arrived at Mr Lynch's, and adds that the

"Captain Lynch just mentioned was the author of the Lynch laws so well-known and so frequently carried into effect some years ago in the southern states in violation of every principle of justice and jurisprudence. Mr. Lynch resided in Pittsylvania in the state of Virginia when he commenced legislator and carried his system into effect: —the detail I had from himself and is nearly as follows.—

The Lynch-men associated for the purpose of punishing crimes in a summary way without the tedious and technical forms of our courts of justice. Upon complaint being made to any member of the association of a crime being committed within the vicinity of their jurisdiction the person complained of was immediately pursued and taken if possible. If apprehended he was carried before some members of the association and examined:—if his answers were not satisfactory he was whipped till they were so. Those extorted answers generally involved others in the supposed crime who in their turn were punished in like manner.—These punishments were sometimes severe and not infrequently inflicted upon the innocent through spite or in consequence of answers extorted under the smarting of the whip. . . .

Mr. Lynch informed me that he had never in any case given a vote for the punishment of death some however he acknowledged had been actually hanged tho not in the common way a horse in part became the executioner: the manner was this.—The person who it was supposed ought to suffer death was placed on a horse with his hands tied behind him and a rope about his neck which was fastened to the limb of a tree over his head. In this situation the person was left and when the horse in pursuit of food or any other cause moved from his position the unfortunate person was left suspended by the neck,—this was called aiding the civil authority.—It seems almost incredible that such proceedings should be had in a civilized country governed by known laws it may nevertheless be relied on. I should not have asserted it as a fact has it not been related to me by Mr. Lynch himself, and his neighbor Mr. Lay one of the original association together with several other Lynch-men as they are called. This self created judicial tribunal was first organized in the state of Virginia about the year 1776 from whence it extended southward as before observed.

Mr. Lynch had the appearance of an antient athlete and had he lived in the times of the Olympic games would probably have figured 'on the *bloody arena*':—he possesses a strong but uncultivated mind and is hospitable and generous to an extreme to which may be added a great stickler for equality and the rights of man as established by law! So contradictory are the ideas and conduct of the only creatures supposed to be endowed with reason and judgment in the universe."

SOURCE: Catharine Van Cortlandt Mathews, *Andrew Ellicott: His Life and Letters* (New York: Grafton, 1908), 220–222.

Further evidence of William Lynch and his "Lynch-men" comes from Edgar Allan Poe. In 1836 Poe edited the *Southern Literary Messenger*. Just a year after the Vicksburg mob created a sensation by hanging five gamblers, Poe announced that he had found documentary proof in support of William Lynch's claim to be the original Judge Lynch in Pittsylvania County, Virginia. The document Poe published in his *Southern Literary Messenger* purported to be the lynchers' original agreement, their organizing document or charter. Given Poe's reputation for literary hoaxes, it seems wise not to accept his "lynchers' charter" uncritically. Nonetheless, it is interesting that the document Poe published excuses mob violence, explaining it as the work of honest men deprived of their property.

14. *Edgar Allan Poe, "Lynchers' Character,"* 1836

Whereas many of the inhabitants of the county of Pittsylvania, as well as elsewhere, have sustained great and intolerable losses by a set of lawless men who have banded themselves together to deprive honest men of their just rights and property, by stealing their horses, counterfeiting, and passing paper currency, and committing many other species of villainy, too tedious to mention, and that those vile miscreants do still persist in their diabolical practices, and have hitherto escaped the civil power with impunity, it being almost useless and unnecessary to have recourse to our laws to suppress and punish those freebooters, they having it in their power to extricate themselves when brought to justice by suborning witnesses who do swear them clear —we, the subscribers, being determined to put a stop to the iniquitous practices of those unlawful and abandoned wretches, do enter into the following association, to wit: that next to our consciences, soul and body, we hold our rights and property, sacred and inviolable. We solemnly protest before God and the world, that (for the future) upon hearing or having sufficient reason to believe, that any villainy or species of villainy having been committed within our neighborhood, we will forthwith embody ourselves, and repair immediately to the person or persons suspected, or those under suspicious characters, harboring, aiding, or assisting those villains, and if they will not desist from their evil practices, we will inflict such corporeal punishment on him or them, as to us shall seem adequate to the crime committed or the damage sustained; that we will protect and defend each and every one of us, the subscribers, as well jointly as severally, from the insults and assaults offered by any other person in their behalf: and further, we do bind ourselves jointly and severally, our joint and several heirs &c. to pay or cause to be paid, all damages that shall or may accrue in consequences of this our laudable undertaking, and will pay an equal proportion according to our several abilities; and we, after having a sufficient number of subscribers to this association, will convene ourselves to some convenient place, and will make choice of our body five of the best and most discreet men belonging to our body, to direct and govern the whole, and we will strictly adhere to their determinations in all cases whatsoever relative to the above undertaking; and if any of our body summoned to attend the execution of this our plan, and fail so to do without a reasonable excuse, they shall forfeit and pay the sum of one hundred pounds current money of Virginia, to be appropriated towards defraying the contingent expenses of this our undertaking. In witness whereof we have hereunto set our hands, this 22d day September 1780.

SOURCE: "Lynch's Law," *Southern Literary Messenger* 2 (May 1836): 389.

There is solid evidence that the Bedford County, Virginia, militia actually lynched Tories during the Revolution. Bedford's militia, including its colonel, planter, and magistrate Charles Lynch (1736–1796), as well as William Preston, William Campbell, Arthur Campbell, and William Edmiston, ran down and hanged miscreants outside the law. And Charles Lynch referred to his work as "lynching." Unlike accounts published long after the fact, these contemporary documents reveal an ugly side to Charles Lynch's extralegal violence. The negotiation between militia leaders and Governor Thomas Jefferson show the governor sharing the militia's growing concern over the Tory threat. But while Jefferson commended Charles Lynch in 1780 for his "activity," the governor also implored his militia to follow the law, importunings which suggest that Jefferson worried about just what his militia soldiers did to their Tory prisoners. He was right to worry. The dialogue among the lynchers shows slight attachment to the due-process values Jefferson advocated. The next nine letters represent the best documentation available of the origins of extralegal American violence attached to the word "lynching." Militia officers exchanged letters with one another and with their governor, Thomas Jefferson.

15. *William Preston to Thomas Jefferson,* March 1780

Sir:

I am sorry to acquaint your Excellency that three Days ago an Information was made to a Magistrate in the County That a Number of men Dissafected to the present Government had combined to disturb the Peace of this unhappy Frontier as soon as the Season would Permit and the british Troops could gain any Footing in So Carolina & were making the Necessary Preparations for that Purpose. That 75 or thereabouts had taken the Oath of Allegiance to the King of Great Britain in one Neighbourhood & carried on a constant Correspondence with all the other Disaffected People not only in this & Washington County but on the Frontiers of No Carolina but that they had Persons employ'd to carry Intelligence to & from our Enemies in Georgia & Elsewhere on the Continent. That there is now fifteen British Commissions in this County and Washington & that these People intended to perpetrate the most horrid murders [on all] Individuals in Authority on this Quarter, with many other Things of the like Nature that would be too tedious to Relate.

SOURCE: Louise Phelps Kellogg, *Frontier Retreat on the Upper Ohio, 1779–1781* (Madison: State Historical Society of Wisconsin, 1917), 143.

16. *Thomas Jefferson to William Preston,* March 21, 1780

Sir:

I am sorry to hear that there are persons in your quarters so far discontented with the present government as to combine with it's enemies to destroy it. I trust they have no grievance but what we all feel in common, as being forced on us by those to whom they would not join themselves. Had any such grievances existed complaint and refusal of redress should have preceded violence. The measures they are now taking expose them to the pains of the law, to which it is our business to deliver them. We must therefore avoid any irregularity which might give them legal means of withdrawing themselves from punishment. I approve much of your most active endeavors to apprehend the guilty and put them into a course of trial. The carrying them out of the country before an examining court is had on them, if their safe custody required it must be yielded to: but if they can be kept safely without it, I should rather approve it. I suppose this may be done by strong guards of militia, which must be summoned, and subsisted and paid at the public expence. You seem to expect that writings may be found about them which will convict them of treason. Should your evidence however not be such as the law required in cases of treason where the punishment is capital, perhaps it may be sufficient to convict them of a misprision of treason which is punishable by fine and imprisonment at the pleasure of the court. I suggest this to you that you may not suppose them absolutely cleared if the evidence will not support the charge of treason.

I think it necessary that you should take the most immediate measures for protecting the lead mines. For this I know none so likely to be effectual as your calling on a sufficient number of the newly recruited soldiers (no matter for what service engaged) from the counties round about, which you are hereby authorized to do, rendezvousing them at the lead mines and putting into their hands the arms taken from the malcontents.

SOURCE: Julian P. Boyd, ed., *The Papers of Thomas Jefferson* (Princeton, N.J.: Princeton University Press, 1951), 3:325. Copyright © 1951 Princeton University Press, 1979 renewed PUP. Reprinted by permission of Princeton University Press.

17. *Col. Arthur Campbell to Major William Edmiston,* June 24, 1780

Dear Sir:

A Letter just received from the Commanding Officer at the Lead-Mines, I am informed that the Tories have embodied themselves up New River, and intend to take that place also that they have killed nine Men, and are committing various outrages. I am also call'd upon in a most pressing manner to send assistance as the Mines is in great danger.

SOURCE: Louise Phelps Kellogg, *Frontier Retreat on the Upper Ohio, 1779–1781* (Madison: State Historical Society of Wisconsin, 1917), 195–196.

The hanging of Zachariah Goss, with "the joint consent of near three hundred men" closely resembles later lynchings. Virginia Militia Colonel William Campbell evidently thought the size of his crowd legitimized the killing.

18. *Col. William Campbell to Col. Arthur Campbell,* July 25, 1780

Sir:

Upon receiving your letter . . . informing me that the insurgents were embodying up New River, and that their design was to destroy the works at the lead mines, I immediately wrote to Captains Edmiston, Lewis and Dysart, directing to order fifteen men out of each of their companies, to assemble at my house early next day, equipped to march with me to the lead mines. . . . We got to the mines next day soon in evening. There I was informed two men had been sent up the river, to discover, if possible, the designs of the insurgents, and that it was expected they would return that night. About an hour and a half before day next morning they came to the mines and informed me that they had been as far as Captain Cox's, where they counted one hundred and five men assembled and in arms, beside a considerable number without arms. . . . I then determined to go up New River with the men who went with me from this county; but some of the Militia officers of Montgomery County being there, they proposed to collect as many men that day as they possibly could, and to be in readiness to march early next day, which we did with about one hundred and forty men. That evening we got about sixteen miles above the lead mines. . . . Next day we continued our route up the river, through the most populous part of the settlement, and found no people at home but the women and children excepting a few very old men. Upon our arrival at Captain Cox's, in the evening, we were informed that about forty of the insurgents, about two hours before, had crossed the river, and taken Captain Cox's son a prisoner. . . . We then followed after them . . . until it became so dark that we could no longer follow their track, and turned off the path, about a quarter of a mile, and tied up our horses in the most silent manner we could, conjecturing the enemy were not far before us. . . . I then concluded they were encamped in the woods, and determined if at all possible to surprise them, and for that purpose set out on foot about two or three hours before day, leaving all our horses tied, where we halted in the evening. In this order we marched about a mile, when we again made a halt, and sent off four or five very trusty men, to find if possible where the enemy lay. I also sent with them a man whom I the day before had caused to come with me. Being informed he had a brother among the insurgents, I imagined he knew something of their schemes and designs, and told him if he did not discover where the insurgents lay, I would put him to death. They returned in about an hour and informed me they had been within twenty yards of the enemy's camp, and was fired upon by one of their sentries. . . .

As soon as it became so light that we could see a small distance around us, we set out a second time toward the enemy's camp on horseback. We got to the side of the glade just as the sun was rising. The morning was very foggy, which prevented our discovering the flight of the enemy, nor did we know they had fled until Captain Cox's son came to us, who in their hurry they had suffered to escape. . . . We had not the fortune to find any but one of them, who was immediately shot. . . .

That night we went again to Captain Cox's where we were next morning met by a party of 130 men under the command of Colonel Cleveland from Wilks county, North Carolina. They had the day before apprehended a certain Zechariah Goss, a fellow who belonged to a party under the command of Samuel Brown and [James] Coyle, two noted murderers, horse-thieves and robbers. Goss was immediately hung, I believe with the joint consent of near three hundred men, and two other villains were very well whip'd. I then detached between sixty and seventy men under the command of Captain Francis, with instructions to collect all the stocks of horses and cattle belonging to the insurgents they possibly could, only leaving to each family one horse creature and what milch cattle were necessary for its support.

SOURCE: Louise Phelps Kellogg, *Frontier Retreat on the Upper Ohio, 1779–1781* (Madison: State Historical Society of Wisconsin, 1917), 236–240.

19. *Thomas Jefferson to Charles Lynch,* August 1, 1780

Sir:

It gives me real concern to find that there is any one citizen in the [common]wealth so insensible of the advantages which himself and his posterity must [derive] from the present form of Governm[ent] . . . they can expect on a [return to] dominion under a foreign State, as to wish to return to it. . . . It remains to determine what shall be done. The most vigorous, decisive measures shou'd be continued for seizing every one on whom probable proof of guilt shall appear. Those who have been the leaders of the combination, who have enlisted others into it, or who have accepted of commissions from the enemy, shou'd be tried before an examining court for high treason, and if found guilty sent here for further trial. . . . Your activity on this occasion, deserves great commendation, and meets it from the Executive. The method of seizing them at once which you have adopted is much the best. You have only to take care that they be regularly tried after[wards]. . . . The attorn[ey for the Common]wealth in your county will doubtless advise you in yo[ur proceedings . . . I] can add nothing but an exhortation to continue the [energy with which you have] begun [to sup]press [these] parricides.

SOURCE: Julian P. Boyd, ed., *The Papers of Thomas Jefferson* (Princeton, N.J.: Princeton University Press, 1951), 3:523. Copyright © 1951 Princeton University Press, 1979 renewed PUP. Reprinted by permission of Princeton University Press.

20. *Col. William Preston to Gov. Thomas Jefferson,* August 8, 1780

Sir:

A most horrid Conspiracy amongst the Tories in this County being providentialy discovered about ten days ago obliged me not only to raise the militia of the County but to care for so a large Number from the Counties of Washington and Botetourt that there are upwards of four hundred men now on Duty exclusive of a Party which I hear Col. Lynch marched from Bedford towards the Mines yesterday. . . . A number of Magistrates were called together from this County and Botetourt to examine Witnesses and enquire fully into the Conduct of those deluded Wretches In which we have been Engaged three Days; & I am convinced the Enquiry will continued at least a fortnight, as there are Prisoners brought in every hour and new Discoveries making. One has been enlarged on giving Security in £100,000 to appear when called for, some have been whipped & others, against whom little can be made appear, have enlisted to serve in the Continental Army. There is yet another Class who comes fully within the Treason Law, that we cannot Punish otherwise than by sending to the best Prisons in the Neighbouring Counties, until they can be legally tried according to an Act of the last Session of Assembly to which however we are strangers, as we have not been able to procure a Copy of the Act & have only heard of it.

Some of the Capital offenders have disappeared whose personal Property has been removed by the soldiers & which they insist on being sold & divided as Plunder to which the Officers have submitted otherwise it would be almost impossible to get men on those pressing Occassions. I would beg your Excellency's Opinion on this head; as also what steps you Judge necessary to be taken by the Officers & Magistrates with the Prisoners, other than what I have mentioned.

SOURCE: Louise Phelps Kellogg, *Frontier Retreat on the Upper Ohio, 1779–1781* (Madison: State Historical Society of Wisconsin, 1917), 241–242.

This letter, from the wife of an apparent lynching victim, shows the ethnic dimension of the violence perpetrated by Charles Lynch and the Virginia Militia, based on "a misunderstanding between Colo Lynch and the Welsh in General."

21. *Nancy Devereaux to Col. William Preston,* August 1780

Dear Colo:

Colo Lynch, with a party of Militia have come from Bedford in quest of Tories, they are now at the Lead Mines, and have in Custoday Several and my Husband among the rest. I am very certain, nothing can be made appear against him, but as there is a misunderstanding between Colo Lynch and the Welsh in General, I am very uneasy at present least my Husband should not have the Strictest Justice done him at the Trial, therefore request the favour of you to send for him, and the Witnesses against him and have him Try'd, at Princes or where yourself and the rest of the Gentlemen are conveined, and then if my Husband should be convicted of any misconduct against the State, I only wish he may get a punishment Suitable to his deserts.

SOURCE: Louise Phelps Kellogg, *Frontier Retreat on the Upper Ohio, 1779–1781* (Madison: State Historical Society of Wisconsin, 1917), 252.

By August, doubts about Charles Lynch's tactics circulated in Virginia. Even his fellow militia officers seemed to think that Lynch might have gone too far.

22. *Col. Charles Lynch to Col. William Preston,* August 17, 1780

Dr Sr:

I was honour'd with yours a few days past, in which you Desire Me to Desist in trying torys &c &c—What sort of trials you have been inform'd I have given them I know not, but I can assure you I only Examine them strictly & such as I believe not Very criminal I set at Liberty. Others I have for a proper trial, some I have kept for soldiers, some as witnesses, some perhaps Justice of this County May require that shou'd be Made Exampels of. . . . I wou'd also request the favour of you to Let Me have a sight of Letters you receiv'd relative to my conduct &c &c.

SOURCE: Louise Phelps Kellogg, *Frontier Retreat on the Upper Ohio, 1779–1781* (Madison: State Historical Society of Wisconsin, 1917), 250–251.

Charles Lynch, in this letter, documents his own use of the term "Lynch's law." He also links his violence to race: his man applied "Lynch's law" to persons accused of "Dealing with the negroes &c."

23. *Charles Lynch to William Hay,* May 11, 1782

Dear Sir.

Since I had the Pleasure of seeing you I went up to the Led mines advising Capt Sanders to Exchange led for Bacon &c. I have received accounts of a fine Prospect of ore, and the Greatest Quantity raisd now Lying on hand that we have Ever had at any one time.—the furnace as I mentioned to you when Down is altogether out of repair;—and by one of the Miners who has Deserted and come to my house Last Evening (for want of Provisions as he says) I understand they await my going up to repair the furnace.—the old miner says Sanders feeds them on bread and water half their time, and Drives hard, & he won not nor cannot stand too it.—the neighboring People always has grumbled at Sanders for being too Light & Close in Exchanging Led for Provisions and the Executive have been inform'd he Lavish'd it away without taking any account of What he Did—I suppose I can discount for that & many more reports,—all the Welchmen, sumer before Last, Enter'd into bond not to Work for the Country unless they should all Be imploy'd and John Jenkins to have management considering the Business cou'd not be carried on with out them—at the same time Jenkins & two more that I fix'd it on saw sworn in with one Jo. Griffet who they Call'd Col Griffet at the head of the insurgents in them Parts—I was then so happy as to find out their schemes & frustrate them I was also able to do without their assistance, by working the furnace turn about with Mr. Sanders, & made more Led out of a charge of Oar then they had Done before—Jenkins who at that time was one of my Principal Men & receiving more wages than any Man I imploy'd,—after their infernal scheems was quash'd,—made some acknowledgements & Promising all that I cou'd ask, I took him into Business again he is of great use about the furnace—cut some of the rest who I am inform'd Made us of hundreds of Pounds of the Proprietors property, before the Country took possession of the mines, and who still was imploy'd Occasionally, being Loosers by the Mistake, I have already mentioned have never ceas'd to say Every thing to the Prejudice of Sanders & those Consern'd, and have gain'd the Ear of some I Did not Expect,—I am convinc'd a Party there is who by Lying has Deceiv'd some good men to Listen to them—they are mostly Torys & such as Sanders has given Lynchs Law too for Dealing with the negroes &c.

I shall await your Answer and Direction, when as you Direct I shall go up immediately & Do the Best I can—Whilst I have the Honor to be your most obt svt &c.

    Chas Lynch

Source: Governors' Letters Received, Library of Virginia, Richmond, Virginia.

The contemporary record of what happened in Revolutionary Virginia may seem confusing and contradictory. By the end of the nineteenth century some had begun to sentimentalize Charles Lynch, smoothing over references to his murderous violence and his ethnic prejudices. The new narratives falsely insisted that he never hanged anyone and therefore did not deserve the opprobrium associated with "Lynch Law."[3] This anonymous 1892 article appeared in the popular lawyers' magazine, *Green Bag*.

24. *"The Lynch-Law Tree,"* 1892

On the lawn of one of the most charming and hospitable homes in southern Virginia stands the old walnut-tree on which lynch law was first administered. It bears the marks of extreme age, and is a picturesque object in the landscape. . . .

It is not generally known that the original lynch law never sentenced an offender to death, but only to be whipped. . . . There is no room for doubt that the term "now become a part of the English language and accepted of all men" was derived from that fearless and honored soldier of the Revolution, Col. Charles Lynch, whose sword hangs on the wall of the lofty hall at Avoca. But that Colonel Lynch should be reputed the father of lynch law, in the modern acceptation of the term is quite another matter, and would be utterly unjust to him. In the year 1780, when the fortunes of the patriots were at low ebb, the Scotch settlers and Tories of Piedmont, Va., conspired to crush the "rebellion." Their efforts were thwarted by the courage, vigilance, and energy of Col. Charles Lynch, Capt. Robert Adams, and Capt. Thomas Calloway, aided by Col. William Preston, all Virginians of wealth and influence. Colonel Lynch, being Chief-Magistrate, had the powers of a judge. He was a man of striking individuality, and "vividly impressed the popular imagination,—so eminently a leader that he naturally and easily took his place at the head of the Whig party in his section of the country."

These gentlemen, ardent patriots, kept a sharp watch upon the loyalists; and when one was discovered, playing in the hands of the enemies of Washington, he was seized, taken to the residence of Colonel Lynch, examined by a court composed of the gentlemen above named and others, and if found guilty, tied to the walnut-trees, given thirty-nine lashes, and made to shout "Liberty forever!" . . . The refrain of a popular song of that section was,—

> "Hurrah for Colonel Lynch,
>   Captain Bob, and Calloway!
> They never let a Tory off
>   Until he shouts for Liberty."

The manner of procedure cannot be said to be lawless and unauthorized, and was considered by most amply justified by the disturbed condition of the country resulting from the repudiation of allegiance to the English Government. . . . no one ever came to his death at the hands of the gallant Colonel Lynch, except on the battlefield. No ghastly body ever dangled from the bare old tree that has battled with the storms of one hundred and fifty years.

SOURCE: "The Lynch-Law Tree," *Green Bag* 4 (1892): 561–562.

Thomas Walker Page, a Virginian, who studied at the University of Leipzig, Oxford University, and the University of Paris, continued the effort to clean up Charles Lynch's reputation. An economist, Page taught at leading American universities, including the University of California, the University of Texas, and the University of Virginia. In 1901 he vigorously defended Charles Lynch, calling him "a brave pioneer" and a "brawny man of peace." Page offers the most detailed biographical sketch of Charles Lynch available, based on documentary research but also on legend and family tradition.

25. *Thomas Walker Page, "The Real Judge Lynch,"* 1901

Charles Lynch was a man whose services to his country as a brave pioneer and righteous judge, as a soldier and a statesmen, are by no means deserving of oblivion, still less of obloquy. It seems, indeed, one of the iniquities of fate that his name should now be universally applied to proceedings that no one would condemn more heartily than he. The records of the court of Bedford County, in Virginia, and those of various Quaker meetings, the journals of the House of Burgesses and the first Constitutional Convention, taken together with family documents and traditions, show him to have been an upright and useful member of society, and a wise and energetic leader at the most important crisis of American history.

Charles Lynch was born in 1736, at Chestnut Hill, his father's estate. . . . There is a tradition that somewhere in the misty past one of his forefathers was mayor of a certain Irish city, where he meted out justice with a hand so stern and swift as to earn him the sobriquet of "Hanging Pat." . . .

In the division of the Irish Immigrant's property, Chestnut Hill, the home he had founded on the James, fell to his eldest son, John. Charles, therefore, was under the necessity of taking his young wife to the family lands that lay nearer the frontier. . . . It required a stout heart and a strong arm to establish civilization in such a country at such a time, but young Lynch was equal to the occasion.

Already the previous year it had been attempted to meet the necessity of a proper government for the scattered settlers by the organization of Bedford County. . . . It was then "Ordered, that the Sheriff of this County impress a sufficient Number of Persons to guard such Persons as from Time to Time shall be arrested and taken into Custody in the County." His duties began immediately, for the next entry is "Ordered, that the Sheriff summon those Persons that have this Daye behaved in a riotous Manner in the Court to appear to Morrow to answer the Same." . . .

Such were the conditions for law and executing justice in the county where Lynch attained to manhood. A sparsely settled frontier region, the beginning of a long and mortal struggle with the French and the savages, the mere form of a court of justice meeting in a place of public entertainment, interrupted by "ryotous behavyour," and presided over by men whose ignorance of "compleat Bodys of the Law" was equaled only by the impotence of the sheriff to prevent "Escaips" of malefactors. Truly, at such a time every log house must be a castle, every man must be his own protector, and justice had no other local habitation than the hearts of the hard-fisted settlers in buckskin breeches who were planting in the wilderness the seeds of civilization. . . .

As a leading Quaker, Lynch found his services in great demand to arbitrate disputes over land, cattle, and other things. There is even a tradition to the effect that he was once called upon to settle a quarrel between the owners of two captive bears, who had bet on a fight between the animals, and disagreed about the result. On that occasion his decision was so unsatisfactory that the disputants turned their wrath from each other upon the umpire. In the struggle that ensued Celtic blood proved too much for Quaker principles, and the brawny man of peace forced the quarrelers to swallow his decision. . . .

Lynch . . . had been made a justice of the peace under a commission from Dunmore in 1774, and when the county court was reorganized according to the ordinance of the [Constitutional] Convention, passed on the 3d of July, 1776, he retained his position. Several of his former associates on the bench, however, were of Tory sentiments, and refused to serve under a republican government. He did not enlist in the army, partly because of his Quaker principles, but chiefly because his presence was imperatively necessary at home. . . . He had to raise and equip troops for the army. . . . He let it be known, however, that neither Quaker principles nor other duties would prevent his going to the front, if his services became more necessary there than at home. Accordingly, we find, in 1778, that the court of Bedford "doth recommend to his Excellency, the Governor, Charles Lynch as a suitable Person to exercise the Office of Colonel of Militia in this County." . . .

In 1780 the British determined to shift the war to the South. . . . Numerous records of the county courts, taken together with other sources of information, show that here, as in many other western counties, there was a strong and influential party opposed to the struggle for independence. . . . They therefore entered into a conspiracy to upset the county organization, and to seize for the use of Cornwallis on his arrival the stores that Lynch had collected. . . . Tradition says that Colonel Lynch was made aware of the conspirators' plans by one of their own number. He had them all arrested, and found among them some of the leading men of the county. . . . The infliction of capital punishment was extremely rare. There were only three instances of it. . . . both custom and sentiment were violently opposed to visiting capital punishment upon the detected Tory conspirators. But fines and warnings would evidently be inadequate. . . . After careful deliberation, Colonel Lynch, as the presiding justice, sentenced them to terms of imprisonment varying from one to five years. . . .

Such was the result of the trial that has made the name of Lynch a byword and a hissing in the tongues of the nations!

In passing these sentences, comparatively mild as they were, the county court was transcending its powers; the General Court alone had jurisdiction in cases of treason.

SOURCE: Thomas Walter Page, "The Real Judge Lynch," *Atlantic Monthly* 88 (December 1901): 731–741.

NOTES

1. James Elbert Cutler, *Lynch-Law: An Investigation into the History of Lynching in the United States* (New York: Longman's Green, 1905), 16.

2. Daniel Leonard, *Massachusettensis: Letters to the Inhabitants of the Province of Massachusetts Bay, 12 December 1774–3 April 1775* (1776; reprint ed., Boston: Gregg, 1972), 3, 12.

3. Some newspapers published an interview with Charles Lynch's granddaughter, celebrating her ancestor's "courage, vigilance, and energy." See *Edgefield [South Carolina] Advertiser,* March 24, 1892.

2

Jacksonian America

Whether Charles or William Lynch first used his name as a verb excites debate primarily academic. The more important inquiry asks who legitimized the idea of summary violence administered outside the law. This question must turn on popular sovereignty since lynchers typically base their legitimacy on the public's claim on ultimate power. This is not so farfetched since, as Edmund Morgan has observed, the fiction of popular sovereignty rests on another fiction: the righteousness, independence, and military prowess of yeomen farmers. If government asserts its authority as an expression of the people's power, one should not be surprised to find that on occasion the public's might breaks free of its bounds, spilling out into the streets. During the revolutionary era, some praised rioting as politics "out-of-doors." Mob violence simply expressed a common good shared by every member of the community, a kind of informal republicanism.[1]

It can be no coincidence that lynching achieved widespread currency at exactly the moment Andrew Jackson's star shined brightest. More than any previous president, Jackson advanced his own power as an expression of ordinary people. And Jackson came into office with an established record as an energetic enforcer of popular values outside law. No one used the phrase Lynch Law to describe Jackson's actions, but early in the nineteenth century Jackson became famous for boldly killing enemies of the public, members of despised populations, without according them due process of law. White Americans admired him for acting decisively outside the pesky constraints posed by law and constitutionalism.

While Jackson served as president, the word "lynching" entered the print culture, joining the national vocabulary for the first time. At the same time, opponents of mob law turned the word to their own use, a tool to condemn their enemies.

After making himself a national hero by defeating the British at New Orleans in 1816,[2] Jackson marched into Florida, attacking the Spanish at Pensacola and then going after the Indians. On April 8, 1818, he hanged two captured Indian chiefs without even the pretense of a trial. The word "lynching" did not circulate widely that year, but a mob law spirit animated Jackson's actions, as it did again on April 29, 1818, when he executed two English subjects, Alexander Arbuthnot and Robert C. Ambrister, accused of siding with the Indians. Americans today would call Arbuthnot and Ambrister "enemy combatants" entitled to due-process protections. For Jackson, their outsider status made it all the easier to cast aside due process of law and hurry them to their deaths. In contrast to the fate of the Indians, however, Jackson felt that he had to give these white men something resembling a trial before execution. But his drumhead court-martial offered no real due process, no chance of appeal or real justice, and rested on no legal authority. Some claim Col. Charles Lynch acted only in technical excess of his authority as a militia officer when he executed Tories. General Jackson's defenders made the same claim for their hero. Those defenders had only a little trouble with Ambrister, first sentenced to death but then only to a whipping, after the court-martial reconsidered its original decision. Jackson had him shot anyway, rejecting his own court's ultimate verdict. He had no authority to hold the court-martial in the first place, or to overturn its leniency, any more than Charles Lynch had authority to try felonies on the Virginia Southside. It seems fair to conclude that Jackson was a lyncher in the same way as Charles Lynch, albeit without the name. And Jackson had far more influence.

Robert Butler, an officer on Jackson's staff, filed a report on Jackson's execution of the Indian chiefs.

26. *Robert Butler to Daniel Parker,*
Adjutant and Inspector General, May 3, 1818

[On] the morning of the 5th . . . the march was resumed for St. Marks, before which it arrived on the evening of the 6th, and, after communicating with the commanding officer, took possession of that fortress on the following morning. Captain McKeever, of the navy, having sailed for St. Marks with some vessels containing supplies for the army, was fortunate enough to entice on board his vessel, in the river, Francis, or Hillishajo, and Homathlamicco, hostile chiefs of the Creek nation, and whose settled hostility has been severely felt by our citizens. The commanding general had them brought on shore, and ordered them to be hung, as an example to deter others from exciting these deluded wretches to future scenes of butchery. A man of the name of A. Arbuthnot was also taken on the arrival of the army, and placed in close confinement.

SOURCE: Robert Butler to Daniel Parker, May 3, 1818, *American State Papers. Documents, Legislative and Executive, of the Congress of the United States* (Washington: Gales and Seaton, 1832), 1:703.

After court-martialing and hanging the two British subjects, Jackson reported on what he had done to his superiors.

27. *Trial and Execution of Alexander Arbuthnot and*
Robert C. Ambrister, 1818

At a special court-martial, commenced on the 26th instant at St. Marks, and continued until the night of the 28th, of which Brevet Major General E. P. Gaines is President, was tried A. Arbuthnot on the following charges and specifications, viz:

Charge 1st. Exciting and stirring up the Creek Indians to war against the United States and her citizens; he, A. Arbuthnot, being a subject of Great Britain, with whom the United States are at peace.

Charge 2d. Acting as a spy, aiding, abetting, and comforting the enemy, and supplying them with the means of war.

Charge 3d. Exciting the Indians to murder and destroy William Hambly and Edmund Doyle, confiscate their property, and causing their arrest with a view to their condemnation to death, and the seizure of their property, they being citizens of Spain, on account of their active and zealous exertions to maintain peace between Spain, the United States, and the Indians.

To which charges the prisoner pleaded not guilty. The court, after mature deliberation on the evidence adduced, find the prisoner, A. Arbuthnot, guilty of the first charge, and guilty of the second charge, leaving out the words "acting as a spy"; and, after mature reflection, sentence him, A. Arbuthnot, to be suspended by the neck until he is *dead*.

Was also tried Robert C. Ambrister, on the following charges, viz:

Charge 1st. Aiding, abetting, and comforting the enemy, and supplying them with the means of war, he being a subject of Great Britain, (who are at peace with the United States,) and late an officer in the British colonial marines.

Charge 2d. Leading and commanding the Lower Creek Indians in carrying on a war against the United States.

To which charges the prisoner pleaded as follows, viz: To the first charge not guilty; to the second charge guilty, and justification.

The court, on examination of evidence, and on mature deliberation, find the prisoner, Robert C. Ambrister, guilty of the first and second charges, and do therefore sentence him to suffer death by being *shot*. The members requesting a reconsideration of the vote on this sentence, and it being had, they sentence the prisoner to receive fifty stripes on his bare back, and he being confined with a ball and chain to hard labor for twelve calendar months.

The Commanding General approves the finding and sentence of the court in the case of A. Arbuthnot, and approves the finding and first sentence of the court in the case of Robert C. Ambrister, and disapproves the reconsideration of the honorable court in this case. It appears from the evidence and pleading of the prisoner that he did lead and command, within the territory of Spain, (being a subject of Great Britain,) the Indians in war against the United States, those nations being at peace. It is an established principle of the laws of nations that any individual of a nation making war against the citizens of another nation, they being at peace, forfeits his allegiance, and becomes an outlaw and pirate; this is the case of Robert C. Ambrister, clearly shown by the evidence adduced.

The Commanding General orders that Brevet Major A. C. W. Fanning, of the corps of artillery, will have, between the hours of eight and nine o'clock, A.M., A. Arbuthnot suspended by the neck, with a rope, until he is *dead*, and Robert C. Ambrister to be shot to *death*, agreeably to the sentence of the court.

SOURCE: *American State Papers. Documents, Legislative and Executive, of the Congress of the United States* (Washington: Gales and Seaton, 1832), 1:734.

Andrew Jackson intended the deaths of Arbuthnot and Ambrister as *spectacle*, "an awful example to the world." He made this point in his report to the Secretary of War, John C. Calhoun.

28. *Andrew Jackson to Secretary of War John C. Calhoun*, May 5, 1818

In Fort St. Marks, as an inmate in the family of the Spanish commander, an Englishman by the name of Arbuthnot was found, unable satisfactorily to explain the objects of his visiting this country, and there being a combination of circumstances to justify a suspicion that his views were not honest[,] he was ordered in close confinement.

The capture of his schooner near the mouth of the Suwaney river by my aid-de-camp, Lieutenant Gadsden, and the papers found on board, unveiled his corrupt transactions, as well as those of Captain Ambrister, late of the British colonial marine corps, taken as a prisoner near Bowlegs town. These individuals were tried under my orders by a special court of select officers, legally convicted as exciters of this savage and negro war, legally condemned, and most justly punished for their iniquities. . . . If Arbuthnot and Ambrister are not convicted as the authorized agents of Great Britain, there is no doubt but that that Government had a knowledge of their assumed character, and was well advised of the measures which they had adopted to excite the negroes and Indians in East Florida to war against the United States. I hope the execution of these two unprincipled villains will prove an awful example to the world, and convince the Government of Great Britain, as well as her subjects, that certain, though slow retribution awaits those unchristian wretches who, by false promises, delude and excite an Indian tribe to all the horrid deeds of savage war.

SOURCE: Andrew Jackson to John C. Calhoun, May 5, 1818, *American State Papers. Documents, Legislative and Executive, of the Congress of the United States* (Washington: Gales and Seaton, 1832), 1:702.

Most Americans could overlook the Indian chiefs more easily than the extralegal executions of two white men. Congressman Henry Clay pointed out that Jackson acted outside the law in all four cases and warned that the United States ran the risk of losing the "great moral battle" for world opinion if it did not condemn Jackson's actions.[3] (The *Annals of Congress* paraphrased Clay's speech rather than publishing it verbatim.) Jackson's most prominent modern biographer, Robert Remini, agrees with Clay, charging that the illegal executions reflected "frontier fears, bigotry, and hatred at their worst."[4]

29. *Henry Clay, "Seminole War,"* January 20, 1819

The first circumstance which . . . fixed our attention, had, Mr. C. said, filled him with regret. It was the execution of the Indian chiefs. How, he asked, did they come into our possession? Was it in the course of fair and open and honorable war? No; but by means of deception—by hoisting foreign colors on the staff from which the stars and stripes should alone have floated. Thus ensnared, the Indians were taken on shore, and without ceremony, without delay, were hung. . . . it was the first instance that he knew of, in the annals of our country, in which retaliation, by executing Indian captives, had ever been deliberately practiced. There may have been exceptions, but, if there were, they met with contemporaneous condemnation, and have been reprehended by the just pen of impartial history. The gentleman from Massachusetts [John Holmes] may tell me, if he pleases, what he pleases about the tomahawk and the scalping knife; about Indian enormities, and foreign miscreants and incendiaries. I, too, hate them; from my very soul I abominate them. But I love my country and its Constitution; I love liberty and safety, and fear military despotism. . . .

The mode of the trial and sentencing of [Arbuthnot and Ambrister] was equally objectionable. . . . No man could be executed in this free country without two things being shown; 1st. That the law condemns him to death; and, 2dly. That his death is pronounced by that tribunal which is authorized by the law to try him. . . . [Clay] denied that any commander-in-chief, in this country, had this absolute power of life and death, at his sole discretion. It was contrary to the genius of all our laws and institutions. . . .

However guilty these men were, they should not have been condemned or executed without the authority of the law. He would not dwell, at this time, on the effect of these precedents in foreign countries.

SOURCE: Henry Clay, Remarks on The Seminole War, January 20, 1819, 15th Congress, 2d sess., House of Representatives, Annals of Congress.

Jackson's defenders carried the day, praising his energy and promptitude. "Whatever degree of force, whatever destruction, whatever punishment" whites needed to inflict on "savages" and their white allies for endangering women and children, "they should be made to feel," one Virginia congressman orated.[5] More white Americans agreed with the Virginian than with Henry Clay. In fact, Americans widely admired Jackson for his decisive illegalities. His example put decisive action ahead of tedious legalities to become a model for lynchers, making him, in a sense, the original Judge Lynch.

In the early years of the nineteenth century, as newspaper readers discovered the power of widely shared knowledge cheaply distributed, ordinary Americans believed that they could rally as a unified public in a single agitation, a great public articulation of consensus, a revision of the old elite vision of the nation as a republic, with citizens acting in a common cause. By 1824, when Jackson first ran for president, many white Americans had made democracy their watchword. These new democrats had no doubt that the "public" possessed ultimate power, if not at the ballot box then on the street. Jackson's opponents wrote elegant newspaper editorials; his followers marshaled large crowds, cheering and chanting with torches behind live eagles. Jackson ran for president in 1824, winning both the popular vote and the electoral vote. He nonetheless did not take office after that election. Since he did not win a majority, the election went to the House of Representatives where John Q. Adams emerged the winner. From Jackson's perspective, the election had been stolen from him by a backroom deal. In 1828 Jackson had the satisfaction of defeating John Q. Adams through the sheer power of his popular appeal.

After winning the presidency, Jackson celebrated by throwing open the White House to the ordinary people he championed. His critics decried his inauguration as a mob spectacle: the rabble scrambled, fought, romped, and jostled. The worst was yet to come. By the time Jackson left office in 1837, to be succeeded by his vice president, Martin Van Buren, the whole nation seemed rocked by disorder. Mob violence erupted in Vicksburg, Mississippi, St. Louis, Cincinnati, New York, and many other cities across the country. Jacksonian democracy had apparently made rioting epidemic. One newspaper declared: "The whole country . . . seems ready to take fire on the most trivial occasion." Another paper moaned about "the present supremacy of the Mobocracy."[6]

When Jackson took office, the word *lynching* circulated largely outside the print culture in the rhythms of ordinary conversation. Travelers encountered the word; a South Carolina novelist fascinated by frontier argot picked it up. In the spring of 1830 the travel writer James Stuart steamed up the Mississippi River. Stuart later wrote of his experiences, including an encounter with frontier mobbing, of which he thoroughly approved. On the frontier, where courts are not well established, the inhabitants could devise "no better scheme" for protecting their property.

30. *James Stuart, "On the Mississippi,"* 1830

In an extensive district of country, where the expence of a police establishment cannot be borne by a few inhabitants, scattered at considerable distances from each other, no better scheme perhaps can be devised than that the inhabitants should, with a view to their security, place themselves under the control of some one of their number, in whom they have confidence. Many instances of this have occurred in Southern and Western America and, in various cases, the newly established state governments have winked at the infliction of public punishment on depredators and criminals by such authorities as those I have mentioned, where it was obviously impossible to have criminals, and the necessary witnesses, carried to a circuit town, owing to its great distance, and to the almost total absence of officers of police. I have heard, and I believe correctly, though I cannot specify my authority, that soon after the war of the revolution, when many lawless acts were committed by the disbanded soldiers in the United States, especially in the mountainous parts of the state of Carolina, the inhabitants deputed powers of this description to an individual of the name of Lynch, who exercised them with such impartiality, that his decisions were almost looked upon as having the force of law. They were said to be pronounced according to Lynch's law; and now, whenever a delinquent is summarily punished by the neighborhood in the way I have mentioned, he is said to be punished by Lynch's law. There are yet, on the western banks of the Mississippi, occurrences which require that this law should be resorted to, and even capital punishment inflicted. Sometimes, however, these self-constituted courts have done wrong; and, in such cases, have been called to account for their proceedings before regular courts of judicature, and had to pay heavy damages. These local courts almost in all cases dissolve themselves as soon as the district is able to support anything like regular police. . . .

In the course of the 10th of April, while we were still in the territory of the Arkansas, and in a very wild part of the river, we stopped to take in wood. I had not intended to go ashore, but Captain Paul, who was obligingly anxious to make me acquainted with every thing that he thought would interest or amuse me, after being ashore, returned to insist upon my accompanying him to the residence of a planter, who was a judge, by which I mean a justice of the peace, in the neighborhood. The judge was a fine old man, in a very comfortable habitation, clean and well kept, and pressed me to join him in a little rye whisky, which turned out to be the best whisky I had seen in the United States—for it is seldom of good quality. I found that Captain Paul's object in getting me ashore was to prevail upon this old gentleman to relate to me an occurrence which took place here a few days ago, and to which he suspected I would not give credit if I had heard it only from him, the captain, at second hand. It seems that several boats, going down the river with the produce of the country a few days ago, had stopped during the night in this neighbourhood; and that in one of the boats a murder had been committed; and the murderer detected almost in the fact.

The people in the boats were excited—the victim was the friend of many of them; and they feared that his death would remain unrevenged if the murderer, whom they had immediately apprehended, was handed over to a very distant Arkansas court, where there was little prospect of any witness attending. They therefore resolved instantly to try him by Lynch's law, and ordered him to be hung not many hours afterwards. Notice of the proceedings was given to the judge, whom I was visiting, but he had no force to prevent the execution of the sentence, had he been so inclined. In point of fact, he, as I was told, rather thought that the example would be productive of good effects, on account of the number of lawless people at present upon the river. No one is more exposed to depredations than the judge himself. His plantation is on the edge of the river; and he has a rather nice orchard and garden, and large stacks of wood for the steam-boats.

SOURCE: James Stuart, *Three Years in North America*, 2 vols. (Edinburgh: Robert Cadell, 1833), 178–179, 266–267.

The South Carolina novelist William Gilmore Simms had an ear for dialogue and a desire to make his novels sound authentic. In 1834, when he first published *Guy Rivers*, he did not expect his audience to know what the word *lynching* meant, so he defined it. Like Stuart, Simms saw little to disparage and, also like Stuart, believed the word had its origins in the Revolution, on the East Coast. More than Stuart, however, Simms emphasized the link between lynching and popular sovereignty. "The regulators are just, simply, you see, our own people," one character explained. Simms and Stuart also agreed that race had nothing to do with lynching, although Simms did identify mob violence with sectional malice. His Georgians punished peddlers for fraud, "coming Yankee over everybody."

31. *William Gilmore Simms, "Guy Rivers,"* 1834

"Why, you must know, 'squire, that the regulators have made out to catch a certain Yankee pedler—one Jared Bunce; and you must know, 'squire, a more cunning and presumptious rapscallion don't come from all Connecticut. They caught the critter not an hour ago. . . . He can cheat you out of your eyes, and you won't know about it, till it's all done, and too late to make a fuss. He's been playing his tricks through the clearing, it's now better than three years, and somehow he always got off; but last year the *regulators* swore for him, and he *cut dirt,* I tell you.

"Who are the regulators?" inquired the youth.

"What, you live in Georgia, and never heard tell of the regulators? Well, that's queer, anyhow. But, the regulators are just, simply, you see, our own people; who, every now and then, turn out,—now one set and now another,—and whenever a chap like this same Jared Bunce goes about, living on everybody, and coming Yankee over everybody, they hunt him up and pay off old scores. Sometimes they let him off with a light hand, but then, you see, it altogether happens according to his behavior. Sometimes they give him Lynch's Law, after old Nick Lynch, who invented it in Virginny, long before your time or mine. Sometimes they ride him upon a rail, and then duck him in the pond. It all depends, you see, upon the humour of the regulators."

"And which of these punishments will they inflict upon the Yankee?"

"Well, now, I can't say—but I take it, he runs a chance of hitting hard agin all of 'em. They've got a long score agin him. He's taken in everybody with his notions. Some bought his clocks, which only went while the rogue was in sight, and after that they came to a full stand. Some bought ready-made clothes, which never lasted long enough for soap and the washerwoman; and there's old Jeremiah Seaborn that swears agin him for a fusee he sold little Jeremiah, the son, that bursted into flinders the very first fire, and tore the boy's hand and arm, there's no telling how. I reckon he's in a fair road for stumps."

"And will they seriously harm the poor fellow, and that too without law?"

The woodman turned more fully to the youth, as if doubting the sincerity, as he certainly seemed not a little surprised at the simplicity, of the question.

"Harm him—poor fellow! I wonder, 'squire, that you should speak so of such a fellow;—a fellow that's got no more soul than my whip-handle, and isn't half so much to be counted on in a fight. Why, he only goes about the country to rob and to defraud; and ha'n't spirit enough, would you believe it, either to get drunk with his friend or have it out with his enemy. I shouldn't myself like to see the fellow's throat cut, but I an't scrupulous to say, I see no harm in his having the benefit of a few hickories, and a dip into the horsepond; and if you knew but half as much of his rogueries as I, you'd soon come over to my opinion."

Ralph knew well how perfectly idle must be any effort in such an argument to overcome the prejudices of the sturdy woodman, in which, from repeated and extravagant impositions of the kind spoken of, the humble classes of the South had been taught but a common spirit. He contented himself, therefore, with a single remark upon the general propriety of forbearance where the laws could administer ample justice. But Forrester had his answer for this also.

"There, again, 'squire, you are quite out. The laws, somehow or other, can't touch these conniving fellows. They run through the country a wink faster than the sheriff's deputies, and laugh at all the processes you send after them. So, you see, there's no justice, no how, unless you catch a rogue like this, and wind up with him for all the gang—for they're all alike, all of the same family, and it comes to the same thing in the end."

SOURCE: William Gilmore Simms, *Guy Rivers: A Tale of Georgia*, 2 vols. (New York: Harper and Brothers, 1834), 1:64–68.

After the fourth of July, 1835, a Vicksburg mob hanged five white gamblers. Newspaper coverage called the Vicksburg killings "lynchings," and spread the word across the country. The Vicksburgers justified their violence on the basis of community sovereignty. "We have never known the public so unanimous on any subject," the *Vicksburg Register* declared. Ostensibly these killings of white people by a white mob had nothing to do with race. Some writers, however, insist that the Vicksburg lynchings tamed the Mississippi Valley frontier, using southern cultural symbols to close out the "flush times" and buckle down to the real work of plantation agriculture. By this account, white Vicksburgers cleaned out the gamblers as part of a larger project of making the Mississippi Valley safe for slavery.[7]

32. *"The Vicksburg Tragedy,"* 1835

The following account of some proceedings of the citizens of this town, which will excite the attention of the public, was prepared by a witness of the acts detailed, and the correctness of the account may be relied on.

And so far as we know, public opinion, both in town and country, is decidedly in favor of the course pursued. We have never known the public so unanimous on any subject.

Our city has for some days past been the theatre of the most novel and startling scenes that we have ever witnessed. While we regret that the necessity for such scenes should have existed, we are proud of the public spirit and indignation against offenders displayed by the citizens, and congratulate them on having at length banished a class of individuals, whose shameless vices and daring outrages have long poisoned the springs of morality, and interrupted the relations of society. For years past, Professional Gamblers, destitute of all sense of moral obligations—unconnected with society by any of its ordinary ties, and intent only on the gratification of their avarice—have made Vicksburg their place of rendezvous—and, in the very bosom of our society, boldly plotted their vile and lawless machinations. Here, as everywhere else, the laws of the country were found wholly ineffectual for the punishment of these individuals, and emboldened by impunity, their numbers and their crimes, have daily continued to multiply. Every species of transgression followed in their train. They supported a large number of tippling houses to which they would decoy the youthful and unsuspecting, and, after stripping them of their possessions, send them forth into the world the ready and desperate instruments of vice. Our streets were ever resounding with the echoes of their drunken and obscene mirth, and no citizen was secure from their villainy. Frequently in armed bodies, they have disturbed the good order of public assemblages, insulted our citizens, and defied our civil authorities. Thus had they continued to grow bolder in their wickedness, and more formidable in their numbers, until Saturday, the fourth of July, (inst[ant]) when our citizens had assembled together with the corps of Vicksburg volunteers, at the barbecue, to celebrate the day by the usual festivities. After dinner, and during the delivery of the toasts, one of the officers attempted to enforce order and silence at the table, when one of these gamblers, whose name was Cabler, who had impudently thrust himself into the company, insulted the officer and struck one of the citizens. Indignation immediately rose high, and it was only by the interference of the commandant that he was saved from instantaneous punishment. He was, however, permitted to retire, and the company dispersed. The military corps proceeded to the public square of the city, and . . . information was received that Cabler was coming up armed, and resolved to kill one of the Volunteers who had been most active in expelling him from the table. Knowing his desperate character—two of the corps instantly stepped forward and arrested him. A loaded pistol, a large knife and dagger were found on his person, all of which he had procured since he had separated from the company. To liberate him would have been to devote several of the most respectable members of the company to his vengeance, and to proceed against him at law would have been mere mockery, inasmuch as, not having had the opportunity of consummating his design, no adequate punishment could have been inflicted on him. Consequently it was determined to take him into the woods and *lynch* him—which is a mode of punishment provided for such as become obnoxious in a manner which the law cannot reach. He was immediately carried out under a guard, attended by a crowd of respectable citizens—tied to a tree, punished with stripes—tarred and feathered, and ordered to leave the city in 48 hours. In the meantime one of his comrades, the Lucifer of the gang, had been endeavoring to rally and arm his confederates for the purpose of rescuing him; which however he failed to accomplish.

Having thus aggravated the whole band of these desperadoes, and feeling no security against their vengeance, the citizens met at night in the Court house, in a large number, and there passed the following resolutions:

Resolved, That a notice be given to all Professional Gamblers, that the citizens of Vicksburg are *resolved* to exclude them from this place and its vicinity; and that twenty-four hours notice be given them to leave the place. . . .

On Sunday morning, one of these notices was posted at the corners of each square of the city. During that day (the 5th) a majority of the gang, terrified by the threats of the citizens, dispersed in different directions, without making any opposition. It was sincerely hoped that the remainder would follow their example, and thus prevent a bloody termination of the strife, which had commenced. On the morning of the 6th, the military corps, followed by a file of several hundred citizens, marched to each suspected house and, sending in an examining committee, dragged out every faro table and other gambling apparatus that could be found. At length they approached a house which was occupied by one of the most profligate of the gang, whose name was North, and in which, it was understood that a garrison of armed men had been stationed. All hoped that these wretches would be intimidated by the superior numbers of their assailants, and surrender themselves at discretion, rather than attempt a desperate defence. The House being surrounded, the back door was burst open, when four or five shots were fired from the interior, one of which instantly killed Doctor Hugh S. Bodley, a citizen universally beloved and respected. The interior was so dark that the villains could not be seen, but several of the citizens, guided by the flash of their guns, returned their fire. A yell from one of the party announced that one of these shots had been effectual, and by this time a crowd of citizens, their indignation overcoming all other feelings—burst open every door of the building, and dragged into the light those who had not been wounded.

North, the ringleader, who had contrived this desperate plot, could not be found in the building, but was apprehended by a citizen, while attempting, in company with another, to make his escape, at a place not far distant. Himself, with the rest of the prisoners, were then conducted in silence to the scaffold. One of them, not having been in the building before it was attacked, nor appearing to be concerned with the rest, except that he was the brother of one of them, was liberated. The remaining number of five, among whom was the individual who had been shot, but who still lived, were immediately executed in presence of the assembled multitude. All sympathy for the wretches was completely merged in defestation and horror of their crime. The whole procession then returned to the city, collected all the faro tables into a pile and burnt them—This being done, a troop of horsemen set out for a neighboring house to the residence of Hord, the individual who had attempted to organize a force on the day of this disturbance, for the rescue of Cabler, and had since threatened to fire the city. He had, however, made his escape on that day, and the next morning crossed the Big Black, at Baldwin's ferry, in a state of indescribable consternation. We lament his escape, as his whole course of life, for the last three years, has exhibited the most shameless profligacy, and been a continual series of transgression against the laws of God and man.

The names of the individuals who perished were as follows: North, Hullums, Dutch Bill, Smith and McCall.

Their bodies were cut down on the morning after execution, and buried in a ditch.

It is not expected that this act will pass without censure from most who had not an opportunity of knowing and feeling the dire necessity out of which it originated. The laws, however severe in their provision, have never been sufficient to correct a vice which must be established by positive proof, and cannot, like others, be shown from circumstantial testimony. It is practiced too, by individuals whose whole study is to violate the law in such a manner as to evade its punishment, and who never are in want of secret confederates to swear them out of their difficulties, whose oaths cannot be impeached for any specific cause. We had borne with their enormities, until to have suffered them any longer would not only have proved us to be destitute of every manly sentiment, but would also have implicated us in the guilt of accessories to their crimes.

Society may be compared to the elements, which, although "order is their first law," can sometimes be purified only by a storm. Whatever, therefore, sickly sensibility or mawkish philanthropy may say against the course pursued by us, we hope that our citizens will not relax the code of punishment which they have enacted against this infamous, unprincipled and baleful class of society—and we invite Natchez, Jackson, Columbus, Warrenton, and all our sister towns throughout the state, in the name of our insulted laws—of offended virtue, and of slaughtered innocence, to aid us in exterminating this deep-rooted vice from our land. The Revolution has been conducted here by the most respectable citizens, heads of families, members of all classes, professions, and pursuits. None have been heard to utter a syllable of censure against either the act or the manner in which it was performed.

An anti-gambling society has been formed, the members of which have pledged their lives, fortunes and sacred honors, for the suppression of gambling, and the punishment and expulsion of gamblers.

Source: *Vicksburg Register*, July 9, 1835.

In Vicksburg whites mobbed other whites. Some historians insist that the Vicksburg troubles had an indirect connection to slavery, but the connection is not obvious. Within months of the Vicksburg hangings the connection between mobbing and slavery became more explicit. Abolitionists seized on the word "lynching," turning it against their enemies. Abolitionists wanted to abolish slavery, but they realized that talking about white southerners' propensity for mob violence helped their anti-slavery cause. They charged that lynching had become a deliberate system of white southern lawbreaking, one based on popular sovereignty rather than the higher law of constitutionalism. Slavery, a lawless institution, encouraged mob violence, lynching, and many other crimes, abolitionists claimed. Abolitionists complained that lynchers endangered the Constitution, a charge often leveled at the abolitionists themselves. They knew that many northerners, while indifferent to the plight of black people, could be aroused with reports of mob violence because they disliked the disorder that lynching represented.

33. *"The Enemies of the Constitution Discovered,"* 1835

At Vicksburg, a number of citizens of the United States were seized and executed without even the pretence of legal authority, contrary to the express letter of the constitution of the United States, which declares, that "no person shall be deprived of life, liberty, or property, without due process of law." Acts equally inconsistent with the constitution and laws of our country have been matters of every day occurrence, but have regarded as comparatively of little moment, until they had gained the co-operation and sanction of men high in authority. . . .

All who have been conversant with the subject must have observed that in most cases of late, the law breaking, or proceedings of Judge Lynch has been carried on in the most systematic manner, with all possible regularity and solemnity. The proceeding is on this wise. A meeting of citizens is called, at which care is sometimes taken to have a large number of boys and drunkards, enough to constitute a *clever mob* who are ready to set up a roar of laughter, cheering, hissing, or yelling at the signal of their leader; when this class attend, every thing is carried by them, and nobody observes whether the voices come from the rabble, or from respectable citizens: of course the proceedings are ascribed to respectable citizens. The most inflammatory speeches are then made, and the rabble understand well that their duty is to act according to the spirit of the speeches, and not according to the letter of the resolutions, because these being matters of record must necessarily be more temperate. It must before have been observed that the officers of Judge Lynch never act in discharge of those *inferior obligations which we owe to the constitution and the laws,* but only of the *higher obligations which we owe to society.*

After the public mind has been excited to the highest pitch and the rabble have become phrensied with rage and desperation, so that they are ready to rush madly upon whatever design the *chief mover* has in view, in order that the design of violating the laws of the land and the rights of citizens, may be accomplished in the most *genteel* and unsuspicious manner, a committee consisting of a large number of citizens, (some drawn unconsciously into the snare) is appointed who advance with professions of pacific intentions, either preceded or followed by the rabble to the spot where the violence is to be committed. . . .

After the Lynching is finished . . . and while the "committee" retire to their homes and are industriously engaged in preparing communications for the public journals in order to forestall public opinion, the "peaceable citizens" assemble together in small squads at the groceries in different parts of the city, where orders are sometimes given, by some higher in the scale of being than they, that intoxicating liquors shall be dealt out to them in large quantities without money and without price. . . .

Sometimes a few of the principal officers of Judge Lynch are called to an account by Judge Law, but their *bond of indemnity* is brought into requisition and their fines are instantly discharged, even in case the latter judge should be so fortunate as to find that his chief officers have not superceded their functions by an appointment under the former. . . .

We have seen the principal features which distinguish the *calm, peaceable, and deliberate* system of law-breaking of the present day, and by taking care to keep them in view hereafter, we shall be enabled to detect the fallacious pretences with which it is too frequently excused or palliated, and to discover its authors from beneath the cloaks with which they are covered.

SOURCE: "Defensor," *The Enemies of the Constitution Discovered, or, An Inquiry into the Origin and Tendency of Popular Violence* (New York, 1835), 11, 48–52.

In 1836 a St. Louis mob numbering in the thousands carried out one of the most famous, and barbarous, lynchings in American history. This account appeared in the abolitionist journal *Boston Liberator*, penned by a writer who witnessed the burning personally, standing at the front of the mob, directly before Francis McIntosh.

Crudely racist newspapers referred to McIntosh as a "yellow fellow" because of his mixed race heritage. He had white and African ancestry. Whites sometimes feared such mulattoes (supposedly yellow in color, in some cases) as especially dangerous because they were thought to combine the cunning of the white race with the savage brutality of the black race. In this instance, whites accused McIntosh of murdering the white deputy of a sheriff.

The St. Louis mob burned McIntosh to death at a time when humanitarians campaigned to at least move state executions indoors.[8] In a society trying to distance itself from pain, this account has pornographic appeal, offering a detailed description of McIntosh's suffering.

34. *McIntosh Burning, 1836*

I have just returned from witnessing the most horrid sight that ever fell to the lot of man, viz: the execution of "Lynch Law" upon a yellow fellow, by the horrible means of a *slow fire.* The cause of this almost unprecedented execution, I will now briefly relate. Deputy Sheriff Hammond, while endeavoring to arrest an offender, was, by the above mentioned yellow fellow, defeated in his intent. During the scuffle, the prisoner escaped. Mr. Hammond then arrested the yellow fellow for his interference and took him before a Justice of the Peace, by whom he was committed. While conducting him to jail, accompanied by our constable, Mr. Mull, the prisoner drew a knife and plunged it into the constable's side. Upon witnessing this, Hammond sprang at the prisoner, who now turned upon him and inflicted a terrible and mortal blow; the point of the knife struck him on the chin, passed through his throat, completely severing the jugular vein; he staggered a few paces and fell dead. The prisoner then fled to a yard or passage way, but being brought to bay by his pursuers, and still retaining his knife, he swore he would kill the first man that attempted to arrest him. His pursuers, perceiving his threatening manner, backed out with the exception of one, who seized the rail, broke it over his head, which slightly stunned him, but soon recovering, he resumed his menacing attitude, when a powerful and courageous man, but just arrived, seized upon a stone and hurled it with herculean force, striking him on the shoulder and dislocating that limb. His arm dropped useless at his side, his knife fell from his grasp, and he was immediately arrested, bound, and carried to prison.

We must now return to the dead and wounded. During the time occupied in the pursuit of the prisoner, the news of the affray had spread over town, and the crowd around Mr. Hammond's body was joined by his son, (an interesting lad about 11 years of age, whose loud and heart-rending lamentations infuriated the already excited spectators. They swore that the murderer should not live another hour. This resolution once formed, they proceeded to the jail where the prisoner was confined. Being too strong for the officers, who could not, under existing circumstances, make much resistance, after forcing three doors they reached the cell that contained the murderer, and led him forth amidst the shouts of the multitude. Some endeavored to quell the tumult, but to no purpose. The friends of Mr. Hammond (and they were many, for he was universally beloved and respected) were determined on revenge—a revenge that may seem to you unwarrantable, but take the case home to yourself, conceive your own brother in the situation of Mr. Hammond, and you will find some palliating considerations to abate the horrid character of this transaction.

The mob conducted the murderer to a pasture back of the city with the intention of hanging him, but some among them cried out, "Burn him." The horrible suggestion was immediately caught at; the moon had now risen bright and clear—the evening was calm and beautiful—too fair a night for the appalling spectacle that was to be witnessed by at least five hundred of our most respectable citizens. They chained the murderer to a tree, and the cry arose, "Let the fire be slow!" They piled shavings and rails around him until they reached the height of about 2 1-2 feet—a match was applied to the shavings—and the murderer commenced singing a hymn, which he continued until the heat became intense, and then these few half-smothered words escaped him, "God take my life!" I had pressed forward until I stood in front of the sufferer—I could not move—it seemed as though some horrid fascination chained me to the spot, and I witnessed all his agony. Never [a] martyr suffered more courageously. Not one single scream escaped him—his chest heaved with the most intense agony, yet all he said was "God take my soul!—God take my life!" in accents so low that none except those immediately about him could catch the sound. He had been burning about fifteen minutes, when someone said, "he feels no pain, he is too far gone"; he immediately answered, "Y-e-s I d-o f-e-e-l i-t!" Never, never can I forget his looks, when with the utmost difficulty he uttered those few words. The fire was so low that his legs and feet were burnt almost to a cinder before his other parts were to any degree affected. The tree to which he was chained was in full blossom, and seemed to smile upon the horrid deed. The horror of that scene can never be effaced from my memory! Imagine a human being chained to a tree—a slow fire burning around him —the boiling blood gushing in torrents from his mouth—his legs burnt to a crisp— yet his head moving from side to side, and occasionally a half uttered groan. But I will not, I cannot, further enlarge upon a sight so horrible—I feel a sickness at my heart, a dizziness in my head, occasioned by witnessing that terrific sight; but I was rooted to the spot, I could not withdraw my eye from the sight before me.

M.C.

SOURCE: *Boston Liberator,* May 21, 1836.

Not long after the St. Louis mob burned McIntosh, Judge Luke Lawless instructed the local grand jury on how to proceed. While denouncing the burning of McIntosh, Lawless really focused his energies, and the jury's attention, on McIntosh's crimes. He thought the mob's violence understandable. "Is not something to be allowed for human sympathies in those appalling circumstances?" Lawless advised the grand jury not to indict anyone for McIntosh's death and expressed outrage at abolitionist influence on his city and state. Judge Lawless thought opponents of slavery to be criminal just as surely as the lynch mob, perhaps more so.

35. *Luke Lawless, Charge to the Grand Jury after McIntosh Burning,* 1836

Gentlemen of the Grand Jury . . . I have reflected much on this matter, and after weighing all the considerations that present themselves as bearing upon it, I feel it my duty to state my opinion to be, that, whether the Grand Jury shall act at all, depends upon the solution of this preliminary question, namely, whether the destruction of McIntosh was the act of the "few" or the act of the "many."

If, on a calm view of the circumstances attending this dreadful transaction, you shall be of opinion that it was perpetrated by a definite, and compared to the population of St. Louis, a *small* number of individuals, separate from the mass, and evidently taking upon themselves, as contradistinguished from the multitude, the responsibility of the act, my opinion is, that you ought to indict them all without a single exception.

If, on the other hand, the destruction of the murderer of Hammond was the act, as I have said, of the many—of the multitude, in the ordinary sense of those words—not the act of numerable and ascertainable malefactors, but of congregated thousands, seized upon and impelled by that mysterious, metaphysical, and almost electric phrenzy, which, in all ages and nations, has hurried on the infuriated multitude to deeds of death and destruction—then, I say, act not at all in the matter—the case then transcends your jurisdiction—it is beyond the reach of human law.

The attempt to punish it, would, in my opinion, be fruitless and, perhaps, worse than that. The foundations of decency might be shaken—the social elements in this City and County thrown into most disastrous collision. For, how are we to indict—upon what evidence—two or three thousand offenders? How try them, if indicted—how convict them, if guilty—how punish them? I repeal if the thousands congregated around the fire were the actions in the fearful tragedy, it would be impossible to punish, and absurd to attempt it.

Now even we select a few and hang them by way of example—if one be indicted, all who are known must be indicted. An autocrat, a despot, a dictator might order his guards to seize and put to death, by the shortest process, any given number as a warning to the rest. Not so here, where we have to deal with two or three thousand American citizens—these cannot be decimated.

Again, if an indictment be preferred against any of the persons who assisted in the burning of McIntosh, the indictment, in my opinion, must be for murder. By the common law, the act would be the highest degree of felonious homicide—unqualified murder. By our criminal code, as amended at the last session of our legislature, the homicide would be murder, at least, in the second degree.

The punishment for the first degree of murder is hanging. The second degree, ten years imprisonment in the State Penitentiary.

. . . [T]he people were comparatively under the influence of a generous excitement. When it is recollected that their respected and beloved fellow citizen, slain in the performance of his duty, lay dead before them—when they saw another worthy Father of a family, and faithful public officer severely, and, to all appearance, mortally wounded —the pavement streaming with the blood of those two unfortunate men—when they heard the shrieks of the widow and her desolate orphans, and added to all this, when their feelings and their understandings were assailed and outraged by the atrocious and savage demeanor of the murderer himself, after he had committed those crimes, and within the grasp of the Sheriff, is it to be wondered at that the people should be moved? Is not something to be allowed for human sympathies in those appalling circumstances? Is there not some slight palliation of that deplorable disregard of Law and Constitution, which is now the subject of our deliberations?

. . . [I]f you arrive at the ultimate conclusion, that the death of McIntosh was the act of the multitude, you will pursue the safest and wisest course, in declining all action with respect to it. The very enormity of this violation of the constitution by popular insurrection will, I firmly believe, have the effect of impressing on the people of Missouri the necessity in future of a stern and a prompt suppression of all attempts to punish by summary popular execution crimes, however atrocious—however flagrant—for which our criminal code has already provided. I am persuaded that the persons themselves who were most actively engaged in this tragic scene, must already regret what they have done—they must perceive that the object which they had in view, namely to punish the murderer and avenge his victims, would have been better attained by leaving him in the jail, to which the magistrate had committed him. If he had been tried by a Jury, convicted and executed—the horror at his crimes would have been unmixed with any other feeling. There could have been no reaction—no pretence for the outcry which now, in all probability, will be raised throughout the Union by the misguided or unprincipled men engaged in the anti-national scheme of abolitionism. The public attention in this state would have been concentrated on what, I am disposed to think, was the exciting cause of McIntosh's crime, and of similar atrocities committed in this and other states by individuals of negro blood against their white brethren.

This abolitionist influence upon the passions and intellect of the wretched McIntosh seems to me to be indicated by the peculiar character of his language and demeanor. His rabid denunciations of the white man—his professions of deadly hostility to the whole white race—his hymns and his prayers, so profanely and frightfully mixed up with those horrid imprecations, seem, I say, to betray the incendiary cause to which I have adverted.

If this be, indeed, the case, the murderer of Hammond was, morally speaking, only the blind instrument in the hands of the fanatics—they, and not McIntosh, would then be responsible in the sight of God and of man. . . .

I hold in my hand a newspaper printed in this city entitled "The St. Louis Observer," and professing to be a paper exclusively devoted to religious objects. . . . I note the following: *"Slavery is a sin and ought to be abandoned"*—*"The Slave-Holder would suppress discussion, because discussion would blast his iniquitous system of oppression"*—*"Oh! There never was such an abandonment of virtue, such prostration of principle, and treachery to the cause of liberty and religion, such truckling to wickedness in high places, to a damning system of oppression, as that which characterizes Pro-Slavery men of modern times."* . . .

It seems to be impossible that, while such language is used and published as that which I have cited from the St. Louis Observer, there can be any safety in a slave holding state. . . .

The danger in Missouri is peculiarly great from this species of incendiary excitement. The negroes are numerous—they are quartered on our farms, in our families—they have on our frontier natural allies—armed bands of savages—with whom they would not fail, if occasion offered, and their minds and passions prepared by the publications in question, to assail the white population.

SOURCE: *Missouri Republican*, May 26, 1836.

A young Illinois lawyer named Abraham Lincoln took the violence in Mississippi and St. Louis as a menace to American constitutionalism. It is important to note that Lincoln was a Whig. He meant to articulate constitutionalism as a counter to the popular sovereignty Jackson championed. Jackson's democratic ideals obviously appealed to a large number of voters; Lincoln hoped that law and constitutionalism could also attract a following. In this speech Lincoln warns that white people as well as blacks have been lynched. White people can find safety only through law, Lincoln warned.

36. *Abraham Lincoln, "The Perpetuation of Our Political Institutions,"* January 27, 1838

In the great journal of things happening under the sun, we, the American People, find our account running, under date of the nineteenth century of the Christian era. We find ourselves in the peaceful possession, of the fairest portion of the earth, as regards extent of territory, fertility of soil, and salubrity of climate. We find ourselves under the government of a system of political institutions, conducing more essentially to the ends of civil and religious liberty, than any of which the history of former times tells us. We, when mounting the stage of existence, found ourselves the legal inheritors of these fundamental blessings. We toiled not in the acquirement or establishment of them—they are a legacy bequeathed us, by a *once* hardy, brave, and patriotic, but *now* lamented and departed race of ancestors. Their's was the task (and nobly they performed it) to possess themselves, and through themselves, us, of this goodly land; and to uprear upon its hills and its valleys, a political edifice of liberty and equal rights;

'tis ours only, to transmit these, the former, unprofaned by the foot of an invader; the latter, undecayed by the lapse of time, and untorn by [usurpation—to the latest generation that fate shall permit the world to know. This task of gratitude to our fathers, justice to] ourselves, duty to posterity, and love for our species in general, all imperatively require us faithfully to perform.

. . . I hope I am over wary; but if I am not, there is, even now, something of ill-omen amongst us. I mean the increasing disregard for law which pervades the country; the growing disposition to substitute the wild and furious passions, in lieu of the sober judgement of Courts; and the worse than savage mobs, for the executive ministers of justice. This disposition is awfully fearful in any community; and that it now exists in ours, though grating to our feelings to admit, it would be a violation of truth, and an insult to our intelligence, to deny. Accounts of outrages committed by mobs, form the every-day news of the times. They have pervaded the country, from New England to Louisiana;—they are neither peculiar to the eternal snows of the former, nor the burning suns of the latter;—they are not the creature of climate—neither are they confined to the slaveholding, or the non-slaveholding States. Alike, they spring up among the pleasure hunting masters of Southern slaves, and the order loving citizens of the land of steady habits. Whatever, then, their cause may be, it is common to the whole country.

It would be tedious, as well as useless, to recount the horrors of all of them. Those happening in the State of Mississippi, and at St. Louis, are, perhaps, the most dangerous in example, and revolting to humanity. In the Mississippi case, they first commenced by hanging the regular gamblers: a set of men, certainly not following for a livelihood, a very useful, or very honest occupation; but one which, so far from being forbidden by the laws, was actually licensed by an act of the Legislature, passed but a single year before. Next, negroes, suspected of conspiring to raise an insurrection, were caught up and hanged in all parts of the State: then, white men, supposed to be leagued with the negroes; and finally, strangers, from neighboring States, going thither on business, were, in many instances, subjected to the same fate. Thus went on this process of hanging, from gamblers to negroes, from negroes to white citizens, and from these to strangers; till, dead men were seen literally dangling from the boughs of trees upon every road side; and in numbers almost sufficient, to rival the native Spanish moss of the country, as a drapery of the forest.

Turn, then, to that horror-striking scene at St. Louis. A single victim was only sacrificed there. His story is very short; and is, perhaps, the most highly tragic, of any thing of its length, that has ever been witnessed in real life. A mulatto man, by the name of McIntosh, was seized in the street, dragged to the suburbs of the city, chained to a tree, and actually burned to death; and all within a single hour from the time he had been a freeman, attending to his own business, and at peace with the world.

Such are the effects of mob law; and such are the scenes, becoming more and more frequent in this land so lately famed for love of law and order; and the stories of which, have even now grown too familiar, to attract any thing more, than an idle remark.

. . . Abstractly considered, the hanging of the gamblers at Vicksburg, was of but little consequence. They constitute a portion of the population, that is worse than useless in a[ny community; and their death, if no perni]cious example be set by it, is never matter of reasonable regret with any one. If they were annually swept, from the stage of existence, by the plague or small pox, honest men would, perhaps, be much profited, by the operation. Similar too, is the correct reasoning, in regard to the burning of the negro at St. Louis. He had forfeited his life, by the perpetration of an outrageous murder, upon one of the most worthy and respectable citizens of the city; and had he not died as he did, he must have died by the sentence of the law, in a very short time afterwards. As to him alone, it was as well the way it was, as it could otherwise have been. But the example in either case, was fearful. When men take it in their heads to day, to hang gamblers, or burn murderers, they should recollect, that, in the confusion usually attending such transactions, they will be as likely to hang or burn some one, who is neither a gambler nor a murderer [as] one who is; and that, acting upon the [exam]ple they set, the mob of to-morrow, may, an[d] probably will, hang or burn some of them, [by th]e very same mistake. And not only so; the innocent, those who have ever set their faces against violations of law in every shape, alike with the guilty, fall victims to the ravages of mob law; and thus it goes on, step by step, till all the walls erected for the defence of the persons and property of individuals, are trodden down, and disregarded. But all this even, is not the full extent of the evil. By such examples, by instances of the perpetrators of such acts going unpunished, the lawless in spirit, are encouraged to become lawless in practice; and having been used to no restraint, but dread of punishment, they thus become, absolutely unrestrained. Having ever regarded Government as their deadliest bane, they make a jubilee of the suspension of its operations; and pray for nothing so much, as its total annihilation. While, on the other hand, good men, men who love tranquility, who desire to abide by the laws, and enjoy their benefits, who would gladly spill their blood in the defence of their country; seeing their property destroyed; their families insulted, and their lives endangered; their persons injured; and seeing nothing in prospect that forebodes a change for the better; become tired of, and disgusted with, a Government that offers them no protection; and are not much averse to a change in which they imagine they have nothing to lose. Thus, then, by the operation of this mobocratic spirit, which all must admit, is now abroad in the land, the strongest bulwark of any Government, and particularly of those constituted like ours, may effectually be broken down and destroyed —I mean the attachment of the People. Whenever this effect shall be produced among us; whenever the vicious portion of population shall be permitted to gather in bands of hundreds and thousands, and burn churches, ravage and rob provision stores, throw printing presses into rivers, shoot editors, and hang and burn obnoxious persons at pleasure, and with impunity; depend on it, this Government cannot last. By such things, the feelings of the best citizens will become more or less alienated from it; and thus it will be left without friends, or with too few, and those few too weak, to make their friendship effectual. At such a time and under such circumstances, men of sufficient tal[ent and ambition will not be want]ing to seize [the opportunity, strike the blow, and over-turn that fair fabric], which for the last half century, has been the fondest hope, of the lovers of freedom, throughout the world.

I know the American People are much attached to their Government;—I know they would suffer much for its sake;—I know they would endure evils long and patiently, before they would ever think of exchanging it for another. Yet, notwithstanding all this, if the laws be continually despised and disregarded, if their rights to be secure in their persons and property, are held by no better tenure than the caprice of a mob, the alienation of their affections from the Government is the natural consequence; and to that, sooner or later, it must come.

Here then, is one point at which danger may be expected.

The question recurs, "how shall we fortify against it?" The answer is simple. Let every American, every lover of liberty, every well wisher to his posterity, swear by the blood of the Revolution, never to violate in the least particular, the laws of the country; and never to tolerate their violation by others. As the patriots of seventy-six did to the support of the Declaration of Independence, so to the support of the Constitution and Laws, let every American pledge his life, his property, and his sacred honor;—let every man remember that to violate the law, is to trample on the blood of his father, and to tear the character [charter?] of his own, and his children's liberty. Let reverence for the laws, be breathed by every American mother, to the lisping babe, that prattles on her lap—let it be taught in schools, in seminaries, and in colleges;—let it be written in Primmers, spelling books, and in Almanacs;—let it be preached from the pulpit, proclaimed in legislative halls, and enforced in courts of justice. And, in short, let it become the political religion of the nation.

SOURCE: Roy P. Basler, ed., Marion Delores Pratt and Lloyd A. Dunlap, asst. eds., *The Collected Works of Abraham Lincoln*, 8 vols. (New Brunswick: Rutgers University Press, 1953), 1:108–115. Permission courtesy of the Abraham Lincoln Association, Springfield, Illinois. This speech was delivered by Lincoln as an "Address Before the Young Men's Lyceum of Springfield, Illinois," January 27, 1838.

NOTES

1. Edmund S. Morgan, *Inventing the People: The Rise of Popular Sovereignty in England and America* (New York: Norton, 1988), 153–267; Paul A. Gilje, *The Road to Mobocracy: Popular Disorder in New York City, 1763–1834* (Chapel Hill: University of North Carolina, 1987), 9–24.

2. Jackson's critics claimed that he acted arbitrarily in New Orleans as well, closing down the state legislature to silence antiwar dissenters. John Spencer Bassett, *The Life of Andrew Jackson* (1911; reprint ed., n.p.: Anchor Books, 1967), 216–218.

3. Henry Clay, Remarks on The Seminole War, January 20, 1819, House of Representatives, *Annals of Congress*, 15th Congress, 2d sess., 631–655.

4. Robert Remini, *Andrew Jackson and His Indian Wars* (New York: Viking, 2001), 156.

5. Alexander Smyth, Remarks on The Seminole War, January 21, 1819, House of Representatives, Annals of Congress, 15th Congress, 2d sess., 689.

6. David Grimsted, *American Mobbing, 1828–1861: Toward Civil War* (New York: Oxford University Press, 1998), 3.

7. Ann Fabian, *Card Shops, Dream Books, and Bucket Shops: Gambling in Nineteenth-Century America* (Ithaca, N.Y.: Cornell University Press, 1990), 34–37; John M. Findlay, *People of Chance: Gambling in American Society from Jamestown to Las Vegas* (New York: Oxford University Press, 1986), 66–69.

8. Karen Halttunen, *Murder Most Foul: The Killer and the American Gothic Imagination* (Cambridge, Mass.: Harvard University Press, 1998), 60–79.

3

Slavery

Historians sometimes date the origins of racial lynching to emancipation.[1] Slaveowners, it is supposed, would not destroy their own property. In 1669, however, Virginia's legislature sanctioned "The Casuall Killing of Slaves," forbidding the punishment of owners when their property "should chance to die" in the "extremity of correction."[2] There is always a question of whether laws really reflect behavior. In this case, it is hard to believe that Virginia passed the statute other than to meet a need.

Sometimes the slaves died in a less "casuall" fashion. Thomas G. Dyer has examined a spate of slave lynchings in Saline County, Missouri. Four slaves died in the space of three days. More slave lynchings might be known, Dyer theorizes, were it not for the lack of source material.[3] In the lynchings Dyer found, the mob leader justified himself in print, claiming that "law that is not based upon public opinion is but a rope of sand." When the law fails, the citizens must act extralegally, a Missouri lynch leader named James M. Shackleford added. Shackleford also drew strength by comparing himself to Andrew Jackson, whom he saw as another mob leader.[4]

In fact, however, white southerners saw their right to kill miscreant black people as a prime privilege of slavery. The roots of lynching intertwine with slavery. The difficulty of defining lynching complicates our ability to understand its role under slavery. If an overseer called on two white men to help him subdue a slave, and that trio beat their victim to death, has a lynching occurred? If such a killing—so clearly the result of community-sanctioned white racism—is not technically a lynching, does the distinction matter?

In colonial Boston authorities executed Tom, "a negro man slave." So, he was not lynched. But the *Boston Gazette*'s description of the incensed mob's brutality to Tom's body sounds very much like a lynching, and, in fact, after slavery, journalists reported that mobs did "lynch" dead bodies.

37. Boston Gazette, *"Tom, A Negro Man Slave,"* 1763

TOM, a negro man slave, condemned the last Assize for attempting a Rape on Mary Ryan, a child, was executed at Fresh-Water. The Mob were so incensed, after he was turned off, that the officers could not stand their Ground from the shower of Snow-Balls, Stones &c. thrown at him; thus were obliged to leave him to their Brutality: After they cut him down they dragged his Body through some of the streets; when the great good Conduct of a single Gentleman soon put a stop to their Inhumanity by seizing the Corpse, and ordering it to be interr'd, judiciously knowing the Law was fulfilled, by the Execution, and consequently that the publick ought to be therewith contented. But it is said the Body has since been taken up and likely to become a

Raw-Head and Bloody-Bones,[5] by our Tribe of Dissecters, for the better Instruction of our young Practitioners.

SOURCE: *Boston Gazette,* December 5, 1763. Thanks to Rob Desrochers for this citation.

In eighteenth-century Georgia a posse chased down six slaves accused of murder. At the spot of capture, the crowd decided to burn one of their captives. The *Norfolk Herald and Public Advertiser* did not call this killing a lynching because the term was not widely known in 1797. It is the availability of the word, not the behavior, that keeps this event off lists of lynchings.

38. Norfolk Herald and Public Advertiser, *"The Sentence Was Immediately Put into Execution,"* February 24, 1797

On Wednesday the 15th instant, a shocking murder was committed at the Plantation of Mr. Hergen Herson in Scriven county. The particulars of which, as far as we are informed, are as follows: Mr. Herson, had purchased in October last, seven men and a woman, from a cargo of Negroes, lately imported, and carried them up to his place in Scriven county, where they appeared to be happy and content, never received hard language or blows from their master. On the morning of the 15th, one of the fellows, came to the dwelling house, requested his master to walk with him to the spot where they had been working, alledging they had finished what was pointed out to them and wanted more. Some little time after, his lady looking out observed one of the fellows strike Mr. William Rae, on the head twice with the club end of his axe; on her screaming with terror, three or four rushed in the house, with axes in their hands, and attempted her life, as also that of a young lady who resided with her, but were prevented by the spirited conduct of the latter, who raised a chair to defend herself. The confusion this threw them in, gave time for her to make her escape; Mrs. Herson, attempting the same, was closely pursued, and saved herself only by the interposition of a fellow and a wench, who had long lived with them, and on finding the fellows return[ed] from the place where they had deposited articles plundered from the dwelling house, advised her to conceal herself under a house. Strick search was made for the unfortunate lady, but happily she remained undiscovered. The faithful fellow having secured her safety, as far as lay in his power, ran to the neighbours and gave the alarm, which occasioned the collection of a few men, who arrived on the spot, found Mr. Rae quite dead, and on searching, discovered Mr. Herson about the spot where he was enticed to examine the work, lying without any other indications of life, [than] that of a laborious breathing, the back part of his skull being driven in by a blow of an axe. In this situation, he remained about twenty hours and expired, greatly lamented by all who had the pleasure of his acquaintance; his character being that of an amiable worthy man. The party immediately pursued, and came up with the murderers, who made resistance, but were overcome, three being killed on the first discharge, and one badly wounded; two surrendered, one of which declared himself the author and contriver of the murder: and after much deliberation, was by the men assembled, condemned to the flames, which sentence was immediately put in execution.

SOURCE: *Norfolk Herald and Public Advertiser,* March 25, 1797.

In the summer of 1835, as Vicksburgers mobbed the gamblers, rumors of a slave uprising spread through Madison County, east of Vicksburg. Whites tortured and hanged their slaves. According to a pamphlet the lynchers published to justify themselves, whites felt "there seemed to be left no alternative but to adopt the most efficient and decisive measures." The pamphlet confessed that the lynchers knew their evidence would not stand up in court. Simms's novel, *Guy Rivers*, published just a year before (and excerpted in the previous chapter), documented frontier folks' distrust of lawyers and institutionalized procedure. The Madison killings seem to confirm Simms's fiction. The killings also raise doubts about the commonly expressed sentiment that slave owners rarely or never lynched their own property.

39. *Thomas Shackelford, "Madison County, Mississippi, Proceedings,"* 1836

About the middle of the month of June 1835, a rumor was afloat through Madison county, that an insurrection of the slaves was meditated. . . . After ascertaining that the report had emanated from a lady residing at Beatie's Bluff, in this county, about 9 miles from Livingston, a number of gentlemen waited upon her, for the purpose of learning upon what grounds or suspicions, she had given publicity to it. The lady, in compliance with their request, informed them that she was induced to believe an insurrection of the negroes was in contemplation, from the following circumstances, and parts of conversation she had overheard among her house girls.

She remarked, her suspicions were first awakend by noticing, in her house servants, a disposition to be insolent and disobedient . . . and in a few days she heard the girls in conversation, and among other similar remarks, she heard one of them say, "she wished to God it was all over and done with, that she was tired of waiting on the *white folks,* and wanted to be her own mistress the balance of her days, and clean up her own house." Soon after, she again heard the same girl engaged in secret conversation with a negro man belonging to a neighbor. From the low tone in which the conversation was carried on, she was unable to hear it all, but gleaned the following remarks: The girl remarked, "is it not a pity to kill such ****." The man replied, "that it was, but it must be done, and that it would be doing a great favor, as it would go to heaven and escape the troubles of this world." . . .

The girls were examined by the gentlemen, and their statements corresponded in every particular with the above communication of the lady. The report of the gentlemen, of course, was that they had good reason to believe that an insurrection of the negroes was contemplated by them, and warned their fellow citizens to be on their guard. . . .

[Citizens assembled at Livingston, the county seat, on June 27 and 30, interrogating slaves. When whipped, some of the slaves confessed knowledge of "a rising of the blacks soon."—ed.]

It was agreed upon by common consent of the citizens assembled in the various meetings, that when the ring-leaders in the conspiracy should be detected, to make examples of them immediately by hanging, which would strike terror among the rest, and by that means crush all hopes of their freedom.

The citizens in the neighborhood of Beaties Bluff were not idle. During the investigations at Livingston, to whom they are mainly indebted for the detection of the conspirators, and of the discovery of their sanguinary and diabolical designs. They had, by their indefatigable exertions, succeeded in detecting the negro ring-leaders, from whom they obtained confessions of their plans, and of some of their white accomplices.

After two days of patient and scrutinizing examination of the negroes implicated at Beaties Bluff, their guilt was fully established, not only by their own confessions, but by other facts and circumstances, which could not leave a doubt on the mind. Each negro was examined separate and apart from the rest, neither knowing that another was suspected or in custody; each acknowledging his own guilt, and implicating all of the others; every one implicating the same *white men,* and the whole of their statements coinciding precisely with each other.

After ascertaining so fully the guilt of these negroes, and the time for the consummation of the designs being at hand; the situation of the country being such as to render consummation so easy; the whole community and the owners of the negroes in particular, demanded the immediate execution of the guilty, and they were accordingly hung on the 2d of July. . . .

The following white men, Cotton and Saunders, were arrested and in custody; and this, too, before the disclosures of the negroes at Beatties Bluff were known. The arrest being made upon circumstances of suspicion and facts, indicating a very strong degree their agency and participation in the plans then hastening to their full development and consummation. And when the disclosures made at Beatties Bluff as above unfolded, were fully made known at Livingston, there seemed to be left no alternative but to adopt the most efficient and decisive measures.

The question became general—what should they do with the persons implicated? Should they hand them over to civil authority? This, it would seem, under ordinary circumstances, to be the proper course. But should that be the course, it was well known that much of the testimony which established their guilt beyond all doubt, would, under the *forms* of the law, be excluded; and, if admissible, that the witnesses were then no more. If, from our peculiar situation, the laws were incompetent to reach their case—should such acts go unpunished? Besides, from what had been seen and witnessed the day before, it was universally believed, and doubtless such would have been the fact, these persons would have been *forcibly* taken, even from the custody of the law, and made to suffer the penalty due to their crimes. Should they even be committed for trial, there was much reason to apprehend that they would be rescued by their confederates in guilt—if not by *perjury* at least by breaking the jail. They had an example of the dreadful excitement on the evening of the 2d July, at Livingston. Immediately after the execution of the negroes at Beatties Bluff was made known in Livingston, it created a most alarming excitement. The two old negro men who were in custody of the committee of examination at Livingston, were demanded by the citizens; and previous to a vote of condemnation, and a full examination, they were forcibly taken by an infuriated people from the custody of those who intended to award them a fair trial, and immediately hung.

The time was near at hand when the intentions of the conspirators would inevitably be carried into effect, if some prompt and efficient means should not be adopted by the citizens to strike terror among their accomplices, and to bring the guilty to a summary and exemplary punishment. It was not believed that the execution of a few negroes, unknown and obscure, would have the effect of frightening their *white* associates from an attempt to perpetrate their horrid designs; which *association* was fully established by the confessions of the accused and other circumstances.

There was no time to be lost, and for the purpose of effecting their object, to arrest the progress of the impending danger, to extend to the parties implicated something like a *trial,* if not *formal* at least *substantial,* and to save them from the inevitable fate of a speedy and condign punishment, the citizens circulated a call for a general assemblage of the community on the day following, at Livingston, which call was obeyed; and, at an early hour the next day, July 3d, there collected a vast concourse of people from the adjoining neighborhoods.

This meeting, thus speedily assembled, (for it was full by 9 A.M.) was composed of at least 160 respectable citizens of Madison and Hinds counties . . . who then and there acting under the influence of the law of self preservation, which *is paramount to all law,* chose from among the assemblage thirteen of their fellow citizens, who were immediately organized, and styled a "Committee of Safety"—to whom they determined to commit what is emphatically and properly called the *supreme law,* the *safety* of the people (or salus populi est summa lex,) and then pledged themselves to carry into effect any order which the committee might make. Which committee were invested, by the citizens, with the authority of punishing all persons found guilty, by them, of aiding and exciting the negroes to insurrection, as they might deem necessary for the safety of the community. . . .

Trial of Joshua Cotton. . . . The committee after receiving his confession, condemned him to be hanged in an hour after the sentence, in order that the news of his execution might be circulated extensively before the night, thinking it would frighten his accomplices from the undertaking.

After his condemnation he made publicly some additional disclosures, which, unfortunately, were not reduced to writing. Under the gallows he acknowledged his guilt and the justness of his sentence, and remarked, "it was nothing more than he deserved." . . . And, lastly, in answer to some person who asked him "if he really thought there would be any danger that night," he said "he did, if they should not hear he was hung." His last words were "take care of yourselves to night and to morrow night," and swung off.

Trial &c. Of William Saunders. . . . The majority of the committee were of opinion that Saunders was guilty, though they had not passed sentence on him, nor did they till Cotton came out and confessed his own guilt, disclosing the name of Saunders as one of his accomplices and chief actors in bringing about the conspiracy; which disclosure was made to the committee in the presence of Saunders; whereupon the committee, by an unanimous vote found him guilty, and sentenced him to be hanged. And, in pursuance of the sentence, he was executed on the 4th with Cotton.

Thus, after all his treachery, he fell victim to his crimes.

Trial of Albe Dean. . . . He was accused by Dr. Cotton, who said "Dean was one of his accomplices, and to be deeply engaged in the conspiracy, as a member of the Murrel *clan.*" After a cool and deliberate investigation of his case he was, by an unanimous vote of the committee, found guilty of aiding and exciting the negroes to insurrection, and sentenced to be hanged.

In pursuance of the sentence he was executed on the 8th of July, with Donovan, and died in dogged silence, neither acknowledging his guilt or asserting his innocence. . . .

Trial of A. L. Donovan, of Maysville, Ky. . . . The committee were satisfied from the evidence before them that Donovan was an emissary of those deluded fanatics at the north—the ABOLITIONISTS. And that whilst disseminating his incendiary doctrines among the negroes, to create rebellion, he had found out that he was anticipated by a band of cut throats and robbers, who were engaged in the same work, not wishing to liberate negroes but to use them as instruments, to assist them *in plunder.* Being of a dissolute and abandoned character . . . and ripe for very rash enterprise, he joined the conspirators with the hope of receiving part of the spoils. If there had been any doubt in the minds of the committee as to his connexion with the conspirators, there being none, he would have been sentenced to be hanged for his attempts at diffusing among the negroes rebellious notions. On the 7th he was condemned to be hanged.

Accordingly at twelve o'clock on the 8th of July he offered up his life on the gallows as an expiation for his crimes. He said, from the gallows, that the committee did their duty in condemning him; that from the evidence they were compelled to do so.

Thus died an ABOLITIONIST, and let his blood be on the heads of those who sent him here.

Trial of Ruel Blake. . . . The confession of Dr. Cotton, was in evidence before the committee, who swore . . . that Blake was deeply concerned and one of the chief men in the conspiracy. . . .

On the 10th of July, in the presence of an immense concourse of people he was executed. He privately commended the verdict of the committee, and said they could not have done otherwise than condemn him, from the evidence before them, and publicly under the gallows made the same declaration.

He protested his innocence to the last, and said that his life was sworn away.

Trial of Lee Smith. . . . From the multiplicity of evidence introduced to establish his good character and the circumstances in addition to the confession of Cotton, not being sufficiently strong, the committee thought they could not punish him. . . . After his discharge he was taken by some of the citizens of Hinds county, (where he lived) and Lynched.

Trial of William Benson. . . . He was considered by the committee a great fool, little above an idiot, and that the best way to dispose of him, would be to *order* him off; which order he complied with.

Trial of Lunsford Barnes. . . . The committee considering his youth, and not being fully satisfied that he was guilty, ordered him to leave the county, which he has done.

. . .

Trial of William and John Earle. These two men were brought from Warren County to Madison by several respectable citizens of that county on the 18th of July.... [William Earle committed suicide while in custody.] After hearing all the testimony in [John Earle's] case ... the committee came to the conclusion that he was *guilty*, but would take no further steps in relation to him, until they could hear from Warren [County]. ... In a few days a guard was sent from the "Committee of Safety" at Vicksburg, requesting the committee of Livingston, to deliver him into their hands, which request was complied with.

With this case the committee adjourned sine die.

SOURCE: Thomas Shackelford, *Proceedings of the Citizens of Madison County, Mississippi at Livingston, in July 1835, in Relation to the Trial and Punishment of Several Individuals Implicated in a Contemplated Insurrection in This State* (Jackson, Mayson, and Smoot, 1836).

At the same time as the violence in Madison County and Vicksburg, abolitionists launched a pamphlet campaign against slavery, sending 175,000 items through the New York post office. The abolitionists hoped to win over white southerners to their cause. Instead, they sparked a backlash. Charles Lynch—not the same Charles Lynch active in revolutionary Virginia but another man of the same name—served as governor of Mississippi from 1836 until 1838. In his inaugural address, the ironically named Lynch took note, indirectly, of the abolitionists' postal campaign. According to Lynch, his state's mob violence demonstrated what abolitionists could expect if they came South. The governor declared that necessity sometimes required "a summary mode of trial and punishment unknown to law."

40. *Governor Charles Lynch, "The Question of Right Admits of No Parley," 1836*

Occurrences of a highly exciting and offensive nature have recently taken place in some of the non-slave holding States calculated, if persisted in, to affect us in the most serious and vital manner. The subject is one of delicacy, and should be approached with courtesy and circumspection. The question of right involved admits of no parley, no intermeddling, no discussion from any quarter—nor can a proposition bearing on this point, either immediate or remotely, be listened to for a moment. In stamping upon these incendiary movements our indignant and decided disapprobation, there can be but one opinion; I will not doubt, nor can I indulge the suspicion, that sister States will tolerate offences of so black a die, and of so fatal a tendency. Precaution and watchfulness on our part, presume neither the one nor the other. Policy seems to enjoin upon us such enactments as may be necessary to bring the offence and its punishment within the pale of the law; and comity requires that they should be predicated on the principles of reciprocity. I persuade myself that an appeal to the justice and the propriety of some arrangement of this character will not be disregarded.

Mississippi has given a practical demonstration of feeling on this exciting subject that may serve as an impressive admonition to offenders; and however we may regret the occasion, we are constrained to admit, that necessity will sometimes prompt a summary mode of trial and punishment unknown to the law. But no means should be spared to guard against and prevent similar occurrences. Nothing but the most manifest, imminent, and unmeditated peril can justify a repetition of such dangerous examples.

SOURCE: *Clinton Gazette*, January 16, 1836.

Abolitionists used stories of white southerners' violence to denounce slavery. In 1839 an abolitionist named Joseph Henry alleged that white Mississippians routinely shot down escaping slaves. While Henry did not call such killings "lynchings," he did describe them as sanctioned by the community. Such extralegal executions, declared legitimate by the neighborhood, blur the line between "murder" and "lynching." Certainly the roots of racial attitudes that would flower in the late nineteenth-century South can be found in such killings. It may be that the chief value of Henry's pamphlet is the light it sheds on white southerners' early ideas about their right to execute blacks outside the law.

41. *Joseph Henry, "A Statement of Facts," 1839*

On Sunday, I think in the month of January or February 1839, about 9 o'clock in the evening, a slave was shot dead in the streets of Vicksburg by a white man, as the citizens were returning from meeting. My informant who witnessed the murder stated to me, that the assassin when interrogated by the citizens as to his motive for shooting the negro, merely declared that he was "one of his d—d runaway niggers whom he had just overtaken," and that this declaration seemed to satisfy everybody, the people appearing to think it perfectly right to kill a slave in such circumstances, just as much as if he had been a dog or other brute animal. No other notice was taken of the affair than to talk about it in private. Shooting of runaway slaves I understood to be very common.

SOURCE: Joseph Henry, *A Statement of Facts Respecting the Condition and Treatment of Slaves in the City of Vicksburg and Its Vicinity, in the State of Mississippi in 1838 and '39* (Medina, Ohio: privately printed, 1839), 7.

Whites only rarely lynched slaves, historians commonly claim. And yet, if three whites beat to death a slave with a shovel, should not that killing be counted as a lynching? One suspects that such killings, when they occurred on remote corners of rural plantations, often went unrecorded. In the case of the slave known only as "Lewis," a grand jury accused three white men with his death. District Attorney Fulton Anderson fashioned a narrative of the killing in his grand jury indictment, littered with "aforesaid's" and run-on sentences. Since this case never went to a higher court, there is no transcript of testimony or any other detailed legal document laying out exactly what happened. Perhaps the sparsity of the documentation, buried in numerous courthouse attics and basements, helps to explain why lynching seemed so rare under slavery.

42. *Fulton Anderson, Grand Jury Indictment, 1846*

The Grand Jurors . . . on their oath present that Arthur Jordan of the county of War-ren laborer Thomas J. Winter late of the county aforesaid laborer and James H. Scott late of the county aforesaid laborer not having the fear of God before their eyes but being moved and seduced by the instigation of the devil, on the first day of July in the year of our Lord one thousand eight hundred and forty six, with force and arms at the county aforesaid to wit in the county aforesaid, in and upon one Lewis a negro man slave in the peace of god and the said state then and there being feloniously willfully and of their malice aforethought did make an assault and that the said Arthur Jordan with a certain iron shovel of the value of one dollar which he the said Arthur Jordan in both his hands then and there had and held, the said Lewis in and upon the back breast sides and stomach of him the aid Lewis, then and there feloniously willfully and of his malice aforethought did strike beat and wound, giving to the said Lewis a negro man slave as aforesaid, then and there by the striking, beating and wounding the said Lewis as aforesaid with the iron shovel aforesaid held as aforesaid in both the hands of him the said Arthur Jordan, in and upon the back breast sides and stomach of him the said Lewis of which said several mortal bruises, the said Lewis from the said first day of July in the year aforesaid until the fifth day of the same month of July in the year aforesaid at the county aforesaid to wit in the County aforesaid, did Lan-guish and languishing did live, on which the fifth day of July in the year aforesaid the said Lewis a negro man slave as aforesaid . . . died and that the said Thomas J. Winter and James H. Scott, then and there feloniously willfully and of their malice afore-thought, were present aiding helping abetting comforting assisting and maintaining the said Arthur Jordan in the felony and murder aforesaid in manner and form afore-said, to do and commit and so the Jurors aforesaid upon their oath aforesaid do say that the said Arthur Jordan the said Thomas J Winter and the said James H Scott . . . did kill and murder contrary to the form of the statute in such case made and pro-vided and against the peace and dignity of the state of Mississippi.

SOURCE: *State v. Arthur Jordan et al.,* Warren County Circuit Court Papers, Old Court House Museum, Vicksburg.

Winter and Scott fled rather than stand trial. While few papers remain from the trial of Arthur Jordan, the lawyers did file drafts of instructions which they hoped that the judge would read to the jury. These documents record how the two sides saw the killing. Few twentieth-century definitions of lynching would not cover three white men, acting together, to beat and kill a slave. Jordan's argument that he acted only in the heat of passion (or not at all) cuts no ice in defini-tional terms. Apologists for mob law in later years commonly claimed that the lynchers acted out of passion, uncontrollable fury at what their victim had done to provoke their wrath.

Lewis resisted his killers, apparently attempting to drown one. One author has written that, "if they chose not to resist a mob, their deaths were called lynchings; if they fought back, it was called a riot."[6] If resistance disqualifies, then Lewis's death cannot be called a lynching, but that would mean following a cynical distinction created by racists.

There is the question of community sanction. The fact that district attorney Anderson convinced a grand jury to indict the three, and brought Jordan to trial, suggests that the white community disapproved of the killing. The word *lynching* usually implies community approval. But the trial jury could not agree on a verdict, and Anderson finally gave up on trying to convict anyone of the killing. The white killers of Lewis went free. These documents are not sufficient to say with certainty if the jury acted on the basis of race, although the instructions reveal that Jordan confessed to the crime. This one case comes at random from a courthouse attic; there must be thousands of such incidents, not recorded at all, or barely recorded.

Even if Lewis's death does not meet some strict lynching definition, it seems quite clear that whites' imagined right to "chastise" black people outside the law, a sentiment that formed a central component of lynching, had its origins in slavery.

43. *Proposed Jury Instructions in Trial of Arthur Jordan,* 1846

Defendant's Proposed Jury Instructions

That if the jury believe from the evidence that Jordan designed inflicting a proper chastisement on the slave for his insubordination & being unable of himself to do it, called in the assistance of Winter & Scott & while about inflicting the chastisement the slave by attempting to drown Scott provoked Scott & Winter to give him the whipping that caused his death & that Jordan protested against the severity of the whipping & inflicted none of the fatal blows, they must find the prisoner not guilty.

That if the jury believe that Jordan, Scott & Winter at first designed inflicting only a proper punishment on the slave for his disobedience; & in consequence of the resistance of the slave & his attempt to drown Scott, Scott inflicted the fatal blows while under the excitement & provocation caused by the attempt to take Scott's life, then they would none of them be guilty of more than manslaughter.

That the confessions of Jordan, introduced by the State, are entitled to the same weight before the jury that the testimony of any other witness would be entitled to; subject only to be overthrown by contradictory circumstances & testimony in the cause.

The prosecutor offered his own jury instruction, emphasizing points he thought would win a conviction. He wanted the jury to hold Jordan responsible for Lewis's death, whether or not he inflicted the fatal blow himself.

Fulton Anderson's Proposed Jury Instructions

If the jury believe that Jordan did not protest until after the mortal blow was given, he is responsible for the death if Scott and Winter were there at his request.

It makes no difference who inflicted the mortal blows if Jordan were present aiding and abetting.

SOURCE: *State v. Arthur Jordan et al.,* Warren County Circuit Court Papers, Old Court House Museum, Vicksburg.

This document suggests that white southerners, even members of Congress, did not hesitate to position themselves as lynchers.

On April 15, 1848, two years after Lewis perished on a Mississippi plantation, seventy-six slaves, aided by three white sailors, tried to escape the District of Columbia by sailing down the Potomac aboard the schooner *Pearl*. The next day armed white men boarded the steamer *Salem* and pursued the escaping *Pearl*. The *Salem* overtook the *Pearl* and took the slaves, and their white helpers, into custody. Authorities charged the three white men with slave stealing and set bail at a thousand dollars per slave. The captured slaves went to the slave pens in Baltimore and Alexandria for sale, where they disappeared into the bowels of the slave system. In Washington thousands took to the streets on behalf of slavery, formed mobs, and attacked the *National Era*, an antislavery newspaper. The Senate's most prominent abolitionist responded by proposing a law against rioting. John Parker Hale of New Hampshire introduced the anti-riot law. Hale had been Liberty Party candidate for president in 1848, withdrawing to become the first antislavery candidate elected to the U.S. Senate. He ran for president again in 1852, on the Free-Soil ticket. At the time he introduced this bill, Hale was the strongest antislavery politician in the country. Hale deliberately modeled his bill on an anti-riot law already in force in the slave state of Maryland. The District of Columbia, governed by Congress, had no anti-riot law, and Hale claimed that he merely wanted to innocently apply a slave state law to the District of Columbia. Southern senators saw through Hale's ploy. Mississippi senator Henry Stuart Foote led the attack on the proposed legislation. Hale's anti-riot law really intended to outlaw lynching, they said, and they did not hesitate to defend lynching, which they thought perfectly legitimate.

Meanwhile two of the white abolitionists went on trial, were convicted, and received lengthy sentences. In 1852 President Millard Fillmore pardoned them, acting only after the Whigs refused to nominate him for a second term and he knew his presidency had come to an end. Privately he wrote, "I shall be abused and misrepresented for pardoning them."[7]

44. *Debate in the Senate*, April 20, 1848

On the Bill introduced by Mr. Hale, relating to riots, and for the Protection of Property in the District of Columbia.

MR. HALE. I wish to make a single remark, in order to call attention of the Senate to the necessity of adopting the legislation proposed by this bill. The bill itself is nearly an abstract of a similar law now in force in the adjoining State of Maryland, and also in many other States of the Union. The necessity for the passage of the bill will be apparent to the Senate from facts which are probably notorious to every member of the body. Within the present week large and riotous assemblages of people have taken place in the District, and have not only threatened to carry into execution schemes utterly subversive to all law, with respect to the rights of property, but have actually carried these threats into execution, after having been addressed, upheld, and countenanced by men of station in society, whose character might have led us to suppose that they would have taken a different course, and given wiser counsels to those whom they addressed. It seems to me, then, that we have approached a time when the decision is to be made in this Capitol, whether mob-law or constitutional law is to reign paramount. The bill which I now propose to introduce simply makes any city, town, or incorporated place within the District liable for all injuries done to property

by riotous or tumultuous assemblages. Whether any further legislation on the part of
Congress will be necessary, time will determine. But I may be permitted to say, that at
the present moment we present a singular spectacle to the people of this country and
to the world. The notes of congratulation which this Senate sent across the Atlantic to
the people of France on their deliverance from thralldom, have hardly ceased, when
the supremacy of mob-law and the destruction of the freedom of the press are threatened in this capital of the Union. . . .

MR. FOOTE. . . . Why is it that this question is continually agitated in the Senate of
the United States—that it is kept here as the subject of perpetual discussion? Is it simply that gentlemen wish to be popular at home? I suppose so. Is it because of their peculiar sympathies for that portion of the population which constitutes slavery as recognized in the South? What is the motive? Is the object to attain popularity? Is it to
gain high station? Is it to keep up a local excitement in some portions of the North,
with the view of obtaining political elevation as the reward of such factious conduct?
But I care not for the motives of such acts. I undertake to say that in no country
where the principles of honesty are respected, would such a movement as that now attempted be promoted, or even countenanced for a moment. I feel bound, on this occasion, to say that the bill proposed could not have any good object. What does it declare? It declares that any attempt on the part of the people of this District, through
the only means which they may have in their power, to protect their property, and
prevent it from being taken from them, either by stealth or open robbery, shall subject
them to be muleted in heavy pecuniary damages! It amounts then, to this: that if,
hereafter, any occurrence similar to that which has recently disgraced the District
should happen, and the good people of the District should assemble and proceed to
the vessel in which their property had been placed, and the captain of which had become the agent in the nefarious transaction, and should then and there dare to use
the only means to prevent that vessel from sailing, and their property from being
taken away before their eyes, they would be compelled to pay heavy pecuniary damages. It is a bill, then, obviously intended to cover and protect negro-stealing! It is a
bill for the encouragement and immunity of robbery! That is its true character. . . .

All must see that the course of the Senator from New Hampshire [Hale] is calculated to embroil the Confederacy—to put in peril our free institutions—to jeopard
that Union which our forefathers established, and which every pure patriot throughout the country desires shall be perpetuated. Can any man be a patriot who pursues
such a course? Is he an enlightened friend of freedom, or even a judicious friend of
those with whom he affects to sympathize, who adopts such a course? . . . I will close
by saying, that if he really wishes glory, and to be regarded as the great liberator of the
blacks; if he wishes to be particularly distinguished in this cause of emancipation, as it
is called, let him, instead of remaining here in the Senate of the United States, or, instead of secreting himself in some dark corner of New Hampshire, whether he may
possibly escape the just indignation of good men throughout this Republic—let him
visit the good State of Mississippi, in which I have the honor to reside, and no doubt
he will be received with such hosannas and shouts of joy as have rarely marked the re-
ception of any individual in this day and generation. I invite him there, and will tell
him beforehand, in all honesty, that he could not go ten miles into the interior, before

he would grace one of the tallest trees of the forest, with a rope around his neck, with the approbation of every virtuous and patriotic citizen; and that, if necessary, I should myself assist in the operation.

SOURCE: Appendix to the *Congressional Globe*, April 20, 1848, 30th Congress, 1st sess., 500–502.

After 1830 northerners routinely used accounts of white southerners' anti-black violence to attack slavery. Most white northerners found it difficult to empathize with persons of a different color and culture, to the great frustration of abolitionists. The same white northerners who cared little for the plight of enslaved black people, prized order. In fact, one problem that opponents of slavery faced was the perception, widespread in the North, that abolitionism threatened disorder and lawlessness. Slavery opponents, after all, criticized an institution sanctioned by the Constitution. Members of the antislavery movement discovered, however, that they could turn white northerners' dislike of lawlessness and disorder against the slave regime of the South. White northerners, unmoved by the plight of African Americans, did react to accounts of white southerners' lawless violence.

Richard Hildreth (1807–1865), born in Massachusetts, son of a minister, campaigned vigorously against slavery as a journalist, novelist, and historian. Hildreth described himself as a driven man, impelled by forces he could not control to rage against the tyranny of slavery. Slave owners, Hildreth complained, had too much power; they lorded over not just the black victims of their despotism but over whites as well, silencing the critics of slavery. In this book Hildreth writes that slavery rendered southern whites "idle, turbulent, hot-headed, and insolent" and prone to lynching not just individuals but, metaphorically, the rights of entire northern states.

45. *Richard Hildreth, "Despotism in America,"* 1854

The framers of the constitution never intended, the people who ratified the constitution never intended, to found a slave-breeding and slavery-propagating republic. The barest suspicion that the constitution could operate to perpetuate the institution of slavery would have caused its indignant rejection by all the northern and by a part of the southern states. The general intent of the framers of the constitution is clearly and comprehensively expressed in its preamble, by which its objects are declared to be "To form a more perfect union, establish justice, insure domestic tranquility, provide for the common defence, promote the general welfare, and secure the blessings of liberty to ourselves and our posterity." Now, to which of these great objects has not the existence among us of domestic slavery proved a stumbling-block from the day the first Continental Congress met down to the current moment? So long as slavery continues, the union of the states never can be perfected; justice is but an empty name; our domestic tranquility will always be in danger—and that even less from the slaves, reluctantly held in bondage, and watching an opportunity to throw off the yoke, than from the idle, turbulent, hot-headed, and insolent among their masters, who, not content with lynching private individuals, and even sovereign states of the Union in the persons of their representatives.

SOURCE: Richard Hildreth, *Despotism in America: An Inquiry into the Nature, Results, and Legal Basis of the Slave-Holding System in the United States* (Boston: John P. Jewett, 1854), 251–252.

By 1855 the abolitionist and publisher of the *Boston Liberator* William Lloyd Garrison regularly reprinted stories of white southerners' violent acts clipped from their own newspapers to argue against slavery. In the article below, Garrison takes his text from the *Memphis News,* the *Memphis Eagle,* and the *Nashville True Whig.* Garrison's message was clear: the constant violence needed to maintain slave discipline damaged the minds of the slave drivers as well as the slaves. The casual use of the whip dulled southern whites' capacity to empathize not only with their human property but with humankind generally, and thus promoted chaotic bloody violence that threatened law and order everywhere.

46. Boston Liberator, *"Southern Outrages,"* 1855

Lynch Law—Probably Murder.—We learn from a passenger on the steamboat *Virginia,* which passed here not long since, that about daylight, after leaving here, at a wood-yard, a man was accused by a watchman of having stolen sixty dollars from a passenger. There was no other evidence against the fellow then that the watchman had seen him near the berth from whence the money was stolen. The passengers and officers of the boat tied the poor man, and leading him ashore, shaved off one side of his head, stripping off his clothing, and stretching him on the ground, one large man standing on his neck, and another on his legs, while two or three stood over whipping him with big sticks for one hour, until he was almost dead.

The lynchers were remonstrated with by one of the passengers, but he was soon given to understand that he would be treated in like manner, if he interfered. The poor man begged his persecutors to kill him at once, and put him out of his misery, but the cowardly villains preferred to torture him to death. We have this statement from a most reliable gentleman, who witnessed the affair himself, and is loud in his denunciation of the officers of the boat. The poor man that was so brutally whipped would not acknowledge the theft. Our informant states, from circumstances which afterward came to his knowledge, that the watchman stole the money himself.—*Memphis News,* 20th ult[imo].

Hanging Negroes in Tennessee, Judge Lynch's Code. Our Tennessee exchanges furnish us with the particulars of the hanging of two negroes, in different parts of that State, under the following circumstances. The first is from the Memphis Eagle:

The negro boy, aged about seventeen, belonging to Mr. Wm. Turner, of the vicinity of La Grange, Tenn., whom we mentioned yesterday morning as having, the day previous, killed the overseer, Mr. James, was apprehended the same day, and taken to La Grange, where he was lodged in the Calaboose for safekeeping. About 1 o'clock yesterday morning, the calaboose was broken open by some persons unknown, the negro taken thence to the scene of the murder, and hung until he was dead—dead—dead! Where, in fact, he was found hanging by his master, yesterday morning.

The other we find in the Nashville True Whig, as furnished that paper by a correspondent writing from Sparta, Tenn., under date of Sept. 26th:

We have been in the midst of a terrible excitement here for the last day or two. Some weeks since, a runaway negro came across a poor defenceless woman on the Cumberland mountain, and murdered her. The circumstances were of such an aggravating

character, that the citizens of the surrounding country determined on his speedy execution. After he was caught, all the preliminary arrangements were made to hang him,
but milder counsel prevailed, and he was for the time delivered over to the hands of
the law. At the present term of the court a true bill was found, yet when his case was
called, in consequence of the excitement, it was continued for one term. The multitude
became apparently ungovernable; so, when our excellent Judge, the Hon. J. C. Georal,
was informed of the fact, he ordered the Sheriff to summon a guard of twelve men to
protect the negro until the next term of the Court. But a large number of citizens of
White county, about dark, repaired to the jail, broke open the doors, after overpower-
ing the guard, took the negro out and carried him to a tree some two or three hundred
yards off, to the execution; before doing which, he was given half an hour to pray. At
this juncture, Parson King, of this place, and Timothy H. Williams, Esq., made short
appeals to the crowd to stay their evil purpose, but to no avail. When the time expired
allotted him, he was swung up, and remained their until this morning.

SOURCE: *Boston Liberator,* October 19, 1855.

Horace Greeley (1811–1872) launched the *New York Tribune* in 1841 as a vehicle to advance his
personal causes, which included opposition to slavery, monopolies, and capital punishment,
and his support for homestead legislation, laws to distribute free land to western migrants.
Greeley's paper, however, for all its progressivism and egalitarian ideology, achieved main-
stream status in a way Hildreth and Garrison never could. Greeley's *Tribune* became the pre-
eminent newspaper in the rural North with a circulation of more than a quarter of a million.
Like Garrison, Greeley used southern lynching stories to arouse northerners against the institution of slavery. According to this 1854 account, whites around Natchez, Mississippi, assembled
four thousand slaves to watch a slave burning.

47. New York Daily Tribune, *"The Burning of a Negro,"* 1854

The burning of a negro alive near the City of Natchez, an account of which appears in
the *Natchez Free Trader,* is one of the most frightful phenomena of the peculiar institution that we have ever had to record, and will match in atrocity gladiatorial and in-
quisitorial times. The slave, according to the account, struck a white man, and the
Democracy of that region, not waiting for "justice" to take its course, inflicted Lynch
law. The victim was chained to a tree, faggots were placed around him, while he
showed the greatest indifference. When the chivalry had arranged the pile, in reply to
a question if he had anything to say, he is reported to have warned all slaves to take
example by him, and asked the prayers of those around. He then asked for a drink of
water, and after quaffing it said, "Now, set fire. I am ready to go in peace." When the
flames began to burn him, in his agony he showed gigantic strength, and actually
forced the staple from the tree and bounded from the burning mass! But he instantly
fell pierced with rifle-balls, and then his body was thrown into the flames and consumed, to show that no such being had ever existed. Nearly four thousand slaves from
the neighboring plantations were present as at a moral lesson written in characters of
hell fire. Numerous speeches were made by the magistrates and ministers of religion

(facetiously so called) to the slaves, warning them that the same fate awaited them if they proved rebellious to their owners.

SOURCE: *New York Daily Tribune,* February 6, 1854.

Whites in Mississippi defended themselves from the *New York Daily Tribune*'s abolitionist attack. On February 25, 1854, the Natchez, Mississippi, *Free Trader* answered Greeley's charges by invoking the same argument that white southerners would use on behalf of lynching fifty years later. The *Free Trader* traced Greeley's story back to an incident that had occurred in 1841. According to the Mississippi newspaper, the lynched men had raped white women. White men had to act on behalf of white women against the black threat, the Natchez paper explained. Greeley's rival, the *New York Times,* reprinted the *Free Trader*'s article.

48. Mississippi Free Trader, *"Men Wept Tears of Blood,"* 1854

The circumstances on which the fiction is doubtless founded, occurred, from the best information we can get, in the Summer or Fall of 1841.

Two runaway slaves, in the Parish of Avoyelles, Louisiana, had for some time eluded capture, and had become a terror to the whites of that thinly-settled region. The first crime of magnitude which they committed was the murder of an old man named Herrington, who was living on Red River, near the Mississippi, with his only daughter, a young woman who assisted him by her labors in obtaining a meager support. The negroes had previously forced a negro woman, belonging to a neighboring planter, to join them. After murdering Mr. Herrington and robbing his house of everything available to them, they forced his daughter to join them, tearing her from beneath the roof where her murdered father lay weltering in his blood, and making her the victim of crimes too horrible to be told. From the house of Mr. Herrington they proceeded up Red River to the mouth of the Cocodra, where was then living a Mr. Todd, with his wife and child, who kept a small store to supply raftsmen. At that time, the two negroes were armed, one with a double-barrel gun and knife, and the other with a rifle and pistol. They demanded food and liquor, which he gave them. After satisfying their appetites, they demanded a free pass. He pretended to comply; and wrote an account of what had transpired at his house, stating his belief that they intended to murder him. They did murder him by beating out his brains. They then departed, taking with them, his child, and his wife, whom they made the victim of the same horrible crimes to which they had devoted the innocent young girl whom they had ruthlessly torn from the home of a murdered father. Miss Herrington seemed to have lost her reason, but Mrs. Todd, it seems, was a woman of great strength of mind, and knowing that so soon as the murders and abductions became known, the neighbors would be out in pursuit, she endeavored to mark a trail for the pursuers by leaving shreds of her dress on the bushes as they passed, and making her little child walk in the mud of the swamp, at times, that its little track might afford indubitable proof of these savage fiends and their unhappy victims.

In a week or ten days, while the party were at a halt, about three miles back of Union Point, which is on the Mississippi River, about thirty-five miles below Natchez, the two negro men fell asleep, one of them with his head in Mrs. Todd's lap, and the negro woman keeping guard. Suddenly, Mrs. Todd perceived the approach of the armed pursuers. She, with admirable presence of mind, motioned to them to be cautious. They advanced silently, and when she thought them sufficiently near, she sprang up "with a shriek of delirious joy," and rushed towards them. The negroes sprang to their feet—one was captured—the other escaped, several shots having been fired at him as he fled.

The party were taken to Union Point. Many of the neighbors were collected. Miss Herrington was a maniac, but the mind of Mrs. Todd was clear and unclouded. She told her story with remarkable clearness and consistency. It was enough to make men weep tears of blood—a series of crimes black enough to be execrated by devils. The people assembled did not need long to deliberate. A summary execution was resolved upon. The captured negro was tied to a tree—faggots were placed around him—and Mrs. Todd herself set fire to his funeral pile. *It was the one who had murdered her husband and first outraged herself!*

About one week afterwards, the other negro was captured and met a similar fate. The negro woman was not executed, Mrs. Todd stating that [the latter] had saved the lives of Miss Herrington and herself several times from these savage fiends.

This is as accurate a history of the transaction as can be given at the lapse of time without reference to old files of newspapers, which we have not been able to obtain. It is drawn from the narrative of several old citizens of that neighborhood, and in part from a gentleman who witnessed the execution and heard Mrs. Todd's tragic and heart-rending story.

Both the negroes made full confession of the horrible crimes. They confessed further that they had lurked around the plantation of another planter of the neighborhood, for the purpose of murdering him also, and of obtaining possession of his wife. We have seen and conversed with a highly intelligent and respectable planter of the neighborhood, who witnessed the execution of the second negro and was opposed to it, thinking it best that the law should take its course. He conversed with the negro from whom he heard a full confession. The same gentleman also informs us that the negroes assembled were far more anxious for the execution than the whites, and that it was with difficulty, after they heard of the crimes he had committed, that they could be restrained from tearing him to pieces—that he himself addressed them to prevent them from taking vengeance on the inhuman fiend. . . .

The circumstances we have detailed are undoubtedly the basis of the late foul abolition calumny. The villainy of the calumny consists in its pretending to relate a recent occurrence—in its assigning as a reason for the "burning of a slave alive," that he "merely raised his hand against a white man," and in the fanciful details of horror with which the scene is pictured. The story of four thousand slaves being assembled, and addresses from magistrates, ministers, &c., is totally false. Not more than thirty slaves, at the utmost, could have been present.

Had the perpetrators of these awful crimes, for which they terribly atoned, been white men instead of negroes, they would have met the same fate; nor is it probable that the story would have been revived at this late day, or that the *philanthropists* of the North would have found time for the expression of sympathy or the outpouring

of indignation. It is only for negro slaves, who crowded into a short space of time a series of crime too black to be given in all their horrid details, that the abolitionist has a
heart to mourn. He does not think of the two households desolated—of an old man
on the brink of the grave, living in quiet seclusion with an only and beloved daughter.
Murdered in cold blood—of an honest trader brutally assassinated after he had min-
istered to the wants of the murderers—of an innocent young girl and a virtuous wife
doomed to a fate which makes the heart shudder. All these things are forgotten by the
negrophilist in his savage sympathy with *the slave!*

If there ever was a case in which summary execution was justifiable, from the character of the crimes committed, the absolute certainty of their commission, and the
necessity of a terrible example, this was one. None ever occurred appealing more
powerfully to every noble feeling, to every generous sympathy, to man's high sense of
inexorable justice. They perished—perished terribly, but justly—and they who read
the story will acknowledge in their hearts the perfect harmony between the crimes
they perpetrated and the fate they met.

SOURCE: *Mississippi Free Trader*, March 8, 1854.

For three days in July 1859 Missouri whites lynched four Saline County slaves. This was no mass
execution. Whites accused the slaves of different crimes and carried out the killings in four separate locations.[8] A magistrate named James M. Shackleford published a defense of the killings
in the local newspaper. Shackleford's 1859 essay made the same points lynchers would make fifty
years later: the black men had endangered white women, the law and courts offered no adequate
deterrent, popular sovereignty justified the violence. On this last issue, Shackleford invoked the
name of Andrew Jackson.

49. *James M. Shackleford, "A Little Mob Law in the State of Missouri,"* 1859

The summary punishment of four negroes, by the people of Saline County, on the 19th
of this month, will excite a profound sensation throughout the country. It is due to
the people of the State that they should know why the people of old Saline—distinguished, as they ever have been, for their devotion to law and order—should take law
into their own hands.

Crime after crime has been recently perpetrated by the blacks. A most estimable
young man had been murdered; another young man, in attempting to correct a slave
whom he had forbidden to come to his place, had his arm cut with a deadly weapon,
and has probably lost the use of his hand for life; the house of a poor, defenceless, delicate woman was broken open, and a rape attempted to be committed upon her; a little girl, about eleven years of age, gathering blackberries, was caught by a naked negro
and dragged into the brush, and a rape attempted upon her. Those crimes following
each other in rapid succession, excited the public mind to the highest pitch. The last
crime perpetrated occurred the day before the meeting of the special term of the
Court to try the negro for the murder of young Hinton. The penalty for rape and for
cutting with a knife is almost universally admitted to be inadequate to the crime. A

spirit of insubordination existed amongst the negro population that required a terrible example to be set them. The people resolved to make the penalty suit the crime; nothing less would satisfy the public mind. The Court met, and the Grand Jury found a bill of indictment for murder in the first degree against the boy for the murder of young Hinton; he was put upon his trial, and speedily found guilty, and sat in the bar of the courthouse awaiting the sentence of death. The Grand Jury brought in a true bill against White's Jim, for an attempted rape. A jury was impaneled to try him. The dinner hour approached, and the Court took a recess. The Sheriff started with the murderer of young Hinton to the jail, and the packed and densely crowded courtroom was immediately vacated, and the people from all quarters rushed to the jail.

When the court met, the people had relieved the Judge of any further labor. The people of Saline county will so continue to act until the Legislature shall do their duty, revise the criminal code, make the penalty adequate to the crime—satisfy the public opinion. Let the law harmonize with it. The law that is not based upon public opinion is but a rope of sand. An enlightened public opinion is the voice of God, and when brought into action it has a power and an energy that cannot be resisted. Abolitionists and negro sympathizers have had a great deal to do in creating a spirit of insubordination amongst our negro population. Every abolitionist ought to be driven out of the country; every free negro should be sold into slavery or go out of the State; no more emancipation without sending them off. These are the remedies I suggest. I have no fears of the action of the people on the 19th being made a precedent for the abuse of illegal power. An enlightened people will ever discriminate in the use of illegal power. If we are advancing in civilization, as I believe we are, the use of this power will become less frequent; the law will have more reverence, because it will be clothed with the sanctity of justice. If we are retrograding, if we are going backwards, the abuse of unlawful power will cure itself; the strong arm of military power will do the work.

People may call it mob law. Well, it was mob law when Jackson drove the Legislature of Louisiana from their halls and closed the doors. It was mob law when he bombarded Pensacola, and hung Arburthnot and Ambrister. It was mob law when the laboring men of Boston disguised themselves as Indians and threw the tea overboard. It was mob law when the people of France hurled the Bourbons from the throne, and crushed out the dominion of the priests and established a new order of things. Incapable of discriminating, they waded through oceans of blood of the innocent as well as the guilty, but they saved France. I know no reason why we should not have a little mob law in the State of Missouri, and County of Saline, when the *occasion imperiously and of necessity* demands it.

SOURCE: *Marshall [Missouri] Democrat*, July 22, 1859.

NOTES

1. Martha Hodes, *White Women, Black Men: Illicit Sex in the Nineteenth-Century South* (New Haven: Yale University Press, 1997), 176–177.

2. William Waller Hening, *The Statutes at Large; Being a Collection of All the Laws of Vir-*

ginia from the First Session of the Legislature in the Year 1619 (New York: Bartow, 1823), 2:270, 481–482.

3. Thomas G. Dyer, "'A Most Unexampled Exhibition of Madness and Brutality': Judge Lynch in Saline County, Missouri, 1859, Part 1," *Missouri Historical Review* 89 (1995): 269.

4. Thomas G. Dyer, "'A Most Unexampled Exhibition of Madness and Brutality': Judge Lynch in Saline County, Missouri, 1859, Part 2," *Missouri Historical Review* 89 (1995): 369, 372.

5. The term *raw-head and bloody-bones,* dating back to the sixteenth century, refers to a children's bugbear, a murderer's apparition.

6. Michael D'Orso, *Like Judgment Day: The Ruin and Redemption of a Town Called Rosewood* (New York: Putnam's, 1996), 55.

7. Richard C. Rohrs, "Antislavery Politics and the Pearl Incident of 1848," *Historian* 56 (summer 1994): 711–718. For this incident, see also Daniel Drayton, *Personal Memoir of Daniel Drayton* (Boston: Bela Marsha, 1854), 22–59.

8. Dyer, "'A Most Unexampled Exhibition of Madness and Brutality,'" 269–289, 367–383.

4

How the West Was Won

By 1860, 350,000 Americans had journeyed across the Oregon Trail, carving deep ruts across southern Wyoming. Tens of thousands more hurried to California, seeking gold. When these migrants left the eastern states, they abandoned institutionalized law. As they crossed the Missouri River, migrants wrote in their diaries that by leaving the United States they had gone outside the law. "Of course," one pioneer wrote, "'*Judge Lynch*' holds the Court out here." Settlers made their own law on the overland trails, writing ad hoc constitutions, enforcing their laws, holding courts, and preserving law and order. "California law," it was said, prevailed.[1]

Justice on the Overland Trail could seem communal, a product of genuine popular sovereignty untainted by prejudice. The memories of the trek West preserved in American popular culture seem untroubled by the racial hate that motivated white southern lynchers, and the prevalence of western lynching has suggested to some that prejudice cannot solely explain American mob violence.

The West, however, was not without its own bigotry. The great outbreaks of western vigilantism in Kansas, California, and Montana all involved racial prejudice, politics or both. Kansans, of course, fought over slavery while San Francisco vigilantes overturned an existing government to substitute their own authority. In Montana, Republicans adopted vigilante tactics to turn Democrats out of power. Throughout this era, the lynchers—of course—claimed legitimacy by saying that they acted on behalf of the whole people.

But, in fact, they never did. Lynch mobs acted for some segment of the population, often racially determined.[2] Elias Ketcham's diary documented the role ethnic prejudice played in westerners' more ordinary crowd violence. Any examination of western lynching must query the role of prejudice.

50. *Elias S. Ketcham, Diary,* January 24, 1853

The shocking news is circulated in our town this evening of the murder of 6 persons by a party of Mexicans or greasers as they are termed. One of the murderers had been taken & hanged & 15 horsemen were in pursuit of the rest. The murderers were seen to pass along the road towards duglasses. It is hoped they will yet be overtaken. Of the victims two were said to be Chinamen & the others Americans, the particulars I have not learned of this horrible tragedy. The pursuers are reported to have destroyed all the Mexican tents or dwellings that came in their way; which believes to be cruel &

unjust. The innocent must suffer for the guilty in that case.—But many persons who are prejudiced say they are all alike, a set of cut throats & should be exterminated or drove out of the country.

SOURCE: Elias S. Ketcham Diary, HM 58269, Department of Manuscripts, The Huntington Library, San Marino. Reprinted by permission.

Congress had sowed the seeds for mob violence when it threw open Kansas Territory to settlement, leaving the question of slavery to be decided by local voting. "Bleeding Kansas" famously pitted slavery's opponents against its defenders. Neither side recognized the legitimacy of any government or legal system acceptable to the other. The abolition side complained that extralegal "armed hordes" from Missouri crossed the border only to vote, tilting the election away from the free soil.

The antislavery side refused to acknowledge the legitimacy of these elections and organized its own, extralegal elections and wrote its own antislavery constitution. In this volatile atmosphere, no governing authority enjoyed true legitimacy, the respect of all political factions.

The pro-slavery side saw the abolitionists as thieves, "negro stealers," seeking to take their property and thus fit subjects for lynching. The antislavery side denounced the legislature as a mob and regularly accused the pro-slavery forces for vigilantism and mobbing as well as criminal acts suitable for lynching.

In June 1855 the Kansas press published news that an abolitionist named Cole McCrea shot and killed Malcolm Clark, a pro-slavery man. McCrea barely escaped a lynching on the spot. Thereafter the pro-slavery side seemed to regret the lost opportunity and continually agitated for the lynching of McCrea. By the time John Brown arrived in Kansas, the lynching epithet freely flew in both directions.

51. Kansas Weekly Herald, *"Resolutions,"* 1855

Pursuant to adjournment of the indignation meeting on the 30th, the citizens of Leavenworth re-convened on Thursday last, at 11 o'clock, Col. A. Payne, presiding, and James M. Lyle, acting as Secretary of the meeting.

The committee appointed to draft resolutions reported the following, through their chairman, J. M. Alexander, which were unanimously adopted,

Resolved, That we regret the death of our esteemed fellow citizen, Malcolm Clark, and most bitterly condemn the cowardly act by which he was murdered; but we would depreciate any violation of the laws of the land by way of revenge, and stand ready to maintain and defend the laws from any violation by mob violence; that we do not deem the time has arrived, when it is necessary for men to maintain their inalienable rights, by setting at defiance the constituted authorities of the country....

Resolved, That no man has a right to go into any community and disturb its peace and quiet by doing incendiary acts or circulating incendiary sentiments; we therefore advise such as are unwilling to submit to the institutions of this country, to leave for some climate more congenial to their feelings, as abolition sentiments cannot, nor will not, be tolerated here; and while we do not say what may be the consequences, for the peace and quiet of the community we urge all entertaining and expressing such sentiments to leave immediately, claiming the right to expel all such as persist in such a course. . . .

Resolved, That a vigilance committee consisting of thirty members, shall now be appointed, who shall observe and report all such persons as shall openly act in violation of law and order, and by the expression of abolition sentiments produce disturbance to the quiet of the citizens, or danger to their domestic relations and all such persons so offending shall be notified and made to leave the Territory. . . .

SOURCE: Leavenworth, *Kansas Weekly Herald,* May 4, 1855.

Pro-slavery newspapers sometimes advocated hanging abolitionists charged with crimes.

52. Squatter Sovereign, *"Hanging is a Death Entirely Too Good for Such a Villain!"* 1855

On Monday week last, at Leavenworth City, Malcolm Clark, formerly of Platte county, Mo., was murdered in cold blood by an abolitionist named McCrea. They were disputing, and while Mr. Clark was in the act of turning, probably to go away, McCrea drew a pistol and shot him through the heart. He died immediately. He did not speak one word after that fatal shot. The murderer escaped his pursuers, and succeeded in placing himself under the protection of the troops at the Fort. He will not live to be tried. An outraged people are anxiously awaiting an opportunity to deal out summary punishment to the offender. Hanging is a death entirely too good for such a villain! Let him be tortured *and his friends hung*! Hope is beyond his reach. Should the technicalities of the law permit the murderer for a while to hope, the fire of indignation which already exists in the hearts of our citizens will need no other fanning to dissipate such a vain conjecture on his part. He may live in hope, but die in despair he surely must. . . .

We call for a settlement of this affair—let us make examples of such outlaws, and their sympathizers, until our fair Territory is ridden of such curses—until honest men can walk the streets of our towns, without the fear of being attacked by Northern cutthroats and hired assassins; until our homes and fire-sides can be made secure from the torch of the incendiary, and our slaves be permitted to remain with us in quietude and contentment. As long as one Abolitionist remains in the Territory, such occurrences will be numerous, both here and in Missouri. Let us begin to purge ourselves of all Abolition emissaries who occupy our dominion, and give distinct notice that all who do not leave immediately, for the East, WILL LEAVE FOR ETERNITY!

SOURCE: Atchison, Kansas Territory, *Squatter Sovereign,* May 8, 1855.

By the summer of 1855 pro-slavery forces dominated the territorial legislature, the law-making body of Kansas. Nonetheless, even after they took over the government, pro-slavery men could not curb their enthusiasm for extralegal violence, according to the abolitionist press. Specifically the pro-slavery men had lynched William Phillips, meaning they had tarred and feathered him.

53. New York Tribune, *"Border Ruffianism,"* 1855

I have just been conversing with a friend of mine who has recently visited the seat of war—western Missouri—and I have learned from him some facts which should be known to the many readers of the Tribune. . . .

My friend of whom I speak is by birth and education a pro-slavery man; yet his good sense and honesty lead him to speak the truth always. He says that western Missouri is at present under a reign of terror more terrible than that of Robespierre, because existing in a land claiming to be free, enlightened and Christianized. The fire-eaters are organized in a secret band, and conspire together in secret meetings. Their hand is against every man who will not loudly advocate their damnable doctrines. Those who are not with them, these slavery propagandists consider to be against them, and no ancient ban of excommunication could be more fearful than their avowed enmity. Whisky is their inspiration, and hemp and tar and feathers are their arguments. They have resolved to hang, burn and destroy, to bully and intimidate, until the curse of slavery shall be fixed on Kansas.

SOURCE: *New York Tribune*; reprinted in *Herald of Freedom*, July 21, 1855.

54. J. Marion Alexander, Letter to the Kansas Weekly Herald, 1855

My dear sir:—I had observed a short article extracted from the Pittsburg *Dispatch*, going the rounds of the Press, in which I was pronounced,—"the originator of the Pro-Slavery Vigilance Committee which lynched Phillips. And committed other outrages." . . . I had not intended to notice any attack upon me by any Abolitionist paper; but as you have had the manliness to speak through your able journal in my defence, and as it is possible that my position may be misunderstood by many of my friends . . . I will say a few words to the Public about myself in connection with the famous article alluded to! . . .

. . . The celebrated "Committee" that applied those forcible corrections to Phillips, originated in this wise. On the night of the Inquest upon the dead body of Malcolm Clark, a portion of the evidence implicated Phillips as having *abetted* McCrea, by urging him on to create a difficulty, and handing him the pistol with which Clark was shot so soon afterwards. Added to this, was the fact, that Phillips stood charged before the community with having committed a *perjury* concerning the late election, in which many of the more honorable Free-soilers could not exculpate him. The attendants on the Inquest, Clark's bleeding corpse before them,—a man in his life, it was impossible to know and not to admire, for he was noble and generous to a fault,—indignantly determined, that Phillips was not a safe man to live in that community, and so appointed a committee on the spot, to notify him to leave the place. The notice was given that night. Now mark: *I knew nothing of this till the next day!* I was present but a few minutes at the incipient stage of the Inquest. . . . But I am fearless to say of that Committee that it embraced the names of young gentlemen of high qualifications and unimpeachable character.

SOURCE: *Kansas Weekly Herald*, September 1, 1855.

With pro-slavery voters dominating every election, antislavery people felt that they truly lived in a lawless hell. The only law in Kansas, they complained, was Lynch Law.

55. *"Our Only Law,"* 1855

The following communication is an extract from a letter written by a Kansas Emigrant to his old chum, a friend in the Far East. . . .

It seems to have become a historical fact that all new countries are first settled by a floating population, discontented and restless spirits, "seeking rest and finding none" in their native place, float[ing] off . . . not very unlike the scum on the surface of a boiling cauldron, and as a matter of course, in this age. . . . Morals in such an age, and in these times, cannot be of an elevated character, nor the conduct of pioneer life regulated by high standards of intelligence and virtue. Hence we have our outbreaks in which passion seizes the reins and drives headlong into the commission of crime. Hence we have no law at least as such; and as was the case on a certain time in ancient Israel, "every man did as seemed good in his own eyes." It is true we have a law, or rather a code of laws, enacted by one political party, and repudiated by the other, which amounts to no law, but rather anarchy, in which "confusion is still more confounded." I will illustrate the state of things here by citing a case that recently occurred not a thousand miles from Lawrence. Lawrence you know is one of the first places in the Territory, where civilization, morality, religion and wisdom converge at a focal point or centre, and from which they again radiate, creating and giving tone and character to public opinion throughout the more distant and sparsely settled sections of this new country, yet not a thousand miles from this metropolitan City, the Sovereign Squatters are in the practice of shooting their neighbors' hogs, cattle and horses, when doing "damage feasan" in their unfenced grain crops, garden and cultivated patches on the prairies. I do not wish to be understood to say that all do this, for the great mass despise so foul a deed, but I do wish to be understood to say that such things are often done, and done here at the reputed centre of Kansas civilization. Nor does outrage in this land without law, stop here. I have said, Kansas is a kind of "Crystal Palace" in which the world is represented in all its commodities and fabrics, and I hope to be pardoned, through the proprietary virtues of truth, when I tell you that the descendants of the Goths and Vandals are also here carrying on their work of destruction and devastation, not only in the killing of cattle and horses, but also in tearing down their neighbors' houses at midnight, throwing out families and furniture on the open prairies, with no shelter except that what the better feelings of a better class of our citizens charitably afford.

It is but a few days since a horse was shot at night, and found dead next morning, for getting into a patch of corn with only a mere shadow of a fence, and this dark deed was done, by the order, if not by the hand, of a gentleman, belonging to one of the learned professions, and within two miles of Lawrence. But the "Sovereigns," to the number of twenty, took this matter in hand, and with a summary process characteristic of "Judge Lynch" brought the transgressor to justice. But here, too, the same fierceness of spirit and impatient impulse, so common in his Honor's Court, manifested itself. Human nature is human nature whether in Kansas or elsewhere—

whether curbed and controlled by law or allowed to develop itself without its salutary and civilizing influences. Those men took the matter into their own hands. The culprit requested time and opportunity to make what defence that the case would admit of. This was denied him on the ground, first, no defence could be made in so clear a case of guilt; and second, on the ground, the court was not prejudiced and would decide right and further that the defence would delay proceedings and take up time, and the court had no more time to devote to the examination. Several of the company moved for the case to be submitted to three references to be the one nominated by the owner of the horse, another by the culprit, and the third by the first two thus to be nominated. This motion was put down on the ground that the company present knew all about the case, and was as competent to award a right verdict in the premises as any three men, that could be selected by the parties, and as every man's mind had already made up on the guilt of the culprit there will be no occasion for postponing proceedings, nor for delaying judgment. . . .

The defendant being a man of sagacity and tact, perceiving his case had to be met, then and there, requested that the damages should be made up and assessed by them on the spot and at once without any further delay. This sudden turn in his policy and not comprehending his tactics as it was said by one man since, to have gratified their conceits, or flattered their vanity into a belief that he still had confidence in their integrity as judges of the case, and it is believed they let him off with a less sum than any other set of men in the Territory would have done.

This is given you as a specimen of Lynch Law, the only law in fact we have in the land, administered by Judge Lynch himself almost within the suburbs of our metropolis. His Judgeship is however very capricious in his administrations of justice. In this instance he did very well, and if he erred at all, it was on the side of clemency and mercy. But still he is said to be capricious, for in the same neighborhood he still allows houses to be torn down without cause or provocation, and widows claims to be "jumped," as it is here called, "without let or hindrance," and not unfrequently where interest concurs, with an approving nod of approbation from the ermine.
J.W.

SOURCE: *Kansas Free State*, October 22, 1855.

On May 24, 1856, in one of the most famous killings in American history, John Brown and seven followers hacked to death five settlers along Pottawatomie Creek. Historians universally call these killings a "massacre" and not a lynching, and Brown's abolitionist group a "militia" rather than a mob. Yet few twentieth-century lynching definitions would not cover Brown's killings. Brown led a group of more than three, acted in the service of justice (as he saw it), and quite obviously acted outside any law. Like the putative original Judge Lynch, Charles Lynch, Brown represented a militia company.

Brown and his men resembled lynchers in another way—perhaps the most important one. They saw themselves as taking the place of courts. A month before the "massacre," John Brown Jr. had gone to court, demanding to know whether the territorial laws would be enforced. One may doubt the sincerity of the demand. Young Brown knew full well that pro-slavery forces wrote the laws and ruled the courts. He wanted to make a point and document illegitimacy and fecklessness before taking the law into his own hands.[3]

The most famous western lynchings came in San Francisco, California. Some writers argue that the San Francisco lynchers should be thought of as "vigilantes" and not as "lynchers." But this early history of the first San Francisco Vigilance Committee reprints a handbill circulated by the vigilantes, a document in which they invoke the name "Judge Lynch" themselves.

Residents of San Francisco organized their first Vigilance Committee in 1851. According to the committee's defenders, five thousand people turned out. "This was not a mob, but the *people*," according to Frank Soule, John H. Gihon, and James Nisbet. The sovereign people have the right to take control of their criminal justice system, when they choose to do so. The following handbill circulated all over San Francisco.

56. *"Citizens of San Francisco,"* 1855

The series of murders and robberies that have been committed in this city, seems to leave us entirely in a state of anarchy. "When thieves are left without control to rob and kill, then doth the honest traveler fear each bush a thief." Law, it appears, is but a nonentity to be scoffed at; redress can be bad for aggression but through the never failing remedy so admirably laid down in the code of Judge Lynch. Not that we should admire this process for redress, but that it seems to be inevitably necessary.

Are we to be robbed and assassinated in our domiciles, and the law to let our aggressors perambulate the streets merely because they have furnished straw bail? If so, "let each man be his own executioner." "Fie upon your laws!" They have no force.

All those who would rid our city of its robbers and murderers will assemble on Sunday at two o'clock on the plaza.

SOURCE: Frank Soule, John H. Gihon, and James Nisbet, *The Annals of San Francisco; Containing a Summary of the History of the First Discovery, Settlement, Progress and Present Condition of California . . .* (New York: D. Appleton, 1855), 316.

In 1856 a new Vigilance Committee again organized. This time the California governor Neely Johnson appealed for federal help. The U.S. Constitution promises federal intervention in cases of "insurrection." Johnson was at pains to make sure that President Franklin Pierce understood the troubles as an "insurrection." The text of this document comes from Johnson's personal papers and includes his crossouts and corrections.

57. *California Governor Neely Johnson to President Franklin Pierce,* 1856

In view of the exciting Condition of affairs in the City and County of San Francisco in this state, I am constrained to call upon the General Government through the intervention of your Excellency for aid and assistance in the enforcement of the <laws> ~~provisions~~ of this state, and that you may the better understand the propriety of <readily> granting such request, I would beg leave to present a brief recital of events which have recently transpired and rendered necessary such application.

As early as the 16th of May last an organization styling themselves the Vigilance Committee was formed in that city secret in its character and to the uninitiated its purposes unknown, except as their insurgent acts have developed themselves. Although the presumption is that the organization had its origin in the events connected with the shooting of Mr. James King by one Casey on the 14th of the same month. Apprehensions were entertained from the incendiary appeals of the Press and <the> Public excitement that an attempt would be made to attack the jail where Casey was confined and rescue him from the officers of the law and deal out summary ~~vengeance~~ punishment to him—in fact an effort was made so to do by a mob prior to this organization—but was resisted successfully. In the meantime the Mayor ~~of the city~~ had called in the Military forces of the City numbering some ten companies for assistance—the sheriff did his utmost to obtain the aid of a posse capable of resisting an anticipated attack. It was found that the response in both case was but limited— not more than fifty or sixty of the Military could be depended on—<several> companies disbanded—joined the Vigilance Committee—forcibly placed in the possession of that organization arms and accoutrements (including the only two pieces of artillery belonging to the state) which had been loaned to them as Volunteer Companies by the State—and not one in ten of those summoned by the sheriff would obey his call. It seemed as if a panic had seized when the people and the fear of this formidable organization impelled law-abiding and law-observing citizens generally to shrink from the responsibility resting on them as citizens owing obedience to the Constitution and Laws of the State. On the 17th of the Month—when it was manifest that neither a military or Citizen force could be obtained to aid the sheriff in defending the jail—an armed body estimated at 3 or 4 thousand marched up there and demanded the delivery of two prisoners Casey and Cora—The sheriff was powerless—The few men he had about him would have constituted no impediment in the way of these superior numbers—and resistance was useless. He was forced to give up the prisoners. A few days later this same body of men from the windows of their place of meeting hung the two men referred to. Furthermore, they proceeded to arrest various individuals, search the houses of many of the best citizens on the most frivolous and groundless pretexts—establishing a system of espionage over the conversation and movements of respectable citizens—male and female, Wholly unknown to the laws or usages of a Republican form of Government. At length for one of the parties arrested by order of this self constituted tribunal, on proper application being made to one of the Judges of our Supreme Court, he issued a writ of *Habeas Corpus.* The sheriff was prevented by the armed resistance of this body of men from serving it and a few days later the party for whom the writ was issued Was—in Company with several other <citizens>—forcibly transported by different modes of conveyance and to different places—report says China, Australia, and the Sandwich Islands. In the meantime one of the number they had arrested and whilst in their custody, learning his sentence of punishment from the Country, Committed suicide in the cell where they had him confined.

On the 3d day of the Present Month I issued a Proclamation (a copy of which I enclose in the form of a printed slip) declaring the ~~city and~~ county <of San Francisco> in a state of insurrection. Genl Wood I had previously in a personal interview detailed the condition of affairs of which <matters> however he was fully informed otherwise. At such interview, he unhesitatingly promised me on the representations made him, that we were almost wholly destitute of Arms and of Ammunition we had none—to furnish on *my requisition* when we wanted them, such arms and ammunition as we desired. Within one or two days after the issuance of my Proclamation—of which I duly notified him—I made a requisition on Genl Wood for certain Arms and Ammunition to be furnished Maj General W. T. Sherman—in Command of the state troops at San Francisco. To my great surprise—he refused—alleging that he had no authority so to do in any ~~event~~ case.

That the necessities of the <case> ~~application~~ were of such an urgent character as should induce a compliance with my request I communicated with him again (a copy of which letter dated June 7th I herewith enclose) To this his reply was as before—a peremptory refusal to furnish any part of such requisition. In the course of this time the Vigilance Committee continued to arm themselves with muskets, a large quantity of which they easily purchased—Guns of various Calibre ranging from 6 to 32 pounders numbering near or about thirty pieces.—erected fortifications in the Central business portion of the City—~~by the military forces~~ proceeded with the trial and conviction of various persons—and now have in their custody several citizens <while> others have been compelled to flee for protection and safety to remote parts of the state. While all these warlike demonstrations are proceeding with members of their organization on the streets and public assemblages, and through the columns of the press controlled and directed by them the most violent harangues and inflammatory appeals are indulged both against the General and State Governments—and at least one of their organs—comes out boldly and defiantly against existing authority and calls upon the People to assemble and form a new government.

The power and authority of the state is set at naught. These unlawful proceedings cannot be arrested—firstly because we are destitute of arms and ammunition whereby to equip a force capable of coping with them—which it is now said numbers 6 or 7 thousand with their sympathizers in large numbers outside. ~~I therefore ask that orders may be transmitted~~ At most we have not muskets and rifles more than sufficient to arm 600 men—ordinance and ammunition we have none. I would therefore <respect> ~~ask that in view of this state of affairs, you~~ most urgently ask that you will <transmit orders> to the officer who is or may be Commanding the Pacific Division, to issue to the State authorities on the requisition of the Executive such arms and ammunition as may be needed for the purpose of suppressing the existing insurrection, or ~~to~~ at least the number and quantity specified in the requisition I made on Genl Wood as appears on the Pt of the <enclosed copy> of the Communication to him of June 7th. ~~found in the copy enclosed.~~ I <would> also urge the importance of transmitting such orders to the officer Commanding this Department to render such assistance in arms and ammunition at any future period as may be required by the State Executive for the purpose of enforcing obedience to the Constitution and Laws—as it is feared the example afforded by the present organization may extend its influence to other localities <in all probability> to ~~maybe~~ renew the <present one even> after disbanding <their forces> ~~For the time being.~~ In conclusion I would add, without the aid which is now sought at the hands of the General Government ~~we are in fact powerless~~

~~and the security of person and property in the City of San Francisco. no guarantee for the protection which the citizen is entitled to by our laws, can be given by the State authorities and this lawless and law-defying body of men can with impunity continue to disregard to the duty they extreme of~~ the State authorities can no longer afford protection to its citizens, or punish the lawless acts this <body of> men have been guilty of, and with impunity they may and doubtless will proceed with their acts of aggression and disobedience towards the Government as will ultimately result in its <entire> destruction.

I would beg leave to refer you to the Hon R. Augustus Thompson recently U. S. Land Commissioner for this state and Col H. Hovman now the Post Master of this city—who are deputed by me to lay this Communication before your Excellency—for a more detailed and minute relation of these affairs, than ~~the character of this~~ can conveniently be embodied in a written Communication.

Your earliest possible attention to this matter is extremely desirable.

> Very Respectfully
> Your obt svt
> J Neely Johnson

SOURCE: Johnson to Pierce, June 19, 1856, John Neely Johnson Papers, Manuscript Department, Bancroft Library, University of California, Berkeley.

News of the California vigilantes reached Kansas. The pro-slavery *Kansas Weekly Herald* fully endorsed the San Francisco proceedings.

58. Kansas Weekly Herald, *"Exciting News from California,"* 1856

The latest advices we have from California are of a most exciting character and depict the recurrence of many of those terrible scenes that disgraced San Francisco in former years. The terrible "Vigilance Committee" has again been compelled to organize itself for purposes of public protection. J. P. Casey, editor of the San Francisco Times, having drawn a pistol on Jas. King, editor of the Evening Bulletin, and shot him dead on the spot, was committed to prison. The mass of the population, feeling that Mr. Casey's influential associations would secure his escape, convened in great numbers, armed themselves, and drilled, nearly three thousand strong, marched to the jail, and compelled the Sheriff to deliver up for immediate trial before the Committee of Vigilance, not only the man Casey, but also the gambler Cora, who, sometime ago, murdered the late U. S. Marshal Richardson in cold blood. Our latest intelligence leave it pretty certain that both the culprits would be hung in the shortest possible time after an impartial but hasty scrutiny into the character of their defence.

The Courts in California, it appears, are utterly incompetent to punish anything like crime, and murder with its kindred offences against society run riot with impunity.—If any condition of things can justify the dreadful resort, by respectable citizens, to the habits and summary proceedings of Judge Lynch, it certainly seems to be when human life is not safe and private property not secure under the more legitimate administration of the laws. When assassins of influence are enabled to twist the legal meshes so as to suit their own operations, when they openly put those to death, with the bowie-knife or the revolver, whose honesty they fear, or whose presence is embarrassing, what can a community do but fall back on its natural rights, and personally maintain that standard of peremptory justice which the exigency demands and the authorities are too corrupt to enforce.

The Vigilance Committee will no doubt be the means of suppressing these disgraceful scenes and making the city of San Francisco once more inhabitable.—To do so and to slough off the dead flesh that mars the healthy action of her social system, let the Vigilance Committee drive out and exterminate the gamblers and thieves, the pugilists and assassins, who have so long invested their city.

SOURCE: Leavenworth, *Kansas Weekly Herald*, June 28, 1856.

During the Civil War Montana lynchers published a landmark on the landscape of lynching literature. Thomas J. Dimsdale had edited the *Montana Post* from 1864 until he died in 1866. Dimsdale, a Republican, justified the work of fellow Republican Sidney Edgerton, chief justice for the Idaho Territory, which included what is now Montana. When Edgerton traveled to the Montana mining camps he said he found crime and violence raging out of control. In fact, the miners, mostly Democrats, had organized their own courts and elected Henry Plummer as sheriff. Edgerton's nephew, Wilbur Sanders, nonetheless organized a vigilance committee. When the vigilantes lynched Plummer and his deputies they claimed the sheriff led a double life, secretly leading a bandit gang. Eliminating the leading Democrat also served Edgerton's political needs.[4]

Though Republicans regularly charged white southerners with lynching and vigilantism, Dimsdale published a powerful defense of Montana vigilantes. He first serialized it in his newspaper and then republished it as a book, *The Vigilantes of Montana*, which is still in print today.

59. *Thomas J. Dimsdale, "The Vigilantes of Montana,"* 1865

"Oh, cursed thirst of gold," said the ancient, and no man has even an inkling of the truth and force of the sentiment, till he has lived where gold and silver are as much the objects of desire and of daily and laborious exertion as glory and promotion are to the young soldier. Were it not for the preponderance of this conservative body of citizens, every camp in remote and recently discovered mineral regions would be a field of blood; and where this is not so, the fact is proof irresistible that the good is in sufficient force to control the evil, and eventually to bring order out of chaos.

Let the reader suppose that the police of New York were withdrawn for twelve months, and then let them picture the wild saturnalia which would take the place of the order that reigns there now. If, then, it is so hard to restrain the dangerous classes of old and settled communities, what must be the difficulty of the task, when, ten-fold in number, fearless in character, generally well armed, and supplied with money to an extent unknown among their equals in the east, such men find themselves removed from the restraints of civilized society, and beyond the control of the authority which there enforces obedience to the law.

Were it not for the sterling stuff of which the mass of miners is made, their love of fair play, and their prompt and decisive action in emergencies, this history could never have been written, for desperadoes of every nation would have made this country a scene of bloodshed and a sink of iniquity such as was never before witnessed.

Together with so much that is evil, nowhere is there so much that is sternly opposed to dishonesty and violence as in the mountains; and though careless of externals and style, to a degree elsewhere unknown, the intrinsic value of manly uprightness is nowhere so clearly exhibited and so well appreciated as in the Eldorado of the west. Middling people do not live in these regions. A man or a woman becomes better or worse by a trip towards the Pacific. The keen eye of the experienced miner detects the imposter at a glance, and compels his entire isolation, or his association with the class to which he rightfully belongs.

Thousands of weak-minded people return, after a stay in the mountains, varying in duration from a single day to a year, leaving the field where only the strong of heart are fit to battle with difficulty and to win the golden crown which is the reward of persevering toil and unbending firmness. There is no man more fit to serve his country in any capacity requiring courage, integrity, and self-reliance, than an "honest miner," who has been tried and found true by a jury of mountaineers. . . .

Finally, swift and terrible retribution is the only preventive of crime, while society is organizing in the far West. The long delay of justice, the wearisome proceedings, the remembrance of old friendships, etc., create a sympathy for the offender, so strong as to cause a hatred of the avenging law, instead of inspiring a horror of the crime. There is something in the excitement of continued stampedes that makes men of quick temperaments uncontrollably impulsive. In the moment of passion, they would slay all round them; but let the blood cool, and they would share their last dollar with the men whose life they sought a day or two before.

Habits of thought rule communities more than laws, and the settled opinion of a numerous class is, that calling a man a liar, a thief, or a son of a b—h, is provocation sufficient to justify instant slaying. Juries do not ordinarily bother themselves about the lengthy instruction they hear read by the court. They simply consider whether the deed is a crime against the Mountain Code; and if not, "not guilty" is the verdict, at once returned. Thieving, or any action which a miner calls mean, will surely be visited with condign punishment, at the hands of a Territorial jury. In such cases, mercy there is none; but, in affairs of single combats, assaults, shootings, stabbings, and highway robberies, the civil law, with its positively awful expense and delay, is worse than useless. . . .

Under these circumstances, it becomes an absolute necessity that good, law-loving, and order-sustaining men should unite for mutual protection and for the salvation of the community. Being united, they must act in harmony, repress disorder, punish crime, and prevent outrage, or their organization would be a failure from the start, and society would collapse in the throes of anarchy. None but extreme penalties, inflicted with promptitude, are of any avail to quell the spirit of the desperadoes with whom they have to contend; considerable numbers are required to cope successfully with the gangs of murderers, desperadoes, and robbers who infest mining countries, and who, though faithful to no other bond, yet all league willingly against the law. Secret they must be, in council and membership, or they will remain nearly useless for the detection of crime, in a country where equal facilities for the transmission of intelligence are at the command of the criminal and the judiciary; and an organization on this footing is a VIGILANCE COMMITTEE.

Such was the state of affairs, when five men in Virginia and four in Bannack initiated the movement which resulted in the formation of a tribunal, supported by an omnipresent executive, comprising within itself nearly every good man in the Territory, and pledged to render impartial justice to friend and foe, without regard to clime, creed, race, or politics. In a few short weeks it was known that the voice of justice had spoken, in tones that might not be disregarded. The face of society was changed, as if by magic; for the Vigilantes, holding in one hand the invisible, yet effectual shield of protection, and in the other, the swift descending and inevitable sword of retribution, struck from his nerveless grasp the weapon of the assassin; commanded the brawler to cease from strife; warned the thief to steal no more; bade the good citizen take courage; and compelled the ruffians and marauders who had so long maintained the "reign of terror" in Montana, to fly the Territory, or meet the just reward of their crimes. Need we say that they were at once obeyed? Yet not before more than one hundred valuable lives had been pitilessly sacrificed and twenty-four miscreants had met a dog's doom as the reward of their crimes.

To this hour, the whispered words, "Virginia Vigilantes" would blanch the cheek of the wildest and most redoubtable desperado, and necessitate an instant election between flight and certain doom.

The administration of the lex talionis by self-constituted authority is, undoubtedly, in civilized and settled communities, an outrage on mankind. It is there, wholly unnecessary; but the sight of a few of the mangled corpses of beloved friends and valued citizens, the whistle of the desperado's bullet, and the plunder of the fruits of the patient toil of years spent in weary exile from home, in places where civil law is as powerless as a palsied arm, from sheer lack of ability to enforce its decrees, alter the basis of the reasoning, and reverse the conclusion. In the case of the Vigilantes of Montana, it must be also remembered that the Sheriff himself was the leader of the Road Agents, and his deputies were the prominent members of the band.

The question of the propriety of establishing a Vigilance Committee depends upon the answers which ought to be given to the following queries: Is it lawful for citizens to slay robbers or murderers, when they catch them; or ought they to wait for policemen, where there are none, or put them in penitentiaries not yet erected?

Gladly, indeed, we feel sure, would the Vigilantes cease from their labor, and joyfully would they hail the advent of power, civil or military, to take their place; but, till this is furnished by Government, society must be preserved from demoralization and anarchy; murder, arson, and robbery must be prevented or punished, and road agents must die. Justice, and protection from wrong to person or property, are the birthright of every American citizen, and these must be furnished in the best and most effectual manner that circumstances render possible. Furnished, however, they must be by constitutional law, undoubtedly, wherever practical and efficient provision can be made for its enforcement. But where justice is powerless as well as blind, the strong arm of the mountaineer must wield her sword; for "self preservation is the first law of nature."

SOURCE: *Montana Post,* August 26, 1865.

NOTES

1. John Phillip Reid, *Policing the Elephant: Crime, Punishment, and Social Behavior on the Overland Trail* (San Marino: Huntington Library, 1997), 28, 103–116.

2. Edmund S. Morgan has said that popular sovereignty is never the many rising against the few but rather a few enlisting many against another few. See Edmund S. Morgan, *Inventing the People: The Rise of Popular Sovereignty in England and America* (New York: Norton, 1988), 169.

3. David M. Potter, with Don E. Fehrenbacher, *The Impending Crisis, 1848–1861* (New York: Harper and Row, 1976), 212–213. David Reynolds defends John Brown against charges that Brown's campaign of violence resembles that of Osama bin Laden or Timothy McVeigh. Reynolds's description of Brown fits the lynching definition promulgated by Fitzhugh Brundage and other scholars. According to Reynolds, Brown acted "under the pretext of service to justice, race, or tradition," which is Brundage's definition. Reynolds links Brown to the Puritan tradition. David S. Reynolds, *John Brown, Abolitionist: The Man Who Killed Slavery, Sparked the Civil War, and Seeded Civil Rights* (New York: Knopf, 2005), 14–28; W. Fitzhugh Brundage, *Lynching in the New South: Georgia and Virginia, 1880–1930* (Urbana: University of Illinois Press, 1993), 291.

4. Plummer may *not* have been living a double life. Although most historians have accepted Dimsdale's story, Plummer's biographers do not. R. E. Mather and F. E. Bozwell, *Hanging the Sheriff: A Biography of Henry Plummer* (Salt Lake City: University of Utah Press, 1987). Frederick Allen, in *A Decent Orderly Lynching: The Montana Vigilantes* (Norman: University of Oklahoma Press, 2004), takes issue with Mather and Bozwell but concedes that the evidence against Plummer was thin.

5

Civil War and Reconstruction

On March 4, 1861, when Abraham Lincoln and the Republicans took power in Washington, they challenged a thirty-year cultural dynasty, Jacksonian democracy. The six presidents following Andrew Jackson, including two Whigs, had had only slight impact on the political and social culture Old Hickory had established. With Lincoln and his fellow Republicans in control, this changed. The national government extended its powers in ways the old hero would never have approved. Under Lincoln, for example, Congress created a central banking authority, an anathema to Jacksonian Democrats. Most important, while Jackson had championed popular sovereignty to such an extent that some thought he legitimized mob law, Lincoln proclaimed himself a constitutionalist. Lincoln claimed to view constitutional principles as a sacred gifts bequeathed intact by the founders. Such constitutionalism tolerated neither secession, "the essence of anarchy," Lincoln said,[1] nor mob law. Lynchers challenged Lincoln's constitutionalism. In the New York City draft riots whites chased down and killed blacks, brutalizing their bodies.[2] In Texas Confederates hanged dozens of Union sympathizers in an incident known as "The Great Hanging."[3]

Lincoln himself sought to attach meaning to memory by memorializing great Civil War battles, as he had done at Gettysburg. After his death, political quarrels over the right to vote, the breaking up of the southern plantations, and the kind of labor system that would replace slavery dominated the halls of Congress and the nation. Leading politicians, and white people generally, did not want to base the nation's Civil War imagination on these issues, but continuing racial violence measured the limits on what the Civil War accomplished. In 1866 rioting erupted in Memphis and New Orleans that killed blacks by the dozens. Violence in other places killed many more. Often these "riots" featured a lynching component, with whites hunting down and hanging or shooting blacks. While the most radical Republicans hoped to expand national power on behalf of citizens' rights, white southerners clung to their right to kill misbehaving former slaves in their neighborhoods, free of outside scrutiny.

In 1866 Congress enacted a civil rights law, one that defined American citizenship ("All persons born in the United States") and spelled out citizens' rights. This law fell short of what the Radicals wanted, and, while the 1866 Civil Rights Act asserted national power against the states, many of its supporters expected the states to continue policing their communities much as they had before the Civil War. The great political question after the Civil War asked what power the states still had.

Reports of white southerners' continued violence against their former slaves argued for greater federal intervention and a further diminution of state power. Such violence also hampered sectional reconciliation and even suggested that the Republican Party's southern strategy had failed. No wonder tallies and reports of mobbing actually offended moderate Republicans, even those serving in the president's cabinet.

60. *Ulysses S. Grant to Edwin M. Stanton*, February 8, 1867

I have the honor to return herewith the copy of a call by the Senate for information as to the violations of the Civil Rights Bill and of a report of the Attorney General, both referred to me by you on the 23d ultimo.

In the reports of officers of outrages committed on the freedmen, reference is rarely or never made to the Civil Rights Bill, and I am accordingly unable to report its violations. I enclose, however, a statement of murders committed in the Southern States as in part pertinent to the inquiry.

Partial List of outrages committed in Southern States, and reported to Head Quarters Armies, U.S. during the year, 1866.

DATE	BY WHOM REPORTED	NATURE OF OUTRAGE
Feby 10, 66	Maj. Saml E. Rankin 8th Iowa V. V. acting Pro. Mar. Selma, Ala	Negro girl, 14 years old, ravished and both ears cut off by a white man Jan 6th near town of Opelika.
Same	Same	Negro woman ravished and one ear cut off. Oct. previous in Macon, Co.
March 2d	Sergt Jos. Rosch, 54th NY V. V. Comdg. Detchm't Aiken, S.C.	Eight colored and one white man murdered in Dist of Edgefield.
April 24th	Major Wm. Davis, Cmdg Detchm't 18th NY Cav. Yorktown, Texas	Sergt Josiah Ripley and Private John O'Brien Co. H 18th NY Cav found murdered on road.
July 3d	Major Genl. O. O. Howard Comr Bureau R. F. & A. L.	Lt. J. B. Blanding, 21st Regt V.R.C. an officer of Freedm Bureau, murdered on night of April 30th at Grenada, Miss.
July 3d	Same	Capt. C. C. Richardson, late of Freedm. Bureau at Thomasville, Ga., shot at twice and wounded by a man upon whom he had imposed a fine while working as Agent of Bureau.
Same	Same	A freedman shot by man named Lovett near Leesburg, Va., about 24th May.
Aug 9th	Gen. T. J. Wood, comdg Dist. of Miss.	Four freedmen murdered in Dist. Grenada.
Sept. 21st	Lt. Webster, Agt Fr. B. Columbia, La.	Maj Thomas, freedman, murdered by his employer, Henry Duke.
Oct. 1	Major Gen. P. H. Sheridan Comdg Dept. Gulf	Two soldiers named Privt Nath. Eglan and John Bull, colored, murdered by Jack Phillips, Dept Marshal, City of Jefferson, Texas on 30th August.
Nov. 16th	Bvt Major James Cronie Agt F. B. for Parishes of Sabine and Natchetoches	Amos Owens, freedman, waylaid by Dr.McNorton and two sons, who beat, shot and left him for dead. Friends of perpetrators took possession of his farm and left his family destitute.
Dec. 6th	Maj. Gen. O. O. Howard, Comr. Bureau &c.	Abraham & Noah Zook murdered by the Broome family near Vicksburg, Miss.
Dec. 22d	Major James T. Watson Genl. Supt. At Jackson, post, Ark.	Colored woman murdered in Jackson Co.

DATE	BY WHOM REPORTED	NATURE OF OUTRAGE
Dec. 24th	Bvt. Major H. Sweeney Genl. Supt. At Helena	Begs for a detachment of troops for protection of freedmen and so enforce payment of their dues, and states that murders and threats to murder have been quite frequent. Three freedmen murdered not long since — no trace of murderers.
Same	Col. Mullivan Cmdg Post of Dover	Negro boy killed.
Dec. 28th	A. E. Habricht, Supt. At Arkadelphia	Peter & Thomas Brinkley, colored, murdered by W. Bruns, near Benton, Ark.
Dec. 31	Bvt. Major Wm. J. Dawes Genl. Supt. Pine Bluff	Robert Stuart, colored, murdered by Frank Williams in Arkansas Co.
Jan. 4 '67	Genl. T. J. Wood, Comdg Dist. Miss.	Mr. Purvis Speer, a British subject, murdered and his house burned in Yazoo Co., Dec. 30th
Same	Same	Capt. King, late of army, killed near Greenville, Washington County

SOURCE: Container 31, The Papers of Edwin M. Stanton, Library of Congress.

61. *Orville Hickman Browning Diary,* February 15, 1867

Friday Feby 15, 1867 Full Cabinet. Mr Stanton presented his report in reply to the resolution calling on the President for information in regard to the execution of the civil rights bill. He the Secy of War, had called on Genl Howard, Commissioner of the Freedman's Bureau, and got from him a report of all the alleged outrages and murders that had been committed on freedmen in the South, compiled from the exaggerated statements of Lieutenants and others, agents of the Bureau, without details or authenticated facts, and insisted that the President should send it in as part of his reply to the resolution. It was a mean, malicious thing intended to compel the President, for the benefit of radical partizans, to send out to the country, endorsed by him as facts, these prejudiced and in many instances false, and in almost all exaggerated statements, or place himself, by refusing to send them to Congress, in a position where they could falsely, but plausibly charge him with the suppression of facts.

The resolution called on the President to say whether any instances of a refusal to execute the provisions of the civil rights bill had come to his knowledge. None of these cases had ever before been reported to him or brought to his notice and Mr Stanbery and myself remonstrated against his sending in such a mass of mere rumors as a part of his report. Stanton was very persistent, and manifestly wanted to do the President an injury. I have no faith in him. He has no sincerity of character, but is hypocritical and malicious. Stanbery and I were equally persistent. The Cabinet sustained us, and it was determined that the President should confine himself to an answer to the resolution, but say, in addition thereto, the truth, that the Secretary of War had today for the first time, reported to him a number of cases, of which he had not before heard, and which he would at once have investigated.

SOURCE: James G. Randall, ed., *The Diary of Orville Hickman Browning, Volume II, 1865–1881* (Springfield: Illinois State Historical Library, 1933), 130. Reprinted by permission.

Gideon Welles's account of the February 15 cabinet meeting. Interlineations appear within angled brackets.

62. *Gideon Welles Diary,* February 15, 1867

There was but one sentiment, I think, among all present, and that of astonishment and disgust at this presentation of the labors of the War Department. The Attorney-General asked what all this had to do with the enquiry made of the President. The resolution called for what information had come to the knowledge of the President respecting failures to execute the law under the civil rights bill, and here was a mass of uncertain material <mostly relating to negro quarrels> wholly unreliable, and of which the President had no knowledge, collected and sent in through Genl Grant as a response to the resolution.

Two or three expressed surprise at these documents. Stanton, who is not easily dashed <when he feels he has power and will be sustained> betrayed guilt, which, however, he would not acknowledge, but claimed that the information was pertinent —was furnished by Genl Grant. If, however, the President did not choose to use it, he could decline doing so. Subsequently he thought the Attorney-General should, perhaps, decide. Seward undertook to modify and suggest changes. I claimed that the whole was wrong and that no such reply could be made acceptable under any form of words.

Randall[4] thought the letter of Stanton and the whole budget had better be received, and that the President should send in that he knew nothing about them when this the Senate's resolution was passed, but that, having since received this information, he would have it looked into, and thoroughly investigated.

Stanton, who showed more in his countenance and manner than I ever saw him, caught at once at Randall's proposition. Said he would alter his report to that effect and went to work with his pencil.

Seward indorsed Randall—said he thought all might be got along with if that course was pursued.

I dissented <entirely> and deprecated communicating this compilation of <scandalous and inflammable> material, gathered by partisans since the action of Congress, <and represented to be> a matter of which the <President> had knowledge <when the resolution was passed>. It would be said at once by mischievous persons that here was information of which Grant complained, but of which the President took no notice. That Congress had called out the information, and Grant communicated it and that there is mal-administration—that this was the purpose of the call— the design, probably of the members who got it up. Stanton looked at me earnestly— said he never was as desirous to act in unison with the President as any one—no matter who,—that this information seemed to him proper, and so <he said> it seemed to Genl Grant who sent it to him; but if others wished to suppress it they would make the attempt but there was little doubt that members of congress had seen this—likely had copies. Finally, and with great reluctance on his part, it was arranged that he would, as the rest of us had done, give, as we had done, all the information called for which had come to his knowledge in answer to the resolution, and that the reports of

Grant & Howard should, with the rumors <scandal> & gossip be referred to the Attorney General for investigation or prosecution if proper.

It was evident, throughout this whole discussion of an hour and a half that all were alike impressed in regard to this matter. McCulloch and Stanberry, each remarked to me before we left, that this was design and intrigue in concert with the radical conspirators at the Capitol. Stanton betrayed his knowledge and participation in it, for though he endeavored to bear himself through it, he could not conceal his part in the intrigue. He had delayed his answer until Howard and his subordinates <scattered over the South> could hunt up all the <rumor of negro quarrels and> party scandal and malignity and pour through Genl Grant on to the President. It would <keep> generate differences between the President and the General, and if sent out to the country under the call for information by Congress, would be used by the Congress to injure the President and perhaps Grant also.

SOURCE: Gideon Welles, Diary, February 15, 1867, The Papers of Gideon Welles, Library of Congress, Washington, D.C.

The Ku Klux Klan began life in the law office of Judge Thomas M. Jones of Pulaski, Tennessee, probably in May or June 1866. The six founders were all Confederate veterans: John C. Lester, James R. Crowe, John B. Kennedy, Richard Reed, Frank O. McCord, and the judge's son, Calvin. McCord edited the local newspaper, the *Pulaski Citizen*. Their most brilliant innovation came in naming their organization, corrupting the Greek word for circle or band, *kuklos*. The founders were public-spirited citizens, and some, it is said, became a bit embarrassed when they saw the Ku Klux Klan turn to racial vigilantism.

In 1868 reports of white southerners' vigilante activity began appearing widely in the press. The 1867 Reconstruction Act required the southern states to organize new governments, with constitutions approved by black as well as white voters. Whites exploded in outrage and seized on the name "Ku Klux Klan" as a name for their vigilante movement.

63. *The Ku Klux Klan, 1868*

For something like six months past, perhaps longer, there has existed in the counties of Giles and Maury, a robed organization under the euphonious sobriquet of the "Kuklux Klan." How or by whom it was organized, we are unable to state; but certain it is that, commencing probably at the town of Pulaski, this secret society has spread out until it embraces nearly all the young men of rebel proclivities in the two counties above mentioned. The organization was represented to outsiders as a harmless conclave of congenial or convivial spirits to encourage tournaments, masquerades, &c. Under this guise the leaders of the "kuklux" held meetings, established their lodges, swept in their members by scores and hundreds, and perfected their plans for terrorizing the whole region, and rendering the lives and the property of Union men unsafe. We doubt not the object of this conclave, which seems to be characterized by the same answers that tempted the rebel leaders, is to drive Union men out of the country, or at least keep them in constant alarm, and to overawe the negroes and prevent them from exercising their rights at the ballot-box.

Having completed their organization, the leaders of this secret society, finding themselves at the head of a large number of ignorant, reckless young men, have felt themselves of late, in a situation to commence operations. The riot at Pulaski was but one of the recent outrages of this villainous rebel crew. We have the facts in connection with a dastardly outrage perpetrated last Saturday upon several unoffending men, which shows conclusively that this secret clan of rebels is assuming an activity toward the accomplishment of their peculiar ends which should make it an object of attention upon the part of the military authorities of this Department.

Last Saturday night a party of some twenty or twenty-five members of the "Kuklux Klan" collected at the town of Lynnville, some twelve miles north of Pulaski, in Giles County, and proceeded to a plantation nearby, upon which is employed a Union man, against whom, it seems, they felt the greatest animosity on account, doubtless, of his outspoken boldness as a Republican. This man, named Frank Dickinson, and four colored men, named respectively Jack White, Ephraim Johnson, Jordan Gregory, and Thomas White, the gang of outlaws took from the house and carried into the piece of woods near by. Here Dickinson, the white man, Jack White and Thomas White, were secured, their hands being tied behind them, after which they were beaten in a terrible manner with beech goads. Four men were engaged at one time in beating one of the colored men, who received not less than one hundred lashes. For some cause the other colored men were not whipped, but were compelled to stand by and witness this outrage upon their companions. After having beaten Dickinson and the two other men to their heart's content, the gang withdrew from the spot. They were all armed with navy revolvers, wore masks, and were commanded by a Major and Lieutenant, the men obeying their leaders as though they were in a regular military organization.

SOURCE: *Nashville Press and Times, January 15, 1868*

Press reports of Ku Klux Klansmen mobbing almost never used the word *lynch,* yet the Klansmen formed mobs, took prisoners from jails, and hanged them in extralegal service to justice. This report appeared in the *Pulaski Citizen,* edited by a Ku Klux Klan founder.

64. *"A Murderer's Mishaps,"* 1868

One day last week, John Bicknell, a worthy ex-Confederate soldier, resident at Columbia, while traveling between Henryville, Lawrence county, and Mount Pleasant, Maury county, was attacked, murdered and robbed by a man named Walker, who with Bicknell's horse, purse and valuables, made his escape, but was afterwards captured and placed in jail at Columbia.—Further we will let the *Banner* of Wednesday tell the story as follows:

At the hour of 10 o'clock on Monday night, a party of about twenty horsemen, well mounted and completely disguised in the Kuklux mask and mantle, rode into Columbia, and proceeded directly to the County Jail. They took the precaution to picket all the streets leading to the jail, and halted every citizen going in that direction. Three of the unknown entered the building and called for the jailer. Mr. White immediately came forward and demanded to know why they were there and what they wanted. One of the number replied, "We want the murderer of John Bicknell." The jailer said, "The prisoner is in the hands of the law; you can get him only through an order from the sheriff." Thereupon the unknown, in a deep guttural voice answered, "we are the law, and this (presenting a navy at the head of the Jailer) is our order." Mr. White at once called upon his wife for the keys and delivered up the criminal, who was immediately seized, taken out, and hurriedly placed behind one of the horsemen. The party then started off at a gallop. . . .

Many were the surmises of the citizens as to the character and object of the rescuing party, some insisting that they were the friends of the prisoner, while others were equally confident that they were friends of the deceased, who were determined to avenge his death. None knew the truth, as the whole affair had been conducted by strangers. Yesterday morning a rumor was rife that the body of the murderer was hanging to a tree in the cemetery, near the grave of Bicknell. Hundreds of curious and credulous persons hurried to the spot only to be deceived by the hoax. The mystery continued as dark and deep as ever, until about 10 o'clock, when a party of citizens from Bear Creek rode into town bringing with them a prisoner who was at once recognized by a large number of persons as the criminal who had been taken from the jail the night before.

The disguised parties who had spirited Walker away have, of course, nothing to say as to the manner of his escape, for any statement from them would expose their connection with the transaction. We are, therefore, left for the fact entirely to the statement of the prisoner which may, as far as his reliability is concerned, be true or false. He says that he was carried after having been bound hand and foot, to a point on Duck River, two miles east of Columbia, and, in that dark, uninhabitable bend, was untied, taken to a high rock on the bluff, overhanging the stream, and told that he had but a few minutes to live, which he might devote to prayer. As he pretended to kneel down, he threw himself into the cold swollen stream beneath, and was fired at at least twenty times while swimming across. Having reached the northern bank exhausted and almost frozen, he made his way to a house in sight, and asked that he might warm and dry himself. He accounted for his condition by saying that he had swam the river while hotly pursued by a band of robbers. A seat near the fire was given him, and while he was warming himself, Mr. Dooley the master of the house, provided himself with a double barreled shot gun and forbade his leaving, on the ground that the manner and hour of his untimely visit were such as to awaken a suspicion that he had been guilty of some evil deed. The stranger protested his innocence until the arrival of Mr. Loftin, father-in-law of Mr. Dooley, who recognized Walker as the man he had seen in the jail at Columbia during the day. Finding himself cornered, the prisoner made a full confession of his guilt. He stated that he had recently been to Memphis, where he had got on a spree and spent all his money, and had also parted with his horse. While wending his way home, foot sore and weary, he stopped at Henryville, bought a quart of mean whisky, drank freely, and, when overtaken by the unfortunate Bicknell, he was drunk and desperate. Without provocation he fired the fatal shot with no other motive than to procure himself of the horse of his victim. . . .

Some of the circumstances connected with the funeral of young Bicknell were so extraordinary in their nature as to merit more than a passing notice. Rain fell during the entire day. . . . This did not, however, prevent the attendance of a large concourse of sympathizing citizens. The corpse was escorted to its last resting place by the Pale Faces and Kuklux; the latter in the weird dress peculiar to their order. At the grave the Pale Faces took charge of the remains and went through a strange but solemn cere-mony. After the last shovelful of earth had been thrown upon the freshly raised mount, the Kuklux, about twenty strong, kneeled around, and, raising their right hands toward Heaven, swore vengeance on the murderer of John Bicknell. They then rose slowly, mounted their horses went off at a brisk gait southward and soon disap-peared from the view of the awe-struck spectators.

Later.—On Tuesday night, Walker was again taken from the jail and this time hung. His corpse was found the next morning hanging to a limb one mile this side of Columbia.

SOURCE: *Pulaski Citizen*, March 6, 1868.

The Klan claimed to eschew politics but in fact served as the military arm of the Democratic Party. White southerners hated the Freedmen's Bureau, an agency of the federal government working on behalf of the freed slaves. Every act of Klan violence made an argument to north-erners that the South could not be trusted to police itself. "There are some who say we will keep the "*Bureau*" here," the Klan's "Great Grand Cyclops recognized. To prevent such a catastrophe, the Cyclops promised not to "harm the poor African." The Klan adopted military forms, styling its communication a "Special Order" addressed to the "First Grand Division."

65. "*Communication from the Great Grand Cyclops,*" 1868

The following communication from the Great Grand Cyclops was handed to us by one of our oldest citizens and most reliable merchants, who found it in his pocket, and who says that he has no idea in the world how it got there. He is inclined to think that it would have been impossible for human hands to put it there without detection. The finder was directed to deliver the document to the editor of the Citizen:

Office, G. G. S., }
Crimson Den, First Moon, 1868. }
SPECIAL ORDER TO FIRST GRAND DIVISION.

To the Grand Giant Commanding

There are those who endeavor to pry into our sacred mysteries. There are spies on the alert. Watch and be silent. There are some who say we are *politicians*. This your Chief depl[or]es for the honor of the Klan. There are some who say we will keep the "*Bu-reau*" here. Your chief here says, for the honor of the Klan, that we will not harm the poor *African*. There are some who say we commit outrages on citizens of our State, this your Chief denies for the honor of the Klan.

Order No. 2. The Grand Cyclops of Den No. 8 in Maury County, will order a coun-cil for the trial of Mamaluka Kaan.

Order No. 3. The Grand Cyclops of all Dens in each Division will order councils for the trial of all members who have been guilty of wearing their costumes outside of their respective Dens. This order is perem[p]tory. All persons are hereby warned against wearing the costume of our Klan. It shall be the duty of all members of the Klan to put down all attempts to bring reproach upon our Klan by malicious persons. By order of the G.G.C.

SOURCE: *Pulaski Citizen,* February 14, 1868.

Lynchings did occur by name during Reconstruction.

66. New York Commercial Advertiser, *"Lynch Law in Maryland,"* 1869

On Monday last a colored man committed an outrage on a young lady, a school teacher near Fort Washington, sixteen miles from Washington City, while she was on her way to, and within 200 yards of, the school house. When found by her friends, she was lying on the ground fearing to move lest the assailant should return, and, finding her alive, kill her. The negro was arrested the same day, taken to Piscataway, where he was identified by the lady, and a committal made out against him, and in charge of Constables John Underwood and Anthony Anderson, he was immediately started in a wagon for Marlboro, the county seat. At his request he was taken to his house to bid his wife good-bye. While the wagon was standing in front of his house it was approached by about twenty men, dressed only in their shirts and drawers, one only in a shirt, and with handkerchiefs with pierced eye holes. After tying Constable Underwood, who had attempted to defend his prisoner and had fired several shots at the lynchers, and removed him from the wagon, they made Deputy Constable Anderson drive the vehicle to a piece of woods a short distance off, where he, too, was put out and tied. The wagon was then driven by one of the maskers under a large white oak tree, and a noose having been adjusted over a horizontal limb, the prisoner, who was handcuffed, was made to stand up, but his head not reaching the noose, he was required to get upon the driver's seat, when the noose was put around his neck and the wagon driven from under him, he springing up at the time apparently with the intention of expediting his death. The rope slipped and the man's feet touched the ground. One of the maskers then jumped upon his shoulders to bear him down, while some of the others swung him to and fro until life was extinct. The party then formed in line, and fired a volley at his body. After swinging for two hours his body was cut down and a coroner's jury was summoned to hold an inquest upon it, who returned a verdict of "death from hanging by unknown persons." The corpse was buried on Hatton Hill.

SOURCE: *New York Commercial Advertiser,* October 14, 1869.

"Our people," the Republican *New York Times* editorialized in 1870, "must become homogeneous in political thought and action." To accomplish this, the *Times* believed, demagogues, North and South, must be silenced.[5] A few months later the *Times* pronounced itself weary of those Republican newspapers that repeated, "with marvelous regularity," reports of "the reign of lawlessness in the South." Republicans advanced such stale and sensational stories only to advance their political fortunes, the *Times* thought. The *Times* wanted to reconcile the sections.[6]

So did Democrats. Eugene Casserly served in the U.S. Senate from 1869 to 1873, representing California from San Francisco. Democrats like Casserly feared that reports of white southerners' violence threatened states' rights and state powers. Casserly and the Democrats wanted reconciliation as well, but with the states' power over policing intact.

67. *Senator Eugene Casserly, "Stale Charges,"* January 18, 1871

I can well understand that there are in the South disorderly and violent men. They are the natural fruits of the war and of your own misgovernment. They are but a handful, easily dealt with by any Government dealing with them in the right spirit . . . It would be a great deal better for the dignity of this body, for the peace of this country, for the good standing of the American people before the enlightened judgment of Christendom, to say at once what is the object of all this exaggerated outcry of outrages in the South; of all this hollow parade of investigations—far better to come directly to the point like men, and let it be understood that no one of the States lately in insurrection will be permitted to come back here until she sends to the Senate and to the House of Representatives men whose party politics shall be acceptable to the accidental party majority in each. . . .

I do not doubt that in parts of the South there are troubles. Considering the terrible ordeal, first of war and then of your misgovernment, it would be wonderful if there were not. But why exaggerate them; why turn them into capital for a party?

SOURCE: *Congressional Globe*, 41st Congress, 3d sess., 571.

On April 20, 1871, Congress passed "an Act to enforce the Provisions of the Fourteenth Amendment to the Constitution of the United States and for Other Purposes," better known as the Ku Klux Klan Act. Previous laws had tried to prevent misconduct by state governments; for the first time this law aimed to punish individuals in federal court for crimes. Many doubted the constitutionality of the new law, despite its title. The language of the Fourteenth Amendment forbade *states* from depriving persons of life, liberty, or property, not private individuals. Eric Foner writes that this law "pushed Republicans to the outer limits of constitutional change."[7]

68. *Ku Klux Klan Act,* 1871

SECT. 2. That if two or more persons within any State or Territory of the United States shall conspire together to . . . go in disguise upon the public highway or upon the premises of another for the purpose, either directly or indirectly, of depriving any person or any class of persons of the equal protection of the laws, or of equal privileges or immunities under the laws, or for the purpose of preventing or hindering the constituted authorities of any State from giving or securing to all persons within such State the equal protection of the laws, or shall conspire together for the purpose of in any manner impeding, hindering, obstructing, or defeating the due course of justice in any State or Territory, with intent to deny to any citizen of the United States the due and equal protection of the laws, or to injure any person in his person or his property for lawfully enforcing the right of any person or class of persons to the equal protection of the laws, or by force, intimidation, or threat to prevent any citizen of the United States lawfully entitled to vote from giving his support or advocacy in a lawful manner towards or in favor of the election of any lawfully qualified person as an elector of President or Vice-President of the United States, or as a member of Congress of the United States, or to injure any such citizen in his person or property on account of such support or advocacy, each and every person so offending shall be deemed guilty of a high crime, and, upon conviction thereof in any district or circuit court of the United States or district or supreme court of any Territory of the Untied States having jurisdiction of similar offences, shall be punished by a fine not less than five hundred nor more than five thousand dollars, or by imprisonment, with or without hard labor, as the court may determine, for a period of not less than six months nor more than six years, as the court may determine, or by both such fine and imprisonment as the court shall determine.

SOURCE: George P. Sanger, ed., *Statutes at Large and Proclamations of the United States* (Boston, 1873), 17:13–14.

In March 1871, over the objections of Casserly and others, Congress created a joint committee of fourteen Representatives and seven Senators to investigate Klan violence. The Joint Select Committee to Inquire into the Condition of Affairs in the Late Insurrectionary States was organized on April 20. Democrats saw the investigation as purely political. Republicans had already passed the Ku Klux Klan Act but probably hoped that the hearings would compile evidence in support of what they had done.[8] The committee heard from Klansmen and their victims, compiling a detailed record of Reconstruction mob violence in one of the largest congressional investigations to date.

Frank Myers of Florida told the committee how the Klan recruited new members.

69. *Testimony of Frank Myers, Jacksonville, Florida*, November 11, 1871

In 1868, when I was living in Alachua County, I joined a democratic club that was being organized at that time; and a short time after I joined it, a proposition was made to me to join what they termed a secret-service club; as I expected to leave the county in a few days, and move into Hernando County, I did not join the secret-service club, as they called it; since that time I have been in Alachua County repeatedly, and in conversation with several of those parties I have been informed that such an organization was completed.

Question. What did you understand was the object of that secret-service club?

Answer. The object of the secret-service club, as explained to me at that time by the party who spoke to me about it, was, in case it became necessary, as they feared it would, to use force or violence to prevent certain parties from exerting too great an influence with the colored population in that county, to be prepared to do it effectually and secretly.

Source: Testimony Taken by the Joint Select Committee to Inquire into the Condition of Affairs in the Late Insurrectionary States, Miscellaneous and Florida, 42d Congress, 2d sess., House of Representatives Report No. 22, part 13 (Washington, D.C.: USGPO, 1872), 156.

Joseph J. Williams, a North Carolina–born planter living in Florida, saw the Ku Klux Klan as a logical extension of antebellum vigilante tradition.

70. *Testimony of Joseph J. Williams, Jacksonville, Florida,* November 13, 1871

Question. How many persons do you suppose belonged to the club in your county?
Answer. I could not say positively, but I suppose three or four hundred. . . .
Question. Then something like one-half of the democrats belong to that organization?
Answer. Yes, sir; and I suppose all would have belonged to it, if it had been convenient. I know some who did not belong to it.
Question. Was there any other business the club was to look after except the inciters of riot among the colored voters.
Answer. No, sir. . . . it was political entirely; that was all that was ever contemplated. . . . [I]t is an organization that could act any day and every day, and would consult together, while the courts met only once or twice a year.
Question. What was the force and vigor of such an organization, if after notifying a man to leave the country and he should not do it—?
Answer. He would have left; no man would have staid in a community of that sort.
Question. Why should he have left?
Answer. He should have been afraid of some disturbance, of being interfered with. A man of that sort who disturbs the peace of the community in which I live would deserve to have something done to him.
Question. We are not talking about that; no doubt he would deserve punishment, but we are now speaking of this mode of doing it.
Answer. Yes, sir; that is so.
Question. Why would they have left; because they would have feared illegal violence?
Answer. Well, before the war, years ago, we had here a very similar process; it never has been resorted to since, but that was twenty-five or thirty years ago. We had down in this country what were called regulators. Whenever they noticed a man to leave he left. If it had not been for this organization, with the men at the head of it, we could not have been protected.
Question. Protected from what?
Answer. From the colored people, and from the men who were urging them on. . . .
Question. The reason why those people would have left after notice was, that they would have anticipated violence from your order? . . .
Answer. Well, I think so, yes. . . .

Source: Testimony Taken by the Joint Select Committee to Inquire into the Condition of Affairs in the Late Insurrectionary States, Miscellaneous and Florida, 42d Congress, 2d sess., House of Representatives Report No. 22, part 13 (Washington, D.C.: USGPO, 1872), 230.

Before the Civil War, westerners had justified their lynching as having been made necessary by inefficient or corrupt courts. When the criminal justice system failed, the people had to act, westerners had insisted. Pride Jones of North Carolina applied this argument to the Reconstruction South.

71. *Testimony of Dr. Pride Jones, Washington, D.C.,* June 5, 1871

Question. What avowal of purpose was made to you by any one connected with the organization?

Answer. The purport of it was this: That barns were being burned, women were afraid to go about the country for fear of being ravished by negroes, and the law should not punish them; there was inefficiency somewhere; they could not get protection, and they got up this organization to protect themselves by punishing a few who were obviously guilty, and thereby preventing others from committing that sort of offense. . . .

Question. In judging whether it was a political organization or not, were you governed by the fact that most of the persons who were victims of these wrongs were of one political party; or how did you account for that?

Answer. I judged it this way; there were papers generally attached to the persons of those who were hung. In one case it would be, "You are hung for barn-burning"; in another case it would be, "You are hung for threatening to ravish" some one; or something to that effect. Those cards were attached to the bodies of the persons who were executed—or rather hung, not executed.

Question. Was there any difficulty, where a person was known to have committed such an offense as barn-burning or violation of chastity, to bring him to justice in the courts? . . .

Answer. Yes, sir; and it was the very general impression throughout the community with everybody that it was a very hard matter to have justice inflicted upon a negro.

SOURCE: Testimony Taken by the Joint Select Committee to Inquire into the Condition of Affairs in the Late Insurrectionary States, North Carolina, 42d Congress, 2d sess., House of Representatives Report No. 22, part 2 (Washington, D.C.: USGPO, 1872), 3–4.

The next witness served as the sheriff of Sumter County, Alabama.

72. *Testimony of Allen E. Moore, Livingston, Alabama,* October 30, 1871

Question. You may state to the committee the particulars of the rescue of a negro from the jail in this place [Sumter County, Alabama], which is said to have occurred in the fore part of the present month.

Answer. I can do so. I will give all the particulars, and you can judge for yourself. I think it was on the 29th of September last, as far as I recollect just now. . . . [My niece] knocked at my door, and says, "Uncle, somebody is calling you at the door." I said, "Who my dear?" and I jumped up. I was sleeping on the back side of the bed near the wall, and before I got out, she said, "La, uncle, the yard is full of men." At this time they kept hammering on the front door. . . . I went . . . to the . . . window . . . and threw up the sash, and didn't have time to fix it, and held the sash raised between my shoulders; threw open the blinds, and held my hand on the outside of the sill of the window, and by that time there was about fifteen or twenty of them; that is my surmise of the number. One of them drew out—as I could see, for the moon was shining almost as light as day—jerked out his pistol, and says, "Doctor Moore, we want Zeke High. We must have him, and we will have him"; and then, at the same time, a man grabbed at my hands, and catched in that way by the middle finger of the left hand [illustrating]. Says I, "Gentlemen, this is a strange proceeding. I thought that a thing of that sort had played out in this country." One of them remarked, "We don't care a damn about its being played out; we want Zeke High. If you won't open the door, give us the keys, or we will have to go the extreme of burning down the house. We are going to have him." . . . they all went inside of the house. . . . This man walked up and gathered me by the arm, and walked to the door that goes to the jail, and says, "Open the door." I says, "You have got all the keys; you can unlock it yourselves." He says, "Here is the key, damn it." Then I unlocked the door and went up and went to the second door. I opened that door. . . . They said, "Show us the cell." I said, "Here it is." I went up and unlocked the top lock of the cell. . . . One of them, the leader, says, "Hold on, Doc, I am going in there to get him out." I says, "That's nothing to me; I am not going in there." And he walked into the cell, I heard a terrible rattling amongst the crockery. . . . The negro had struck him with one of these night mugs as he walked in. . . . I heard a tremendous lick, then heard the manure and everything splashing on the floor, and the fellow jumped back and says, "God damn it, boys, he has ruined me," I asked him, "Where did he hit you?" He says, "God damn it, Doc, he has knocked out two of my front teeth." . . . After they got up there, they pushed this prisoner, this negro boy, Lewis, into the cell, and made him pull the negro Zeke out. They pushed him in until he got him by the leg, and they catched him and hauled him out. I heard them tramping down the stairs, and just as I came to my wife's door, going out into the passage, they came down the basement floor of the jail where I staid, in the lower story. There they struck a trot with him . . . ; and that, gentlemen, was the end of their taking him out of jail. I can tell you where I found him, and how I recognized him and knew it to be the same negro. The next morning it was all over town, of course, and created a great deal of excitement. I took a crowd of men, next morning—I knew it was not worth while to take a crowd that night—but after I got through my evidence, I will explain that. I took about twenty or thirty men. I said, "I want you to hunt this swamp; I am satisfied from the way these fellows acted they would kill him in ten minutes, for one prisoner told me this morning that he wanted to put on his clothes and they told him it was not worth while—that they would kill him in ten minutes." Well, some of them found him over here, in sight of this place. There is an old steam mill there. They had taken him down between that mill and the river, and shot him. He was shot worse than any piece of flesh I ever saw. He was shot, really, from the top of his head, plumb to the soles of his feet. . . .

Question. Would there have been any trouble in summoning a posse that night, and following this crowd? . . .

Answer. There would have been no trouble in summoning them, but not a damned man would have gone.

Question. Why not?
Answer. Fear of bodily harm.

Source: Testimony Taken by the Joint Select Committee to Inquire into the Condition of Affairs in the Late Insurrectionary States, Alabama, 42d Congress, 2d sess., House of Representatives Report No. 22, part 10 (Washington, D.C.: USGPO, 1872), 1565–1572.

By denying that they had committed any criminal offense, victims of the Klan highlighted the organization's political purpose.

73. *Testimony of William Coleman (Colored), Macon, Mississippi, November 6, 1871*

Question. Where do you live?
Answer. I live in Macon.
Question. How long have you lived here?
Answer. I came here about the last of April.
Question. Where did you come from?
Answer. I came from Winston County.
Question. What occasioned your coming here?
Answer. I got run by the Ku-Klux. . . .
Question. Tell how it occurred. . . .
Answer. Well, I don't know anything that I had said or done that injured any one. Further than being a radical in that part of the land, as for interrupting any one, I didn't. . . .
Question. Did the Ku-Klux come to your house? . . .
Answer. They came about a half hour or more before day, as nigh as I can recollect by my brains, being frightened at their coming up in this kind of way. They were shooting and going on at me through the house, and when they busted the door open, coming in and shooting, I was frightened, and I can only tell you as nigh as my recollection will afford at this time that it was about a half hour to day.
Question. What did they do to you?
Answer. None of the shot hit me, but they aimed to hit me; but I had one door just like that at the side of the house and the other at this side, and there was the chimney, and there was my bed in that corner opposite, and they came to that door first (illustrating) and hollered, "Hallo"; bum, bum, bum, on the lock. I jumped up and said "Hallo." Then one at the door said, "Raise a light in there." "What for; who is you?" I said. He says, "Raise a light in there, God damn you; I'll come in there and smoke my pipe in your ear." He said that just so. I said, "Is that you, Uncle Davy?" Says he, "No, God damn you, it ain't uncle Dave; open this door." Says I, "I am not going to open my door to turn nobody on me that won't tell me who they are before I do it. Who are you?" He says, "God damn you, we didn't come to tell you who we are." I was peeping through a little crack in the door. . . .
I saw men out there standing with horns and faces on all of them, and they all had great, long, white cow-tails way down the breast. I said it was a cow-tail; it was hair,

and it was right white. They told me they rode from Shiloh in two hours and came to kill me. They shot right smart in that house before they got in, but how many times I don't know, they shot so fast outside; but when they come in, they didn't have but three loads to shoot. I know by the way they tangled about in the house they would have put it in me if they had had it. They only shot three times in the house. The men behind me had busted in through the door; both doors were busted open. By the time the fellows at the back door got in the door, these fellows at the front door busted in, and they all met in the middle of the floor, and I didn't have a thing to fight with, only a little piece of ax-handle; and when I started from the first door to the second, pieces of the door flew and met me. I jumped for a piece of ax-handle and fought them squandering about, and they were knocking me with guns, and firing balls that cut several holes in my head. The notches is in my head now. I dashed about among them, but they knocked me down several times. Every time I would get up, they would knock me down again. I saw they were going to kill me, and I turned in and laid there after they knocked me down so many times. The last time they knocked me down I laid there a good while before I moved, and when I had strength I jumped to split through a man's legs that was standing over me, and, as I jumped, they struck at me jumping between his legs, and they struck him, and, he hollered, "Don't hit me, God damn you," but they done knocked him down then, but they hadn't knocked him so he couldn't talk. I jumped through and got past him. They didn't hit him a fair lick, because he was going toward them, and it struck past his head on his shoulder. If it had struck his head, it would have busted it open. I didn't catch that lick. I got up then; they had shot their loads. I grabbed my ax-handle, and commenced fighting, and then they just took and cut me with knives. They surrounded me in the floor and tore my shirt off. They got me out on the floor; some had me by the legs and some by the arms and the neck and anywhere, just like dogs string out a coon, and they took me out to the big road before my gate and whipped me until I couldn't move or holler or do nothing, but just lay there like a log, and every lick they hit me I grunted just like a mule when he is stalled fast and whipped; that was all. They left me there for dead, and what it was done for was because I was a radical, and I didn't deny my profession anywhere and I never will. I never will vote that conservative ticket if I die.
Question. Did they tell you they whipped you because you were a radical?
Answer. They told me, "God damn you, when you meet a white man in the road lift your hat; I'll learn you, God damn you, that you are a nigger, and not to be going about like you thought yourself a white man; you calls yourself like a white man, God damn you."

SOURCE: Testimony Taken by the Joint Select Committee to Inquire into the Condition of Affairs in the Late Insurrectionary States, Mississippi, 42d Congress, 2d sess., House of Representatives Report No. 22, part 11 (Washington, D.C.: USGPO, 1872), 482–483.

The Republican William W. Murray served as U.S. Attorney for the Western District of Tennessee. Constant vigilantism and mobbing ravaged Tennessee. Maintaining order was the job of the states and not the national government, a right jealously guarded by the states and their representatives. Nonetheless Murray believed that he could use the Ku Klux Klan Act to prosecute such violence.

The danger Murray faced was that the courts might declare the Klan Act unconstitutional. The Fourteenth Amendment protected individual citizens' rights against state action, not against other citizens. Murray believed he had figured out a way around that problem, which he explained in a letter to his boss, the attorney general.

74. *William W. Murray to Alphonso Taft*, September 25, 1876

Hon L. B. Eaton, US Marshal for this District, informed me that you desired to see a copy of an indictment sustained by our Circuit Court, drawn under Section 2, Act of April 20, 1871. I herewith enclose copy of said Indictment, the first; third and Fourth Counts of which were sustained by the Court. We insisted for the prosecution that Article 14, of the amended Constitution of the United States . . . was first addressed to the Legislative Department of the States, and secondly, to the Executive and Judicial Departments. That the words in said Article, "that no state shall make," is addressed alone to the Legislative Department, and that the words "or enforce," must apply to the Executive and Judicial Departments. We further insisted that the citizens of the several states, by virtue of article 14, was entitled to the equal protection of the laws of the states, whenever such citizens, for the time being, was in the custody of the laws of such States. In other words, that whenever a citizen had committed an offence against the laws of the State in which he lived, and for which offence he had been placed in the custody of the proper officer of the Executive Department of such state, that it then became the duty of such officer to see that such citizen had the equal protection of the laws of such state, and in as much as this duty was thrown upon such officer; by the provision of said Article 14, that Congress must have the power to punish a conspiracy, the object of which was to present such State officer from securing to such citizen the rights guaranteed to him by the laws of the state.

That if this was not so, that said Article 14 had made it the duty of such officer to perform acts, in which the citizen was vitally interested, without any power in the government, to punish parties who might conspire together for the purpose of preventing said officer from performing the duties so enjoined upon him. In further illustration of our views on this subject, suppose that in one of the States, laws existed upon the State Books which were obnoxious to the provisions of said Article 14, and that the Legislature of such State was to meet and introduce a Bill for the express purpose of complying with the requirements of said amendment, now suppose, that while such Legislature was so engaged that a number of persons should conspire together for the express purpose of preventing such Legislature from passing Laws which said article made it their duty to pass.

We admit that Congress must have power to pass the necessary Laws to punish such conspirators. You will see that we followed the words of Section 2, act of April 20, 1871, and charge that the parties went in disguise &c and that the offence was committed on account of Race, Color &c, all of this was rejected by the Court as surplusage, and, we think, properly. The Indictment . . . was sustained by Judge Ballard, of Kentucky, after three months deliberation; Judge Emmons concurring fully with Judge Ballard. A number of the parties were tried and acquitted, for the reason, that the prosecution was compelled to rely alone on the testimony of an accomplice as the identity of the parties; they all being in disguise when the offence was committed. Judge Emmons charged the Jury that they could not convict upon the uncorroborated testimony of an accomplice, as to any material fact in the case.

I have caused the arrest of several parties in the District, charged with the same offence as set forth in said Indictment, and I do not think I will have any difficulty in making the proof, as the offence was committed in daylight, and the parties were not disguised.

I have reference to the late difficulty at Alamo, Crockett County, Tennessee, the particulars of which, I supposed you have learned through the press.

I am not aware of this question having been made in any other District in the United States, and I am exceedingly anxious that the same should be considered by the Supreme Court of the United States. While I have only given you an outline of our argument before the Court, I hope the same will enable you to instruct me in reference to the cases growing out of the Alamo difficulty.

I will add that the Counsel for the Defendants in the Gibson County case were among the ablest in this District, and argued the question at great length before the Court.

SOURCE: Box 998, Letters Received, Western Tennessee, Source Chronological Files 1871–84, January 1871–1876, General Records of the Department of Justice, RG 60, National Archives, College Park, Maryland.

Murray indicted Roland Green Harris, the sheriff of Crockett County, Tennessee, and his deputies.

75. *Grand Jury Indictment of Roland Green Harris and Others,* November 1876

The Grand Jurors of the United States within and for the Western District of Tennessee in the Sixth Judicial Circuit of the United States duly elected, empanelled, sworn and charged to inquire within and for said District in said Circuit upon their oaths present . . . that . . . R. G. Harris, E. D. Harris, James W. Harris, Tobe Harris, Milton Harris, Sidney Harris, Virgil M. Tucker, W. A. Tucker, A. J. Tucker, Samuel Hudgins, Nathan Brown, W. A. Powell, John Hunt, William Best, William Crandall, Charles L. Miller, Hugh McGavock, W. W. Hannell, A. J. Collinsworth, and S. W. Brassfield . . . within the jurisdiction of this court unlawfully and with force and arms did conspire together and with certain other evil disposed persons whose names are to the Grand Jurors aforesaid unknown then and there for the purpose of depriving one P. M. Wells, the said P. M. Wells then and there being a citizen of the United States and of the state of Tennessee of the equal protection of the laws, in this, to wit; that theretofore . . . the said P. M. Wells having been charged with the commission of a certain criminal offence against the laws of said state, the nature of which said criminal offence being to the Grand Jurors aforesaid unknown and having upon such charge been then and there duly arrested by the lawful and constituted authorities of said state, to wit, by one William A. Tucker, the said William A. Tucker then and there being a Deputy Sheriff of said county, and then and there acting as such; and the said P. M. Wells having been so then and there arrested as aforesaid, and being so as aforesaid under arrest, and in the custody of the said Deputy Sheriff, then and there aforesaid, then and there thereby and by virtue of the laws of said state became and was entitled to the due and equal protection of the said laws and was then and thereby entitled under and by virtue of and according to the laws of said state to have his person protected from violence while he the said P. M. Wells was so then and there under arrest and in custody as aforesaid: And the Grand Jurors aforesaid upon their oaths aforesaid do further present that [the defendants named above] did . . . conspire together as aforesaid then and there for the purpose of depriving him the said P. M. Wells of his right to the due and equal protection of the laws of said state and of his right to be protected in his person from violence while so then and there under arrest as aforesaid . . . unlawfully beating, bruising, wounding, and killing him the said P. M. Wells contrary to the form of the statute in such case made and provided against the peace and dignity of the United States of America.

SOURCE: Case 1415, Circuit Court of the United States, Western District of Tennessee. R.G. 21, National Archives, Atlanta Regional Archives Branch.

As the Supreme Court considered the Harris case, the justices could see white southerners harden in their commitment to mob law. At the end of February 1880 a Colleton County, South Carolina, mob seized and hanged Louis Kinder, charged with rape. On March 5 the *Charleston News and Courier* published a letter of protest from Carlos Tracy. "This State reeks with blood," Tracy warned, adding that the killers of even the most guilty criminals had themselves committed murder. Tracy asked the governor to proceed at once to "the scene of great outrage" and put down mob law. The newspaper spurned Tracy's views. When mob law represents the will of the people, the *News and Courier* said, it articulated a national tradition.

76. Charleston News and Courier, *"Lynch Law and Mob Law,"* 1880

Our opinions on the subject of lynching negroes who commit outrages on women are tolerably widely known. They are not new and they have been often times expressed.

In our view it is better by far, if such is the alternative, to have "The man on horseback" than to refrain from punishing, in the only deterring and effective way, the brutes who do violence to the women of South Carolina. This, too, will be the decision of every husband, father and brother, in the State, who knows the danger and the inability of the Courts to remove it.

We have no fear, however, that the people of the Eastern or Western States will be shocked at the lynching which moves Mr. Tracy so deeply. They know how it is themselves, and do as the South Carolinians have done. The difference is that they apply the halter or bullet with less reason in the West, and in the East have not always the desired opportunity.

Lynch-law, as applied to Louis Kinder, is not mob-law. The brute put himself outside the pale of the law, and was dealt with accordingly. On the general lines of opposition to lawlessness, we go entirely with Mr. Tracy, but it will be a woeful day for South Carolina when crimes of a particular class are only punished, if punished at all, after a long imprisonment, a tedious trial and the procrastination which lawyers practice on behalf of their clients. The fear of judgment and perdition does not suffice to make men virtuous. They sin on, intending to repent in time to save themselves when they are surfeited with wrong. There would be a different state of things, if the punishment followed the offence as swiftly as in the case of the negro who was rightfully lynched in Colleton.

SOURCE: *Charleston South Carolina News and Courier,* March 5, 1880.

In 1882 the Supreme Court rejected Murray's theory. The Court seemed to say that the national government had no power over lynchers.

77. *Justice William B. Woods, Opinion of the U.S. Supreme Court, in* United States v. Harris, *1882*

MR. JUSTICE WOODS delivered the opinion of the court.

The language of the amendment does not leave this subject in doubt. When the State has been guilty of no violation of its provisions; when it has not made or enforced any law abridging the privileges or immunities of citizens of the United States; when no one of its departments has deprived any person of life, liberty, or property without due process of law, or denied to any person within its jurisdiction the equal protection of the laws; when, on the contrary, the laws of the State, as enacted by its legislative, and construed by its judicial, and administered by its executive departments, recognize and protect the rights of all persons, the amendment imposes no duty and confers no power upon Congress.

SOURCE: 106 U.S. 629 (1882).

NOTES

1. "Lincoln's First Inaugural," in *A Compilation of the Messages and Papers of the Presidents,* ed. James D. Richardson (New York, 1897), 7:3206–3210.

2. Iver Bernstein, *The New York City Draft Riots: Their Significance for American Society and Politics in the Age of the Civil War* (New York: Oxford University Press, 1990).

3. Richard B. McCaslin, *Tainted Breeze: The Great Hanging at Gainesville, Texas, 1862* (Baton Rouge: Louisiana State University Press, 1994).

4. Alexander Williams Randall (1819–1872), a former Wisconsin governor, served as postmaster general.

5. *New York Times,* March 2, 1870.

6. Ibid., July 26, 1870.

7. Eric Foner, *Reconstruction: America's Unfinished Revolution, 1863–1877* (New York: Harper and Row, 1988), 454–455.

8. Allen W. Trelease, *White Terror: The Ku Klux Conspiracy and Southern Reconstruction* (Baton Rouge: Louisiana State University Press, 1971), 392–400.

The Gilded Age
Shall the Wheel of Race Agitation Be Stopped?

Late-nineteenth-century America was a great time to be a journalist. Ink was cheap; paper cost little; the post office subsidized bulk mail; and improving technology made printing presses increasingly efficient at a lower cost. No other business needed so little money to get started.[1] It was also a time when whites tightened the screws on their apartheid regime. White racists excluded blacks from the voting booth and formalized segregation through law. In this ravenous time derided by Mark Twain and Charles Dudley Warner as *The Gilded Age,* African American journalists dared to imagine themselves not just denouncing white racism in print but doing so before a national audience.

In the Gilded Age the word *lynching* appeared in newspaper columns with increasing regularity, so much so that some editors worried that their readers had become numbed by its constant use. At the same time that the word *lynching* reached unprecedented numbers of newspaper readers, journalists racialized it. When the *Chicago Tribune* began publishing an annual tally of lynchings in 1882 editors found more whites lynched than blacks. This was true for the last time in 1885, when the *Tribune* counted ninety-seven white lynchings and only sixty-eight "colored." Even adding six "Chinamen" to the "colored" total would not have pushed the nonwhite victims ahead of whites. The next year the balance shifted. The *Tribune* reported sixty-two whites lynched against seventy-one blacks. By 1890 the *Tribune* described Gilded Age lynching as mostly southern and directed almost exclusively at blacks. "How the Colored Man Has Suffered" ran one headline.[2] Monroe Work at the Tuskegee Institute continued what the *Tribune* started, collecting newspaper reports of lynchings, collating the results, and publishing regular statistical reports. Even whites accepted the Tuskegee Institute's counts as authoritative. The *Tribune* and the Tuskegee Institute have long been a source for students of lynching, but African American journalists also compiled a history of Gilded Age lynching in the columns of their papers. This chapter draws on that history in the belief that it illuminates the black experience.

Born a slave in Florida, Timothy Thomas Fortune migrated North in 1881. Arriving in New York City, he edited the *New York Globe* and then the *New York Freeman.* Closely allied with Booker T. Washington, Fortune advocated industrial education and self-improvement. But Fortune also said things that Washington would never say, insisting African Americans should shoot to kill when threatened by white people.[3] W. E. B. Du Bois's biographer calls Fortune's career "meteoric" and notes that Du Bois was an early admirer. Booker T. Washington's biographer thought Fortune's alliance with Washington a mystery but notes that the mercurial Fortune needed Washington's steadiness.[4]

78. *T. Thomas Fortune, "Fiendishness in Texas,"* 1885

We abhor all crime, whether perpetrated by outlaws or men who pose as "the best people of the town." The practice of Southern white men in lynching colored men on suspicious and circumstantial evidence is becoming infamous, intolerable and inexcusable, and the only way to stop it is for colored men to retaliate by the use of the torch and the dagger. We know this is extreme doctrine, but the prevalence of lynch law, or murder by mobocracy justifies it in the enunciation and in the practice.

When white men become so vindictive and savage that they defy the law and hang men by the wholesale on circumstantial evidence colored men have a right to retaliate, however barbarous the argument they may use. *A black man is just as good as a white man,* and if the white man can dispense with law in the investigation and punishment of crime the colored man can do the same in protecting himself from violence, outrage, and usurpation of his common rights.

"War of the races!" do you yell? Who cares anything about the "war of races" where rights are trampled under the feet of outlaws who pose as the salt of the earth? Better have a war of extermination than that violence, murder and open defiance of law should be permitted to pollute every rivulet of Constitutional and common right.

The white man who stabs or lynches a colored man should be stabbed and lynched in return, for he who appeals to the sword should die by the sword. . . .

There must be a period put to this infamous practice of lynching. Let the law take its course. Black men and women are outraged every hour in the day by Southern white men, but they are not lynched and the law scorns to lay its dainty fingers upon them. Are colored men to endure this always? We protest against it, and if no other remedy be suggested, we will preach an eye for an eye and a tooth for a tooth. There is a limit at which patience ceases to be a virtue. It is not right that any man should suffer until he has been proven to be guilty of crime.

SOURCE: *New York Freeman,* July 4, 1885.

African American journalists celebrated the heroics of those black men and women who dared resist white lynchers. Edward E. Cooper, editor of the *Indianapolis Freeman* from 1888 to 1893, promoted his race, once calling on his readers to vote for the "ten greatest Negroes." Cooper hoped that Nelson Jones's story would encourage more blacks to arm themselves and shoot back at white mobs.

79. Indianapolis Freeman, *"A Georgia Outrage,"* 1890

Never before in the history of this State has there been such a feeling of unrest as now exists among the colored people, especially in the rural districts. The Baxley outrage, the East Point whipping affair, and the Jesup episode, along with the brutal shooting of a man named Nelson Jones, because he refused to leave his home, wife and children, Loundes county, when ordered to do so by white ruffians, has made life not

worth living. Your correspondent called to see the man Nelson, who was so brutally
shot, and found him lying with twenty-nine bullet holes, and he tells a

Heart Rendering Story

He says for some reason the whites of the county took an idea that he was advising
the blacks against the interests of the whites he was ordered to leave the county or he
would be whipped, and if he refused to be whipped, he would be killed. He told the
man who informed him that he had done nothing to any one, and did not mean to
leave his wife, children and crop, and that he would stand to the bitter end. He bought
a Winchester rifle and went home. Just before night a white man came down to his
house ostensibly on business, but really to spy out his house and its surroundings,
preparatory to their nocturnal visit. Jones says he went home and informed his wife
of what he had seen and heard, and told her to prepare for the event. He closed up his
house, ate his evening meal, and he and his family retired, with his rifle in a convenient place. He says all went well until about between 1 and 2 in the morning, when
his dogs began to bark. He awoke, he said, from a frightful dream, awoke his wife, and
told her that there was someone near the house and caused her to get up. He got up
and got his gun and prepared for the fray. The dog ceased barking (having been driven away), and a low rumbling sound was heard of human voices, which grew louder
and more distinct, until they could be plainly heard. In the next minute or two a voice
could be heard saying "charge, boys!" and six or eight men came against the door of
his cabin with the end of a ten-foot rail, and shattered the door almost to splinters.
No one entered, however, and Jones stood in one corner of his cabin awaiting devel-
opments. He did not have to wait long, however, for in a few minutes a blazing ball of
cotton saturated with Kerosene was thrown through the now open door into the
house, to light it up that they might see to kill him from the outside. Jones was standing behind the partition and quite out of sight of his would-be slayers. The ball struck
the opposite side of the house, rebounded, and rolled between his feet. He snatched
his wife's apron which was near, and threw it on the ball and put it out. They threw
another, and still another, until they had thrown five of these lighted balls, which he
managed to put out each time without allowing them to get a shot at him. A short
pause followed the throwing of the fifth ball, which was followed by a large wad of the
same material, thrown right on his bed among his three little children. This set the
bed clothing on fire, and the house was in great danger. Seeing that it was necessary
for him to act at once or have the house burned down over his wife and children, he
decided to face death and save his loved ones. This decided, he raised his rifle and
fired in the direction from which the last ball of fire came. There was a death-like still-
ness for a few seconds, and then the firing commenced on the outside. Seeing that to
remain longer in the house would endanger the lives of all, he boldly made a dash for
the door amid a shower of bullets, and, reaching the outside, he faced the enemy and
used his Winchester as long as he could raise it to his shoulders. He retreated and fell
among the corn rows not far away, with fourteen (14) bullets in his body, one of
which broke his hip, eleven went in his right leg and thigh, and two through his jaw.

The ruffians were afraid to approach him, but continued to shoot at long range. Fearing that should he not keep them at bay they would discover his condition and finish him, he rolled over on one side, wounded as he was, and managed to get his hand on a revolver with which he kept them at a distance. Though there were about thirty in the gang, yet they did not have the courage to approach one Negro who allowed himself to have a little pluck. The brutes left Jones, as they wanted to get to their homes before daylight, and the next morning his wife found him where he fell. He was taken up by friends, and fearing that the mob would come back and finish him, they took him to the city of Valdosta, Ga., where they felt he would be more safe. The case was reported to the county officers who expressed their regrets at the affair, and promised him aid and protection. He and his wife and four children were placed in a house not more than two hundred yards from the county court-house, where they remained for a week or more, during which time he was visited by the grand jury of that county, who pretended to be anxious to get some clew to the parties who assaulted him. After hearing enough from him to find out that he knew too much for the safety of some of their friends, they left him with the promise that they would call and see him again. Well, they did call again, but they came at night as they had done in the past, with shot guns and a ball of fire, and there, right under the eyes of the court-house, and within hearing of the Judge and Sheriff, the house where the half dead man was staying was visited by a second mob, the door broken down, a fire ball thrown into the house that they might see to kill him, and fifteen more buckshot poured into his already lacerated body. This time they would have finished him, but for the indomitable courage which saved him in the former struggle. Fearing that something might happen, he had requested his wife to place a pistol and rifle along side of him in the bed. Hence, when the door flew open, he raised his pistol and shot out the two balls left from the previous night of horror and then shot three balls from his Winchester rifle. But for these shots fired by Jones they would never have left him alive that night, but they knew he was a man of courage, and like Brown of Jesup fame, they knew him.

I have taken considerable space to write up this item, as I believe the Afro-American everywhere, while deploring the sufferings of this man and the advantages taken of him, will be proud to know of his manly courage and pluck he has shown against such great odds. If we had more men of the Nelson Jones stamp, we would be far better off. After the last mentioned occurrence, and seeing that if he remained in that section of the country he would be killed (as those who committed the deed considered his presence a continual rebuke), he was brought to this city, Savannah, where he now is with some prospect of recovery. Aside from the fact that he has 29 bullet holes in him, and 15 bullets in his body now and still alive, there is still another feature about the thing that seems wonderfully proverbial: namely that while the house in both instances, the furniture and even the bedding was literally riddled with balls, yet not his wife nor either of his children got as much as a scratch from a ball. He says that a ball passed through his wife's gown, but did not take effect.

"B"

SOURCE: *Indianapolis Freeman*, February 8, 1890.

In 1890 the intensely ambitious Charles H. J. Taylor became editor of the Kansas City *American Citizen,* one of the largest black newspapers in the West. Taylor, born a slave near Marion, Alabama, educated at the University of Michigan, hungry for political office, proclaimed his paper "A National Organ Published in the Interest of Tariff Reform and the Negro's Political Freedom." Taylor's call for tariff reform reflected his ardent support for the Democratic Party. After Abraham Lincoln and emancipation, African Americans strongly supported the Republican Party. Many of his black contemporaries thought that this political treason made him an Uncle Tom, a view shared by some historians today.[5] Taylor's Democratic politics did not prevent him from frequently, and bitterly, denouncing lynching.

80. *Charles H. J. Taylor, "Is God Dead?"* 1892

It gives me great pain to read in every daily paper which visits my office of some poor black man being seized by a mob and lynched without even the semblance of law. The unlawful murderers, not satisfied with this, riddle the body of the poor Negro with bullets. Too often after the poor man is dead investigation proves that the wrong man was killed. The matter is laughed off by the cowardly outlaws with the sentence, "Only another Negro less." My God! When will this thing end, and where?

There is no earthly excuse for mob law in the case of a black man in this country. Every white man who takes part in such an affair writes himself down a coward and a brute. It matters not to me whether the colored man be innocent or guilty, in this country, as at present governed, there is no excuse for a mob to break down the doors of a jail, or intercept officers and take the poor man and hang him.

On last Sunday night while men and women, in large numbers, were on their way home from church a mob stopped them in Pine Bluff, Ark., to have them see a Negro named John Kelly sent into eternity at the end of a rope, one end of which had been thrown over the cross-pin of a telegraph pole. As if to defy the law and civilized government these violators of law hung him right in front of the Court house. Kelly when called upon to speak declared that he was innocent of having killed a white man named J. T. Adams, for whose death he was made to suffer in this brutal way. Nor was this mob of brave (?) men satisfied. Kelly's body was raised forty feet into the air and riddled with bullets. Still these men of southern chivalry, who are only brave among babies or sick women, were not satisfied. Hell was open and his Satanic Majesty bid his intoxicated sons to find them still another victim. Some little devil in the crowd yelled out, "Lynch Culbert Harris, Kelly's accomplice!" A rush was made for the jail, an entrance was effected by means of axes and Harris was pointed out by the other prisoners. Poor Harris on bended knees pleaded for a few minutes to speak, but the mob hurried him to the Court house and as the clock in the Court house tower tolled quarter to 11 he was jerked into the air. Simultaneously 100 shots were heard and Harris was a corpse.

This happened in Pine Bluff, Arkansas, where one Negro named Jones owns, they say, all the street car lines. This happened in a town of churches. This happened where lives the brave Duke of the *Echo,* and the town is still allowed to stand. This happened in the state of the great lawyer, Garland, ex-attorney general. My God! Can such damnable outrages continue? Is there no efficacy in prayer? In the electric light glare, in front of the Court house, before 10,000 persons, says the press dispatch, was the hellish deed enacted. Shame on the state, shame on the governor, shame on the lawmakers, shame on every man and woman who wields the least bit of influence in relation to the Arkansas state government, if you remain silent.

It is not pretended that these men would have escaped the penalty attaching to the crimes alleged against them, if found guilty. Why should there be the least excuse for mob-law against the poor Negro in this country? The whites of Arkansas, and for that matter, of every state in the Union, control entirely the state machinery. They have every judge, every prosecuting attorney, a majority of every jury, the governor—all power is in their hands, now where is the shadow of defence for such cowardly and damnable conduct?

For shame! That a mob should be allowed in a country claiming to lead the world on religious lines to take unarmed men and hang them without any kind of trial. In the United States Senate these same whites of whom these ruffians come have been referred to as a "noble race," a "kingly race"; yes indeed, such "nobleness" and kingly bearing" would disgrace hell. . . .

There are some things beyond mortal knowledge. One is, how a class of people with bibles and churches can use a defenceless people who live among them to fell their timbers and improve their lands and after these people have served them faithfully, repay their kindness, subserviency and almost slavish humbleness by hanging them to the nearest tree on the slightest pretext. I have no respect for a God Who will not eternally damn such people. I have traveled in heathen lands, where ignorance and superstition held full and uncontested sway, but I have never met a heathen so abandoned as to be willing to tie a man to a stake and burn him alive without at least having by heathen methods satisfied himself that the individual was guilty. . . .

Missionary societies raising money, sending the gospel and missionaries to China and to Africa, would be in much better business if they would send the gospel of the "golden rule" and real Christian men, armed with whatever may be necessary to knock hell out of these buzzards of civilization, to the south. No contagious disease is so afflicting and hurtful to a country as a band of organized men whose creed is to do everything in their power against law and order. . . .

I would say go to Africa but I do not want to send you to a worse place than the south. Worse because you know nothing of African dialects, habits or customs. Worse because you are known by tradition there to have been sold into slavery here. Finally worse because you are a *new creation*. I mean that you are not at all African; no more African are you than is the great-grandchild of a German father by an Irish mother is Irish or German. This country is your home. What then must you do? There are several ways to settle this unpleasant state of affairs. . . . Our gray-haired *statesmen* of the race may have a plan. If they have a plan they are great criminals not to have proposed it. In the meantime assure each white man you meet, in this country, of influence, that you are only asking for our people in the south the treatment which you would die to secure to him if he was found in blackest Africa. Ask each white preacher, lawyer, congressman or senator you meet to answer this question, as it relates to our people in the south and to him as an agent of Heaven: *IS GOD DEAD?*

We can educate sentiment in favor of justice! Let's do it. *IS GOD DEAD?* For my Country and Race,

    C. H. J. Taylor

SOURCE: *Kansas City American Citizen*, February 19, 1892.

Black newspapers regularly chastised white officials for failing to uphold the law. African Americans saw the law as the only barrier between their lives and whites' conviction that they had a right to kill misbehaving blacks. According to the leading historian of the Haymarket tragedy, Illinois Governor John Peter Altgeld "had earned the reputation of being a thoroughly honest public servant, and one who was unafraid to voice his convictions or to act upon them."[6] When he pardoned anarchists charged in the Haymarket bombing, progressives all over the country hailed him as a hero. But his sympathies did not lead him to act on behalf of Samuel J. Bush, burned alive in Decatur, Illinois. When Altgeld refused to intervene at all, the *Indianapolis Freeman* sarcastically saluted his "prompt action."

81. Indianapolis Freeman, *"America's Scarlet Crime,"* 1893

Finds its Votaries North as Well as South—Full Particulars of the Lynching of Bush at Decatur, Ill.—Governor Altgeld's Prompt Action in the Matter

Decatur, Ill., Special.

On Friday one Samuel J. Bush, a Negro late from the South, was taken from the county jail in this city, and lynched in a most brutal manner by a mob of lawless white murderers. The crime for which Bush was so foully murdered, is alledged to have occurred in Mt. Zion township, fifteen miles southeast of here, where, it is alledged, that he made a criminal assault upon the wife of one Vest. This was Wednesday, May 31st. Since that time organized men on horse back and afoot, armed to the teeth, have been scouring the country for miles around. Late Thursday night he was arrested a few miles from Sullivan and was brought to Decatur Friday morning on the 11 o'clock train. Officers here had been informed by telegraph of his arrest and were at the depot to meet him. A crowd of about six hundred people were also there and many ugly threats were made, but no one seemed ready to offer any violence. The poor trembling wretch was taken from the train shaking like a leaf, surrounded on all sides by a curious crowd. At the command of the police the crowd fell back and Bush was hurried to a carriage waiting near by, and rapidly driven to the county jail. The crowd was at the jail and Bush was so scared that he could hardly walk.

    Some one in the crowd cried, "Kill him!" but nothing else was done. Bush was half pushed, half dragged up the stone steps in the jail office, from where he was soon hustled to his cell. All day long hundreds of people thronged the streets in front of the jail, and discussed the crime and capture. They boldly talked of lynching and no effort was made by the officers to disperse them. Mayor Moffet called upon Deputy Sheriff Harry Medkiff, who was in charge of affairs at the jail, Sheriff Perl being in Chicago, and told him if he needed assistance to call upon him and he should have all he wanted. W. B. Woodford, the colored lawyer, visited the jail early in the morning after the arrest and had a talk with Medkiff about the prisoner and what would be done in case an attempt was made to lynch him. Midkiff assured him that every effort would made to protect, and that if he was taken out it would be over his dead body.

To a reporter who visited Bush in the jail, he said his home was in Alabama, and that he had been in this county about six weeks looking for work. That he was at the Vest home, but did nothing to the woman. He said he asked her for a drink of water and that she seemed scared; that he told her not to be afraid, he would not hurt her; that then the woman rushed out of the house and down the road screaming, and that the first thing he knew a body of armed men were dashing down the road; he became frightened and run and hid in the woods. While there a detachment of the searching party past him and he heard them talking of lynching him, and that then he resolved to get out of the country.

During the afternoon he wrote a long letter to his cousin in the South, asking for money with which to hire a lawyer. He told him he was in a bad fix and was liable to be lynched. He begged and implored him to assist, asserting that all he wanted was a fair trial and he would prove his innocence. The letter, Attorney J. M. Gray was to send to his cousin. As the day wore away the crowd grew larger and more noisy, and Bush more apprehensive. Still the more conservative men seemed to think that there was no danger. About 7 o'clock one thousand men, to say nothing of the boys and women and girls, were near the vicinity of the jail; word had come to town that the mob from Mt. Zion would be there at 11 o'clock. About 8 o'clock it commenced to rain. This drove some of the crowd home, but hundreds still remained. The colored citizens now became apprehensive. Twenty-five or thirty of them called upon Chief of Police W. W. Mason, and asked to be armed and placed in the jail. Mr. Mason informed them that he would arm them in a short time and slip them into the jail. The Negroes waited for some time, but Mason did not return. They then went to the jail to Midkiff, going around the back way, thus scattering the crowd who were throwing rocks at the window in the back of the jail. At the back entrance they found Deputy Murfee and asked him for Midkiff; he told them that they could not see him. They told Murfee what they wanted, and he told them to rest easy, that Bush was in Springfield. They then returned and found Mason, who also informed them that Bush had been taken to Springfield and that there was a guard of sixty armed men at the jail which was sufficient. With this the Negroes were satisfied and most of them began to disperse.

Nine, ten, eleven, twelve, one o'clock came and yet no mob. The crowd became restless; now and then a solitary rider on horse-back gallops by the jail and then rides back toward the east. At 1:45 about forty-five men were seen approaching from the east marching three abreast. The crowd began to cheer, the mob made straight for the west entrance of the jail where they demanded admittance, which was denied. With one or two blows of the sledge hammer the door flew open and the mob rushed into the office of the jail. Not the slightest resistance was offered. Midkiff had ordered the chief of police to have his entire regular force at police headquarters, not one hundred feet distance, so that if he needed them they would be ready. But they were not called. They heard the cheering of the now furious mob and the blows of the sledge, and came out to see what the matter was. By this time the mob had demanded the keys from Midkiff, and upon being refused, had attacked the big iron door that guards the entrance to the jail corridor. Chief Mason, followed by one or two of his men, forced their way into the office of the jail, and Mason mounts a chair and in the name of the law, commands the mob to stop. He was soon pushed out the door and some villain kicked him down the steps. After that the mob had smooth sailing, no further resistance was offered save by the doors alone. The dozen guards on the inside did not a thing. They smoked cigars and coolly laughed and talked, Midkiff amongst them. As each door fell the cheer by the mob inside was answered by the crowd outside. After an hour of hard labor every barrier was removed, nobody save Mason had attempted to check them. The militia had laid upon their arms in their hall waiting for orders form Midkiff, but none had come.

Prisoners in the jail were pale and trembling. The maddened mob dashed up to Bush's cell. The wretch, more dead than alive, was pulled out from within his mattress stark naked, then a terrible yell went up that chilled the blood of the uninterested listeners on the outside. He was hurried out to the street to the corner across from the court house in front of the Brunswick hotel, and there in the glare of the electric light was he hanged. Straight to a telegraph pole came the mob, at the foot of the pole some one said let him pray, and the poor wretch sank upon his knees and prayed that he might meet his murderers in heaven. He protested his innocence and begged to be taken to the land where there was no trouble. The mob then became impatient and cried out, "String him up, he gave the woman no time to pray," etc.

The rope having been adjusted, someone mounted the pole, put the rope over a guy wire and Bush was speedily drawn up. When about six feet from the ground the rope broke and he fell with a sickening thud upon the brick pavement, badly bruising his head. The rope was quickly tied, a hack was called and Bush was placed upon it already half dead, and commanded to stand up to which he replied, "I can't gentlemen." The rope was drawn up, the hack drawn out and Bush swung into eternity.

At 1:45 the body was cut down by Coroner Bendure, and the inquest is still in progress at this writing. Bush was buried in the potter field Saturday. After Bush was pronounced dead by Drs. Spaulding and Heil, the mob cheered and then left as silently as they came. . . .

Our colored people are generally indignant. No resistance was offered. Officer Leech said: "Do you suppose we would shoot good citizens for a worthless 'nigger.'" But the end is not yet. Illinois disgraced, law violated and a human being murdered by a band of midnight assassins must not go unpunished. Let every citizen of this country who wishes to put a stop to this high-handed manner of murdering Negroes, who have a cent to spend in a good cause, send it to W. B. Woodford.

SOURCE: *Indianapolis Freeman,* June 10, 1893.

In 1893 a mob in Texas tortured and then killed Henry Smith, charged with raping Myrtle Vance. Whites carefully documented Smith's death photographically but also justified themselves in a two-hundred-page book, *The Facts in the Case of the Horrible Murder of Little Myrtle Vance.*[7] Every element in this publication repeated some component that whites had established in earlier lynching apologias. The writer sentimentalized Vance as a "vivacious little bit of human sunshine." Defenders of lynchings typically claimed that the original crime angered the citizenry beyond control, and this author wrote that the little girl's disappearance "fired" the population to a "frenzy." When authorities arrested Smith, whites in Paris built a gallows. The crowd seized Smith, paraded him, and then tortured him with red-hot irons. The lynchers' own book did not fail to recount the torture, telling how Smith's "roars of agony rend the frozen air."

Ida B. Wells investigated the Smith lynching; Robert C. O. Benjamin wrote about it in his book, *Southern Outrages*.[8] The *Indianapolis Freeman* published an account by W. L. Anderson. Anderson made no effort to argue for Smith's innocence but insisted instead that only law separates civilization from barbarism. Anderson also rallied black youth to an apocalyptic vision, "a war of extermination" if whites cannot step away from such barbarities.

82. *W. L. Anderson, "The Texas Horror,"* 1893

Graphic Reflection on this Ultra Southern Heinousness

America Fast Inviting the Fate of Rome and Other Fallen Powers—Mercy, Justice and Humanity Cry Halt

Of all the horrifying occurrences that ever disgraced and blotted the human character of a nation, none has ever happened so revolting, so sickening in all its details as the one perpetrated upon the person of Smith, the colored man accused of raping and murdering Myrtle Vance, a four-year-old white girl at Paris, Texas. How true as to whether he was guilty or innocent of the crime charged against him, is beyond my power to determine. Though if he was guilty, no law moral or otherwise could justify that hellish cabal who threw aside every instinct of humanity to gratify the vengeful spirit prompted by no reason that God will condone. We who are far removed from the scene of the awful outrage have no imagination that could conceive the demonical passion that would cause one man to premeditate thrusting a white heated rod of iron into the vitals of another; for it is a fact in this case that every form of punishment meted out to Smith was fixed hours before the man was caught. Now picture, if you can, a pitiless horde of the flower of Texas chivalry with minds and desires fixed on one consuming purpose and that the torture of a fellow being for the supposed commission of a crime, for which the law makers of that commonwealth have fixed a lawful penalty—imagine those self same lawmakers disregarding the very statutes they created to conserve the public safety—to throw themselves into that blood-thirsty throng, offering every assistance in their power to make the ultimate object of the affair a success. Fix these things firmly in your minds; draw your own conclusion and I dare say that the deductions you will make will leave you to believe that hell is a better place of residence than Texas. If Smith was actually guilty of the crime for which he was so cruelly maltreated he deserved every punishment that the laws of Texas have fixed for that grade of crime. Therefore, I would offer nothing in defense of the individual; nor did the offense that he is said to have committed, without regard to its brutality, excuse the actions of the persons participating in the butchery. Law is provided for men, that men may be protected from each other. It is the safeguard between civilization and barbarism that keeps down the baser passions of men to that degree wherein it is made possible for them to exist together in harmony. It equalizes the plea of life to such a condition that the weak are assured protection against the strong. But to be a living thing of good it must receive the moral support of all men who live under its regime. And sovereign it should reign over all. Even greater than the people, for the people should not control the law, but the law the people. By this Paris affair, you can easily comprehend the ill resultant from a law that is slave and not the master of a situation. There are countless episodes, occurring in the South somewhat similar to the one in Texas, probably not so savage in treatment but all alike as to summary punishment for crimes that a good many times exist only in the brains of the lynchers. To-day I sat in my chamber, reading editorial excerpts from the different journals of the country concerning the torture of Smith, and also the associated press report which gave the uncanny happening a most vivid significance by detailing every time Smith's flesh was seared with the heated poker. So realistic was the statement that when I read of the red glowing rod being pushed into the man's eyes it seemed to me that I was present at the scene of action. In fancy I saw his body withering under the application of burning brands. I saw a frenzied demon, time and again, drop coals of fire in the eyeless caverns of the poor wretch. I looked upon a sea of faces; I saw some seamed and furrowed from rage, round ruddy-cheeked children and stern looking men and women whose faces denoted that life with them was not yet at the meridian mark. But not one face in the vast concourse looked a pitying reflection from the soul within for the suffering mortal being slowly tortured to death before their eyes. . . .

I am one of the great army of black youth of this country who feels, with the intuitive instinct of the oppressed, that a crisis is imminent. I feel that the youth of which I am one is to be the savior of the Negro race. Each moment the plan of action becomes more unified. Two formulas are to be chosen: from one prayers for a peaceful solution, begging for a consideration of the Golden Rule by all mankind, the other craves the application of force let it be a war of extermination if it must be, for it is better to die fighting for liberty, if death as a sacrifice means a probable rectifying of the ills done the living. Repetition of the Paris, Texas, murder will go a great way toward the selection of the latter formula as a means of attaining the end for which we so wistfully pray.

SOURCE: *Indianapolis Freeman, February 18, 1893*

Born to slave parents in 1863, John Mitchell Jr. founded the *Richmond Planet* in 1884. Mitchell grew up in Richmond, but he used his newspaper to build a national audience. He also presented himself as a heroic crusader against mob violence, visiting rural courthouses and jails, defending condemned prisoners. At age twenty-two he strode into Charlotte County after a mob had killed Richard Walker, daring the lynchers to attack him.[9]

In this article Mitchell insisted that the national government should intervene against mob violence and warned that the nation could not well export "the blessings of civilization" overseas while lynching at home.

83. Richmond Planet, *"The Lynching in Kansas,"* 1901

Lynching is no longer a local but a national evil. If it be a national evil, then national remedies should be applied to eradicate it from our form of government.

The burning of Fred Alexander (colored) at the stake in Leavenworth, Kansas, is as astounding as it was inhumane and cruel. Were the evidence not so overwhelming and uncontradicted, it would be difficult to believe that in a community where prize fights are not permitted that a brutal exhibition of the animal passions should be made to all the world.

Sheriff Everhardt took Alexander from the penitentiary where he was safe and carried him to the city jail where he was not safe.

The most remarkable part of the whole affair is that United States troops are quartered at Leavenworth, Kansas. The mob was supreme. And this too in the face of the constitutional provision which declares that cruel and unusual punishments shall not be inflicted upon any of the people thereof.

Fred Alexander was charged with attempting to commit a criminal assault upon Eva Roth (white) and was supposed to have assaulted and killed Pearl Forbes (white).

There was no evidence whatever relative to the last specified charge. It was all supposition.

But even had he been guilty of all of them what excuse could be given for the saturating of his body with kerosene oil and the burning of his person at the stake?

Could a Christian do such a thing? Could a community laying claim to civilization permit such an exhibition of fiendishness?

It is needless to comment upon the sufferings of the victim, of how they struck him with fists, hammers and blunt weapons, of how he pleaded for his life, of how even after he was convinced that he must die, he proclaimed to all of the world his innocence.

Is it possible that the American nation will longer tolerate this crowning infamy of the 19th Century and the ushering disgrace of the 20th? We shall see. It marks us as a nation of barbarities....

We are indeed a sorry lot to be talking about carrying the blessings of civilization to the Chinese, the Filipinos, the Puerto Ricans, the Hawaiians and the Cubans.

The army of 100,000 men is needed at home. But what are they worth here when the noise from the violators of the law was heard by the United States troops at Leavenworth, Kansas, and they were not permitted to go even a dozen yards to prevent a murder.

If burning at the stake has become a national method of punishment for citizens of African descent, the sooner they prepare for it the better.

A thousand times was it more preferable for Fred Alexander to have died fighting for his life than to have surrendered to a cowardly sheriff, who after disarming him, turned him over to a cruel, heartless mob.

The colored men at New Orleans who died fighting set the pace for all colored men in the world. Do like white men have done—sell your lives as dearly as possible and when the end comes go shouting home to heaven—or the other place.

It will at least give us a record for bravery and serve to check the onward march of the white cowards who would submit us to nameless tortures. Burned at the stake in the face of his declared innocence! What is government but a sham? What is the appeal of the Law but a re-echoing mockery of the one making it?

Lynch-law must go!

SOURCE: *Richmond Planet,* January 19, 1901.

In 1901 Mitchell reminisced about his long campaign against mob violence. Complaining that "educated colored men" remained indifferent to lynching, Mitchell urged his race to agitate against "the iron wheel of oppression." Mitchell had urged blacks to violently resist lynch law throughout his newspaper career. In 1890 he wrote, "Whenever a Negro is forced to cross the River of Death by a cowardly Bourbon cut-throat, he should strive to the utmost to have that Bourbon accompany him." By the time he published that editorial, Mitchell already had coined his slogan: "Lynch law must go!"[10] In 1901 he urged every Negro to get a shotgun and a rifle[11] and complained that "colored men" have been "cowed, browbeaten" so much that "only in isolated cases can any be found with the nerve to do and die."[12]

84. *John Mitchell Jr., "Shall the Wheels of Race Agitation Be Stopped?"* 1902

For twenty years, I have waged an unceasing crusade against lynching and all forms of lawlessness. As I sit writing this article, my mind goes back to the stirring scenes through which I have passed. I have lived here in the Southland and I have cried aloud, although the lawless elements seemed to have spared not....

"Shall the wheels of race agitation be sopped?" Come to the Southland and feel the iron wheel of oppression. Look at cultured men and women in convention assembled. It is only here and there that any number of the race can be found to have the hardihood to speak out upon these burning questions and take the chance of being prematurely sent to the other world.

The educated colored man, as a rule, will discuss every subject under the sun in meeting assembled, except politics, lynchings and kindred outrages. To do so is to invite ostracism and to bring forward a gentle hint from some unknown quarter that he is a dangerous Negro and a fit subject for removal either by fight or by the shot-gun route.

A bitter experience has taught me these things. I was born here, and here I expect to remain, either above the earth or within its bosom.

"Shall the wheels of race agitation be stopped?" Not while the evidences remain that this race-agitation has done so much good in imbuing a few Afro-Americans with manhood. The right to life, liberty and the pursuit of happiness is an inherent one. The man who defends that right to the death is a hero. The man who yields it up without a struggle is a coward. The latter, whether white or black, is not popular in this country at the present time....

I indulge in the hope that I shall see the day before I close my eyes in death that the black man will fire upon a white mob with the same certainty and deadly accuracy that a white man would fire upon a black mob. I hope to see a union of the liberty-loving, law-abiding elements of both races combined to put down the lawless elements of whatever nationality and of whatever clime.

Feeling as I do to-day, I would shoulder my rifle or sling on my Colt to protect a white man against a mob with the same alacrity that I would to accord a colored man the same favor. It is the principle which is at stake. "Shall the wheels of race agitation be stopped?" I cannot believe that the thoughtful men of the country would for an instant tolerate such a proposition. Already we have had practical examples of the awakening of the country to the enormity of the offense against the laws. The lynching of colored men has led to the lynching of white ones. The foundations of civilization have been shaken, until protests against lynching have come from the gate-way to Hell, if not Hell itself—I refer to Texas. The Governor of Alabama has spoken out in language too plain to be misunderstood, and the Governor of Georgia has marshaled the militia of that state in an effort to uphold the laws. The recent fight to the death in the neighborhood of Atlanta has clarified the atmosphere, so to speak. . . .

I have never lost faith in my people. They have been hampered by poverty and blinded by ignorance, but—the day is now breaking . . . let us remember . . . the morning cometh. For my part, when the end shall come to me and the sun's setting rays tell me of the dissolution of the body and the ear bring to my failing senses the last strains of earthly music, if I can scan the pages of my race's achievement and see thereon the recorded efforts of a manly people, if the agitators have laid down their pens and stilled their voices and Judge Lynch has retired from the field, then and not until then shall I nod approval and join in the refrain of the faithful, declaring that the wheels of race agitation shall be stopped.

SOURCE: John Mitchell Jr., "Shall the Wheels of Race Agitation Be Stopped?" *Colored American Magazine* 5 (September 1902): 386–391.

African American women vigorously fought against mob law. In 1894 the Boston Woman's Era Club launched *The Woman's Era*, a national magazine. Two years later black women organized the National Association for Colored Women primarily to fight lynching. Black club women criticized black as well as white men. Deborah Gray White argues that they felt they were equal to black men, feeling entitled by their own endurance to the leadership positions they claimed. According to White, black women like Ida B. Wells felt conflicted, "gender tension was the price black women paid for their feminism." They might advance feminist principles, but they did so against a competing notion that patriarchy should be the basis for blacks' racial progress. Insisting on protection subjected their men to mob violence, at one end of the scale, and belittlement, at the other.[13]

Near the end of her life Ida B. Wells penned her autobiography, which lay unpublished until 1970. According to Wells, she took little notice of lynching until whites killed her three friends in 1892. This may be unlikely, since by 1882 Wells had read T. Thomas Fortune and other black militants for years. In any case, this narrative makes the argument that white lynchers acted to smite economic competition.

85. *Ida B. Wells, "A Lynching at the Curve,"* 1892

While I was thus, carrying on the work of my newspaper happy in the thought that our influence was helpful and that I was doing the work I loved and had proved that I could make a living out of it, there came the lynching in Memphis which changed the whole course of my life. I was on one of my trips away from home. I was busily engaged in Natchez when word came of the lynching of three men in Memphis. It came just as I had demonstrated that I could make a living by my newspaper and need never tie myself down to schoolteaching. Thomas Moss, Calvin McDowell, and Henry Stewart owned and operated a grocery store in a thickly populated suburb. Moss was a letter carrier and could only be at the store at night. Everybody in town knew and loved Tommie. An exemplary young man, he was married and the father of one little girl, Maurine, whose godmother I was. He and his wife Betty were the best friends I had in town. And he believed, with me, that we should defend the cause of right and fight wrong wherever we saw it. He delivered mail at the office of the *Free Speech,* and whatever Tommie knew in the way of news we got first. He owned his little home, and having saved his money he went into the grocery business with the same ambition that a young white man would have had. He was the president of the company. His partners ran the business in the daytime.

They had located their grocery in the district known as the "Curve" because the streetcar line curved sharply at that point. There was already a grocery owned and operated by a white man who hitherto had had a monopoly on the trade of this thickly populated colored suburb. Thomas's grocery changed all that, and he and his associates were made to feel that they were not welcome by the white grocer. The district being mostly colored and many of the residents belonging either to Thomas's church or to his lodge, he was not worried by the white grocer's hostility.

One day some colored and white boys quarreled over a game of marbles and the colored boys got the better of the fight which followed. The father of the white boys whipped the victorious colored boy, whose father and friends pitched in to avenge the grown white man's flogging of a colored boy. The colored men won the fight, whereupon the white father and grocery keeper swore out a warrant for the arrest of the colored victors. Of course the colored grocery keepers had been drawn into the dispute. But the case was dismissed with nominal fines. Then the challenge was issued that the vanquished whites were coming on Saturday night to clean out the People's Grocery Company.

Knowing this, the owners of the company consulted a lawyer and were told that [because] they were outside the city limits and beyond police protection, they would be justified in protecting themselves if attacked. Accordingly the grocery company armed several men and stationed them in the rear of the store on that fatal Saturday night, not to attack but to repel a threatened attack. And Saturday night was the time when men of both races congregated in their respective groceries.

About ten o'clock that night, when Thomas was posting his books for the week and Calvin McDowell and his clerk were waiting on customers preparatory to closing, shots rang out in the back room of the store. The men stationed there had seen several white men stealing through the rear door and fired on them without a moment's pause. Three of these men were wounded, and others fled and gave the alarm.

Sunday morning's paper came out with lurid headlines telling how officers of the law had been wounded while in the discharge of their duties, hunting up criminals whom they had been told were harbored in the People's Grocery Company, this being "a low dive in which drinking and gambling were carried on: a resort of thieves and thugs." So ran the description in the leading white journals of Memphis of this successful effort of decent black men to carry on a legitimate business. The same newspaper told of the arrest and jailing of the proprietor of the store and many of the colored people. They predicted that it would go hard with the ringleaders if these "officers" should die. The tale of how the peaceful homes of that suburb were raided on that quiet Sunday morning by police pretending to be looking for others who were implicated in what the papers had called a conspiracy, has been often told. Over a hundred colored men were dragged from their homes and put in jail on suspicion.

All day long on that fateful Sunday white men were permitted in the jail to look over the imprisoned black men. Frenzied descriptions and hearsays were detailed in the papers, which fed the fires of sensationalism. Groups of white men gathered on the street corners and meeting places to discuss the awful crime of Negroes shooting white men.

There had been no lynchings in Memphis since the Civil War, but the colored people felt that anything might happen during the excitement. Many of them were in business there. Several times they had elected a member of their race to represent them in the legislature in Nashville. And a Negro, Lymus Wallace, had been elected several times as a member of the city council and we had had representation on the school board several times. Mr. Fred Savage was then our representative on the Board of Education.

The manhood which these Negroes represented went to the county jail and kept watch Sunday night. This they did also on Monday night, guarding the jail to see that nothing happened to the colored men during this time of race prejudice, while it was thought that the wounded white men would die. On Tuesday following, the newspapers which had fanned the flame of race prejudice announced that the wounded men were out of danger and would recover. The colored men who had guarded the jail for two nights felt that the crisis was past and that they need not guard the jail the third night.

While they slept a body of picked men was admitted to the jail, which was a modern Bastille. This mob took out of their cells Thomas Moss, Calvin McDowell, and Henry Stewart, the three officials of the People's Grocery Company. They were loaded on a switch engine of the railroad which ran back of the jail, carried a mile north of the city limits, and horribly shot to death. One of the morning papers held back its edition in order to supply its readers with the details of that lynching. . . .

Mr. Fortune met me in Jersey City, according to agreement. He greeted me with "Well, we've been a long time getting you to New York, but now you are here I am afraid you will have to stay." "I can't see why that follows," said I. "Well," he said, "from the rumpus you have kicked up I feel assured of it. Oh, I know it was you because it sounded just like you."

"Will you please tell me what you are talking about?" I asked. "Haven't you seen the morning paper?" he replied. I told him no. He handed me a copy of the *New York Sun* where he had marked an Associated Press dispatch from Memphis. The article stated that, acting on an editorial of the *Commercial Appeal* of the previous Monday morning, a committee of leading citizens had gone to the office of the *Free Speech* that night, run the business manager, J. L. Fleming, out of town, destroyed the type and furnishings of the office, and left a note saying that anyone trying to publish the paper again would be punished with death. The article went on to say that the paper was owned by Ida B. Wells, a former schoolteacher, who was traveling in the North.

Although I had been warned repeatedly by my own people that something would happen if I did not cease harping on the lynching of three months before, I had expected that happening to come when I was at home. I had bought a pistol the first thing after Tom Moss was lynched, because I expected some cowardly retaliation from the lynchers. I felt that one had better die fighting against injustice than to die like a dog or a rat in a trap. I had already determined to sell my life as dearly as possible if attacked. I felt if I could take one lyncher with me, this would even up the score a little bit. But fate decided that the blow should fall when I was away, thus settling for me the question whether I should go West or East. My first thought after recovering from the shock of the information given me by Mr. Fortune was to find out if Mr. Fleming got away safely. I went at once to the telegraph office and sent a telegram to B. F. Booth, my lawyer, asking that details be sent me at the home address of Mr. Fortune.

In due time telegrams and letters came assuring me of Mr. Fleming's safety and begging me not to return. My friends declared that the trains and my home were being watched by white men who promised to kill me on sight. They also told me that colored men were organized to protect me if I should return. They said it would mean more bloodshed, more widows and orphans if I came back, and now that I was out of it all, to stay away where I would be safe from harm.

Because I saw the chance to be of more service to the cause by staying in New York than by returning to Memphis, I accepted their advice, took a position on the *New York Age,* and continued my fight against lynching and lynchers. They had destroyed my paper, in which every dollar I had in the world was invested. They had made me an exile and threatened my life for hinting at the truth. I felt that I owed it to myself and my race to tell the whole truth.

So with the splendid help of T. Thomas Fortune and Jerome B. Peterson, owners and editors of the *New York Age,* I was given an opportunity to tell the world for the first time the true story of Negro lynchings, which were becoming more numerous and horrible. Had it not been for the courage and vision of these two men, I could never have made such headway in emblazoning the story to the world. These men gave me a one-fourth interest in the paper in return for my subscription lists, which were afterward furnished by me, and I became a weekly contributor on salary.

The readers will doubtless wonder what caused the destruction of my paper after three months of constant agitation following the lynching of my friends. They were killed on the ninth of March. The *Free Speech* was destroyed 27 May 1892, nearly three months later. I thought then it was the white southerner's chivalrous defense of his womanhood which caused the mob to destroy my paper, even though it was known that the truth had been spoken. I know now that it was an excuse to do what they had wanted to do before but had not dared because they had no good reason until the appearance of that famous editorial.

For the first time in their lives the white people of Memphis had seen earnest, united action by Negroes which upset economic and business conditions. They had thought the excitement would die down; that Negroes would forget and become again, as before, the wealth producers of the South—the hewers of wood and drawers of water, the servants of white men. But the excitement kept up, the colored people continued to leave, business remained at a standstill, and there was still a dearth of servants to cook their meals and wash their clothes and keep their homes in order, to nurse their babies and wait on their tables, to build their houses and do all classes of laborious work.

SOURCE: Ida B. Wells, *Crusade for Justice: The Autobiography of Ida B. Wells,* ed. Alfreda M. Duster (Chicago: University of Chicago Press, 1970), 47–50, 61–63. Reprinted by permission of the University of Chicago Press.

NOTES

1. Ann Field Alexander, *Race Man: The Rise and Fall of the "Fighting Editor," John Mitchell, Jr.* (Charlottesville: University of Virginia Press, 2002), 29.

2. *Chicago Tribune,* January 1, 1891.

3. Emma Lou Thornbrough, *T. Thomas Fortune: Militant Journalist* (Chicago: University of Chicago Press, 1972), 3–79; David Domke, "Journalists, Framing, and Discourse about Race Relations," *Journalism and Mass Communication Monographs* 164 (1997): 1–55; Jean M. Allman and David R. Roediger, "The Early Editorial Career of Timothy Thomas Fortune: Class, Nationalism and Consciousness of Africa," *Afro-Americans in New York Life and History* 6 (1982): 39–52; Donald E. Drake II, "Militancy in Fortune's *New York Age,*" *Journal of Negro History* 55 (1970): 307–322.

4. David Levering Lewis, *W. E. B. Du Bois: Biography of a Race, 1868–1919* (New York: Henry Holt, 1993), 38–39; Louis R. Harlan, *Booker T. Washington: The Making of a Black Leader, 1856–1901* (New York: Oxford University Press, 1972), 192.

5. Randall B. Woods, "C. H. J. Taylor and the Movement for Black Political Independence, 1882–1896," *Journal of Negro History* 67 (1982): 122–135.

6. Paul Avrich, *The Haymarket Tragedy* (Princeton, N.J.: Princeton University Press, 1984), 417.

7. *The Facts in the Case of the Horrible Murder of Little Myrtle Vance and Its Fearful Expiation at Paris, Texas, February 1, 1893, with Photographic Illustrations* (Paris: P. L. James, 1893), 5, 6, 7, 9, 12, 13, 15–17, 19–24.

8. Linda O. McMurry, *To Keep the Waters Troubled: The Life of Ida B. Wells* (New York: Oxford University Press, 1998), 184; Robert C. O. Benjamin, *Southern Outrages: A Statistical Record of Lawless Doings* (n.p.: 1894), 38–42.

9. Alexander, *Race Man,* 1–53; Michael Honey, "One View of Black Life in the South during the 'Nadir': The Richmond *Planet,* 1865–1900," *Potomac Review* 2 (1981): 28–38.

10. *Richmond Planet,* July 12, 1890.

11. Ibid., February 9, 1901.

12. Ibid., March 30, 1901.

13. Deborah Gray White, "The Cost of Club Work, the Price of Black Feminism," in Nancy A. Hewitt and Suzanne Lebsock, eds., *Visible Women: New Essays on American Activism* (Urbana: University of Illinois Press, 1993), 247–269; Dorothy Salem, *To Better Our World: Black Women in Organized Reform, 1890–1920* (Brooklyn: Carlson, 1990), 29–53.

7

State Sovereignty and Mob Law

American citizens looked first to their state government for protection against mob violence. Historians have sometimes underestimated the states' determination to carry out this mission. No doubt many governors and legislatures did nothing, but other state legislators probably acted sincerely when they passed their numerous laws against lynching. They acted knowing that the real work came when county sheriffs and state militia tried to enforce these statutes, a tough job. State officers trying to prevent lynching violence knew that they enraged many ordinary citizens when they shielded violent offenders from extralegal justice. As the last document in this chapter shows, through the lynching era, state officers never really overcame this problem.

And, of course, black prisoners charged with rape posed a special problem. Guarding a rapist seemed to say that the forms of law mattered more than the protection of women against rape. This challenged deeply rooted, traditional gender roles. Men, and many women, insisted that women had a right of protection against rape that overwhelmed any constitutional responsibility the states might assert to maintain order. Even proponents of state power who were genuinely committed to putting down mob violence had trouble overcoming this argument.

States generally divided (and many still do)[1] laws against lynching into three categories: some laws held communities responsible for property damage; others defended state facilities; and still others removed from office sheriffs who would not defend their prisoners against lynch mobs. This Massachusetts law, holding communities responsible for rioting, illustrates the first category. Property owners could be compensated for losses that resulted from rioting on the theory that the local government should have suppressed the mob and prevented the property loss. The whole community is taxed to pay for the damage done by the mob. If bystanders did nothing, they still deserved blame for not intervening.

86. *Massachusetts, An Act concerning Riots,* 1839

Whenever any property, of the value of fifty dollars or more, shall be destroyed, or be injured to that amount, by any persons to the number of twelve or more, riotously, routously, or tumultuously assembled, the city or town within which said property was situated, shall be liable to indemnify the owner thereof to the amount of three fourths of the value of the property so destroyed, or the amount of such injury thereto; to be recovered in an action of the case in any court proper to try the same: *provided,* the owner of such property shall use all reasonable diligence to prevent its destruction, or injury, by such unlawful assembly, and to procure the conviction of the offenders.

SOURCE: Acts and Resolves Passed by the Legislature of Massachusetts, in the Year 1839. Published by the Secretary of the Commonwealth (Boston: Dutton and Wentworth, Printer to the State, 1839), 21–22.

Some states passed laws aimed at the lynchers themselves, the second category. These laws almost always defined lynching as breaking open a jail, an attack on the government itself.

87. *North Carolina, An Act to Protect Prisoners, 1893*

Every person who shall conspire to break or enter any jail or other place of confinement of prisoners charged with crime or under sentence, for the purpose of killing or otherwise injuring any prisoner confined therein; and every person who engages in breaking or entering any such jail or other place of confinement of such prisoners with intent to kill or injure any prisoner, shall be guilty of a felony, and upon conviction thereof or upon a plea of guilty shall be fined by the court having jurisdiction of the offence, not less than five hundred dollars, and imprisoned in the state prison or the county jail not less than two nor more than fifteen years.

SOURCE: Public Laws and Resolutions of the State of North Carolina Passed by the General Assembly at Its Session of 1893. Began and Held in the City of Raleigh on Wednesday, the Fourth Day of January, A.D. 1893 (Raleigh: Josephus Daniels, State Printer and Binder, 1893), 440.

The third category of laws encouraged sheriffs to defend their prisoners rather than simply hand them over to the mob. Sheriffs failing to fend off lynchers could be fired from their jobs.

88. *Kansas, An Act Providing for the Suppression of Mob Violence, 1903*

If any person taken from the hands of a sheriff or his deputy having such person in custody and shall be lynched, it shall be evidence of failure on the part of such sheriff to do his duty, and his office shall thereby and thereat immediately be vacated.

SOURCE: State of Kansas, Session Laws, 1903, Passed at the Thirtieth Regular Session—the Same Being the Thirteenth Biennial Session—of the Legislature of the State of Kansas (Topeka: W. Y. Morgan, State Printers, 1903), 376.

89. *Tennessee, An Act to Punish Sheriffs Who Permit Prisoners in Their Custody to Be Put to Death by Violence, 1881*

Be it enacted by the General Assembly of the State of Tennessee, That any sheriff who either negligently or willfully, or by want of proper diligence, firmness, and promptness in the use of all the powers with which he is vested by law, allows a prisoner to be taken from the jail of his county, or to be taken from his custody and put to death by violence, shall be guilty of a high misdemeanor in office, and on indictment therefor and conviction thereof, shall be fined at the discretion of the court, and shall also, by the judgment of the court, forfeit his office and be declared forever incapable of holding any office of trust or profit in this State.

SOURCE: Acts of the State of Tennessee, Passed by the Forty-second General Assembly, 1881 (Nashville, Tenn.: Tavel and Howell, Printers to the State, 1881), 54.

State officials sometimes vigorously resisted mobs, guarding their prisoners to the death.[2] In 1883 a Confederate veteran named Thomas Goode Jones commanded Alabama National Guard troops dispatched to Birmingham. Just a week after a mob lynched Lewis Houston for rape in that city, Birmingham whites turned out again, this time to lynch Wesley Posey, jailed for raping a nine-year-old white girl. Colonel Jones and eighty-five soldiers came into Birmingham after dark; the streets around the jail boiled with armed and angry men determined to kill Posey.

90. *Thomas Goode Jones, "Report to the Governor,"* December 11, 1883

The command left the cars at the foot of Fourteenth Street, and marched to the city hall, where Company K, Birmingham Rifles, Capt. Sam S. Thompson, and Company M, Birmingham Artillery, Capt. R. J. Lowe, all under command of Major W. J. Cameron, were under arms, awaiting my arrival.

It was quite dark and impossible to sift the numerous reports as to the strength, location and immediate designs of the mob. A considerable portion of it was known to be in possession of the jail, and around the court house. Owing to circumstances hereafter referred to, this mob was hourly growing bolder. Many who were taking part in it, and some who disavowed connection with it, became much excited and very indignant at the appearance of what they called "the foreign military."

The court house and jail are on the same square, and it was essential not only to the majesty of the law, but to the protection of the prisoner when brought back, that the troops should have possession. Remaining on the defensive at the city hall would have impaired the morale of the command, encouraged the mob, and, perhaps, invited attack. The whole command was accordingly moved to the court house as soon as I could familiarize myself with the ground.

The jail itself was found in possession of several men who stated they had been "sworn to protect the prisoner when brought back," and therefore could not leave. I showed these men the governor's instructions, and ordered this guard as well as the crowd around the jail to disperse. Some of this guard assented, but others of them lingered about the jail and made incendiary remarks to the troops and the crowd. Thereupon Captain E. A. Graham was directed to disperse the crowd at the point of the bayonet, which he did promptly and thoroughly. The crowd gave back very stubbornly, and several of them drawing pistols and all the while engaging in abuse of the troops and making violent threats. Captain A. B. Garland, Jr., in the meantime had effectually and speedily cleared the sidewalks and a portion of the street in front of the jail door and to its right. On the corner of Third avenue and Twenty-first street there was a dense crowd, extending a considerable distance down the street and on the vacant ground of the square, diagonally opposite the court house on the right as one comes out. This assemblage was increased by crowds who followed the troops from the city hall, and was variously estimated at from four hundred to a thousand in number. In the darkness, which was relieved only by lights from adjacent houses and a gas light on the opposite corner, I could form no accurate judgment of its strength, except that it outnumbered the troops fourfold at least; nor could I judge how many came from curiosity, and were averse to violence to the military. Those immediately in front were among the most violent of the rioters, and many of these commenced to draw and cock their pistols, and exhibited great anger, while the crowd, on the opposite side of the street, was being driven from the vicinity of the jail and court house. Many of these lawless men were under the influence of liquor. Stones were being thrown at the troops. A single shot from a drunken man's pistol would have caused a volley from the mob into the troops. I was loath to fire upon this dense mass, when innocent and guilty would suffer alike; but it was evident the crisis was at hand. Capt. Thompson promptly wheeled his company to the right to confront this mass and check it. Risking the safety of the command, perhaps, too far, I determined to give this crowd one more warning before firing, and implored all law abiding citizens to leave it. The warning seemed to have little effect. Capt. Thompson's command was promptly brought to a "ready," when a prominent official, no wise connected with the crowd, but endeavoring to make his way through it to reach me, was recognized with other citizens. This caused a momentary pause. The officials and other citizens taking in the situation, hastily got out of the way, and the crowd, which a moment before was ready to fire, followed the example, and fled in great haste and disorder, many of whom soon gathered again, a block further off.

This gave us undisputed possession of the court house and jail, and sentinels were thrown out in every direction around it. Patrols were sent out to bring in squads of men who were halting citizens on their way to their homes, but could come up with them only in one instance, when the squad being ordered to disperse instantly on pain of being fired on, ran hastily away. Having properly posted the command, I endeavored to learn the status of affairs, which was as follows:

A few days before this a negro named Houston had been taken out of jail by a mob and hanged. On Monday a mob attacked the jail for the purpose of hanging the prisoner, Wesley Posey. Company "K," Birmingham Rifles, Lieutenant F. M. Iron commanding during the sickness of Captain Thompson, had been ordered in the jail by the sheriff to protect the prisoner. The sheriff had removed the prisoner. This mob broke down the door and searched the jail, some of them insulting the military and rubbing pistols in their faces. The troops, knowing that the prisoner had gone, and being without orders from any civil authority, refrained from firing. Under the circumstances, self-defense would, perhaps, have justified the troops in firing on this mob without orders.

SOURCE: *Birmingham Iron Age*, December 20, 1883.

Few state officers matched Jones's courage. In 1886 the newspaper editor John Gordon Cashman gloomily assessed white Mississippians' attitudes toward lynching. Cashman campaigned against mob violence on the pages of his newspaper, the *Vicksburg Evening Post*, vacillating between confidence in the public's innate decency and deep depression over human depravity. This editorial documented one of Cashman's darker moods, a moment when he frankly confronted his fellow citizens' "cold blooded apathy." Cashman complained that "fearful and appalling SILENCE" followed lynchings in Mississippi. Few white southerners would admit what Cashman knew: tolerance for lynch law demoralized the white South, corrupting its morals and moral principles. Cashman, however, was too much a part of the system himself to attack the source of the problem: racial hatred.

91. *John G. Cashman, "Law and Order,"* 1886

The recent killing in Carroll county of some thirteen negroes in a Court room at Carrollton during the progress of a trial, by a band of white men one hundred strong, is shocking in the extreme.[3]

The present instance may be regarded as rather an extreme expression of a lawless sentiment which, reluctantly we are compelled to admit, pervades this State to an alarming extent. And what is infinitely worse, there is no improvement in this respect; on the contrary the evil increases and grows with a good lusty growth from year to year.

We may pass by the incident in Senator George's[4] county without any special comments, for there are so many killings, lynchings, mob hangings, even the burning of victims in this State—so little of protest or public criticism, such a lack of public indignation, and so much cold-blooded apathy and indifference on the part of officials who are sworn to execute the law—that to discuss the details of any special instance would be of little if any value, perhaps a waste of time. . . .

Some good people have been patiently waiting for years for a great outburst of public indignation in favor of law and order. Others, less sanguine, have been more modest and have simply hoped in a mild kind of way for a few feeble protests against violence and lawlessness; while others of a bolder thought have hoped for some horror great enough to waken the conscience of the people of this State and bring them to their senses. But this may prove an idle hope.

Not long ago a boy fourteen years old [*sic*] had his poor little hands handcuffed and then literally roasted off in a red-hot stove to force him to testify that his father had thrown a railroad train from the track. Martyr-like he bore this fire test until the flesh and manacles fell from his hands, and then he accused his father who was promptly tied to a tree and riddled with bullets by the mob.[5] On another occasion, a negro was literally burned at the stake for an actual or alleged crime.

And yet the publication of these crimes was greeted with the silence of the grave.

Newspapers in the State could be named that have not only condoned, but have openly advocated mob law in a class of cases which we will not name, where juries are but too willing to convict upon the weakest sort of proof—where the vengeance or justice of the law, in lawful methods, follows swiftly up on the crime. But a judicial trial is too slow, and the hanging on a lawful gallows waits too long upon the criminal for these mob-law newspapers and self-constituted judges and executioners. In one instance, it is reported an old man was hung by a mob in great haste, and two weeks afterward the lynchers suffered all the mortification of the discovery that they had made an error of judgment and hung the wrong man.

The greatest monster of crime, rage, malice; of cowardice and stupidity, the Prince of all the hosts of merciless tyrants, JUDGE LYNCH, Circuit Court and hangman, all in one, with hangman's noose and fagots held aloft, is the most conspicuously commanding and majestic personage in the State of Mississippi. He is too jealous of his power to concede the pardoning power to the Chief Executive; too infallible in judgment to tolerate an appeal to the three learned gentlemen who adorn the Supreme Court bench; so eager to play the hangman that he is jealous of the Sheriff's legal prerogatives in this respect; and so brave of heart as to defy the law that theoretically defines his crime as murder, or of such facetious turn of mind or nimble fancy as to treat this silent statute as Pickwickian in its grim humor.

And what are we going to do about it? Does the press denounce it? (There is an improvement in this respect, as evidenced by extracts which we give elsewhere.) Do public meetings of law-abiding citizens express a public sentiment against it and demand its suppression?

Are there any law officers from Chief Executive down, who lift their hands against his blood-stained Majesty, Judge Lynch?

Are there any leading politicians in public life, in this State, who speak out against this thing?

Who are answerable for the law and order of the State? And when are we to have quiet and peace, and law and order?

Has a lyncher ever been convicted, or even arrested or indicted since the days of Stone's administration?

The Vicksburg Commercial-herald asks The Post to "point out the connection" of Gov. Lowry[6] in this matter. What can a Governor ("who is in Jackson,") do? What can't he do! He is the chief conservator of the peace, by virtue of his office. How utterly powerless then must be the smaller fry of Sheriffs, Constables and Justices of the Peace? When a convict escapes, a reward is offered for his re-capture. Could not proclamation be made and a reward offered for the arrest of one "lyncher?" It could be paid out of the Contingent fund. Even this would be something. It would at least give some variety to the fearful and appalling SILENCE that surrounds the performance of our King. Does he wear a mask and hide himself in dark corners, and shroud himself in great and impenetrable mystery? No, like a King, that he is, he walks with head erect and face uncovered, in the broad light of day; and if we do not cry "vive le Roi," we, at all events, stand hushed and mute in the presence of His Majesty.

SOURCE: *Vicksburg Evening Post,* March 22, 1886.

Lynching meant more than white southerners attacking black southerners. In 1890 the New Orleans police chief David C. Hennessy died at the hands of an assassin. Authorities arrested and tried eight Italians. When a jury failed to convict the accused men, a mob broke into the New Orleans jail and hanged eleven Italians. In 1977 one writer called this incident the worst lynching in American history.[7] Henry Cabot Lodge blamed the lynchings on unrestricted immigration.[8] More lynchings of Italians followed.[9]

Southerners often defended themselves by saying that northerners also participated in lynchings. In October 1894 a black man named William Dolby raped a white woman in Fayette County, Ohio. Authorities arrested Dolby on October 6 and hastily tried him the next day. Dolby plead guilty and the court sentenced him to twenty years, the maximum sentence possible in Ohio.

Fayette County officials had good reason to move swiftly with Dolby's indictment, trial, and conviction. Angry mobs formed around the courthouse. To prevent a lynching, Governor William McKinley dispatched National Guard troops to Washington Court House, the county seat. The angry mob forced troops inside the courthouse and then fashioned a battering ram. The soldiers, commanded by A. B. Coit, fired through the wooden doors, killing six and injuring ten. To this day the immense wooden courthouse doors remain riddled from the gunfire.

Angry whites gossiped that Coit had been drunk when he ordered his men to fire through the doors. A civil trial acquitted Coit, and an army investigation cleared him of all charges.

92. "A Lynching in Ohio," 1895

We find, from the evidence, that early in October, 1894, a respectable white woman, residing in Fayette county, was criminally assaulted by a colored man named William Dolby, who was arrested October 14, and on the 16th was committed to jail at Washington C[ourt] H[ouse] His arrest and confinement having become known, crowds gathered at that place in such numbers, and made such threats as to cause the sheriff of that County to fear that an attempt would be made to take said Dolby from his possession and hang him. The sheriff, therefore, early in the evening of said day duly ordered Captain W. L. Vincent, commanding Company "E," of the 14th Regiment, and stationed at Washington C. H., to assemble his company and report to him at the jail, to aid him in protecting the prisoner. This order was promptly obeyed, but the crowd continued to increase in number and still threatening to lynch the prisoner Dolby, the sheriff wired Governor McKinley to send additional troops to his assistance. In compliance with this request, orders were duly issued to Col. A. B. Coit, commanding the 14th Regiment of Infantry, O. N. G., directing him to assemble two companies of his regiment and report to the sheriff of Fayette county, to act in aid of the civil authorities. This order was also promptly obeyed, and with parts of Companies "A" and "B" of his regiment Col. Coit reported to the sheriff at Washington C. H. at about 6 o'clock on the morning of the 17th of October. The force under his command, including Company "E," consisted of nine officers and seventy-six enlisted men. Upon his reporting to the sheriff, he was informed by him of the situation as above stated, and was also directed by him to take charge of the protection of the prisoner and public property and to use such proper means therefore as he might deem best. A line of guards was at once established around the outer edge of the court house grounds and so maintained until about 3 o'clock in the afternoon, but citizens were allowed free access to the court house by the usual walks and entrances. During the forenoon of the 17th, Judge Maynard, then holding court at Washington C. H., called a special grand jury, which at about 1 o'clock, after a short session, returned an indictment against the prisoner, Dolby. It was then arranged that the prisoner should be arraigned in the afternoon, it being understood that he would plead guilty. It was further arranged to sentence him at once and to take him under escort of the troops to the penitentiary by train, leaving Washington C. H. about 4:30 that afternoon. About 3 o'clock, having been notified by the sheriff that he desired to take the prisoner to the court room, Col. Coit withdrew his guards from their previous position, and after placing a few at each of the other entrances and in the court room, with the remainder be formed a double line from the jail to the north entrance of the court house. The crowd north of the court house at this time was variously estimated by witnesses as being from 300 to 2,500, but it was large enough and threatening enough to warrant all the precaution taken. While the prisoner was being taken through the lines a desperate and nearly successful attempt to lynch him was made by the crowd, several of the soldiers and of the mob being injured, but none seriously. The prisoner was duly arraigned, plead guilty, and was sentenced to the penitentiary for twenty years, but the size and temper of the crowd then assembled about the court house were such that both Col. Coit and the sheriff, though believing that they could then take the prisoner to the train, thought it could only be done at the sacrifice of life, which might be avoided if a larger number of troops was sent to their assistance, and they thereupon decided to send for such reinforcement and await their arrival before leaving the court house. The three doors in the basement and the south and west doors on first floors were barricaded as well as the means at hand would permit, and guards were stationed at these points; at the windows in the basement, and at the north entrance to the court house, which was kept open for the passage of such as had business therein. About this time orders were given by Col. Coit to the troops to fire should the doors be broken in; of this, warning was given by Col. Coit to the crowd on the outside, and from the time that the prisoner was sentenced until a few moments before the firing, which occurred at about seven o'clock in the evening, the crowd was ordered at different times by the sheriff, Col. Coit, Maj. Speaks and others to disperse. In these efforts they were seconded by Rev. Mr. McNair, Mills Gardner and others, but without any effect except to call down upon the sheriff and officers the anger and threats of the crowd to hang them as well as the prisoner. The mob, for such it had become, continued to increase, noticeably so, early in the evening, when large crowds occupied the streets surrounding the yard and many were in the yard on both the north and south sides. This crowd was composed almost entirely of people who were anxious to hang the prisoner Dolby, or were willing to have him hung, and it was impossible for any one to tell how few there were of one class, or how many of the other. The crowd on the grounds on the south side, numbering 800 to 1,000 men, became so boisterous and so threatening that Maj. Speaks, who was looking after the guard on that side, while Col. Coit was at the north door, several times from a balcony in the second story and over the south entrance, ordered the mob to disperse and warned them that if they attempted to break in the door at that point the troops stationed inside would fire. Maj. Speaks gave such an order and warning just prior to the firing. He also sent warning to the people occupying stores on the south side of the street opposite the south side of the court house to shut up their places of business and get out of the way. In the meantime an incendiary fire had been started near the court house for the evident purpose of drawing the troops thereto and thereby weakening the guards. Attempts had also been made to break into the east and west basement doors. About seven o'clock, and immediately after an ineffectual attempt to break in the south doors with heavy sledge hammers, a party of men bearing an oak timber, twenty feet, ten and one-half inches long, nine and one-half inches wide, and four and one-half inches thick and weighing 260 pounds, and using same as battering ram, struck three heavy blows upon one of the double doors at the south entrance of the court house, bursting it open. As it was forced open, a volley was immediately fired by the guard stationed at that door, killing five of those within the grounds at that point and wounding about twenty others. After this the mob was so incensed and became so in earnest in its threats to blow up the court house that guards were stationed at the windows and on the balconies and no one allowed to approach the building, until about four o'clock in the morning of the 18th, when additional troops arrived and the prisoner was taken to the depot and thence to the penitentiary.

We find from the evidence that from the time of their arrival at Washington C. H., on the morning of the 17th, up to early in the afternoon, officers and men were allowed to go outside the guard lines for their meals; that while so outside some of them did visit saloons or the bars at restaurants, where they were subsisted and did drink there; that one enlisted man became intoxicated and unfit for duty, and three others were more or less under the influence of liquor. We find from the evidence that Col. Coit himself drank liquor but once and then upon the advice of the surgeon of his regiment, and as furnished by him. The evidence clearly shows that neither Col. Coit nor any of the officers under his command at Washington C. H., were in the slightest degree under the influence of liquor on that occasion, nor were any enlisted men except the parties referred to above. We do not approve the visiting of saloons or bars, nor the permitting of troops outside the guard line on such occasions. We find also that during the forenoon of the 17th, certain of the troops were allowed to stack their arms in the court house yard and to hang their accoutrements thereon, and that such stacks, containing the arms of nearly one-half of the command, were carelessly and imprudently left without any guard, except the guard then on duty on the outer edge of the grounds, at some distance from these stacks, and this at a time when there was a crowd around the grounds, and the people generally allowed to pass to and from the court house.

We find that in their general behavior, during all the time they were at Washington C. H., the officers and men, with the exception above stated, conducted themselves in a soldierly manner, and that they were as cool and collected as could be expected of troops under such circumstances.

SOURCE: *Annual Report of the Adjutant General to the Governor of the State of Ohio for the Year Ending November 15, 1895* (Columbus: Westbote, 1896), 17–20.

For many, the male duty to protect women outweighed any state responsibility to control mob violence. Gender trumped the states' police powers. Rebecca Latimer Felton articulated this on August 11, 1897, at the annual meeting of the Georgia Agricultural Society.

Felton stepped up to speak amid a statewide debate over lynching. On July 20 a small mob had lynched a white dentist, W. L. Ryder, accused of murdering Sallie Emma Owen after she spurned his advances. This lynching of a white man caused a sensation. Newspaper editorialists, leading lawyers, and ministers took advantage of the opportunity to again denounce mob law. Governor William Yates Atkinson repeated his demands that the legislature give him more power to punish any state officer failing to prevent a lynching. He now offered a five hundred dollar reward for the first two lynchers captured and one hundred dollars for every subsequent lyncher. Pinkerton detectives joined the chase.[10]

Meanwhile, the lynching of African Americans continued apace. Two days after Ryder died, a mob hanged Oscar Williams. That same day a Kentucky mob killed Ephraim Brinkley, and an Alabama mob killed Jim Speaks. So many died at the hands of Judge Lynch around the country in late July that the *Atlanta Journal* published a box score, listing the names of lynched men and the dates of their deaths.[11] The African Methodist Episcopal Bishop Henry M. Turner recommended fasting and prayer in the face of whites' raging "mania for lynching."[12]

The lynchers themselves defended their violence, posting a note on Oscar Williams's body, calling his death "a rebuke" to a mayor who had called on the national guard. Ryders's lynchers sent a piece of their rope to the *Atlanta Journal.* An attached note claimed it came "from the Ladies, he got What he deserved."[13] When DuPont Guerry wrote articles criticizing lynching, Hooper Alexander shot back that the tendency of blacks to rape made lynching unavoidable.[14]

As this debate raged, Rebecca Latimer Felton weighed in with a speech entitled "Needs of the Farmers' Wives and Daughters."[15] Felton made a feminist argument, pointing out that females made up half of Georgia's farming population. About men she said, "I wish I had the power to put them over the cook stove and wash pot, until they would be willing to say 'our crop,' 'our house,' 'our farm,' and 'our' everything else." She demanded that Georgia men "throw open the doors of the university to women." Georgia women should be allowed to compete for the same degrees as men, "upon the same plane, and without favoritism."

In the most famous portion of her speech, however, Felton demanded that men lynch rapists to protect their women. The *Savannah Morning News* acknowledged that Felton's call for more lynchings received applause but added that "the applause was not general, and there were many who thought it a discordant note and out of place in an otherwise harmonious symphony."[16]

93. *Rebecca Latimer Felton, "Needs of the Farmers' Wives and Daughters," 1897*

I hear so much of the millions sent abroad to Japan, China, India, Brazil, and Mexico, but I feel that the heathen at home are so close at hand and need so much that I must make a strong effort to stop lynching, by keeping closer watch over the poor white girls on the secluded farms; and if these poor maidens are destroyed in a land that their fathers died to save from the invader's foot, I say the same lies with the survivors who fail to be protectors for the children of their dead comrades.

I do not discount foreign missions. I simply say the heathens are at your door, when our young maidens are destroyed in sight of your opulence and magnificence, and when your temples of justice are put to shame by the lynchers rope. If your court houses are shams and frauds and the law's delay is the villain's bulwark, then I say let judgment begin at the house of God and redeem this country from the cloud of shame that rests upon it!

When there is not enough religion in the pulpits to organize a crusade against sin; nor justice in the court houses to promptly punish crime; nor manhood enough in the nation to put a sheltering arm about innocence and virtue—if it needs lynching to protect woman's dearest possession from the ravenous human beasts, then I say lynch a thousand times a week if necessary.

The poor girl would choose any death in preference to such ignominy and outrage and a quick death is mercy to the rapist compared to the suffering of innocence and modesty in a land of Bibles and churches, where violence is becoming omnipotent except with the rich and powerful before the law.

The crying need of women on the farms is security in their lives, in their homes. Strong able-bodied men have told me they stopped farming and moved to town because their women folks were scared to death if left alone.

I say it is a disgrace in a free county when such things are a public reproach and the best part of God's creation are trembling and crying for protection in their own homes. And I say, with due respect to all who listen to me, that so long as your politics takes the colored man into your embraces on election day to control his vote; and so long as the politicians use liquor to befuddle his understanding and make him think he is a man and a brother; when they proposed to defeat the opposition by honey-snuggling him at the polls, and so long as he is made familiar with their dirty tricks in politics, so long will lynchings prevail because the causes of it grow and increase.

SOURCE: *Atlanta Journal,* August 12, 1897.

The governor of Georgia took issue with Felton's analysis. By repeating his call to the legislature for increased power to combat lynchers, he thumbed his nose at Felton. But Atkinson's racism limited his ability to refute Felton's message. He could not make himself challenge her basic point: black criminality endangered white women.

94. *Georgia Governor W. Y. Atkinson, "Government, Crime, and Lynching,"* October 27, 1897

The graver crimes are of alarming frequency and more seriously affect that portion of our population who reside outside the towns and cities. In these sections, the crime of burglary, arson and rape have become more frequent than in the years of disorder which followed the civil war.

The frequency of the offense of rape has become alarming in the extreme, and seriously interferes with the security and comfort of living in the country. There are now in the penitentiary seventy-eight convicts for assault to rape, and eighty-one for rape.

Of all crimes known to our law, these two are the most villainous. Their frequency has terrorized the people residing in rural districts, and so aroused their fear and resentment that it has been impossible in many of these cases to induce them to await the action of the courts....

In dealing with this question, the people of the Southern States are, of all people, in the most trying position. Here, a large per cent. of our population has been clothed with the rights and privileges of citizenship before receiving the training necessary to prepare them for the duties and responsibilities of so important a position. If the same population had been placed among the people of any other section of the Union, they would have the same problem to deal with which now confronts us, and would find just as much human nature among their people as is exhibited by ours.

Notwithstanding the anomalous condition which exists here, our people deplore mob violence, but should be more determined in insisting upon leaving to courts and juries the punishment of violators of the law.

If defects exist in the law, the remedy is not to ignore and violate the law, but to amend it. The citizen cannot be justified in trampling upon law and assuming the functions of judge, jury and executioner.

It is the duty of the citizen to leave to the government, under which he lives, the righting of wrongs, and the punishment of crime. The man who ignores this obligation and assumes, with his own hand to punish crime, becomes a criminal.

The evil to which I allude is not restricted to this State or section, but is national.

The frequency of such occurrences within the last few years is calculated to alarm every citizen who realizes the dreadful results to which it leads; or the enormity of the crime against human rights, government and civilization. To denominate these offenses lynchings do not make them less lawless or barbarous.

It is an attack upon government itself—a conflict between the forces of anarchy and law. It is fundamentally wrong, because it defies government, ignores law and punishes without law or evidence. Under our government, laws are made and un-made at the will of the majority. If there are unwise laws, the people can repeal, if [there is] a need for one, the people can enact. Any organized effort to set at naught our laws and punish crime without and in defiance of the law is itself criminal. It is worse than criminal. In its very essence, it is treason against the majority and against government. . . .

I feel the more deeply upon this question because from the best information I can secure, I believe, that during my administration there have been in this state several men lynched who were not guilty of the crimes with which they were charged. How many, can never be known, for their tongues are hushed, and they are denied an opportunity to prove their innocence. I am informed that one man, whom the mob believed to be guilty, was shot down. A question then arose as to his identity and he was salted down like a hog, shipped to the location of the crime and found to be the wrong man—an innocent man. . . .

Lynch law has not been restricted to cases where the charge was an outrage upon a female. In Texas a man was lynched simply to suppress his evidence; in Kentucky, because he was objectionable to the neighborhood, and in Indiana five men were lynched for burglary. In our State, in the last three years, seven men have been lynched for murder, and one man and one woman because they were suspected of arson.

When Charge Is Rape

Even had it been confined to offenses committed upon females it could not be justified:

To adopt it, in these cases, is to put the life of every man in the power of any woman who might for any reason desire his death. When such crimes are charged the passion of the people is more deeply stirred than by any other, and the mob is quick to act.

Yet, viewed from the standpoint of reason and not of passion, there is less excuse for lynching in such cases than in any other. Delay cannot be given as a reason, nor a fear that justice will be defeated. At Monticello and Columbus the men were taken out of the court room during the trial and lynched. In most cases they are taken from the custody of officers of the law, when they know that the court will convene and give a speedy trial. For this offense, above all others, the courts are quick to try, and, if guilty, the juries certain to convict.

It is not then that they fear delay or the acquittal of the guilty, but it is a defiance of law. It is a desire to substitute passion for evidence and vengeance for justice.

SOURCE: *Journal of the Senate of the State of Georgia at the Regular Session of the General Assembly at Atlanta, Wednesday, October 27, 1897* (Atlanta: Geo. W. Harrison, State Printer, 1897), 27–33.

After Felton delivered her infamous address a black newspaper editor in Wilmington, North Carolina, published a rebuttal. Alexander Manly charged that Felton (according to the best record of his editorial, a transcript made by a white man, he mistook her name as "Fellows") had exaggerated the rape threat. "White girls of culture and refinement" often welcomed black lovers, Manly wrote. Manly's editorial struck a match to the dry kindling of white discontent with North Carolina's interracial government. The Wilmington race riot followed, in which whites killed an untold number of blacks.[17]

95. *Alexander Manly, "Mrs. Fellows's Speech,"* 1898

A Mrs. Fellows from Georgia, makes a speech before the Agricultural Society, at Tybee, Ga., in which she advocates lynching as an extreme measure. This woman makes a strong plea for white womanhood and if the alleged crimes were half so frequent as is oftimes alleged, her pleas would be worthy of consideration.

Mrs. Fellows, like many other so called Christians, loses sight of the basic principle of the religion of Christ in her plea for one class of Religion as against another. If a Missionary spirit is essential for the uplifting of the poor white girls, why is it? The morals of the poor white people are on a par with their colored neighbors of like conditions, and if one doubts the statement, let him visit among them. The whole lump needs to be leavened by those who profess so much Religion, thus showing them that the presence of virtue is an essential for the life of any people.

Mrs. Fellows begins well for she admits that education will better protect the girls on the farm from the assaulter. This we admit and it should not be confined to the white any more than to the colored girls. The papers are filled often with reports of rapes of white women; and the subsequent lynching of the alleged rapists. The editors pour forth volumes of aspersions against all negroes because of the few who may be guilty. If the papers and speakers of the other race would condemn the commission of crime and not try to make it appear that the negroes were the only criminals, they would find their strongest allies in the intelligent negroes themselves, and together would root the evil out of both races.

We suggest that the whites guard their women more closely, as Mrs. Fellows says, thus giving no opportunity for the human fiend, be he white or black. You leave your goods out of doors and then complain because they are taken away. Poor white men are careless in the matter of protecting their women, especially on farms. They are careless of their conduct toward them, and our experiences among poor white people in the country teaches us that the women of that race are not any more particular in the matter of clandestine meetings with colored men than are the white men with colored women. Meetings of this kind go on for some time until the woman's infatuation, or the man's boldness, bring attention to them, and the man is lynched for rape. Every negro lynched is called "a big, burly, black brute", when in fact many of those who have thus been dealt with had white men for their fathers, and were not only not "black" and "burly" but were sufficiently attractive for white girls of culture and refinement to fall in love with them, as is well known to all.

Mrs. Fellows must begin at the fountain head if she wishes to purify the stream. Teach your men purity. Let virtue be something more than an example for them to intimidate and torture a helpless people. Tell your men that it is no worse for a black man to be intimate with a white woman than for a white man to be intimate with a colored woman.

You set yourselves down as a lot of carping hypocrites; in fact, you cry aloud for the virtue of your women, when you seek to destroy the morality of ours. Don't think ever that your women will remain pure while you are debauching ours. You sow the seed—the harvest will come in due time.

SOURCE: *Wilmington Daily Record,* August 18, 1898. Transcript in Col. Thomas W. Clawson, "The Wilmington Race Riot of 1898," Louis T. Moore Collection, Archives and Records Section, North Carolina State Archives, Raleigh.

After Governor Atkinson left office in 1898, to be succeeded by Allen D. Candler, the state lid on mob violence slipped even further. Atkinson's appeal for state law over lynch law failed to prevent white Georgians from torturing, burning, and mutilating the man known as "Sam Hose." Like Atkinson, Candler denounced lynching but also worried about black criminality.[18]

96. *"Sam Hose,"* 1899

Newnan, Ga., April 23. In the presence of nearly two thousand persons, who sent aloft yells of defiance and shouts of joy, Sam Hose, a negro, who committed two of the basest acts known to crime, was burned at the stake in a public road one and one-half miles from here this afternoon. Before the torch was applied to the pyre the negro was deprived of his ears, fingers and other portions of his anatomy. The negro pleaded pitifully for his life while the mutilation was going on, but stood the ordeal of fire with surprising fortitude. Before the body was cool it was cut to pieces, the bones were crushed into small bits and even the tree upon which the wretch met his fate was torn up and disposed of as souvenirs. The negro's heart was cut in several pieces, as was his liver. Those unable to obtain these ghastly relics direct paid fortunate possessors extravagant sums for them. Small pieces of bone went for 25 cents and a bit of the liver crisply cooked sold for 10 cents. One of the men who lifted the can of kerosene to the negro's head is said to be a native of the Commonwealth of Pennsylvania. His name is known to those who were with him, but they refuse to divulge it. The mob was composed of citizens of Newnan, Griffin, Palmetto and other little towns in the country round about Newnan, and all the farmers who had received word that the burning was to take place.

The Hon. W. Y. Atkinson, former governor of Georgia, met the mob as he was returning from church and appealed to them to let the law take its course. In addressing the mob he used these words: "Some of you are known to me, and when this affair is finally settled in the Courts you may depend upon it that I will testify against you." A member of the mob was seen to draw a revolver and level it at Governor Atkinson, but his arm was seized and the pistol taken from him. The mob was frantic at delays, and would hear nothing but burning at the stake.

Hose confessed to killing Cranford, but denied that he outraged Mrs. Cranford. Before being put to death the negro stated that he has been paid $12 by "Lige" Strickland, a negro preacher at Palmetto, to kill Cranford. To-night a mob of citizens is scouring the country for Strickland, who has left his home, and will lynch him if caught.

Sam Hose killed Alfred Cranford, a white farmer, near Palmetto, and outraged his wife, ten days ago. Since that time business in that part of the State has been suspended, the entire population turning out in an effort to capture Hose.

Governor Candler has been asked to send troops here to preserve order for a day or two, as it is feared the negroes may wreak vengeance, many threats to that effect having been made.

Hose has been on the farm of the Jones brothers, between Macon and Columbus, since the day after he committed his horrible crime. His mother is employed on the farm, and to her little cabin he fled as a safe refuge. She fed him and cared for him, but it is not believed that she knew he was being hunted for by the authorities. The Jones brothers were not aware of the crime until a few days ago, and were not sure that he was the much wanted man. Saturday morning one of the Jones boys met Hose and as he was talking to him noticed that his "ginger" face was ebony black, but just below the collar of his shirt the copper color was discernible. It was evident that the negro had blackened his face, and the Jones[es] became convinced that he was the negro for whom the authorities, assisted by bloodhounds, had been scouring the country for ten days, and they determined to arrest him. Sunday morning they brought the negro into Macon and put him aboard the Central of Georgia train, with the intention of bringing him to Atlanta. At Griffin someone recognized Hose and sent word to the Newnan, the next station, that the negro was on the train bound for Atlanta. When Newnan was reached a great crowd surrounded the train and pushed into the cars. The Jones boys were told that the negro could be delivered to the sheriff of Campbell County there, and that it was not necessary to take him to Atlanta. This was acceded to, and the negro was taken off the train and marched at the head of a yelling, shouting crowd of five hundred people to the jail. Here they turned him over to Sheriff Brown, taking a receipt for the prisoner, thus making themselves sure of the $250 reward for the "arrest and delivery to the sheriff of Campbell County of one Sam Hose." Word was sent to Mrs. Cranford, at Palmetto, that it was believed Hose was under arrest and that her presence was necessary in Newnan to make sure of identification. In some way the news of the arrest leaked out, and as the town had been on the alert for nearly two weeks the intelligence spread rapidly. From every house in the little city came its occupants, and a good-sized crowd was soon gathered about the jail.

Sheriff Brown was importuned to give up the prisoner and finally, in order to avoid an assault on the jail and possible bloodshed, he turned the wretch over to the waiting crowd. A procession was quickly formed and the doomed negro was marched at its head through several streets of the town. Soon the public square was reached. Here former Governor Atkinson, of Georgia, who lives in Newnan, came hurriedly upon the scene and standing up in a buggy importuned the crowd to let the law take its course. Governor Atkinson said:

"My fellow citizens and friends, I beseech you to let this affair go no further. You are hurrying this negro on to death without an identification. Mrs. Cranford, whom he is said to have assaulted, and whose husband he is said to have killed, is sick in bed and unable to be here to say whether this is her assailant. Let this negro be returned to the jail. The law will take its course, and I promise you it will do so quickly and effectually. Do not stain the honor of the State with a crime such as you are about to perform."

Judge A. D. Freeman, also of Newnan, spoke in a similar strain and implored the mob to return the prisoner to the custody of the sheriff and go home. The assemblage heard the words of the two speakers in silence, but the instant their voices had died away shouts of "On to Palmetto! Burn him! Think of his crime!" arose, and the march was resumed.

Mrs. Cranford's mother and sister are residents of Newnan. The mob was headed in the direction of their house and in a short time reached the McElroy home. The negro was marched in the gate and Mrs. McElroy called to the front door. She at once identified the African and her verdict was agreed to by her daughter, who had often seen Hose around the Cranford place. "To the stake," was again the cry and several men wanted to burn him in Mrs. McElroy's yard. To this she objected strenuously and the mob, complying with her wish, started for Palmetto.

Just as they were leaving Newnan word was brought that the 1 o'clock train from Atlanta was bringing 1,000 people to Palmetto. This was thought to be a regiment of militia and the mob at once decided to burn the prisoner at the first favorable place, rather than be compelled to shoot him when the militia put in sight.

Leaving the little town, whose Sunday's quiet had been so rudely disturbed, the mob, which now numbered nearly 1,500 people, started on the road to Palmetto. A line of buggies and vehicles of all kinds, their drivers fighting for position in line, followed the procession at the head of which, closely guarded, marched the negro.

One and a half miles out of Newnan, a place believed to be favorable for the burning was reached. A little to the side of the road stood a strong pine tree. Up to this the negro was marched, his back placed to the tree and his face to the crowd, which jostled closely about him. Here, for the first time, he was allowed to talk. He said: "I am Sam Hose. I killed Alfred Candler, but I was paid to do it. Lige Strickland, the negro preacher at Palmetto, gave me $12 to kill him." At this a roar went up from the crowd as the intelligence imparted by the wretch was spread among them. "Let him go on. Tell all you know about it," came from the crowd. The negro, shivering like a leaf, continued his recital. "I did not outrage Mrs. Cranford. Somebody else did that. I can identify them. Give me time for that."

The mob would hear no more. The clothes were torn from the wretch in an instant. A heavy chain was produced and wound around the body of the terrified wretch, clasped by a new lock, which dangled at Hose's neck. He said not a word to this proceeding, but at the sight of three or four knives clashing in the hands of several members of the crowd, which seemed to forecast the terrible ordeal he was about to be put to, he sent up a yell which could be heard a mile.

Instantly a hand grasping a knife shot out, and one of the negro's ears dropped into a hand ready to receive it. Hose pleaded pitifully for mercy, and begged his tormentors to let him die. His cries were unheeded. The second ear went the way of the other. Hardly had he been deprived of his ears before his fingers, one by one, were taken from his hand and passed among the members of the crowd. The shrieking wretch was quickly deprived of other portions of his anatomy and words, "Come on with the oil," brought a huge can of kerosene to the foot of the tree, where the negro, his body covered with blood from head to foot, was striving and tugging at his chains. The can was lifted over the negro's head by three or four men, and its contents poured over him. By this time a good supply of brush, pieces of fence rail and other firewood had been placed about the negro's feet. This pyre was thoroughly saturated and a match applied.

A flame shot upward and spread quickly over the pile of wood. As it licked the negro's legs, he shrieked once, and began tugging at his chains. As the flames crept higher and the smoke entered his eyes and mouth, Hose put the stumps of his hands to the tree back of him, and with a terrific lunge forward of his body severed the upper portion of the chains which bound him to the tree. His body, held to the tree only as far as his thighs, lunged forward, thus escaping the flames, which roared and crackled about his feet. One of the men near the burning negro quickly ran up, and, pushing him back said: "Get back into the fire there," and quickly connected the disjoined links of the chain. The road for half a mile on each side of the burning negro was black with conveyance, and was simply impassable. The crowd surrounded the stake on all sides, but none of those nearer than one hundred feet of the centre were able to see what was going on. Yell after yell went up and the progress of the flames were communicated to those in the rear by shouts from the eye-witnesses.

The torch was applied about half-past 2 and at 3 o'clock the body of Sam Hose was limp and lifeless, his head hanging to one side. The body was not cut down. It was cut to pieces. The crowd fought for places about the smouldering tree, and with knives, secured such pieces of his carcass as did not fall to pieces. The chain was severed by hammers, the tree chopped down and such pieces of the firewood as had not burned, were carried away as souvenirs.

Atlanta, Ga., April 23. One special and two regular trains carried nearly 4,000 persons to Newnan to witness the burning of Sam Hose, or to visit the scene of the horrible affair. The excursionists returning to-night were loaded down with ghastly reminders of the affair in the shape of bones, pieces of flesh and parts of the wood, which was placed at the negro's feet.

One of the trains, as it passed through Fort McPherson, four miles out of Atlanta, was stoned—presumably by negroes. A number of windows were broken and two passengers were painfully injured.

SOURCE: *Charleston News and Courier*, April 24, 1899.

In 1901 Alabama assembled a constitutional convention to disfranchise the states' African American voters. Some at the convention urged that the new constitution protect blacks from lynching in exchange for giving up the right to vote. Thomas Goode Jones, who had stood up to Birmingham mobs as a colonel in the Alabama National Guard, spoke forcefully on behalf of a constitutional measure against lynching.

97. *Report of Debate at the Alabama Constitutional Convention,* June 22, 1901

Debate on Lynching and Duties of Sheriffs

Mr. Sollie spoke against the proposal. He said that he was opposed to lynching, but that the proposition before the Convention would put the blame on one person where the blame should be imposed on the, entire State.

Mr. Jones (Montgomery).—***In its enforcement civilization religion and good government are alike promoted. Without it all languish and wither. Let us be frank with ourselves. Every time a citizen rises up and appeals for the law, some man says some Negro has committed an unmentionable crime, and, therefore, the sacredness of all law must be cast to the wind.

People in Alabama, who have not taken the trouble to keep pace with events, will be startled to be told that in the last ten years over one hundred citizens of Alabama have been taken by mobs from sheriffs and jails, and murdered. Yet such is the case, such is our bloody record. And yet over two-thirds of those people were not guilty of a crime I will not mention, because of fair listeners in the gallery.

Some years ago down in Butler County, a tax collector was murdered. A mob went to the jail and took two white men out and, in flagrant contempt of law and the court, hung them in front of the Court House door that the judge of an Alabama court, when he went in to deal out its justice, must be informed by the swinging bodies, how little people recked of law or courts.

We all recognize what I might call "justifiable humanity," when a criminal is caught red-handed in the act with the screams of his victim still vibrating in the air that wise and good men may be moved to acts of lawless vengeance. But when a prisoner is once in the hands of the law, it should be taught all men that the prisoner, like the ark of the covenant, is sacred, and that the profane hand which touches either will be palsied.

Why is it of all men on earth who are entrusted with the keeping of others, that a standard of honor must be made for officers different from all others, and that he should take no risk. Mr. President, the minister of the gospel who would fail to see the veriest stranger, much less one of his own congregation who is stricken with a deadly disease, because of personal fear, would be outlawed and scourged for all time. We see locomotive engineers every day standing by the throttle and risking their lives to save their passengers. We have seen captains of ships standing on the bridge that the women and children might be saved and going down to death in the waters. What policeman would be allowed to wear his uniform five minutes if he refused to make an arrest, at the risk or loss of life? What man would have respect for the Alabama State Troops, no matter what the odds, if they allowed a mob to take a prisoner from them? Such a standard as is claimed for sheriffs has no recognition in any laws of honor. It is a false standard of duty; if I may be pardoned for saying it, a cowardly standard of duty.

Mr. Jones.—*** Mob violence is a thing which grows by what it feeds on. Here and there, searching the public records, are cases which all men admit are excusable excuses outside the forms of law. ***We see lynchings almost every week not for the one crime, but for any crime. Some man is suspected of burning a house, and the honor of the State and the peace of the County is invaded. A lawless mob leads the suspect out to death; and so it goes from bad to worse. In all these cases the guilty go unwhipt of justice.

Two-thirds of the executions of prisoners by mobs are due to one of two things, either the cowardice of the Sheriff—and I don't think there have been many cases of cowardice—or to a willingness for the mob to succeed, from the false conviction that a Sheriff in fighting for them is not fighting for law but for some worthless prisoner. In county after county, everybody but the grand jury knows who did the deed. Case after case of this sort has happened without ever being brought to the bar of justice. There is no prosecution. No strong voice ever condemns it. We owe it to ourselves, we owe it to our children, we owe it to our God, to put a stop to this base indifference to murder, and making excuses for men who will not risk anything for the preservation of human life and the honor of the State.***

The gentlemen from Wilcox (Mr. Jenkins) makes the argument you must not have a law to punish the Sheriff for failing to defend a prisoner after he is in the possession of the law, because forsooth sometimes people will want to hang a rapist. Let us build up a sentiment that when a man is in the hands of the law he is sacred, sacred from lawless violence, sacred for justice's sake. Every citizen in Alabama is interested. All of our civilization is based on the idea that "no man can be deprived of life, liberty, or property without due process of law." Without its enforcement there can be no civilization—no government worthy of the name.

Public opinion is powerful. It makes war or it makes peace. It protects the helpless when no other power can do so.*****

We are thought to be disbelievers in the sanctity of human life—if that life happens to be that of a Negro. We are looked upon as tacitly consenting, if not openly approving, the right of any body of men to mete out death, without trial or evidence, if the suspect can be found, not for rape alone, but for any offense against the laws. As Southern men, let us ask ourselves how far appearances justify the belief. Have we stopped mobs at rape? Is not the thirst of mob violence for blood as great in many lesser crimes? And are not our courts open? Is justice administered by our judges or by our own juries? How many of these outbreaks and assaults upon officers and jails have been punished? We know and the world knows. Does it not behoove us to pause and consider? To devise some remedy? To strike some blow for the sanctity of human life and the honour of our State?

These mob executions are brutalizing our children, blunting our religion, and undermining our civilization. Can any one within the sound of my voice rise up and say this is not true? We are undermining all noble ideals of duty and manhood. When we [say that in] some places, that a Sheriff is not bound to take any risks, even to loss of life and limb, in defense of a prisoner, we abdicate all our past and bow down and worship false and base standards of duty. Why should not the Sheriff die at his post, as well as the locomotive engineer, or the priest, or the doctor, or the soldier? (Applause)

We are setting a baleful example to our young sons, who are coming up around us, if we teach that when a prisoner is given to an officer, that officer is free to desert his post of duty, because there may be danger in it. ***that it will go out from these halls that the law shall be executed, that we despise mob violence, and we intend that human life shall be regarded as sacred and be taken only by the law. (Applause.)

SOURCE: Association of Southern Women for the Prevention of Lynching Papers (microfilm).

On January 23, 1906, someone raped a white woman near Chattanooga, in Hamilton County, Tennessee. Sheriff Joseph Shipp arrested and jailed Ed Johnson for the crime. Mobs formed and roamed the streets, but the court system did its work: a grand jury indicted Johnson, and a petit jury convicted him in a mob so dominated by a mob mentality and out-of-control racism that no juror would have dared vote to acquit. In this tumult, the judge sentenced Johnson to death. Johnson's attorneys appealed to the U.S. Supreme Court, pointing out, quite accurately, that the state had not given their client a fair trial. Justice John Marshall Harlan found merit in this appeal and stayed the execution.

On March 19 the clerk of the Supreme Court telegraphed the news to Shipp that Harlan had called off Johnson's execution and that he should now consider Johnson a federal prisoner. All over Chattanooga whites did not bother to hide their anger on hearing news of this federal "intrusion" in their affairs. A mob gathered, broke into the jail, took Johnson, and hanged him from the Tennessee River bridge.

The mob that hanged Johnson challenged the authority of the Supreme Court, and it did so facing little or no resistance from Shipp and his deputies. Shipp gave a newspaper interview in which he confessed his disdain for the Supreme Court. In Washington the justices talked among themselves and worried about just how to react to such an obvious and deliberate affront to their authority. The Justice Department wanted to prosecute the lynchers under the 1871 Enforcement Act, a move that would have expanded federal authority over mob violence. The justices rejected that option and, instead, found Shipp in contempt of their Court. He served ninety days.

98. *Justice Melville W. Fuller, Opinion of the U.S. Supreme Court, in* United States v. Shipp, 1909

On May 28, at Birmingham, Alabama, defendant Shipp himself, in an interview, reported and printed the next morning in The Birmingham Age-Herald, said:

"'The first I knew of the mob was through a telephone message I received from The Chattanooga Times office, for they had cut the wires at the county jail immediately upon their arrival. I dressed as quickly as possible and went to the jail, and found a crowd of about seventy-five people around it, most of them being in disguise. I made my way through the crowd into the jail and began remonstrating with them against taking any drastic steps. They seized me and took me upstairs, locking me up in a bathroom. The members of the mob told me they meant no violence to me. I argued with them against doing anything at all, since the law had so far taken its proper course. I am frank to say that I did not attempt to hurt any of them, and would not have made such an attempt if I could. In the first place, I could have done no good, as I was overwhelmed by numbers.

"'The Supreme Court of the United States was responsible for this lynching. I had given that negro every protection that I could. For fourteen days I had guarded and protected him myself. The authorities had urged me to use one or two military companies in doing so, but I told them I would land the negro in jail, which I did, individually.

"'Many nights before the lynching there had been a sufficient guard around the jail. I had looked for no trouble that night and, on the contrary, did not look for it until the next day. That night no one was on duty except the jailer, which is the usual guard at our jail, as well as in other counties.

"'In my opinion the act of the Supreme Court of the United States in not allowing the case to remain in our courts was the most unfortunate thing in the history of Tennessee. I was determined that the case should be put in the hands of the law, as it was. The jury that tried the negro Johnson was as good as ever sat in a jury box.

"'The people of Hamilton County were willing to let the law take its course until it became known that the case would not probably be disposed of for four or five years by the Supreme Court of the United States. The people would not submit to this, and I do not wonder at it.

"'These proceedings in the United States Supreme Court recently appear to me to be only a matter of politics. I do not wish to appear in the light of defying the United States court, but I did my duty. I am conscious of it, thoroughly conscious of it, and I am ready for any conditions that may come up.'"

The testimony of the reporter that Shipp made these statements was corroborated by the evidence of another reporter who interviewed Shipp on the following day regarding them, and is not denied by Shipp except in an immaterial particular. From this it appears that defendant Shipp looked for trouble on the twentieth, but, as he says, not that night; that he did not attempt to hurt any of the mob, "and would not have made such an attempt if I could."

He evidently resented the necessary order of this court as an alien intrusion, and declared that the court was responsible for the lynching. According to him, "the people of Hamilton County were willing to let the law take its course until it became known that the case would not probably be disposed of for four or five years by the Supreme Court of the United States." "But," he added, "the people would not submit to this, and I do not wonder at it." In other words, his view was that because this court, in the discharge of its duty entered the order which it did, that therefore the people of Hamilton County would not submit to its mandate, and hence the court became responsible for the mob. He took the view expressed by several members of the mob on the afternoon of the nineteenth and before the lynching, when they said, referring to the Supreme Court, that "they had no business interfering with our business at all." His reference to the "people" was significant, for he was a candidate for re-election and had been told that his saving the prisoner from the first attempt to mob him would cost him his place, and he had answered that he wished the mob had got him before he did.

It seems to us that to say that the sheriff and his deputies did not anticipate that the mob would attempt to lynch Johnson on the night of the nineteenth is to charge them with gross neglect of duty and with an ignorance of conditions in a matter which vitally concerned them all as officers, and is directly contrary to their own testimony. It is absurd to contend that officers of the law who have been through the experiences these defendants had passed through two months prior to the actual lynching did not know that a lynching probably would be attempted on the nineteenth. Under the facts shown, when the sheriff and his deputies assert that they expected a mob on the twentieth, they practically concede the allegation of the information that they were informed and had every reason to believe that an attempt would be made on the evening of the nineteenth or early on the morning of the twentieth.

In view of this, Shipp's failure to make the slightest preparation to resist the mob; the absence of all of the deputies, except Gibson, from the jail during the mob's proceedings, occupying a period of some hours in the early evening; the action of Shipp in not resisting the mob and his failure to make any reasonable effort to save Johnson or identify the members of the mob, justify the inference of a disposition upon his part to render it easy for the mob to lynch Johnson, and to acquiesce in the lynching. After Shipp was informed that a mob was at the jail, and he could not do otherwise than go there, he did not and in fact at no time hindered the mob or caused it to be interfered with, or helped in the slightest degree to protect Johnson. And this in utter disregard of this court's mandate and in defiance of this court's orders.

SOURCE: 214 U.S. 386.

Shipp faced a real dilemma. Any sheriff daring to protect a black prisoner from an inflamed mob risked bringing down the wrath of the voters on his own head. In Baker County, Georgia, authorities accused two black men, Oscar Gordon and Oscar Gordon Jr., of murdering a white man. Their attorney, Delacey Allen, asked for a change of venue and called on the sheriff to make the case that racial hatred was rampant in the county. When he testified, Jack Griffin Sr. had been sheriff for twelve years. As this excerpt shows, Sheriff Griffin presided over a county particularly prone to lynching, though he did not want to admit it.

99. *Sheriff Jack Griffin Sr., Testimony in* State v. Oscar Gordon and Oscar Gordon Jr., July 1933

Q.: Tell the court what were the threats made to you regarding this crime.

A.: There have been several different ones to caution me that a bunch was going to kill me.

Q.: Why did they say they were going to kill you?

A.: They seemed to think I was upholding Oscar Gordon and his boy and they had it in for me.

Q.: Let me ask you for your own sake right here, have you any desire for anything but justice in this particular case?

A.: No, sir, I say if Oscar Gordon and his boy killed him they ought to suffer and I am willing to do my duty towards it.

Q.: Will you state to the court whether you are or are not upholding them in this supposed crime?

A.: No, sir, I am not upholding them.

Q.: You have heard some of the people who lived in that community, you have heard that some of them have made threats that they would kill you because of the fact that they through you were upholding them?

A.: Not all of them were living in that community.

Q.: Some of them lived in that community and some in other communities in this county?

A.: Not all of them lived in this county.

Q.: Some were from outside the county?

A.: Yes, sir.

Q.: You have had threats communicated to you that people residing in this county threatened to kill you because of your supposed upholding of the negroes in this crime?

A.: Yes, sir.

Q.: Do you or did you know a negro by the name of T. J. Thomas?

A.: Yes, sir.

Q.: Was he out at the home of Oscar Gordon the night Mr. Pat Kirksey was killed?

A.: I heard he was.

Q.: It is a generally accepted fact in the community that he was there?

A.: Yes, sir.

Q.: Some statements have been made that he tried to help do this killing?

A.: I have heard a little of that the last few days, all I have heard has been lately.

Q.: I will ask if you know where T. J. Thomas is?

A.: Yes, sir, he is dead.

Q.: Was he lynched?

A.: Yes, sir.

Q.: After the night when Mr. Pat Kirksey was killed?

A.: Yes, sir.

Q.: It is generally accepted in this county that white people did that?

A.: Yes, sir.

Q.: Feeling then was pretty high towards all those negroes, was it not, who were out there and supposed to have taken part in this killing?

A.: Yes, sir, I think so.

Q.: It must have been if they threatened to kill you because they thought you upheld the negroes? Did you know a negro by the name of Rich Marshall?

A.: Yes, Sir. Richard Marshall.

Q.: Was he lynched in this county?

A.: Yes, sir.

Q.: It is generally accepted that he was lynched by white people?

A.: I don't know.

Q.: You know he was lynched.

A.: Yes, sir.

Q.: Where was the dead body found?

A.: Tied to a tree near Barnett's bridge.

Q.: About when was the dead body found?

A.: I think it was on the night of the 16th.

Q.: Of June?

A.: Yes, sir.

Q.: 1933?

A.: Yes, sir.

Q.: After Mr. Pat Kirksey was killed at the home of Oscar Gordon?

A.: Yes, sir.

Q.: . . . If that case were tried here and I asked you to help us select a jury could you with reasonable certainty select men who were not in that mob?

A.: No, sir.

Q.: You don't know of your own knowledge all the men who were in that mob?

A.: No, sir, not all of them.

Q.: You needn't go into that. You need not name them. In your opinion could those negroes come down here and get what is called a fair and impartial trial in this county?

A.: I think so, as fair here as anywhere the crime had been committed.

Q.: May I state, sir, that I agree with you, but in your opinion, knowing what is fair and impartial, and knowing that the minds of a considerable part of the county are inflamed over this recurring difficulty between the whites and blacks, is it your opinion that these two defendants, Oscar Gordon and Oscar Gordon Jr., can get an absolutely fair and impartial trial in this county?

A.: I think so.

Q.: Isn't what you really think, sir, let me ask you if you really think they would get as fair a trial here as they could get in any other places where the same thing had taken place?

A.: I think so. . . .

Q.: Assuming that these negroes were brought back here for trial and that from some technical point of the law that they were turned aloose in this county, in your opinion would it be safe for them to remain in this county?

A.: I don't think so.

Q.: In the event they were acquitted and turned aloose do you think it would be safe for them to remain in this county?

A.: No, sir.

Q.: Do you think any violence would be done them?

A.: Yes sir.

Q.: Do you think they would be lynched?

A.: Yes, sir. . . .

Q.: Were these negroes arrested on June 4th or about that time?

A.: Yes, sir.

Q.: Were they placed in your custody?

A.: Yes, sir.

Q.: Where did you take them?

A.: I sent them to Camilla.

Q.: Why did you send them to Camilla?

A.: I had information that likely they would lynch them that night, and that a crowd would come and try to take them and I didn't want to have any trouble.

SOURCE: Criminal Evidence Record, July term 1933, Baker Superior Court, Baker County Courthouse, Newton, Georgia.

NOTES

1. At the beginning of the twenty-first century prosecutors in South Carolina and Virginia discovered their states' old lynching laws and began using them again, often against black youth gangs.

2. *New York Times*, August 17, 1873, July 15, 1884.

3. For the Carrollton massacre, see Christopher Waldrep, *The Many Faces of Judge Lynch: Extralegal Violence and Punishment in America* (New York: Palgrave Macmillan, 2002), 103–107.

4. James Zachariah George served as the U.S. senator from Mississippi from 1880 until his death in 1897. Born in Georgia, he moved to Carrollton in 1826.

5. See *Vicksburg Evening Post*, December 29, 1884, regarding the thirteen-year-old son of Jordan Parker, tortured with a red-hot stove until he accused his father of train wrecking. When the *New Orleans Times-Democrat* first reported the story, Cashman could not believe it: "We are assured that this story is utterly unfounded, and that no violence or injury was inflicted upon the boy." In fact, the story was true, as this editorial reflects.

6. Confederate veteran Robert Lowry served as governor from 1882 to 1890.

7. Richard Gambino, *Vendetta: A True Story of the Worst Lynching in America, the Mass Murder of Italian-Americans in New Orleans in 1891, the Vicious Motivations Behind It, and the Tragic Repercussions That Linger to This Day* (Garden City, N.Y.: Doubleday, 1977).

8. Henry Cabot Lodge, "Lynching Law and Unrestricted Immigration," *North American Review* 152 (1890): 602–612.

9. *Correspondence Regarding the Lynching of Certain Italian Subjects*, Senate Report, 56th Congress, 1st sess., Document No. 104.

10. *Atlanta Journal*, July 20, 21, 27, 28, 29, 1897; August 3, 1897.

11. Ibid., July 22, 1897.

12. Ibid., July 26, 1897.

13. Ibid., July 27, 1897.

14. Ibid., July 29, 1897.

15. For Felton's life, see LeeAnn Whites, "Rebecca Latimer Felton and the Wife's Farm: The Class and Racial Politics of Gender Reform," *Georgia Historical Quarterly* 76 (summer 1992): 354–372.

16. *Savannah Morning News*, August 12, 1897.

17. H. Leon Prather Sr., "We Have Taken a City, A Centennial Essay," in David S. Cecelski and Timothy B. Tyson, eds., *Democracy Betrayed: The Wilmington Race Riot of 1898 and Its Legacy* (Chapel Hill: University of North Carolina Press, 1998), 15–39.

18. W. Fitzhugh Brundage, *Lynching in the New South: Georgia and Virginia, 1880–1930* (Urbana: University of Illinois Press, 1993), 201–202.

8

Western Lynching in an Industrializing Age

After the Civil War American business expanded. From old industries modern corporations grew, building extensive and powerful bureaucracies. Railroad companies became America's first truly big business. Railroad tracks quadrupled between 1870 and 1890, many of them heading West. Iron and steel production scrambled to keep up with the demand. The railroads rationalized transportation, dividing the country into time zones and standardizing the tracks. For many Americans the West now seemed more tightly connected to the rest of the country. Gustavius Swift built new links between east and west by constructing a fleet of refrigerated railroad cars that allowed him to centralize beef processing. Industrialization, some have written, brought with it a "great bourgeois revolution" that empowered lawyers as it regularized commerce and agriculture. Institutions arose to discipline persons to meet middle-class expectations. The rowdy western gunslinger began to seem like an artifact of some earlier age.[1]

All this accelerated sentimentalizing of the "Old West" and led American men to seek new ways to establish their manhood, including violence. One student of western lynchings, Stephen J. Leonard, recently calculated that, "between 1882 and 1902, Montana, Wyoming, Colorado, New Mexico and Arizona formed a kind of lynching belt that outdid most of the South in lynchings on a per capita basis." Leonard writes that lynching persisted in Colorado because while respectable people in cities turned against lynching, new towns, with weak law enforcement, kept springing up.[2] This repeats the frontier argument that W. J. Cash and Edward Ayers have applied to the South.

In 1887 Hubert Howe Bancroft expounded the classic westerners' defense of extralegal jurisprudence in a massive two-volume behemoth that recounted in great and positive detail the actions and movements of the 1850s San Francisco Vigilance Committees. In 1851 and 1856 San Francisco citizens banded together, organizing extralegal police patrols, staging trials, and executing persons accused of crimes. The regularly constituted authorities, the vigilantes charged, had been corrupted and failed to keep good order. Bancroft stoutly supported the San Francisco vigilantes, but the rise of bourgeois sensitivities brought "mob" violence into disrepute, associating it with the laboring classes. He essentially made a class argument: when good people became vigilantes, then their violence deserved respect. They do not oppose the law; they *are* the law. A "tumultuous rabble," on the other hand, does not truly represent "the people" and therefore does not deserve the name "vigilance committee." Bancroft carefully distinguished between lynchers and vigilantes, although he conceded that, as a word, "lynching" had gotten into bad odor through the happenstance of usage.[3] Bancroft's arguments were not original to him or unique to California. In the midst of the Revolution, John Adams had made a remarkably similar argument. Tyrants can be dethroned by the people, Adams wrote, and then explained: "We do not mean by the word *people*, the vile populace or rabble of the country . . . but the greater and more judicious part of the subjects."[4] In 1887 Bancroft continued Adams's argument.

100. *Hubert Howe Bancroft, "Popular Tribunals," 1887*

It was on the western frontier of the United States, and during the last half century, that the popular tribunal in its broadest proportions was reached. All that time and before it, beginning just back of the English plantations, this frontier had been shifting, extending farther and farther to the westward, until the valley of the Mississippi was reached. Upon this border, as upon the edge of mighty fermentations, accumulated the scum of the commonwealth. The spirit of evil was ever strong, and government was weak. Society there was low and brutal, and the lynchers were not always much better than the lynched. After Missouri and Arkansas for a time had constituted the frontier, a leap was made by war and western progress to California, and the popular tribunal, seemingly purified by the passage, settled upon the newly found goldfields. Here, at the Ultima Thule of western migration, the institution found itself in an element totally different from any it had ever before enjoyed. The people were active and able; many of them were educated and intelligent; most of them were honest. But there were some rogues present, else enginery for punishment had never been required. It was then that the popular tribunal assumed respectability and took a new name. The somewhat besmeared terms mob law, lynch-law, and the like, were discarded, and the more pleasing titles of Regulators, Committee of Safety, and Committee of Vigilance were adopted.

In Nevada, Utah, Montana, and Idaho, in all frontier settlements, before the machinery of territorial legislatures and law courts was in working order, before laws were framed or executed, a tribunal formed of citizens was found necessary to prevent wholesale robbery and murder. Order-loving men, as were they who composed these tribunals, were backward enough in assuming the unwelcome duties, usually taking no steps to organize until after a score or two of murderers had escaped punishment. Each new western state, as it began to be settled, attracted thither villains of every dye, who kept the community in constant fear until it purged itself by the swift and sure executions of mobocracy or vigilance committees.

What then has the popular tribunal here become? What is a vigilance committee, and what mobocracy? The terms vigilance committee, mob-law, lynch-law, are not, as many suppose, synonymous. In some respects they are diametrically opposed in principle and in purpose. The vigilance committee is not a mob; it is to a mob as revolution is to rebellion, the name being somewhat according to its strength. Neither is a tumultuous rabble a vigilance committee. Indeed, prominent among its other functions is that of holding brute force and vulgar sentiment in wholesome fear. The vigilance committee will itself break the law, but it does not allow others to do so. It has the highest respect for law, and would be friendly with the law, notwithstanding the law is sometimes disposed to be ill-natured; yet it has a higher respect for itself than for ill-administered law. Often it has assisted officers of the law in catching offenders, and has even gone so far as to hand insignificant and filthy criminals over to courts of justice for trial rather than soil its fingers with them.

The doctrine of Vigilance, if I may so call the idea or principle embodied in the term vigilance committee, is that the people, or a majority of them, possess the right, nay, that it is their bounden duty, to hold perpetual vigil in all matters relating to their governance, to guard their laws with circumspection, and sleeplessly to watch their servants chosen to execute them. Yet more is implied. Possessing this right, and acknowledging the obligation, it is their further right and duty, whenever they see misbehavior on the part of their servants, whenever they see the laws which they have made trampled upon, distorted, or prostituted, to rise in their sovereign privilege and remove such unfaithful servants, lawfully if possible, arbitrarily if necessary. The law must govern, absolutely, eternally, say, the men of vigilance. Suffer inconvenience, injustice if need be, rather than attempt illegal reform. Every right-minded man recognizes the necessity of good conduct in human associations, to secure which experience teaches that rule is essential. In a free republican form of government every citizen contributes to the making of the laws, and is interested in seeing them executed and obeyed. The good citizen, above all others, insists that the law of the land shall be regarded. But to have law, statutes must be enacted by the people; governments must be administered by representatives of the people; officials, to be officials, must be chosen by the people. Law is the voice of the people. Now it is not the voice of the people that vigilance would disregard, but the voice of corrupt officials and bad men. Law is the will of the community as a whole; it is therefore omnipotent. When law is not omnipotent, it is nothing. This is why, when law fails—that is to say, when a power rises in society antagonistic at once to statutory law and to the will of the people—the people must crush the enemy of their law or be crushed by it. A true vigilance committee is this expression of power on the part of the people in the absence or impotence of law. Omnipotence in rule being necessary, and law failing to be omnipotent, the element here denominated vigilance becomes omnipotent, not as a usurper, but as a friend in an emergency. Vigilance recognizes fully the supremacy of law, flies to its rescue when beaten down by its natural enemy, crime, and lifts it up, that it may always be supreme; and if the law must be broken to save the state, then it breaks it soberly, conscientiously, and under the formulas of law, not in a feeling of revenge, or in a manner usual to the disorderly rabble.

SOURCE: Hubert Howe Bancroft, *Popular Tribunals*, 2 vols. (San Francisco: History Company, 1887), 1:7–10.

In the same year that Bancroft published *Popular Tribunals* citizens around the northern California town of Colusa hanged and shot Ho Ah Heung, a Chinese man they called Hong Di. The *Chico Enterprise* had campaigned against the Chinese presence in California for some time and did not hesitate to applaud the lynching. Colusa had a long history of lynching. In 1867 the *Colusa Sun* reported that a mob of family men had hanged a Spaniard and an Indian, both charged with rape. "The gentlemen" in the mob, the newspaper reported, "felt that if these fellows were permitted to escape that no white woman would be safe."[5]

On April 7, 1887, Ho Ah Heung carried his repeating rifle to the kitchen where he worked as a cook for the Joseph Billiou family. On that day he shot into the dining room, killing Julia Billiou, Joseph's wife, and wounding the Billiou's hired hand, William Weaver. Heung then ran. White posses searched for him in the several Chinese camps along the Sacramento River. One posseman, James Hagan, ransacked cabins at a place called "Mr. Young's camp." According to the notes of his later testimony, Hagan went to a cabin and "called to Chinaman," demanding admittance to the cabin's dim interior. After patiently waiting twenty minutes, or even half an hour, Hagan later claimed, "the door partly opened" before "a man run out of the cabin with a gun." Hagan shot the man down, only to turn the body over and find he had killed the wrong Chinese man. A coroner's jury listened to his story and voted to "fully exonerate" Hagan.[6]

Whites captured the fugitive on May 22. Jailed, Ho Ah Heung confessed, saying he acted after discovering Julia Billiou in the barn with Weaver when Joseph Billiou was in San Francisco. Weaver threatened Heung, vowing to kill him before Joseph returned. Although he had killed Julia Billiou, Heung admitted, he had meant to kill Weaver. The local newspapers refused to print this story but hissed to its readers that Heung had dared defame his victim. Other newspapers, however, did print Hong's confession, and it circulated through Colusa, stirring up more anger against Heung.[7]

When a trial jury failed to order Heung executed, the victim's family immediately objected and tried to storm the courtroom.[8] Authorities blocked that attempt, but a day later a mob entered the jail and killed Heung. According to the *San Francisco Chronicle*, "everyone" in Colusa approved the lynching.[9] The *Chico Enterprise* published a list of the jurors with a hangman's noose drawn around their names.[10] Other newspapers justified the lynching in the same way: this was an act of "the people." In this case Bancroft's popular sovereignty argument justified a racially motivated lynching in the presence of a working criminal-justice system. Southern lynchings followed the same formula.

101. *Chico Enterprise, "The People Execute the Law,"* 1887

A dispatch from Colusa this morning over the Pacific Postal line says that the excitement at Colusa continued to increase in intensity, and farmers came in from all directions determined to execute the law, notwithstanding the verdict of the jury. A force of nearly 2,000 men met and organized under competent leaders. They were calm and determined, and at 12:40 they moved upon the jail. There was a formidable opposition to their entrance, but the more formidable appearance of the men demanding justice seemed to over-awe the guard at the jail, who were easily overpowered, and the way to the Sheriff's office was made easy. Hong Di was confined in what is called the "trap," chained hand and foot, and was got out of the jail without difficulty. The guard being guarded by the citizens offering no resistance. [sic] The prisoner was then taken to the turntable of the narrow-gauge railroad, where he was asked why he killed Mrs. Billou. He confessed that he was drunk and did not know what he was doing.

HE WAS STRUNG UP BY THE NECK,

And in five minutes was taken down, but an examination showed the heart still to be beating, and up he went again, until he was pronounced dead, and he was then left for the Coroner to take charge of.

We confess that we have nothing to say against the action of the people of Colusa. This was a case in which the prisoner had a fair trial, and was found guilty of murder in the first degree. His crime was a cold-blooded murder. His victim was an amiable woman, wife and mother. The law gives the jury the privilege to fix the punishment at imprisonment for life, and one crank (Gay) on the jury brought the other eleven to his terms, and the verdict had the recommendation of "imprisonment for life." The people were not satisfied—the extreme penalty was demanded, and the people executed the law. "He that sheddeth man's blood, by man shall his blood be shed."

Special to the Enterprise

(From Our Own Reporter)

Jury yesterday morning brought in a verdict of murder in the first degree with imprisonment for life. Great excitement prevailed and a rush was made for the prisoner in Court but the crowd was repulsed by the Sheriff's posse. Excitement grew stronger all day and about five o'clock the Colusa Guard was ordered out by the Governor. The company reported for duty fifty strong at eight o'clock, and were posted around the jail. Sentries were put out, and the Court House yard and walks proclaimed under martial law. The company held the place until 11:30 when they were relieved by the Sheriff and returned to the Armory.

Word was passed around that Hong Di had been removed from jail, which rapidly spread. Wagons had been rolling into town all evening, loaded with men, and a mob was fully organized one hundred strong, armed to the teeth. The mob did not believe the story and made a rush for the jail at 12:30.

The front door was not locked, and they took complete possession.

Hong's place of concealment was guessed by the leaders and no attempt was made to break down cell doors. Under the jail is a small, dark cell, reached by a trap door. Under a bed, in a back room, Hong was found, nearly dead with terror. He was hauled out by the struggling mob, marched rapidly up Fifth, and thence to Main street, to the depot, followed by thousands of people.

A noose was placed around his neck and the rope was thrown over the turntable. Hong was pressed to talk and said Weaver had always been good to him, that he was drunk when he did the shooting. He was soon strung up and hung for twenty minutes, while the crowd cheered. The mob then left.

The body was cut down by the Coroner this morning and an inquest held. The verdict was that he came to his death by hanging at the hands of unknown men. The verdict attributes the deed to the verdict of the trial jury, brought in yesterday, and censures that jury with scorching language. The town is wild with excitement and delirious with joy. The only feeling in the community is that the lynching was a righteous deed.

SOURCE: *Chico Enterprise,* July 15, 1887.

102. Red Bluff News, *"A Righteous Execution,"* 1887

The lynching of Hong Di at Colusa is indorsed by nearly all the people and the papers of the State, so far as there has been an expression of opinion. Two newspapers, the Sacramento *Bee* and the San Francisco *Examiner,* are notably vehement in denouncing the act, however, and work themselves into a very fury of passion in their attack upon the people of Colusa county. It is a habit of the *Bee* to indorse lynch law either in the headings which it puts upon dispatches relating to such events or in its comments upon them. It is but a short time since the *Examiner* advocated the election to the Presidency of a man who headed an organized mob in San Francisco that hanged criminals who had not been tried. Why have these papers so suddenly and so savagely changed front?

The crime of Hong Di was one peculiarly atrocious. With rifle and axe and butcher knife sharpened like a razor, he had prepared for his fearful work. But he partly failed, and, in fear, fled out into the night. After skulking for weeks, he was arrested and quietly handed over to the officers of the law. Then the infamous wretch, in the wild hope of excusing his crime, most foully lied about his dead victim,—a noble woman, beloved in her neighborhood, whose virtues are proclaimed by all who knew her— and in this infamous lie he had the co-operation of the two papers named above and of the Chinese Consul. They became *particeps criminis* with him, accessories after the fact. These four—Hong Di, Fred. Bee, the other *Bee*, and the *Examiner*—danced the witches' dance around poor Mrs. Billou's grave, and we can still see them casting slander and defamation into the seething cauldron, and can hear their unholy incantation, "Like a hell broth, boil and bubble." The trial of the assassin came on. The verdict was a shock to the moral sense of the State. The law failed, justice was disregarded, infamous slander was excused, the foulest murder was to go virtually unpunished. Indignant and righteously moved to right a wrong, the County of Colusa rose up and executed the murderer. We applaud the act. Hong Di is silent now, but the *Examiner* and the *Bee* are frothing at the mouth and cursing, and soon we shall hear the clamor of the other Bee. It matters little. Justice has been done, rude but right. All men who respect womanly virtue and rebuke defamation of the dead will uphold the course of the grand County of Colusa. Hong Di deserved his fate. So perish all murderers of benevolence and assassins of reputation!

SOURCE: *Red Bluff News*, reprinted in the *Chico Enterprise*, July 15, 1887.

Bancroft defended vigilantism as the western frontier faded into sentimentalized memory. By 1887 the buffalo had been nearly exterminated and railroad traffic routinely crossed the plains. On the northern plains cattle barons organized the landscape for profit. In London the Anglo-American Cattle Company had formed in 1879. Two years later James S. Brisbin published *The Beef Bonanza, or How to Get Rich on the Plains*. More corporations followed the Anglo-American Cattle Company. By 1890 the census showed 3,125 farms in Wyoming, and foreign capital financed large cattle operations. The Wyoming cattlemen acted "more like captains of industry than Texas cowboys," Richard Slotkin has written.[11]

In addition to the cattle barons, a variety of settlers migrated to Wyoming, a crowd of mustered-out soldiers, prospectors, townsfolk, real cowboys, urban cowboys, and farmers. They established homesteads and turned their tiny herds onto the open range, where they mingled with the big herds. At roundup time, a small-time rancher could increase his herd by picking up unbranded calves and calling them his own. The big ranchers began calling all the smaller operators "rustlers" and complaining that it did no good to take rustlers to court because "rustler juries" always acquitted. In 1891 some of the large cattlemen had decided to organize a private army to attack the small settlers, the "rustlers."[12] Historians call the resulting violence between large and small ranchers the "Johnson County War."

Sam Travers Clover of the *Chicago Herald* wrote a fictionalized account of his involvement in the Johnson County War, thinly disguising himself as "Paul Travers" and the *Chicago Herald* as the *Chicago Mercury*. Clover described himself as hearing of the lynching party by chance, and then approaching a big cattleman for permission to join the expedition. Clover joined the lynchers, promising to publish the story from their point of view. The *Herald* had no trouble supporting western lynching, and it sympathized with racial lynchers as well. When Ohio whites lynched an African American named Henry Corbin, the *Herald* applauded, referring to Corbin as "the black fiend" and warning that "the first insult offered by a colored man will be met with a stringent rebuke."[13] The *Herald* carried this same spirit to its reports on western violence.

103. *Sam Travers Clover, "The Johnson County War,"* 1892

[Travers] now resolved to present his letter of introduction to Mr. Baird, and boldly ask his intercession and indorsement, with a view to gaining admission to the lynching party.

"Do you know I have been trying to solve your mission here for three days or ever since you arrived," confessed Mr. Baird, when the ice had been broken, and Paul had frankly told all he knew and the ambitions he cherished. "Your suspicions, I don't mind stating, in confidence, are based on facts, but whether I can swear you into the company is doubtful. This is no fife-and-drum mission, and I should think a newspaperman the last person to be taken along." But Paul was prepared for that argument, and had a good answer ready to refute it.

"Now see here, Mr. Baird," he reasoned, "your people are starting out on a lawbreaking expedition, but, as they believe, in a righteous cause. They claim that justice is a farce in the cattle counties toward the Big Horn range, which compels the association of stock-growers to organize and administer a taste of Judge Lynch's court.

"You must admit that a tremendous howl will be raised by the newspapers inimical to your interests, and all sorts of wild-eyed stories will be afloat concerning the operations of the regulators. If I go along as a non-combatant, friendly to the interests of the expedition, it stands to reason I will not give you the worst of it in my published reports. In telling the story, at least there will be no disposition to turn public sympathy from you, and as the truth will be better than the distorted yarns put in circulation by the rustler sympathizers, your side certainly will be the gainer by having a veracious, disinterested reporter in the ranks. . . . The *Mercury* has sent me here to join your party, and I'd rather get the news at firsthand than hang around the camp picking up chance gossip in lieu of facts."

There was subtle reasoning in Paul's presentation, and he noted with secret joy that Mr. Baird appeared to be impressed.

SOURCE: Samuel Travers Clover, *On Special Assignment: Being the Further Adventures of Paul Travers; Showing How He Succeeded as a Newspaper Reporter* (Boston: Lothrop, 1903), 228–229.

In his newspaper article, Clover explained that "for upwards of ten years the reputable cattle owners and stockmen of Wyoming have borne with an equanimity past all belief the continuous raids and depredations committed by the cattle thieves that infest this region." Clover went on to charge that the courts had failed to maintain the law, often because county officials had joined with the cattle rustlers, "sharing the profits of their nefarious business."[14]

The more famous defense of the Johnson County lynchings came from Owen Wister. An easterner who went west to escape racial diversity, Wister created the quintessential cowboy character in his fictional Virginian. To distinguish western lynchings from the more barbaric southern variety, he invents this scene between a former federal judge and the naïve Molly Wood who imagines that all mob law must be treated as evil. Wister did not agree. Wister imagined a difference between white southerners' lynching in the South and his white southerner's lynching in Wyoming. Yet the Virginian fought to establish civilization, a job he thought best accomplished by people of the right class and race.[15]

Not everyone familiar with the Johnson County War agreed with Wister. Asa Shinn Mercer took a critical look in *The Banditti of the Plains, or the Cattlemen's Invasion of Wyoming*. Later, Jack Schaefer wrote another novel about the Johnson County War, one that took the side of the small ranchers rather than the wealthy landowners Wister favored. Schaefer titled his book, which became a movie in 1953, *Shane*.[16]

104. Owen Wister, "The Virginian," 1902

Judge Henry . . . had been a federal judge; he had been an upright judge; he had met the responsibilities of his difficult office not only with learning, which is desirable, but also with courage and common sense besides, and these are essential. He had been a stanch servant of the law. And now he was invited to defend that which, at first sight, nay, even at second and third sight, must always seem a defiance of the law more injurious than crime itself. . . .

"I sent him myself on that business," the Judge reflected uncomfortably. "I am partly responsible for the lynching. . . ."

"Judge Henry," said Molly Wood, also coming straight to the point, "have you come to tell me that you think well of lynching?"

He met her. "Of burning Southern negroes in public, no. Of hanging Wyoming cattle thieves in private, yes. You perceive there's a difference, don't you?"

"Not in principle," said the girl, dry and short.

"Oh—dear—me!" slowly exclaimed the Judge. "I am sorry that you cannot see that, because I think that I can. And I think that you have just as much sense as I have." The Judge made himself very grave and very good-humored at the same time. The poor girl was strung to a high pitch, and spoke harshly in spite of herself.

"What is the difference in principle?" she demanded.

". . . I consider the burning a proof that the South is semi-barbarous, and the hanging a proof that Wyoming is determined to become civilized. We do not torture our criminals when we lynch them. We do not invite spectators to enjoy their death agony. We put no such hideous disgrace upon the United States. We execute our criminals by the swiftest means, and in the quietest way. Do you think the principle is the same?"

Molly had listened to him with attention. ". . . Both defy law and order."

"Ah, but do they both? Now we're getting near the principle."

"Why, yes. Ordinary citizens take the law in their own hands."

". . . Out of whose hands do they take the law?"

"The court's."

"What made the courts?"

"I don't understand."

"How did there come to be any courts?"

"The Constitution."

"How did there come to be any Constitution? Who made it?"

"The delegates, I suppose."

"Who made the delegates?"

"I suppose they were elected, or appointed, or something."

"And who elected them?"

"Of course the people elected them."

"Call them the ordinary citizens," said the Judge. "I like your term. They are where the law comes from, you see. For they chose the delegates who made the Constitution that provided for the courts. There's your machinery. These are the hands into which ordinary citizens have put the law. So you see, at best, when they lynch they only take back what they once gave. Now we'll take your two cases that you say are the same in principle. I think that they are not. For in the South they take a negro from jail where he was waiting to be duly hung. The South has never claimed that the law would let him go. But in Wyoming the law has been letting our cattle-thieves go for two years. We are in a very bad way, and we are trying to make that way a little better until civilization can reach us. At present we lie beyond its pale. The courts, or rather the juries, into whose hands we have put the law, are not dealing the law. . . . And so when your ordinary citizen sees this, and sees that he has placed justice in a dead hand, he must take justice back into his own hands where it was once at the beginning of all things. Call this primitive, if you will. But so far from being a *defiance* of the law, it is an *assertion* of it—the fundamental assertion of self-governing men, upon whom our whole social fabric is based."

SOURCE: Owen Wister, *The Virginian* (New York: Macmillan, 1902), 432–436.

The hired Texans that traveled to Johnson County left behind a state with its own history of lynching violence, much of it directed at Mexicans. But while mob violence long plagued the Texas-Mexico border, most students of mob law have neglected Mexican lynchings. The historians William D. Carrigan and Clive Webb have asserted that, between 1882 and 1930, a Mexican caught in Texas faced a greater statistical risk of lynching than a black southerner. These Mexican lynchings cannot be excused as having been made necessary by frontier conditions. They occurred long after authorities had established courts.[17] State department officers periodically investigated reports of lynchings carried out by white Americans against Mexican citizens. The government routinely paid two thousand dollars to the families of foreign nationals lynched by American citizens.

105. *Alvey A. Adee to Consul-General Donnelly,* August 16, 1897

SIR: On October 6, 1895, Juan Montelongo and a child named Pedro Suaste were killed by shooting in Lasalle County, Tex. At the same time Nicolasa Bautista, wife of

Florentino Suaste was wounded. Five days later Florentino Suaste was taken from jail and lynched at Cotulla.

In regard to the killing of Montelongo and Suaste's child, and for the injury inflicted upon Suaste's wife, there is a direct conflict between the Mexican and American statements of facts.

The Mexican contention is that Suaste and Montelongo (Mexicans) were attacked by an American cattleman named Saul, and by Deputy Sheriff Swink, and that Montelongo and Suaste's child were killed and Suaste and his wife injured in the affair. It is alleged that Suaste, after receiving his wound, fired in self-defense at Saul and killed him. Suaste, his wife, and another little child, and also Montelongo's wife, were arrested and taken to the jail at Cotulla, from which Suaste was soon afterwards taken at night by a mob, shot, and hanged. The women were detained about a month, when they were released.

The facts as developed by the investigation of the grand jury of Lasalle County, and reported by the district attorney, are that Saul surprised the Mexicans while killing one of his cattle, and they being armed, he notified Swink, deputy sheriff, who accompanied him in pursuit of the thieves (it is admitted by Mexico that Montelongo did kill Saul's calf); that when they overtook the Mexicans Saul dismounted from his horse, and while in the act of uncovering the meat in the wagon was shot by Montelongo; that Swink and Saul then both opened fire on the Mexicans with pistols and killed Montelongo; after which Suaste took Montelongo's rifle and fired the shot which killed Saul, Swink in the meantime wounding Suaste, the rifle falling from Suaste's hands being picked up by his wife, who, attempting to use it, was also shot by Swink and that the child mentioned was accidentally killed in the general shooting.

In a note of the 30th ultimo the Mexican minister at this capital states that he is instructed by his Government to request of the United States Government indemnity for the alleged murder of Juan Montelongo and Pedro Suaste, the lynching of Florentino Suaste, and for the injuries indicted on Nicolasa Bautista, as well as for the imprisonment to which the latter, her minor children, and Montelongo's wife were subjected at Cotulla.

Although the claim for indemnity has not been established, it nevertheless appears due to Mexico that a detailed investigation and report be made.

You are therefore instructed without delay to visit the place, investigate the affair, and collect evidence on the spot. You will also ascertain whether proper efforts were made by the county authorities to apprehend the guilty parties.

SOURCE: U.S. Congress, *Lynching of Florentino Suaste*, January 9, 1901, 59th Congress, 2d sess., Report No. 1832.

106. *"Report of Consul-General Donnelly,"* September 13, 1897

I shall begin with an account of the affair as it appears from my investigation, subsequently treating in detail such portions thereof as are matters of controversy.

Origin of the Trouble.

On the afternoon of October 6, 1895, the Mexicans named, while traveling in Lasalle County, Tex., entered upon the ranch of one U. T. Saul, killed a calf belonging to him and leaving the hide, head, and entrails in the brush, carried away the carcass. Under the laws of Texas this was a crime punishable by confinement in the State penitentiary of not less than two or more than four years.

(R. S. Texas, art. 882.)

Discovery of the Crime.

Before sundown the same day Joseph Hocut, foreman of the ranch, came across the evidences of the crime, and at once sent Woodlief Thomas, an employee, to notify Mr. Saul, at Cotulla.

The Pursuit.

Saul summoned Deputy Sheriff Swink and a State Ranger and, with Thomas, started after the thieves. A short distance from Cotulla they met some Mexicans with a covered wagon, which they searched and found nothing. These told them they had passed another party of Mexicans with two wagons going south. Thomas and the ranger left the party at this point, and Saul and Swink continued the chase.

The Shooting.

After about two hours' ride the Montelongo party were overtaken. They were armed with Winchesters; the officer and Saul with pistols. In the affray that followed Montelongo was killed and Florentino Suaste, Nicolasa Bautista, Pedro Suaste, and Saul were wounded, the last two mortally.

After the Shooting.

Deputy Swink, who was uninjured, at once sent for a physician, a justice of the peace, and the State Rangers. The doctor looked after the wounded, the justice held an inquest on Montelongo, and the rangers took the surviving Mexican in custody, conveying them to the Cotulla jail in the morning.

Inquest and Examining Trial.

Saul died while being taken to Cotulla. An inquest was regularly held on his body, which found "That on the 6th day of October, 1895, Florentino Suaste, Casimira Reyes, and Nicolaso Bautista, with malice aforethought, did shoot deceased with a gun, inflicting upon the body of deceased, just above the left nipple, it gunshot wound, from the effects of which the said deceased died."

An examining trial of the accused was subsequently held. The papers of this trial are missing but from the statement of the justice and the attorney who acted therein it satisfactorily appears that the proceedings were fairly conducted and that on the evidence submitted Suaste was committed without bail and the women held on bond.

The Lynching.

Saul's death aroused much public feeling. He was a man of means, highly thought of, and left a wife and four children. Threats of lynching were publicly made, and the captain of the State Rangers placed men on guard at the jail. These, however, were withdrawn within three days. On the night of October 11, when the jail was in the sole care of the jailer, Suaste was seized by a party of three or four men and put to death by shooting and hanging.

Action of the Authorities.

There was an inquest held on Suaste's body, which found that his death was caused by parties unknown. The grand jury at the November term, 1895, investigated both the killing and lynching, but the evidence taken by them does not appear to have been reduced to writing, and their only action of record in the matter was a recommendation to the court for the release of Nicolasa Bautista and Casimira Reyes. This was done, November 5, 1895.

The grand jury for the May term, 1896, also considered the lynching and took the testimony of the jailer, Nicolasa Bautista, and Casimira Reyes, but no indictments were found.

Matters of Controversy

Of the foregoing account several important features are matters of more or less controversy, to wit: (1) The stealing of the calf, (2) the shooting, (3) the lynching, (4) the action of the authorities.

I therefore shall consider each separately in the light of the evidence.

Stealing the calf. While it is admitted by the Mexicans that a calf was killed by Montelongo (Inst. No. 97, of August 16), Casimira Reyes says it was found on the road; that they looked for its owner with a view of working out its value, and Nicolasa, through her attorneys, claims that in any event Montelongo alone was responsible for the killing. This contention is not borne out by the facts. The hide, head, and entrails were not discovered on the road, but 150 yards from the road, in the brush. No inquiry appears to have been made by them anywhere as to the ownership, and the carcass was found in their possession where they were overtaken, fully 7 miles from where the calf was killed. There is, besides, their own testimony at the inquest held on the body of Saul. "We did kill a calf" was the voluntary statement of Suaste. "My husband and Juan (meaning Montelongo) together killed a calf," swore Nicolasa Bautista. "I don't know what they did with the hide. We each took half of the meat."

This testimony I take to be conclusive of their common guilt.

The shooting.—Other than the parties concerned there were no witnesses to the shooting.

The night was dark, the road remote. Only the survivors can know or tell the details, and these, unfortunately, tell conflicting stories. Swink declares the Mexicans the aggressors; the Mexicans put all the blame on the Americans. Swink's statement stands alone, while on the Mexican side the voluntary statement of Suaste at the inquest is substantially confirmed by the Mexican women. But this seeming preponderance of evidence in favor of the Mexicans is overcome by the fact that several subsequent statements, made by these women vary from the first in most important details. At the inquest Suaste puts the blame on Saul and virtually exonerates Swink. He declared that the dead American shot him and Montelongo and that he did not see the other American (Swink) shoot at all. Nicolasa tells the same story, saying that the other American (Swink) did not shoot at all; that he slipped to one side. "I did not see him have a pistol." Casimira Reyes says the large man (Saul) did all the shooting. "I did not see the other man (Swink) shoot at all." But in her petition to the circuit court of the United States in and for the western district of Texas, in an action for damages against Swink, Casimira declares that her husband was killed by gunshot wounds inflicted at the hands of Saul and Swink, and in her verbal statement to me in San Antonio she made out Swink to be the chief assailant.

It is proper to consider also the credibility of the parties. Swink and Saul bear good characters. As much can not be said for Montelongo and Suaste. Swink was an officer of the law—had made many arrests without trouble. Saul was a man of means, a good citizen, and particularly remarked in the community for his amiability and indisposition to violence. Of Montelongo I could learn little. He was the common Indian type of Mexican laborer. He had admittedly stolen a calf. Suaste, his accomplice, was of the same type, but with more of a record. He appears to have been a deserter from the Mexican army. There is even serious doubt of his marriage with his alleged wife, Nicolasa, as there is no record thereof in the town where she stated such marriage to have occurred. Nicolasa herself is alleged by a witness to have admitted that she was not married.

Conceive, as we may, the situation a moment before the tragedy: On the one side the owner of the stolen property and an officer of the law. On the other side Montelongo and Suaste overtaken, conscious of their crime, the stolen property in their possession, knowing by long residence in Texas the consequence of arrest, with rifles in their hands or in reach. From which side was apt to spring the impulse of murder?

The lynching. There are few even in Cotulla callous enough to justify the lynching. There are many, however, who profess to believe that it only anticipated the action of the law; that Suaste, by the murder of Saul, had forfeited his life to the State, and that lynching saved the cost of his trial and execution; but, while ready to give ear to every opinion in my quest for facts, I must say I heard nothing that palliates the crime of lynchers. Crime it was, deliberate and indefensible. The courts had not passed upon his alleged offense. He was in the custody of the law, and therefore in the law's protection. His dead friend, his dead child, the wounded mother of his children, his own condition, shot as he was in four places, all the circumstances made the act particularly cruel and revolting.

Action of the authorities. There can be no just criticism of the authorities in the matter of the arrest or imprisonment. Suaste and the women were duly committed on the finding of the inquest and after an examining trial held in the manner provided by the law, and the minor children were neither arrested nor imprisoned, but were permitted to remain with their mother as an act of charity; but there is grave question whether the authorities made adequate efforts to prevent the lynching or to apprehend and punish its perpetrators. Captain Brooks, of the State Rangers, whom I know to be a trustworthy man and officer, seems satisfied with what was done. He admits having been beguiled into the belief that public feeling had quieted down and there was no danger. The sheriff may have shared his opinion; but to my knowledge the proposed lynching was heralded by the press throughout the State—was expected from day to day and finally consummated as a matter of course. I remember the occurrence vividly owing to the feeling it excited among the Mexicans here and my conviction that the governor of the State (who subsequently displayed much energy in preventing a glove fight) should call out the militia, to Cotulla.

Within four days of their incarceration Suaste and his family were left to the sole protection of Lewis Underwood, the jailer, a man neither physically nor mentally strong. There was no resistance to the lynchers. The case with which they entered and seized their prey was described to me by the jailer himself, with many chuckling comments on his own discretion in making no outcry and not saying anything of the lynching until the next morning. The authorities have been charged with negligence —a negligence so gross as to well arouse suspicion of collusion. They knew the threats. They knew the sanguinary record of the town. Twice before from that same jail men had been taken by mobs and done to death, once in broad daylight, the whole populace onlookers or participants. Surely, under the circumstances, a proper regard for the safety of the prisoner should have moved the sheriff to keep his deputies at the jail or within call for a longer period than four days, instead of leaving it so that anyone could enter without resistance.

It would have been some palliation of their failure to prevent the lynching and would have done much to suppress the talk of collusion had there been active and earnest efforts made to find and punish those who were guilty of it. Such efforts do not satisfactorily appear. Captain Brooks states that he followed every clew, but did not succeed in finding any proof of guilt. Several of the deputy sheriffs told me the same story. On the other hand, Mr. Smith, editor of the local paper, holds [that] "it is not possible a man could be taken from that jail in the middle of the town by so many and shot and hanged without their leaving some traces"; and many who would not permit me to quote them spoke in the same strain. The grand jury met the following month and considered the matter. On the jury were many of the most prominent citizens of the county, but they made no indictments, nor is there any record as to whom they examined. The grand jury, at the May term, 1896, also took up the case and examined the jailer, Nicolasa Bautista, and Casimira Reyes, but nobody was indicted.

It may not be proper in this connection to state that it would be out of the usual course of Lasalle County grand juries if any indictments had been made—three lynchings from that same jail, and not a single instance of punishment for the perpetrators. Grand juries nowhere rise above the level of the community. The very justice of the peace who held the inquest and examining trial and committed Suaste without bail (I am reliably informed) was the leader in a former lynching. But he is none the less popular. I did not meet the gentleman who held the office of sheriff at the time. He was not in the county during either of my visits. It is known, however, that he has been charged with complicity in the lynching, and he is now a defendant in an action for damages growing out of it and pending in the United States circuit court of western Texas. But I have met the then district attorney. It might be presumed that this gentleman could fully inform me of the facts, and particularly as to the measures taken by the authorities. A district attorney is the legal advisor of the county, the heart and soul of a grand jury; his the brain that plans and the energy that prosecutes; by his zeal, courage, and intellect may be gauged the standard of a county's criminal procedure.

But Mr. Walton seemed to have no knowledge of the case. I need only refer to his verbal statement. He was not present at the inquest or examining trial. He was in Cotulla during the session of the grand jury which considered the killing and lynching, but "court was in session" and he "gave the proceedings of the grand jury little attention." "I have no recollection," said he, "of the nature of the testimony produced before the grand jury. I know there were no indictments." He knew there were no indictments, and this is positively the only reliable information obtainable from him or others—there were no indictments. I mean no reflection on the district attorney. His district includes many counties and an enormous territory. It may have been impossible for him to give any one county or case that close attention which is common from such officer in more settled communities. But the fact remains—the grand jury that considered the killing of Montelongo and Pedro Suaste and the lynching of Florentine Suaste was without effective counsel and active cooperation of the district attorney. The grand jury saw fit to place its proceedings under seal—why is a mystery, for when I had the seal broken by order of the district judge they disclosed nothing. No list of witnesses summoned, no record of witnesses examined, no line of testimony taken! Even the second grand jury which considered the matter shows only the testimony of three witnesses.

There can be but one conclusion from all this—the county authorities did not do their full duty.

Given a grand jury of honest and sensible men, a district attorney resolute and brainy, a sheriff capable and trustworthy, one session at Cotulla would in my opinion reach the root of this whole disgraceful business.

From the facts and for the reasons set forth, I find as follows:

1. The Mexicans, Juan Montelongo and Florentino Suaste, accompanied by the women and children named, on the 6th day of October, 1895, in Lasalle County, Tex., committed the crime of cattle stealing.

2. In the effort of Mr. Saul, the owner of the stolen property, and a deputy sheriff to effect their arrest, shooting took place, resulting in the death of Saul, Montelongo, and a child, and the wounding of Florentino Suaste and Nicolasa Bautista.

3. It is the reasonable presumption from all the circumstances that the Mexicans opened fire to resist capture and that the Americans returned fire in self-de-

fense. This presumption is not overcome by the conflicting and varying statements of the survivors.

4. The arrest and imprisonment of the Mexicans after the shooting was in due form of law and by the proper officers.

5. The minor children of the Mexicans were neither arrested nor imprisoned, but permitted to accompany and remain with their mother as an act of charity.

6. The lynching of Florentino Sauste could have been prevented by reasonable precaution on the part of the county authorities.

7. It does not satisfactorily appear that proper efforts have been made to apprehend and punish the guilty parties.

> Joseph G. Donnelly,
> Counsul-General

SOURCE: "Lynching of Florentino Suaste," January 9, 1901, Senate Report No. 1832, 56th Congress, 2d sess.

The simmering trouble along the U.S.-Mexican border boiled over after revolutionaries toppled the Mexican government in 1910. Francisco Madero ousted Porfirio Diaz, the dictator of Mexico. Victoriano Huerta soon rose against Madero and seized the government on February 19, 1913. Three days later Madero was murdered, an act that led Venustiano Carranzo and Pancho Villa to turn against Huerta. Under pressure from Carranzo and Villa, Huerta fled Mexico, leaving Carranzo and Villa to fight over the country.

The revolutionaries positioned themselves as opponents of American lynching. Their enemies, including Prócoro F. Gutierrez, editor of the *Mexican Herald,* routinely promoted mob law or so the revolutionaries said. This article attacking Gutierrez comes from *Regeneración,* a newspaper founded by Ricardo Flores Magon and his brother, Enrique, in 1900.

107. *Los Angeles* Regeneración, *"A Swine,"* 1914

He was born in the manure. Fattened on the corn of Texas lynchers, today, as he crawls, he gathers the refuse from the houses of the Mexican proletariat. He had to have a name so they gave him one: Prócoro F. Gutierrez.

He was known in San Marcos, hated by every sensible man, the swine contents himself by denouncing Mexican *libertarios* [literal translation: libertarians] to the henchmen of the drunken bumpkin who tyrannizes the barbarous state.

[He is] a servant and sweeper at a printing press [belonging] to a bourgeois who exploits a journalistic rag known as the *Mexican Herald.* In volume 21 of said paper, which he decided to send us and in which an open letter demands that "one cleanse one's reputation," we read a short article entitled "The adulterous woman." It reads as follows: "The adulterous woman should be punished as she had been in the Middle Ages. She should be taken to the public square and executed without compassion, etc." That is to say, in the vulgar style of Texas lynchings that he is accustomed to witnessing and perhaps even, with a lit torch, dancing around the victim, shrieking and singing the "hue" or the macabre dance without making the slightest protest because he is a coward, because he is very vile and criminal to bribe similar bar-

barisms as those committed against our proletariat and racial brothers in Barbaric Texas.

In Prócoro's complaint—referring to the revolutionaries who struggle for land and liberty, he adds: "If they would not insult Mexico and [the] tri-color flag, I would have no reason to get into this with you because my newspaper is instructive, not political."

In another part, the barbarian says, "I will need to demand from you proof before the law."

The human monster forgot to say if the law with which he threatens us is the law of the lynch bandit, which is the law being used by the one who fattens him when it comes to avenging the racial hatred that exists in the barbarian state against Mexican workers or the law of flight of Porfirio Díaz y de Madero.

Before finishing, let us hear some more of Prócoro's words about the adulterous woman: "The laws that punish a man for seducing a married woman are not justice: the woman is guilty in every case, because she invites the man to commit the crime."

We do not advise the woman to commit what Prócoro calls a "crime"; much less that she ought to be publicly burned. On the contrary we advise that she educate herself so that she can shed the yokes that oppress her: the law and religions, in such a way using all her faculties, moral as well as intellectual. This is the purpose of *Regeneración*.

SOURCE: Los Angeles *Regeneración*, January 24, 1914.

The Magon brothers repeatedly used their newspaper, *Regeneración*, to criticize white Texans and Texas police as lynchers. But the Magons sometimes advocated mob law themselves.

108. *Los Angeles* Regeneración, *"At the Last Hour,"* 1914

In one of our previous issues we talked about the crime committed by a Texas cop on the worker Fermin Alcorta whom he came across in the Mineral del Belto. This comrade fell into the bad graces of a Texas official, who arrested him without a motive while he was in a bar and on his way to the jail in the town of Bastrop, assassinated him in the most cowardly manner, since comrade Alcorta was not carrying any kind of weapon. Since the barbaric state of Texas has a double standard in its application of justice, the murderous policeman was released [after posting] $300 in bail and today he prances around in the streets of Dallas. The Libertarian group "Sol Proletario" ["Proletariat Sun"] in Phelan, Texas, has taken on the defense of the murdered comrade, who lived in Austin and was only passing through Mineral [del Belto], and is committed to ensuring that the assassin pay for the crime he committed. We have come to a point in Texas, when only armed rebellion will put an end to so much crime. Confronted with increased assassinations, what other remedy is there, if not armed struggle, to stop them? Texas tries to deport Mexican workers; the so-called courts of justice only give their services to those who have the money to pay for them. What to do? What can our brothers do? Nothing, except armed rebellion. Force against force. Against armed crime, armed justice. The day will come when the bodies of white bandits will hang from the mezquite groves of the state, when the groves themselves will shake from the death rattles of every Texas assassin who has denied to

Mexicans the right to life in the savage southern state. To be ready for that day, each and every Mexican worker must arm himself. When the cry of rebellion is raised, there is nothing left to do but fight. Oh, bourgeoisie Texas bandits: each and every one of you will pay, as many tears and as many sufferings as you have visited upon thousands of men, women, and children who year after year till your riches in the fields of cotton.

SOURCE: Los Angeles *Regeneración,* January 24, 1914.

Followers of Victoriano Huerta wrote the "Plan of San Diego," calling for an armed uprising against the United States. Most along the Texas-Mexican border thought the plan preposterous. One judge suggested that a conspirator should be tried for lunacy rather than any crime against the United States. A few months after American authorities picked up a copy of the plan, however, reports circulated that Mexican "bandits" had raided ranches on the American side of the border. The problem frightened many Anglos, and ranchers moved their families to town. One raiding party burned a railroad bridge near San Sebastian. Although the plan failed to liberate any territory, some Americans thought it justified lynching any Mexicans who might be following it. Some newspapers advocated vigilantism, and lynchings followed.[18]

109. *"Plan of San Diego,"* 1915

We who in turn sign our names, assembled in the Revolutionary Plot of San Diego, Texas, solemnly promise each other, on our word of honor, that we will fulfill, and cause to be fulfilled and complied with, all the clauses and provisions stipulated in this document, and execute the orders and the wishes emanating from the Provisional Directorate of this movement, and recognize as military Chief of the same, Mr. Agistin S. Garza, guaranteeing with our lives the faithful accomplishment of what is here agreed upon.

1. On the 20th day of February, 1915, at two o'clock in the morning, we will arise in arms against the Government and Country of the United States of North America, one as all and all as one, proclaiming the liberty of the individuals of the black race and its independence of Yankee tyranny which has held us in iniquitous slavery since remote times; and at the same time and in the same manner we will proclaim the independence and segregation of the states bordering upon the Mexican Nations, which are: Texas, New Mexico, Arizona, Colorado, and Upper California, which states the Republic of Mexico was robbed in a most perfidious manner by North American imperialism.

2. In order to render the foregoing clause effective, the necessary army corps will be formed, under the immediate command of military leaders named by the Supreme Revolutionary Congress of San Diego, Texas, which shall have full power to designate a Supreme Chief, who shall be at the head of said army. The banner which shall guide us in this enterprise shall be red, with a white diagonal fringe, and bearing the following inscription: "Equality and Independence," and none of the subordinate leaders or subalterns shall use any other flag (except only the white flag for signals.) The aforesaid army shall be known by the name of: "Liberating Army for Races and People."

3. Each one of the chiefs will do his utmost, by whatever means possible, to get possessed of the arms and funds of the cities which he has beforehand been designated to capture, in order that our cause may be provided with resources to continue the fight with better success, the said leaders each being required to render an account of everything to his superiors, in order that the latter may dispose of it in the proper manner.

4. The leader who may take a city must immediately name and appoint municipal authorities, in order that they may preserve order and assist in every way possible the revolutionary movement. In case the Capital of any State which we are endeavoring to liberate be captured, there will be named in the same manner superior municipal authorities, for the same purpose.

5. It is strictly forbidden to hold prisoners, whether special prisoners (civilians) or soldiers; and the only time that should be spent in dealing with them is that which is absolutely necessary to demand funds (loans) of them; and whether these demands be successful or not, they shall be shot immediately, without any pretext.

6. Every stranger who shall be found armed, and who cannot prove his right to carry arms, shall be summarily executed, regardless of his race or nationality.

7. Every North American over sixteen years of age shall be put to death; and only the aged men, the women, and the children shall be respected; and on no account shall the traitors to our race be spared or respected.

SOURCE: 812/23116, Records of the Department of State Relating to Internal Affairs of Mexico, 1910–1929, M274, microfilm, National Archives, College Park, Maryland.

Pascual Orozco Jr., born 1882, participated in the Mexican Revolution, fighting against Porfirio Diaz and then siding with Victoriano Huerta against Francisco Madero. After Huerta fled Mexico in 1914, American authorities arrested the putative Mexican president and Orozco. Orozco escaped only to be hunted down and killed by an American posse in 1915. The next two selections document the reactions of Spanish-language newspapers to the "lynching" of Pascual Orozco.

110. *"Pascual Orozco and the Fugitive Law,"* 1915

A new stain has fallen on the so decadent Yankee civilization, with the death of General Pascual Orozco, head of the "colorados," whose body has been found riddled by four bullet wounds on land in Big Bend County, Texas. The shots were fired by thirty "American Rangers," and the entry wounds show that Orozco as well as his companions were shot in the back.

In our country when a death occurred under those circumstances it was said that the deceased had been a victim of the fugitive law, of that law that already began to be a thing of the past when unruly gentlemen (and not unruly ones, to be fair) made themselves responsible for exhuming it and putting it into force again, an iniquitous and cruel law that consisted in shooting without running any risk to one or several individuals with four treacherous shots, covering then the method and the cowardice of the act with the official report that they had been killed trying to escape.

We believed that civilized men of the cultivated American Union had enough to be ashamed of with the repugnant and loathsome Lynch Law, whose application which has always been a commonplace thing in this country and is now, unfortunately, all too frequent in the border towns neighboring our country, in which a day doesn't go by that you don't find bodies of Mexicans hanging from trees like macabre fruit, sacrificed by a people that, indignant for real or supposed offenses, make victims of their savage rage not only the guilty but also the innocent, not only our countrymen but even those of their own nationality. We believed, we say, that Lynch Law was sufficient to satiate the anger of the men of this cultivated Republic, but as if that weren't enough, they have imported the "ley fuga" from Mexico to apply it precisely to those who believed they had made themselves safe from it in the territory of the Union.

This type of crime, as that of lynchings, usually remains unpunished; the only thing we can attribute this to is the blindness of the public, and the powerlessness (connivance, we would say) of the authorities to avoid it; but in the present case, if, as everything indicates, a murder has been committed, and that [murder] by elements and individuals that are said to be representative of justice, then not even that recourse could be seized, and the crime would appear in all its horrible nakedness and of such monstrosity for being a mass murder, that even the cannibals in the heart of Africa would feel ashamed.

It is necessary that this people, whose governors boast they are just and altruistic, open their eyes to the light of reason and abandon the bad path in which is situated their hate and their contempt for those of our race.

It is said that the Texas revolution, which costs the American Government a few deaths, began with an injustice committed against a Mexican and his companions in Brownsville, the death of Pascual Orozco. If it becomes clear that a trap was set for them, it will cause more serious fears in the district.

Justice and equality are not exactly the principles which have governed the actions of the American people towards us, and if we add this certain deed that apparently constitutes an assault, it would not be farfetched for hatreds to increase instead of diminishing.

We believe and we hope that light will be shed on the subject and from that will be inferred that the death of those five Mexicans is the result of a crime that will not remain unpunished, like the worst of all the impunities, covered, in order to justify it, with official sanction.

SOURCE: San Antonio, *La Epoca*, September 3, 1915. Translated by Pamela Waldrep and Jarbel Rodriguez.

111. *"Reprisals Feared for the Death of Pascual Orozco,"* 1915

On Monday at 3 in the afternoon General Pascual Orozco and three of his companions, whom a patrol of American Rangers had pursued since Sunday, were surprised in Cañon Verde. General Orozco and his companions were unprepared and unaware of any pursuit so that they did not realize what awaited them until they received the first volley that killed General Orozco, pierced by 4 bullets. His companions all received four to eight bullet wounds in the back, which confirms the belief that they were taken by surprise. The bodies of the four Mexicans, that have been embalmed to transfer them to this town, have not yet arrived.

There are some serious fears that this will provoke uprisings among the Mexicans, and the American inhabitants have urgently written the Governor asking him to send sufficient forces, specifically in front of the Rio Verde Canyon, but Salinas operates throughout Mexican territory with a group of "colorados" numbering no fewer than 700 men and it is not a remote possibility that he may try to avenge the death of his leader.

Even when the Americans assure that Orozco died in combat, no one believes this because of the location of the wounds as well as the fact that none of the attackers received a single wound, and Orozco and his companions were notable shots.

SOURCE: San Antonio *La Epoca*, September 3, 1915. Translated by Pamela Waldrep and Jarbel Rodriguez.

In 1940 Walter Van Tilburg Clark (1909–1971) took a far more critical view of lynching than either Bancroft or Wister. Although born in Maine, Clark grew up in Nevada. His first novel, *The Ox-Bow Incident*, established his reputation as the premier literary figure of the West. Critics praised his work but found that it did not fit with most formulaic western writing. Reviewers recognized that Clark's novel was more a parable than a typical "Wild West" potboiler. Clark used the form of the western novel to indict white southerners' racial lynching along with the western variety. Clark also attempted a short story, never published, about a southern lynching told from the point of view of the victim's African American mother.[19] Clark's western novel attacks lynching more indirectly than did the short story, his writing representing more twentieth-century angst than nineteenth-century history. By the time Clark penned his narrative, Americans had begun to fear the loss of individual identity and responsibility in an increasingly bureaucratized culture. The lyncher's confession reveals Clark's insight into the mob mentality: the rank-and-file members of mobs simply went along with the crowd, afraid to speak up or glad when they could not. Clark saw this as the great danger of twentieth-century American life. Clark urged his readers to see law as "something in itself," "the spirit of the moral nature of man," "an existence apart, like God."

112. *Walter Van Tilburg Clark, "The Ox-Bow Incident,"* 1940

"Art, just when they were going to hang them, when the ropes were up, what was it I was thinking?"

"How would I know? A man thinks about funny things at a time like that. Every man's would be different. Maybe a song you heard once. I don't know."

"What would you think?" he insisted.

Like all of us, I suppose. That you wished it didn't have to be done; at least not there in front of you. Or that it was all over, and the poor bastards were dead and happy."

"You didn't think it could be stopped?" he asked.

"It was too late for that."

"You didn't think of using your gun?"

That surprised me. "On what?" I asked.

"Tetley," he said.

"You mean . . ."

"No, just to force him to take them back for trial."

"No," I said finally, "I don't think I did. It was all settled. I had a kind of wild idea for a moment, but I didn't really think of it. You get those wild ideas, you know, out of nothing, when you have to do something you don't much like. I didn't really think of it, no," I said again.

"Did you have a feeling it would have worked? That you could have turned the whole thing right then? Or that somebody could have?"

I thought. "No," I said, "I guess not. I guess I just thought it was settled. I didn't like it, but it was settled."

"It should have been stopped," he said, "even with a gun."

"I can see that now."

"I could see it then," he said.

"You didn't even *have* a gun."

"No," he said, "no, I didn't," as if admitting the ultimate condemnation of himself.

After a moment I admitted, "I guess you're not twisting it; I guess I am. I don't see what you've got to feel bad about."

"I thought of all that," he said. "Do you see? I knew Tetley could be stopped then. I knew you could all be turned by one man who would face Tetley with a gun. Maybe he wouldn't even have needed a gun, but I told myself he would. I told myself he would to face Tetley, because Tetley couldn't bear to be put down, and because Tetley was mad to see those three men hang, and to see Gerald made to hang one of them. I told myself you'd have to stop him with fear, like any animal from a kill."

"You were right," I said. "I wasn't thinking much then; but you were right."

"It doesn't matter whether I was right or not. Do you know what I felt when I thought that, Croft?"

I thought he was going to answer his own question, and let it go. But he didn't.

"Can't you guess, Croft?" he begged. "No," I said slowly, "I can't, what?"

"I was glad, Croft, glad I didn't have a gun."

I didn't look up. I felt something rotten in what he was saying, or maybe just that he was saying it. It was obscure, but I didn't want to look at him.

"Now do you see," he said triumphantly, like all he had wanted to do was make himself out the worst he could. "I knew those men were innocent. I knew it as surely as I do now. And I knew Tetley could be stopped. I knew in that moment you were all ready to be turned. And I was glad I didn't have a gun."

He was silent, except that I could hear him breathing hard over what he seemed to consider an unmerciful triumph, breathing as if he had overcome something tremendous, and could begin to rest now. I could hear the talking downstairs again too. There wasn't much laughing now, though. For some reason I was relieved that there wasn't much laughing, as if, coming at that moment, even from downstairs, it would have been too much.

SOURCE: Walter Van Tilburg Clark, *The Ox-Bow Incident* (New York: Random House, 1940), 297–300. Reprinted by permission of Walter Van Tilburg Clark Estate.

NOTES

1. David A. Johnson, "Vigilance and the Law: The Moral Authority of Popular Justice in the Far West," *American Quarterly* 33 (1981): 558–586.

2. Stephen J. Leonard, *Lynching in Colorado, 1859–1919* (Boulder: University Press of Colorado, 2002), 7, 32.

3. Johnson, "Vigilance and the Law," 558–586.

4. John Adams, "Novanglus," in Charles Francis Adams, ed., *The Works of John Adams, Second President of the United States* (Boston: Charles C. Little and James Brown, 1851), 4:82.

5. *Colusa Sun,* August 10, 1867.

6. Inquisition over the body of an unknown Chinaman shot near Butte City, April 13, 1887, Colusa County Archives, Colusa County Courthouse, Colusa, California.

7. Michele Shover, "Chico Women: Nemesis of a Rural Town's Anti-Chinese Campaigns, 1876–1888," *California History* 68 (December 1988): 228–243.

8. *San Francisco Chronicle,* July 11, 1887.

9. Ibid., July 12, 1887.

10. *Chico Enterprise,* July 15, 1887.

11. Richard Slotkin, *Gunfighter Nation: The Myth of the Frontier in Twentieth-Century America* (New York: Atheneum, 1992), 171.

12. Helena Huntington Smith, *The War on Powder River: The History of an Insurrection* (Lincoln: University of Nebraska Press, 1966), 7–120.

13. *Chicago Herald,* January 29, 1892.

14. Ibid., April 13, 1892.

15. Slotkin, *Gunfighter Nation,* 169–183.

16. Jack Schaefer, *Shane* (Boston: Houghton Mifflin, 1949).

17. William D. Carrigan and Clive Webb, "The Lynching of Persons of Mexican Origin or Descent in the United States, 1848–1928," *Journal of Social History* 37 (2003): 411–438.

18. Benjamin Heber Johnson, *Revolution in Texas: How a Forgotten Rebellion and Its Bloody Suppression Turned Mexicans into Americans* (New Haven: Yale University Press, 2004), 71–85; James Sandos, "The Plan of San Diego: War and Diplomacy on the Texas Border, 1915–1916," *Arizona and the West* 14 (1972): 5–24.

19. Warren Van Tilberg Clark, "Learning Is Fire," Warren Van Tilburg Clark Papers, Special Collections Department, University Library, University of Nevada, Reno, Nevada.

9

The Limits of Progressive Reform

Early-twentieth-century investigative journalists, exposing social evils and calling for reform, should have been the terror of lynchers. Journalists, called "muckrakers," wired their reports to their magazines and newspapers, electrifying the nation with their shocking revelations about child labor, corrupt police, filthy food preparation, and bribed politicians. Reformers transformed these reports into calls for new legislation based on the muckrakers' revelations. As the Progressives looked about for causes, lynchers tortured and mutilated thousands. The National Association for the Advancement of Colored People (NAACP) primed the pump with its own muckraking investigations. Nonetheless, when it came to lynching, the Progressives' switchboard remained strangely silent.

Racism explains this in large part, but it is also true that industrialization set the Progressive agenda, distracting reformers from all else. Rural problems, especially one common for centuries, flowing from the sovereign power of ordinary people, could hardly compete with the frightening menace posed to American democracy by newly concentrated corporate power. The heart of Progressive reform lay in the belief that American industrialized life could be made better through governmental intervention. Progressive-era social scientists investigated a host of urban ills—immigration, women's and children's labor, prostitution, and gambling. Ida M. Tarbell researched the Standard Oil Corporation; William Hard looked at industrial accidents and child labor; and Lincoln Steffens exposed political corruption. One recent U.S. history textbook notes with enthusiasm: "Hardly a sordid corner of American life escaped the scrutiny of these tireless reporters."[1] In fact, these journalists took hardly any interest in lynching at all, a barbarous old relic of the preindustrial age.

Muckraking journalists, as they came to be called after a speech by President Theodore Roosevelt, wrote for magazines with a national circulation. These national writers hardly touched lynching or racial violence at all. One who did, Ray Stannard Baker, went to the scene of lynchings to find out the facts, in classic muckraking style.

Baker journeyed to Statesboro, Georgia, after a mob had burned alive two men named Will Cato and Paul Reed, charged with murdering Henry Hodges, his wife, and three children on August 16, 1904. Newspapers reported a spectacle that, even after a generation of well-publicized lynchings, shocked white readers. National Guard troops with unloaded rifles had guarded the prisoners; one man threw himself against the soldiers, opening a breech in the line. Two hundred wildly cheering whites poured into the hole. The crowd found Reed and Cato, put ropes around their necks, and hustled them into a throng now numbering five hundred. The crowd chanted "burn them, burn them" as Cato begged to be hanged or shot. After a member of the mob made a speech recounting the crime against Hodges and his family, the crowd piled wood around Cato and Reed and then backed away so a photographer could take a picture before the wood was ignited. One reporter, who was apparently present, thought the scene "beggar[ed] description." The "frenzied" crowd, "crazed with hatred . . . rent the air" with cheers, he wrote. As flames consumed his oil-covered body, Reed twisted and writhed, unsuccessfully trying to choke himself, to escape the pain. Cato's heavy hair, soaked with oil, went up in flames first, the hemp rope around his neck becoming a column of fire. According to the reporter, "a thrill of horror ran through the frames of the more timid" in the cheering crowd.[2]

The black-owned national monthly news magazine, the *Voice of the Negro,* declared public opinion in Bulloch County at "a low ebb." The *Voice* accused the white public of generally supporting the brutality, "with all its cannibalism."[3] If anything, the *Voice* understated the situation. After the last flames consumed the flesh of Cato and Reed, mobs of whites armed with whips roamed the countryside looking for more African Americans to attack. For their part, blacks hid in the weeds, away from their homes, leaping onto passing trains to flee the area.[4] The *Mobile Register,* a white newspaper, lamented that mob "madness" had cost the town an opportunity "to demonstrate that the people were supporters of the law."[5]

Baker disagreed with such gloomy assessments. When he arrived and looked around, he found that Statesboro looked like any other wholesome American town. He looked for ways to explain how morally healthy and civic-minded white southerners could turn to lynching. The problem, he thought, lay in the "worthless" or "floating" Negro more than the white population. In coming to this conclusion, Baker came perilously close to duplicating the excuses offered by the lynchers themselves. He blamed the victims.

113. *Ray Stannard Baker, "What Is Lynching?"* 1905

You and I imagine that a lynching somehow could not possibly take place in our town; our people are orderly and law-abiding; our officials, whatever may be said of their politics, may be depended upon to do their duty; you and I are truly civilized. And conversely, we imagine that the people in towns where lynchings occur must be somehow peculiarly barbarous, illiterate, lawless. A lynching, like death, is a great way off until it strikes us.

I have just been visiting a number of "lynching towns" in this country, both in the South and in the North. I went primarily to formulate, if I could, a clear idea of what one hundred and fifty lynchings a year—the average in the United States for the last twenty-two years—might really signify, to discover in what way a lynching town is different from my town or your town, what classes of citizens constitute the mobs, and what is the underlying cause of such murderous outbreaks.

And as I visited the various towns I was more and more impressed with a sense of their homely familiarity; they were all American towns, just like yours and mine. I saw no barbarians. On Sunday morning I heard the church bells ringing, on weekdays there was the same earnest political buncombe; I found the same sort of newspapers and fraternal societies and woman's clubs, the same talk—and nothing but talk—of "political graft" in this gas deal or that water company, the same soaring local pride over the tallest stand-pipe, or the most wonderful spring, or the greatest factory.

In each successive place they pointed out the telegraph-pole or tree from which the mob's victim had dangled, or the stake at which he was burned to death; they showed me the jails which had been broken open; they told me the awful and gruesome details of the crimes committed. And I heard and saw these things with a strong sense of the unreality of it all; one cannot easily believe that such upheavals could really happen in these orderly, busy, familiar American towns. Yet they have happened, both in the North and in the South, with incidents of unimaginable horror and brutality; and they will happen again—next time, perhaps, in your town or mine. No, lynching is not a crime of barbarians; it is not a Southern crime, nor a Western crime, nor a Northern crime; it is an American crime.

Of one hundred and four lynchings last year (1903), ninety-one were in the South, and thirteen in the North and West. And not all the victims, by any means, were negroes; seventeen were white men, one a Chinaman, and two were women....

Statesboro: Where Two Negroes Were Burned Alive

Statesboro, Georgia, where two negroes were recently burned alive under the most shocking circumstances, is a thrifty county seat of some two thousand five hundred people, located about seventy miles from Savannah. For a hundred years a settlement has existed here, but it was not until people discovered the wealth of the turpentine forests and of the sea-island cotton industry that the town became highly prosperous....

In short, this is a healthy, temperate, progressive, American town—a country city, self-respecting, ambitious, with a good future before it—the splendid future of the New South.

Character of the Negro Population

About forty per cent of the population of the county consists of negroes. To most Northerners a negro is a negro; but one of the first things to impress a visitor in the South is the fact that there are two very distinct kinds of negroes—as distinct as the classes of white men. The first of these is the self-respecting, resident negro. Sometimes he is a land-owner, more often a renter; he is known to the white people, employed by them, and trusted by them. The Southerner of the better class, indeed, takes a real interest in the welfare of the home negro, and often has a real affection for him. In Statesboro, as in most of the South, a large proportion of the negroes are of this better class. On the other hand, one finds everywhere large numbers of the so-called "worthless negroes," perhaps a growing class, who float from town to town, doing rough work, having no permanent place of abode, not known to the white population generally. The turpentine industry has brought many such negroes to the neighborhood of Statesboro. Living in the forest near the turpentine-stills, and usually ignorant and lazy, they and all their kind, both in the country districts and in the city, are doubly unfortunate in coming into contact chiefly with the poorer class of white people, whom they often meet as industrial competitors. White bricklayers, for instance, work with negro bricklayers, and the trade jealously which inevitably arises is slowly crowding the negro out of the skilled trades and forcing him, more and more, to the heavy toil of manual labor. This industrial friction (a more important factor in the negro problem, perhaps, than is commonly recognized), added to the historic contempt of the negro for the "poor white" and the hatred of the poor white for the negro, constitutes a fertile source of discord. Even after making due allowance for the bitter problems of "social equality," negro franchise, and negro crime, all of which go to make up what is called "race prejudice," it is safe to say that if there were only the better class of whites in the South and the better class of negroes, there would be no such thing as a negro problem.

Danger from the Floating Negro

In all the towns I visited, South as well as North, I found that this floating, worthless negro caused most of the trouble. He prowls the roads by day and by night; he steals; he makes it unsafe for women to travel alone. Sometimes he has gone to school long enough to enable him to read a little and to write his name, enough education to make him hate the hard work of the fields and aspire to better things, without giving him the determination to earn them. He is often under the domination of half-educated negro preachers, who sometimes make it their stock in trade to stir their followers to greater hatred of the whites. He had little or no regard for the family relations or home life, and when he commits a crime or is tired of one locality, he sets out unencumbered to seek new fields, leaving his wife and children without the slightest compunction. . . .

Influences Tending to Prevent Future Lynchings in the South

[I]n the South . . . people everywhere, led by the best newspapers and the energetic younger men—the men who are developing the resources of the New South in such an astonishing way—have not only awakened to the gravity of their problem, but that they are making a genuine fight for social self-restraint, for the breaking up of the old prejudices, in short, the replacing of mob-license by the orderly execution of the law. When I went South I shared the impression of many Northerners that the South was lawless and did not care—an impression that arises from the wide publication of the horrible details of every lynching that occurs, and the utter silence regarding those deep, quiet, and yet powerful moral and industrial forces which are at the work of rejuvenation beneath the surface. I came away from the South deeply impressed . . . that the South is making fully as good progress in overcoming its peculiar forms of lawlessness as the North is making in overcoming *its* peculiar forms. Indeed, I do not know where in this country to-day there can be found a healthier or more patriotic growth of the civic consciousness than in the more progressive cities of the South.

SOURCE: Ray Stannard Baker, "What Is Lynching? A Study of Mob Justice South and North," *McClure's Magazine* 24 (January 1905): 299–430.

The most sordid Progressive-era exposé of lynching came not from a muckraker like Ray Stannard Baker but from a conservative Mississippi Democrat and Confederate veteran. Down at the bottom of the Mississippi Delta, the editor of the *Vicksburg Evening Post* needed no Progressive impulse to stand against lynching and made no excuses for lynching. John Gordon Cashman had been campaigning against lynching for decades when the Progressive era rolled around. In 1904 a lynching incident deep in Mississippi's Delta country inspired his most famous effort to expose the horrors of lynching. Cashman's coverage of the Luther Holbert lynching began with a routine news story.

114. *"Both Lynched: Holberts, Man and Woman, Captured Near Itta Bena,"* 1904

News reaches here that Luther Holbert and his wife, who murdered Mr. James Eastland,[6] at Doddsville, last week, were captured near Etta Bena in Yazoo, early Sunday morning, after a desperate fight.

The woman was dressed in men's clothes, and was equally as desperate as her husband. Both were lynched.

SOURCE: *Vicksburg Evening Post*, February 8, 1904.

Newspapers all over the country carried stories similar to Cashman's first article. His second article, however, contained grisly details other papers generally did not report. African American writers picked up this second story and ran with it. Mary Church Terrell quoted the *Evening Post* article in the May issue of *North American Review*.[7] In 1905 Sutton E. Griggs paraphrased it in his novel, *The Hindered Hand; or, The Reign of the Repressionist*, and Benjamin Brawley quoted Terrell's version of Cashman's article in *A Social History of the American Negro* (1921).[8] NAACP leader Walter White's 1929 book, *Rope and Faggot*, relied on Brawley's quote of Terrell's transcript of the *Post* article.[9] Cashman's article became emblematic of all lynching, white racial depravity at its worst. And most writers repeating Cashman's story incorrectly assumed that, as a white Mississippian, Cashman must have favored the violence. Italics indicates the portion quoted by Terrell.

115. *"Most Horrible Details of the Burning at the Stake of the Holberts,"* 1904

A citizen from the Doddsville neighborhood, who witnessed the burning of the Holberts, last Sunday was in the city this morning and told of some new horrors connected with the terrible event that have not yet been printed. He said the affair was probably the most terrible one of its kind in history. *When the two negroes were captured they were tied to trees and while the funeral pyres were being prepared they were forced to suffer the most fiendish tortures. The blacks were forced to hold out their hands while one finger at a time was chopped off. The fingers were distributed as souvenirs. The ears of the murderers were cut off. Holbert was severely beaten, his skull was fractured, and one of his eyes, knocked out with a stick, hung by a shred from the socket. Neither the man nor woman begged for mercy, nor made a groan or plea. When the executioners came forward to lop off fingers, Holbert extended his hand without being asked. The most excruciating form of punishment, consisted in the use of a large corkscrew in the hands of some of the mob. This instrument was bored into the flesh of the man and the woman, in the arms, legs and body, and then pulled out, the spirals tearing out big pieces of raw, quivering flesh, every time it was withdrawn. Even this devilish torture did not make the poor brutes cry out. When finally they were thrown on the fire and allowed to be burned to death, this came as a relief to the maimed and suffering victims.*

SOURCE: *Vicksburg Evening Post*, February 13, 1904.

Cashman based his famous article on an anonymous source. He also published a less well-known account after interviewing another editor.

116. *"Editor J. A. Richardson Talks about Indianola Post Office and Doddsville Burning,"* 1904

J. A. Richardson, editor of the Indianola Tocsin, is in Vicksburg today en route to New Orleans where he will take in the Mardi Gras festivities. Mr. Richardson states that there was not very much rejoicing at Indianola when President Roosevelt decided to appoint a postmaster there to succeed Minnie Cox, the negress. The local post office maintained by the people of Indianola, mail being taken from and delivered to the nearby post office of Heathman, has worked so smoothly that the people are getting along nicely and with no discomfort. Of course the expense has been greater.

Mr. Richardson was present when Luther Holbert and his wife were burned at the stake last Sunday for the murder of James S. Eastland, a prominent planter of Sunflower county. Mr. Richardson rode horseback from Indianola to the scene of the execution, near Doddsville, a distance of about thirty miles, going in his capacity of correspondent for some of the big city papers. Speaking of the thrilling event, Mr. Richardson said this morning:

"After one of the most thrilling and persevering human chases ever had in the history of Mississippi extending over four counties and lasting over eighty hours Luther Holbert and his wife were captured in a dense cane brake on a plantation just below Shepardtown about four o'clock Saturday evening. They had been discovered by a small boy who was passing through who reported the fact to Mr. E. L. O'Neal and Victor Lavender, who being heavily armed went out there and captured Holbert and his wife. They surprised the murderers and easily caught the woman but Holbert broke and ran and was wounded twice in the left leg before he was finally halted.

"The capture was full of excitement as the race had been and the captors turned their prisoners over to the pursuing posse headed by deputy sheriff Allen of our county. With him were Harry Williams and his faithful negroes who had striven so hard to capture them. The rifle and pistol of the murderers were secured and turned in with them.

"They were quickly tied and taken back toward Itta Bena by the Deputy Sheriff. The deputy made a stout effort to hold the murderers but the pressure was too great and he being overpowered yielded to superior numbers and the prisoners were taken in charge by the mob who quickly placed them in a spring wagon and drove hurriedly through the country toward Doddsville reaching thereabout 3 p.m. in the afternoon.

"They were taken to the cabin where the murder of James S. Eastland was committed and preparations were immediately made to burn the prisoners.

"A stump in the yard was selected the expiating stake and Holbert's wife was prepared for the fire, when a good hot fire was made she was chained to the stump and her husband was compelled to witness her death agonies. The fire was started by a brother of the murdered man.

"After she had died the [] Holbert was thrown on the flames [] kicked out and broke away but he did not run far however, before he was caught and willing hands again threw him on the fiercely burning flames which quickly consumed him.

"They bore their fate with a bravery worthy of a better cause but it sufficed them nothing. Blood ran from every pore in their body, but they murmured not; not one comment escaped them, not a single groan. They went to their death without repenting of their crime or complaining of their crime's avengers.

"Sheriff Anderson of this county did all in his power to prevent the burning of the murderers but he was absolute powerless in face of the determined citizens that opposed him. Everything at Doddsville is at present quiet and all the citizens have returned to their homes and no trouble is even thought of."

[The last three paragraphs are printed so closely to the interior binding, that some words do not appear on the microfilm.—Ed.]

SOURCE: *Vicksburg Evening Post,* February 13, 1904.

Progressivism took its inspiration not only from the sciences but from evangelical Protestantism as well. The Progressives went after social wickedness with social science—and evangelical zeal.[10]

If the Progressive movement sprang from religious roots, some thought lynching did as well. Walter White, the secretary of the NAACP at the time, doubted that lynching could flourish under any religion other than Christianity. Christianity alone drew the color line and Christian nations despoiled Africa, White wrote in *Rope and Faggot: A Biography of Judge Lynch.* White did not really explain just why he thought Christianity peculiarly promoted slavery, but he did compare evangelical revivals ("disturbances") to mob violence. "Bible-beating, acrobatic, fanatical preachers" stirred "orgies of emotion" not unlike frenzied lynch mobs. In fact, "frenzy" is the word White used to describe evangelical emotionalism, the same word used by journalists to describe the Statesboro mob.[11] More recently Orlando Patterson thought it no accident that some (not most or many) lynchings occurred near churches, adding that since Christians attached great "mythic and ritual significance" to trees, that explained why so many lynchers used trees to hang their victims. Bridges also carried important symbolic value for lynching ritualists.[12]

Blaming evangelical Christianity for lynching may remind twenty-first-century readers of those who question the relationship between Muslim extremism and mob violence. In 2004 the crowd that burned alive and then hanged four American civilians in Falluja during the Iraq war reminded one *Wall Street Journal* writer of American lynchers.[13]

In 1905 E. T. Wellford, a Presbyterian pastor in Virginia, asked Christians to consider the similarity between the crucifixion of Christ and lynchings. Wellford identified American lynching as spectacle, human sacrifice carried out as a religious ritual. Wellford wrote that if Christ had been legally executed, then Christianity is a blasphemy. The illegality of his crucifixion makes Christianity holy; Christ was lynched, Wellford insisted, or Christianity is a fraud. Since Reverend Wellford did not think his religion a fraud, he worked to prove that Christ died at the hands of an illegal mob. Wellford, in contrast to Walter White, insisted that Christians should see all lynching as an affront to their religion, a continuation of Christ's crucifixion. Christian lynchers, Wellford believed, simply misapplied their own religion.[14]

117. *E. T. Wellford, "The Lynching of Jesus,"* 1905

The populace has tasted blood. They are conscious of their physical power. The savage spirit of barbarity has been revived, men must be broken afresh to law and order as the wild horse to harness. The unbridled spirit of an unmanageable mob has run away with law and justice. The "Reign of Terror" has sprung up in America. . . .

To this disastrous condition of affairs is added the humiliating spectacle of governmental participation. The officers of the law, sworn to execute justice to all and favor to none, are found calmly surveying the scene or actively encouraging it! To mob violence is added judicial murder!

Not infrequently the awful realization dawns, when too late to make amends, that the tortured creature was as harmless as a babe. Fury had vented its wrath upon a vicarious sacrifice and the innocent had suffered for the guilty! . . .

Lynch law is usually credited as an American product. The most awful application of it, however, belongs to the first century. There is to be found *par excellence* the unauthorized mob, there the most innocent victim, there the law most flagrantly defied, there the judicial and military branches of government most actively engaged, there the most deliberate anarchy, there the most excruciating agony. The lynching of Jesus excels in brutality, and in the slaughter of the innocent, all succeeding offences. So long as the twentieth century looks on with unstirred sympathy and passes by the mobbing of Jesus with unconcern and apathy, so long will similar deeds be repeated, in any land, with impunity. If the public conscience does not resent the greatest it will not take cognizance of the less.

SOURCE: E. T. Wellford, *The Lynching of Jesus: A Review of the Legal Aspects of the Trial of Christ* (Newport News: Franklin Printing, 1905), 12, 14, 17, 18.

The most brutal mob killings of African Americans imaginable regularly appeared on the pages of American newspapers through the Progressive period. None of these spectacles, however, attracted the attention devoted to the killing of Leo Frank. Not just the public but academics have made Leo Frank's death the most important Progressive-era lynching.

The first tiny ripples across the American consciousness surfaced with the murder of thirteen-year-old Mary Phagan in Atlanta, Georgia, on April 26, 1913. Atlanta police failed to identify the actual killer, an African American named Jim Conley, and instead fastened on Leo Frank, the Jewish manager of the factory where Phagan worked.

If Conley had beaten Phagan to death fourteen months before rather than after William Randolph Hearst had purchased the *Atlanta Georgia*, Leo Frank might be a forgotten man today. Hearst, a sensationalist, hated minorities and did not hesitate to use his papers to aggravate racial tensions. But it is not exactly clear if Hearst's prejudices fueled the *Georgia*'s lurid coverage. Hearst's Atlanta staff seemed more interested in selling newspapers than promoting prejudice. Nonetheless, by firing public sympathy for the young and photogenic (with retouching) Mary Phagan, Hearst's men elevated her to iconic status, the very essence of rural innocence in an industrializing age, and fired the public's zeal to punish her killer and everything he represented.

118. *Herbert Asbury, "Hearst Comes to Atlanta,"* 1926

William Randolph Hearst bought the Atlanta *Georgian* in February, 1912, and immediately seduced journalism in that pearl of the Southland with banner lines, photograph layouts and Advice to the Lovelorn. . . . He shot the doddering and decrepit *Georgian* full of comic strips, headlines and syndicate features, and for a little while Atlanta took him to her bosom and fawned upon him; journalistically he soon had the town by the tail and was swinging her high, wide and handsome, to the extreme distress of the *Constitution* and the *Journal*, whose editors had never before known the terrors of competition with America's journalistic wild-cat. . . .

II

The Frank case, which developed probably the greatest news story in the history of the State, if not of the South, broke late one Saturday night about a month after I reached Atlanta: [Foster] Coates was in charge of the *Georgian* when Mary Phagan was found murdered in the basement of the plant of the National Pencil Company, where she worked and of which Frank was manager: Coates saw the possibilities of the story immediately, and aroused Mike Clofine. Clofine saw even more than Coates had seen, and before noon the next day every reporter on the *Georgian* staff was working furiously, while the staffs of the *Constitution* and *Journal* were slumbering peacefully in church or otherwise wasting the Sabbath. On Monday morning the *Constitution* printed a half column or so about the crime, and the *Journal*, in its first edition, had even less. And had not Hearst owned the *Georgian*, it, too, would have published half a column, and in a few days the story probably would have died a natural death.

But the *Georgian* devoted three pages to the mystery, and our first edition was on the street about eight o'clock in the morning. We had pictures, in somber but artistic layouts, on every page—pictures of the murdered girl, of her father, her mother, her grandfather, sisters, uncles, aunts and cousins; pictures of her birthplace in Marietta, of her home in Atlanta, of the pencil factory, of the chief of police, and of a trolley-car conductor who thought he had seen someone acting suspiciously—all sorts of pictures. Across the front page was a screaming banner line of noble proportions, with smaller lines below it, and a leaded editorial demanding the arrest and punishment of the murderer. We had a drawing of the murderer himself, prepared by one of the artists from descriptions of various eager citizens who thought they had seen someone who might have been the man, and a diagram of the basement of the pencil factory, showing where the body was found and where it had been dragged, and so forth.

We printed stories of previous child murders, stories about and interviews with every member of the murdered girl's family—thousands of words. My own contribution was an interview with Mary Phagan's grandfather in Marietta. It went something like this: "'By the living God of my fathers!' cried the aged man as he stood bareheaded in the doorway of his modest cottage, unmindful of the pelting rain which mingled with his tears as they ploughed great furrows in his gaunt and withered cheeks, 'I shall not rest until I have had vengeance upon the murderer of my innocent child! I swear it!'" It was not raining, either, although it might well have been.

Our paper was, in modern parlance, a wow. It burst upon Atlanta like a bomb and upon the *Constitution* and *Journal* like the crack of doom. And especially did it burst upon the *Journal*. The editors of that paper had expected the *Georgian* to do something a bit unusual, but they had not anticipated anything even remotely resembling our performance. They were dazed, but they were soon awakened by the plaintive cries of their circulation managers, who reported tearfully that *Georgian*s were selling like the proverbial hot cakes, while *Journal*s could not be given away. They lifted what they could of the *Georgian*'s stories for their second and subsequent editions, and within half an hour after we were on the street the whole *Journal* staff was clamoring at the flabbergasted police, who had expected to make a quiet little investigation and forget it. The case presented a tough problem, and they were not very keen on tough problems.

III

Leo M. Frank was a tall, thin, nervous young Jew, widely known and well-connected in Jewish circles in Atlanta, and in Brooklyn, where his mother lived. He was not arrested until several days after the murder, but meanwhile Atlanta was quite frantic with excitement. People gathered in groups on the street corners, reading the *Georgian*'s screaming headlines and soaking their brains in our weird and exciting stories. In some quarters there was resentment against the Hearst method of handling the story, but on the whole the population thoroughly approved of us, because we certainly did provide snappy reading matter and fine pictures to look at. There was much talk of lynching, but it was aimless talk, directed against no one in particular; the general opinion seemed to be that a Negro must be guilty, and the police did all they could to find a darky on whom they could fix the crime. But for once they failed.

Foster Coates made a blunder when Frank was accused of the crime and taken to Police Headquarters. He put an extra on the street, of course—and wrote a banner line for it which said without qualification that the strangler had been arrested! The type was even larger than we used when we tried to convince the citizenry that there was news when there was none. The line was a blunder of the sort that is made every day in newspaper offices, but it had far-reaching consequences. The Jews of Atlanta considered it a deadly insult to their race; they said the *Georgian* had called Frank guilty before his trial, and that it showed the existence of an organized conspiracy to railroad him to the gallows. Immediately they raised the cry of persecution; they came singly and in groups to the office and demanded that the editors denounce the police and insist on Frank's immediate release, declaring that he was being persecuted because he was a Jew. This was not true then, but it became true later on.

There has been a lot of wild writing and talking about Frank's martyrdom, but the fact is that there was no sentiment against him because of his Jewish birth and religion until the Jews themselves raised the issue. Then, quite naturally, the people of Atlanta began referring to Frank as "that damned Jew," and they began to grow annoyed at the insistence of the Jews that manufactured evidence was being used against him. Yet if Frank had been an Italian they would have called him "that damned wop," and if he had been a Negro they would have said "that damned nigger," and no one would have complained that his arrest was an insult to the Italian or Negro races. If the Jews had been content to regard Frank as a man suspected of murder, entitled to a fair trial and nothing more, instead of as a Jew on the threshold if martyrdom, hounded by Christians thirsting for his blood, there would have been little or no anti-Semitic feeling in Atlanta.

The *Journal* and the *Constitution* paid no attention to the demands of the Jews, and for a long time the *Georgian* ignored them also. But pressure was soon brought to bear in New York, and little by little the editorial and news columns of the *Georgian* began to veer toward Frank, although evidence was constantly piling up against him; indeed, toward the end we worked as hard trying to prove his innocence and build up sentiment for him and against the Negro, Jim Conley, who had confessed to helping Frank hide the body, as we did to legitimate news of the case. The *Constitution* and the *Journal* turned more or less against Frank, though never violently so, largely because the *Georgian* had taken the opposite position. . . .

SOURCE: Herbert Asbury, "Hearst Comes to Atlanta," *American Mercury* 7 (January 1926): 87–95. Used by permission of Legion for the Survival of Freedom, Inc., P.O. Box 2739, Newport Beach, California 92659.

When Frank's jury convicted the defendant, Georgia's senior senator, Hoke Smith, denounced the trial as a mob-dominated sham and declared that a death sentence from such a court amounted to judicial murder. The former congressman and Populist Tom Watson struck back at his rival, accusing Smith of coddling rich criminals. Watson attacked Frank as well, but only secondarily. C. Vann Woodward's biography of Watson carefully reviews the aging Populist's howling anti-Semitism and his obsession with the Frank case, and emphasized the public's receptiveness. "Eager crowds" met trains to grab Watson's newspaper. Great stacks "melted like snowflakes" in the urban centers. Circulation soared. Woodward at least implicitly credited Watson with stirring up Georgians' lethal enmity for Frank. According to Leonard Dinnerstein's authoritative account of the Frank lynching, Watson switched his focus to Frank, and became obsessed with anti-Semitism, only after his readers responded powerfully to the bigotry he originally downplayed.[15]

If that were so, then Watson did not really lead Georgians into a violent hatred of Frank. They already believed in Frank's guilt before Watson ever wrote a word. Rather, Watson, one of the most powerfully popular politicians in Georgia, reassured rural whites in their instincts against Frank. After Frank's conviction, Watson published many lengthy articles in his magazine and his newspaper, building a case designed to warn Governor John M. Slaton not to disturb the verdict. Woodward reports that Watson sent an emissary to the governor, begging for Frank's execution.[16] Some of his articles came perilously close to openly calling for a lynching.

119. *Tom Watson, "Rise! People of Georgia!"* 1915

People of Georgia! Are you going to sit still, and let them run this thing over you?

Are you going to allow a clamorous minority, make a mockery of Justice, a farce of jury trial, a bye-word of our Laws?

Are you going to provide encouragement and justification *for future lynchings*, by allowing Big Money to annul the well-weighed findings of unimpeachable jurors, whose verdict rests on unimpeachable testimony, and bears the approval of the highest court in the world?

Are you going to allow them to fling a Pandora's box into Georgia politics, from whose open lid there will come bitter animosities, and troubles, for years to come?

What right will any Hebrew have to say hereafter that there is prejudice against his race, if they fling down the gauntlet at our feet, and say, by deeds that speak louder than words, *that no criminal of that race shall hang*?

The case has been taken away from the courts and is apparently to be tried again, on the hustings, in the editorial rooms, in school houses, in miscellaneous gatherings, in pamphlets, in telegrams, in circulars, in petitions, in hearings before the Prison Commission.

Every office-holder, or office-seeker, whose constituency embraces Jewish bankers, editors, or voters, will cheaply throw an anchor to windward by asking for the ravisher, sodomist, and murderer, Leo Frank.

Legally, this man's guilt has been *adjudicated*.

Legally, he can not be tried again.

Legally, he must be executed.

Let no Prison Commission, or Governor, be deceived. Let no one make a mistake about the deep, intense and bitter feeling that prevails among the plain people of Georgia.

The clamor of paid lawyers, is one thing: the manufactured howl of hysteria, is another: the perfunctory appeals of place-holders and place-hunters, isn't worth hell's room: the petitions signed by the indifferent, the duped, the coerced, and the misled, are mere waste of ink and paper.

This is Georgia's case: and Georgia means to control it.

SOURCE: *Jeffersonian*, June 3, 1915.

When Governor Slaton commuted Frank's sentence, he thwarted not only the law but also the will of the people, Watson charged. A wealthy Jewish conspiracy had bribed the governor; only lynching would right the wrong, Watson implied—or very nearly said directly.[17]

Two months after the commutation, on August 16, 1915, a mob broke into the Georgia penitentiary, seized Frank, and then hanged him from a tree. Watson thoroughly approved the killing as an act of popular sovereignty, more legal than the commutation.

120. *Tom Watson, "The Voice of the People Is the Voice of God!"* 1915

If democracy does not mean just that, let us abandon our Republican form of Government, kiss the Pope's foot, and ask him to appoint a "divine right" king to rule over us!

Give us one of the Hohensollerns[18] who bought his crown from the House of Hapsburg; or give us a Hapsburg who bought *his,* from a Medieval Pope.

If we have got to abandon democracy, let us go the whole hog, and have a monarch who is a partner to the Pope and the Almighty.

Democracy means, that ALL POWER IS IN THE PEOPLE!

The right to establish government, choose rulers, make laws, found institutions, reward merit, and punish crime, *is in the People.*

The People *delegate* these powers, but never surrender them.

Our highest law declares that the People *cannot* surrender these inherent, inalienable powers.

Just like any other principal who appoints an agent, and is betrayed by that agent, *the People may ignore the act of a recreant agent, and do FOR THEMSELVES what the agent failed to do.*

The Sheriff gets his authority to hang a man from the Law, but the Law got it from the People.

Therefore, the power remains in the People, who have only *delegated* it to an agent.

When the Sheriff kills, it is not his act: *it is the act of the People,* performed through their statutory law.

Look at your Bible, and see whether this has not been so, from of old.

What was the avenger of blood, but the private citizen who could take a life for a life, if the murderer could not outrun him to the City of Refuge?

Our Germanic and British ancestors never hesitated to put to death, swiftly and without a trial, men who were caught red-handed.

When high officials prove themselves to be unfaithful servants of the People, what are the People to do?

If officers of the Law persistently violate the Law, what are the People to do? . . .

Let our rulers try to remember that, under our form of government, *the People rule, BY AGENTS.*

Let those agents have a care!

Let them not usurp powers which the People have *not* delegated.

If they want more power than is given them by Law, let them ask their masters for it.

Their masters are THE PEOPLE!

And let us labor under no mistake as to what happened in Georgia. It was this:

A Vigilance Committee, instead of a Sheriff, carried out *a sentence which remained in full force and effect.*

SOURCE: *Jeffersonian,* August 26, 1915.

Some writers felt that the Frank case excited passions because of its gendered aspects: the case occurred at a time when female behavior and family relations seemed in flux. Converting Phagan into the essence of female purity and nineteenth-century virtue scored points for those defending traditional gender hierarchies against "the leveling potential of social change."[19]

Born April 11, 1865, the radical feminist Mary White Ovington learned radical socialism at the knee of her abolitionist grandmother. The old woman influenced Ovington deeply with talk of the pro-slavery mobs she encountered and her opposition to lynching.[20] Ovington saw the Frank lynching as an opportunity to make a feminist point. Elite white males had cared little for the working poor, until they found they could use the death of one to their own advantage. Like Wellford, Ovington sees religious symbolism at work, but here she makes Phagan the victim of crucifixion.

121. *Mary White Ovington, "Mary Phagan Speaks,"* 1915

You care a lot about me, you men of Georgia, now that I am dead.
You have spent thousands of dollars trying to learn who mutilated my
    body.
You have filled the columns of your newspapers with the story of my
    wrong.
You have broken into a prison and murdered a man that I might be
    avenged.
But why did you not care for me when I was alive?
I was a child, but you shut me out of the daylight.
You held me within four walls watching a machine that crashed through
    the air,
Endlessly watching a knife as it cut a piece of wood.
Noise fills the place—noise, dust and the smell of oil.
I wish some of the thousands of dollars that you spent on the trial might
    have kept me in school.
A real school, the kind you build for the rich.
I worked through the hot August days.
When you were bossing the girls, or shooting birds,
Or lounging in doorways cursing the nigger;
And you never paid me enough to buy a pretty dress.
You sometimes spoke coarsely to me when I went to and from my work;
Yes, you did, and I had to pretend I liked it.
Why did you despise me living and yet love me so now?
I think I know. It is like what the preacher told me about Christ:
People hated Him when He was alive,
But when He was dead they killed man after man for His sake.

SOURCE: *The New Republic* 4 (August 28, 1915): 101.

The most effective Progressive-era muckraking came from the National Association for the Advancement of Colored People, which had its own national publication, *The Crisis.* Walter

White had joined the NAACP in 1918, and immediately went to Estill Springs, Tennessee, where whites had burned alive Jim McIlherron.[21] Walter White had blonde hair, blue eyes and light-colored skin; he could infiltrate the heart of white racism and report back, much as Ida Tarbell could ingratiate herself with sources knowledgeable about the Standard Oil Company. After Tennessee, White next went to Georgia, where he investigated the grisly Mary Turner lynching.

White's writing appeared in *The Crisis*,[22] but his Georgia research reached an audience outside the NAACP subscriber base through the backdoor. Stephen Graham, a prolific travel writer from Scotland who preferred writing about Russia, came to the United States, tramping around the countryside. His description of the Mary Turner lynching closely follows reporting by Walter White for *The Crisis*.[23]

122. *Stephen Graham, "Mary Turner Lynching," 1918*

As far as Georgia is concerned, this record disposes of the theory that lynching only takes place when white women have been attacked. As a matter of fact, the commonest motive for lynching of Negroes throughout the United States has been shown to be mob-condemnation of violence—not of lust. By far the greatest number of lynchings are for supposed murder. The mob lynches the Negro as a man shoots his dog when the latter has turned on him. Formerly attacks on women provided the greater number of cases. If the Negro were fool enough ever to make eyes at a white woman he risked his life. Many innocent admirations and misunderstandings have resulted in lynchings. As for rape, the Negro who commits it is bound to come to a violent end. Very few escape lynching, and the South claims that whatever immunity it enjoys from Negro sexual crimes is due to the deterrent of lynch law. It claims that if the criminals were merely dealt with according to the law sexual crimes would speedily multiply. . . .

To cite an exceptional affair, one might well take the happenings in Brooks and Lowndes Counties, Georgia, in May 1918. Here a white bully, a farmer, with a spite against Negroes, had been in Court and paid the fine of thirty dollars for gambling which had been pronounced against a certain coloured man called Sidney Johnson, and the latter had been sent to his estate to work off the debt. This is an example of the abuse of the law for keeping Negroes still in a state of slavery—a characteristic example of peonage.

Johnson did the work to pay off the fine, but the farmer[24] held him to a great deal more. Eventually the Negro feigned sickness as an excuse for not continuing. The farmer thereupon came to his house and flogged him. It must be supposed this roused the devil in Johnson; he threatened the farmer, and he paid a return visit to the white man's house, fired through the window, killing him and dangerously wounding his wife. He fled, and at once the usual lynching committee was formed. For a whole week they hunted for Johnson, who had gone into hiding. During that time they lynched eleven Negroes, of whom one was a woman.[25]

The farmer had given cause for hatred. He had constantly ill-treated his labourers. On one occasion he had flogged a Negro woman. Her husband had stood up for her, and he had him arrested and sentenced to a term of penal servitude, i.e. put in the chain-gang. The mob concluded that this man must have shot the farmer for revenge, and they accordingly lynched him. He was shot to death. His wife would not be quieted, but kept insisting that her poor husband had been innocent. The mob therefore seized her. They tied her upside down by her ankles to a tree, poured petrol on her clothing, and burned her to death, white American women will perhaps take note that this coloured sister of theirs was in her eighth month with child. The mob around her was not angry or insensate, but hysterical with brutal pleasure. The clothes burned off her body. Her child, prematurely born, was kicked to and fro by the mob, and then . . . Well, that is perhaps sufficient. There are many details of this crime which cannot be set down in print. But all these facts were authenticated and submitted to the Governor of the State. The point that struck me was the pleasure which was taken by the mob in the sufferings which it was causing, It was drunk with cruelty. Here was little idea of a deterrent. Here was no question of racial prudence. From the point of view of the natural history of mankind, it put those white denizens of Georgia on a lower level than cannibals.

It was America's glorious May, when she was pouring troops into Europe and winning the war; hundreds of thousands of Negroes were clad in the uniform of the Army and were fighting for "freedom and justice" in Europe. The moral eloquence of the President was in all men's minds. America had the chance to take the moral leadership of the world.

But away back in Georgia the mob pursued its horrible way. At length they found the original Johnson, who had committed the murder, and he defended himself to the last in a house, with gun and revolver, and died fighting. His dead body was dragged at the back of a motorcar through the district, and then burned.

SOURCE: Stephen Graham, *Children of the Slaves* (London: Macmillan, 1920), 203–208.

Hugh Dorsey, prosecutor of Leo Frank, profited enormously from that case. In 1916 demand for him to enter the gubernatorial race "swept the state like a prairie fire."[26] Dorsey served until 1921, and sat as governor when the Mary Turner mob that Walter White investigated rampaged through south Georgia. Dorsey declared martial law and sent in state troops to restore order. His critics, however, charged that since he had essentially promoted lynching in the Leo Frank case, and lynchers had supported his candidacy, he had a special responsibility to curb the state's appetite for mob law.[27]

The Colored Welfare League of Augusta, Georgia, asked Dorsey to use the powers of his office to stop lynchings. Dorsey responded by chastising the blacks for not condemning the crimes that sparked lynchings. For their part, the Georgia's white newspapers soon returned to running stories about "Hun Atrocities," including the bayoneting of babies and "the crucifixion of captured soldiers."[28]

123. *Hugh Dorsey Answers the Colored Welfare League of Augusta*, 1918

Unfortunately, your resolutions and similar protests heretofore emanating from representative organizations of your race, dealing with kindred subjects, are silent concerning this supreme outrage upon law and civilization, which too often provokes

communities to substitute summary vengeance for the form of organized justice recognized by law. I trust your organization will, by concerted action with similar organizations of your race, disseminate this doctrine. That personal outrages and violence, especially against helpless women and children, will not be tolerated by any civilized community, but will provoke prompt retaliation of community vengeance
which is difficult, if not impossible, to control, and that the surest way to discourage
lynching is to convince the lawless element that such provocative outrages will not be
tolerated. . . .

I am confident that the failure of your resolutions to incorporate this doctrine was
inadvertent, and I am equally sure you will be prompt to avail your organization of
the only practical method by which they can be of real assistance to the executive department of this state in its efforts to discourage lynchings and maintain supremacy
of our courts.

SOURCE: *Augusta Chronicle*, May 25, 1918.

A year after the Georgia lynchings, in October 1919, the newspapers that white people read ran
frightening headlines saying that Arkansas whites had—just barely and fortunately—crushed
a "well-organized Negro uprising." This news came at a time when Americans had grown accustomed to reports of urban racial violence. In the summer and fall of 1919 race rioting had
erupted in Washington, D.C., Chicago, Omaha, Knoxville, and Indianapolis.

The Arkansas trouble started shortly before midnight, September 30, when whites and
blacks exchanged gunfire outside Hoop Spur Church. One white man, Will Adkins, died in the
fighting.[29] The white newspapers' hysterical reporting said that "Negro rioters" were so out of
control that they had even fired on the Arkansas governor Charles Brough. One white reporter
later claimed that whites massacred 856 blacks in the "riot." The NAACP put the number killed
at 250 and reported that the stench of their rotting bodies carried for two miles.[30]

The NAACP's Walter White investigated the violence in Phillips County and wrote that it resulted from whites' exploitative sharecropping system combined with their irrational fear of organized labor. What whites called an "uprising" was actually a movement to organize something called the Progressive Farmers and Householders Union of America. Sharecroppers
hoped for a fairer price for their cotton.[31] Meanwhile, Arkansas hurried nearly one hundred defendants to trial and sentenced twelve to death.

The Arkansas Supreme Court reversed half the death sentences the following March. In their
haste the jurors had failed to write the verdicts properly. But the court affirmed the other convictions, even though those verdicts seemed oddly written as well.

The six defendants who were lucky enough to win before the state supreme court got new
trials, where they promptly received a fresh round of death sentences in May 1920. But the
Arkansas Supreme Court again reversed those convictions, this time because no blacks served
on the juries.

Meanwhile, the other defendants, the ones who lost before the Arkansas Supreme Court in
the first place, filed habeas corpus petitions before the Pulaski County Chancery Court in Little Rock, claiming, accurately, that the Arkansas state courts had denied them due process of
law. Frank Hick's petition narrated whites' efforts to lynch him, in and out of court. This petition began a process that ended up in the U.S. Supreme Court.

124. *Frank Hicks, Petition for Writ of Habeas Corpus,* May 2, 1921

Your petitioner, Frank Hicks, states that he is a citizen of the State of Arkansas, and is now residing in Little Rock, confined in the Arkansas State Penitentiary, within the jurisdiction of this court; that the defendant, E. H. Dempsey, is the Keeper of the Arkansas State Penitentiary, and as such, is unlawfully restraining your petitioner of his liberty, and will, unless prevented from so doing by the issuance of the Writ herein prayed for, deprive him of his life on the 10th day of June, 1921, in violation of the Constitution and Laws of the United States, and of the Constitution and laws of the state of Arkansas.

Petitioner further says that he is a Negro, of African descent, black in color, and that prior to the time hereinafter mentioned was a citizen and resident of Phillips County, Arkansas, at Elaine; that on the ___ day of October, 1919, he was arrested, placed in the Phillips County jail, and thereafter, until his trial was kept in close confinement upon an alleged charge of murder in the first degree for the killing of one Clinton Lee, a white man, said to have occurred on October 1st, 1919; that said Clinton Lee was killed, as he is informed, while a member of a posse of white men who were said to be attempting to quell a race riot, growing out of the killing of W. A. Adkins on the night of September 30, 1919, at Hoop Spur, in said County and State; that said Adkins, as he is advised, was killed under these circumstances and conditions; Petitioner and a large number of the members of his race were peaceably and lawfully assembled in their church house at or near Hoop Spur, with no unlawful purpose in view, and with no desire or purpose to injure or do any wrong to any one; that while no desire or purpose to injure or do any wrong to any one; that while they were thus assembled, white persons began firing guns or pistols from the outside into and through said church house, through the windows and shooting the lights out therein; causing a great disturbance and stampede of those assembled therein; that the white persons so firing on said church came there in automobiles, of which there were several, and came for the purpose of breaking up said meeting; that said Atkins was killed either by members of his own party or by some other person unknown to your petitioner; that the white men sent out the word to Helena, the County seat, that said Adkins had been killed by the Negroes, shot down in cold blood while on a peaceable mission, by an armed force of Negroes, assembled at said church, which caused great excitement all over the City of Helena and Phillips County; that the report of said killing spread like wild fire into other Counties, all over the State of Arkansas, and into other States, notably the State of Mississippi; that early the next day a large number of white men of said county armed themselves and rushed to the scene of the trouble and to adjacent regions, the vicinity of Elaine being one of them, and began the indiscriminate hunting down, shooting and killing of Negroes; that in a short time white men from adjoining Counties and from the State of Mississippi likewise armed themselves[,] rushed to the scene of the trouble and began the indiscriminate shooting down of Negroes, both men and women, particularly the posse from the state of Mississippi, who shot down in cold blood innocent Negro men and women many of whom were at the time in the fields picking cotton; that highly inflammatory articles were published in the press of Arkansas and especially of Helena and throughout the United States, in which the trouble was variously called a "race riot," "an uprising of the Negroes" and a "Deliberately planned insurrection among the Negroes against the whites of that part of Phillips County"; that the officers of Phillips County, especially the sheriff, called upon the Governor of the state, and the Governor in turn called upon the Commanding Officer at Camp Pike for a large number of United States soldiers to assist the citizens in quelling the so called "race riot," "uprising" or "insurrection"; that a company of soldiers was dispatched to the scene of the trouble who took charge of the situation and finally succeeded in stopping the slaughter.

Your petitioner further says that, he, together with a large number of his race, both men and women, were taken to the Phillips County jail, at Helena, incarcerated therein and charged with murder; that a Committee of Seven composed of leading Helena business men and officials, to-wit: Sebastian Straub, Chairman, H. D. Moore, County Judge, F. F. Kitchens, Sheriff, J. G. Knight, Mayor, E. M. Allen, J. E. Horner and T. W. Keesee was selected for the purpose of probing into the situation and picking out those to be condemned to death and those to be sentenced to the penitentiary; that said Committee assumed charge of the matter and proceeded to have brought before them a large number of those incarcerated in jail and examined them regarding their own connection and the connection of others charged with participation in said trouble; that if evidence unsatisfactory to said Committee was not given they would be sent out and certain of their keepers would take them to a room in the jail which was immediately adjoining and a part of the courthouse building where said Committee was sitting, and torture them by beating and whipping them with leather, whips or straps with metal in them, cutting the blood at every lick until the victims would agree to testify to anything their torturers demanded of them; that there was also provided in said jail, to further frighten and torture them, an electric chair, in which they would be put naked and the current turned on to shock and frighten them into giving damaging statements against themselves and others, also strangling drugs were put up their noses for the same purpose and by these methods and means false evidence was extorted from Negroes to be used and was used against your petitioner.

Petitioner further says that on every day from October 1st until after his trial on November 3rd, 1919, the press of Helena State of Arkansas carried inflammatory articles giving accounts of the trouble which were calculated to arouse and did arouse bitter feeling against your petitioner and the other members of his race, . . . that shortly after being placed in jail, a mob was formed in the City of Helena, composed of hundreds of men, who marched to the County jail for the purpose and with the intent of lynching your petitioner and others, and would have done so but for the interference of the United States soldiers and the promise of some of said Committee and other leading officials that if the mob would stay its hand they would execute those found guilty in the form of law. . . .

Petitioner further says that large crowds of white people bent on petitioner's condemnation and death thronged the courthouse and grounds and streets of Helena all during the trial of petitioner and the other Negro defendants; that on account of the great publicity given his and the other cases, on account of his being charged with connection with an insurrection against the white people, and that four or five white men were killed, on account of the fact that he is a Negro and those who run the courts, the Judge upon the bench, the Sheriff the Clerk and all the jurors being white men, on account of the fact that it was stated and widely published that the purpose of the negroes was to kill the whites and take their property, and on account of all the race prejudice which normally exists and which was enhanced a thousand fold at that time, by bitterness beyond expression, it was impossible for him to get a fair and impartial trial in said court before a jury of white men. . . .

Petitioner further says that the entire trial, verdict and judgment against him was but an empty ceremony; that his real trial and condemnation had already taken place before said "Committee of Seven"; that said Committee, in advance of the sitting of the court, had sat in judgment upon his and all the other cases and had assumed and exercised the jurisdiction of the court by determining the guilt or innocence of those in jail, had acquired the evidence in the manner herein set out, and decided which of the defendants should be electrocuted and which sent to prison and the terms to be given them and which to be discharged; that when court convened the program laid out by said Committee was carried through.

SOURCE: Frank Hicks, Petition for Writ of Habeas Corpus, May 2, 1921, *Frank Hicks v. E. H. Dempsey, Keeper of the Arkansas State Penitentiary,* Pulaski Chancery Court, in State of Arkansas, Ex Rel. Attorney General and *E. H. Dempsey, Keeper of the Arkansas State Penitentiary v. J. E. Martineau, Chancellor, Frank Hicks, Frank Moore, Ed Hicks, J. B. Knox, Ed Coleman, and Paul Hall,* case 2531, Arkansas Supreme Court Briefs and Records, University of Arkansas, Little Rock/Pulaski County Law Library.

The Arkansas attorney general did not dispute the facts alleged in this petition, saying, instead, that the petition did "not allege facts to entitle the [defendants] to the relief prayed for in [the] petition."[32] The U.S. Supreme Court, in a decision by Oliver Wendell Holmes, said that, in fact, Arkansas had tried to legally lynch the men. The Supreme Court decision did not guarantee freedom for the defendants but only a new trial conducted by the same state courts that had railroaded them in the first place.

Nonetheless, by the time Holmes wrote his decision, Arkansas authorities had lost their enthusiasm for the Elaine cases. Arkansas compromised on those defendants who had won before the U.S. Supreme Court, knocking the charges down to second-degree murder and then releasing the prisoners for time served. These men left prison in 1925. Shortly after the U.S. Supreme Court decision, the Arkansas Supreme Court released those defendants whose case was not heard before the U.S. Supreme Court, finding that two terms of state court had passed without trial. Of the men sent to prison, all but eight went free in 1923 and authorities released the remainder in 1925.[33]

In 1921, a few months after Republican Warren G. Harding replaced Democrat Woodrow Wilson as president, Mitchell G. Hall wrote to the new president. Harding had shown little interest in taking a strong stand on race during his campaign. A black man and a Republican, Hall nonetheless hoped that the new president might take action on the lynching problem. Harding, however, pursued a "lily-white" southern strategy, hoping to win white voters to the Republican cause.[34]

125. *Mitchell G. Hall to the U.S. Attorney General, 1921*

Sir

I have just read in The Atlanta (Ga) Sunday Journal that Senator Harris[35] was telling you how law abiding the citizens of Georgia are. I am a native southerner I have voted the republican ticket since twenty one years old but what I am going to say concerning criminal condition in this state is not due to political or sectional hate. About six years ago, I was on the Seaboard train going to Savannah I saw two or three dead bodies hanging to telegraph poles in a distance of three or four miles. About five years ago a colored man was lynched openly in this town and the man who it was said tied the victim to the buggy and drove it out to the lynching bee was appointed a Superior Court Judge. About four years ago a colored man was lynched about six miles from this place and his body burnt young boys on their way to Sunday School ashes of the burned victim in their pockets and showing the ashes around the Church. This state has what is known as a labor contract law, but it only applies to the colored laborer that virtually enslaves him unless he pays himself out of debt he owes the landlord. I was book keeper four or five years in the U.S. Marshals office for the Southern District of Georgia, I resigned and came to this place, served two years as postmaster under president Harrison and was removed by president Cleveland. I afterward served as postmaster 4 years under president McKinley and four years under president Roosevelt. I hope you will consider what I am letting you [know] as private as I have to live down here and have many personal friends among the democrats. No colored person can sue or prosecute a white man in these Georgia courts. If you should desire more information in future command me.

> Very respectfully
> Mitchell G. Hall
> Cordele, Georgia
> May 16, 1921

SOURCE: File 158260.140, straight numerical files, Department of Justice, Record Group 60, National Archives, College Park, Maryland.

As the Elaine riot defendants worked though Arkansas's criminal justice system, the *Norfolk Guide and Journal* monitored their progress, eagerly crediting the NAACP with providing the legal firepower that ultimately freed every defendant. Plummer Bernard Young edited the *Norfolk Guide and Journal*. One generation removed from slavery, Young had taken over the *Guide and Journal* in 1909, when the paper had a circulation of just five hundred readers. A dogged accommodationist, Young admired Booker T. Washington. His father, also a journalist, had thought his fellow black journalist, T. Thomas Fortune, too radical and that northerners generally did not understand southern realities. P. B. Young stuck with his father's stance through the rise of W. E. B. Du Bois, through World War I, through the Red Scare (when the U.S. Attorney General accused black leaders and leading journalists of being "Bolsheviks"), and through the rise of the NAACP. Young led the NAACP in Norfolk, even though his conservatism and determination to work within the white system sometimes contradicted NAACP policy.

Young's accommodationist position did not prevent him from denouncing lynching violence. Perhaps his reports carried more weight than those of his rival, the *Richmond Planet*. Young sold more papers than Mitchell. In fact, after World War I the *Journal and Guide* had the largest circulation of any black paper in the South. And Young was "more temperate, better organized, and factually more reliable" than his rival.[36]

126. Norfolk Journal and Guide, *"New Wrinkle in Mobbery,"* 1925

The Sussex County delegation furnished adherents of lynch law something new in the technique of evading apprehension by removing the scant remains of its victim into another county, beyond the jurisdiction of its own coroner, legally blocking even the possibility of any effective grand jury action; and the neighboring county coroner promptly obliged, aided, and abetted the Sussex county mobocrats by burying the remains as soon as they were found, after the usual formality of pronouncing that the man who was hanged, shot and burned came to his death at the hands of parties unknown.

All of which was unnecessary. The Sussex county coroner would have done the same thing. The only plausible pretext we can attribute to the Sussex citizens for the removal of the remains so precipitately is that they heard Governor Trinkle was on his way to Waverly to make an inspection and they wanted to clean up the public square before he got there.

The lynching is regretted. The crime which provoked the lynching is just as deeply regretted. It is deplorable that there are human perverts at large who will so outrage society, and that there are normal citizens who will so quickly lose their self-control as to trample under their feet all of the orderly processes of law which are of their own making. But such is our civilization. And such is our shame. If the man committed the crime he deserved the death penalty. He would have gotten it at the hands of a Virginia court, swiftly and surely. His crime is avenged. But there are at large in the county 2,000 first degree murderers, if the newspaper estimate of the size of the mob is correct, who will never be punished.

The lynching was a particularly atrocious one. Georgia recently burned a man alive, and Tennessee recently hanged and riddled with bullets the body of a fifteen year old boy. In the Waverly performance Georgia and Tennessee surrender the belt to Virginia. The Old Dominion hanged, perforated with shots, and then burned its man.

Lynchings have been rare in Virginia. But of late we are coming upon evil days. There is a growing intolerance, fomented by various societies and groups, purporting to be operating in the name of expediency. The calm, educated, sophisticated mind can absorb their teachings and insidious propaganda without going out and lusting for human blood, but the masses cannot. And it is the masses, the average man, that loses equilibrium when poise and restraint are most needed.

That is something worth thinking about. It is something that should command the thoughtful attention of the lawful authorities, the church, the press and the school.

SOURCE: "No Wrinkle in Mobbery," *Norfolk Journal and Guide*, March 28, 1925. Reprinted by permission.

NOTES

1. James A. Henretta, David Brody, Susan Ware, and Marilynn S. Johnson, *America's History*, 4th ed. (Boston: Bedford/St. Martin's, 2000), 642.

2. *Birmingham Age-Herald*, August 17, 1904.

3. "The Finale of the Statesboro Disgrace," *Voice of the Negro* 1 (December 1904): 588.

4. *Birmingham Age-Herald*, August 18, 1904.

5. *Mobile Register*, reprinted in *Vicksburg Evening Post*, August 19, 1904.

6. James Eastland was the uncle of James O. Eastland, born in 1904 and destined to be a U.S. senator.

7. Mary Church Terrell, "Lynching from a Negro's Point of View," *North American Review* 178 (May 1904): 854.

8. Sutton E. Griggs, *The Hindered Hand; or, The Reign of the Repressionist* (Nashville: Orion, 1905); Benjamin Brawley, *A Social History of the American Negro: Being a History of the Negro Problem in the United States* (New York: Macmillan, 1921), 317–318.

9. Walter White, *Rope and Faggot: A Biography of Judge Lynch* (1929; reprint ed., Notre Dame: University of Notre Dame Press, 2001), 35–36; Frank Shay, *Judge Lynch: His First Hundred Years* (New York: Ives Washburn, 1938), 103–105.

10. Richard L. McCormick, "The Discovery That Business Corrupts Politics: A Reappraisal of the Origins of Progressivism," *American Historical Review* 86 (April 1981): 247–274.

11. Walter White, *Rope and Faggot: A Biography of Judge Lynch* (1929; reprint ed., Notre Dame: University of Notre Dame Press, 2001), 40–43.

12. Orlando Patterson, *Rituals of Blood: Consequences of Slavery in Two American Centuries* (New York: Basic Civitas, 1998), 204–206.

13. *Wall Street Journal*, April 5, 2004; for a news account of the Falluja lynching, see *New York Times*, April 1, 2004.

14. Donald G. Mathews, "The Southern Rite of Human Sacrifice," *Journal of Southern Religion* 3 (2000). Available online at http://jsr.as.wvu/edu/jsrlink3.htm.

15. C. Vann Woodward, *Tom Watson: Agrarian Rebel* (1938; reprint ed., New York: Oxford University Press, 1979), 437–446; Leonard Dinnerstein, *The Leo Frank Case* (1968; reprint ed., Athens: University of Georgia Press, 1987), 97–99.

16. Dinnerstein, *The Leo Frank Case*, 97–99; Woodward, *Tom Watson*, 440.

17. Tom Watson, "The Celebrated Case of the State of Georgia vs. Leo Frank," *Watson's Magazine* 21 (August 1915): 182, 208–209, 211, 230.

18. The Hohenzollern family ruled Brandenburg with Berlin as their capital. After the Thirty Years War, the Hohenzollerns consolidated and expanded power.

19. Nancy MacLean, "Gender, Sexuality, and the Politics of Lynching: The Leo Frank Case Revisited," in W. Fitzhugh Brundage, ed., *Under Sentence of Death: Lynching in the South* (Chapel Hill: University of North Carolina Press, 1997), 158–188. This case has attracted numerous authors in addition to Dinnerstein. See, for example, Steve Oney, *And the Dead Shall Rise: The Murder of Mary Phagan and the Lynching of Leo Frank* (New York: Pantheon Books, 2003); Robert Seitz Frey and Nancy S. Thompson, *The Silent and the Damned: The Murder of Mary Phagan and the Lynching of Leo Frank* (1988; reprint ed., New York: Cooper Square Press, 2002); Jeffrey Melnick, *Black-Jewish Relations on Trial: Leo Frank and Jim Conley in the New South* (Jackson: University Press of Mississippi, 2000).

20. Mary White Ovington, *Black and White Sat Down Together: The Reminiscences of an NAACP Founder* (New York: Feminist Press, 1995), 5.

21. Walter White, "The Burning of Jim McIlherron, an N.A.A.C.P. Investigation," *The Crisis* 16 (May 1918): 16–20.

22. Walter White, "The Work of a Mob," *The Crisis* 16 (September 1918): 221–223.

23. Kenneth Robert Janken, *White: The Biography of Walter White, Mr. NAACP* (New York: New Press, 2003), 32–33.

24. The farmer was Hampton Smith of Brooks County. See *Augusta Chronicle,* May 19, 1918.

25. The mob lynched Will Head and Will Thompson as accomplices to the murder of Hampton Smith (*Augusta Chronicle,* May 19, 1918). The Georgia press reported that the mob hanged Mary Turner on May 19 (*Augusta Chronicle,* May 20, 1918; *Atlanta Constitution,* May 20, 1918). The *Chronicle* reported that Eugene Rice, and Hayes Turner had also been lynched (*Augusta Chronicle,* May 21, 1918). Valdosta police and sheriff's deputies killed Sidney Johnson in a gun battle (*Augusta Chronicle,* May 23, 1918). In a separate incident a mob almost ninety miles north of Valdosta killed Him Cobb, a black man charged with beating to death a farmer's wife (*Augusta Chronicle,* May 23, 1918). The total of all these published lynchings was seven.

26. Quoted in Dinnerstein, *The Leo Frank Case,* 159.

27. Oney, *And the Dead Shall Rise,* 614, hails Dorsey as "Georgia's most progressive governor of the time." Academic writers have been less kind. W. Fitzhugh Brundage, *Lynching in the New South,* 236, describes Dorsey as "typically not a bold critic of Georgia's race relations." Robert L. Zandrando, in *The NAACP Campaign against Lynching, 1909–1950* (Philadelphia: Temple University Press, 1980), 58, wrote that, as governor, Dorsey "had not always responded as forthrightly to mob violence as the NAACP had hoped." But after he left office he took a stronger stand.

28. *Augusta Chronicle,* May 25, 1918.

29. It is still not clear if the whites or the blacks fired first. Grif Stockley, *Blood in Their Eyes: The Elaine Race Massacres of 1919* (Fayetteville: University of Arkansas Press, 2001), 3–60; Richard C. Cortner, *A Mob Intent on Death: The NAACP and the Arkansas Riot Cases* (Middletown, Conn.: Wesleyan University Press, 1988), 5–16.

30. *Birmingham News,* October 3, 1919; *Vicksburg Evening Post,* October 3, 1919; Stockley, *Blood in Their Eyes,* 35–38; Cortner, *A Mob Intent on Death,* 30–31.

31. Walter White, "'Massacring Whites' in Arkansas," *The Nation,* December 6, 1919, 715–716.

32. Cortner, *A Mob Intent on Death,* 131.

33. *Banks v. State,* 143 Ark. 154 (1920); *Hicks v. State,* 143 Ark. 158 (1920); *Ware v. State,* 146 Ark., 321 (1920); *State v. Martineau,* 149 Ark. 237 (1921); *Moore et al. v. Dempsey, Keeper of the Arkansas State Penitentiary,* 261 U.S. 86 (1923); *Norfolk Journal and Guide,* June 30, July 21, November 24, 1923; January 24, 1925.

34. Richard B. Sherman, *The Republican Party and Black America from McKinley to Hoover, 1896–1933* (Charlottesville: University Press of Virginia, 1973), 145–173.

35. William J. Harris, elected to the U.S. Senate from Georgia as a Democrat in 1918, served until his death on April 18, 1932.

36. Henry Lewis Suggs, *P. B. Young: Newspaperman, Race, Politics, and Journalism in the New South, 1910–1962* (Charlottesville: University Press of Virginia, 1988), 43–46.

Federal Law against Mob Law

Normally in American life the states rather than the national government protected the health and safety of U.S. citizens, but the southern state governments tolerated mob law against their black citizens. African Americans petitioned the federal government for relief.

At the end of the nineteenth century the national government flexed its muscles in new ways. In 1894, when workers at the Pullman railroad car factory outside Chicago went on strike, the national government intervened. Federal troops marched, breaking the strike even as the governor of Illinois protested the intrusion. Four years later the United States exhibited its strength on the world stage as it had at home. American soldiers defeated Spain in Cuba and then went into a lengthy war against Filipino revolutionaries led by Emilio Aquinaldo.

Little of this expanded national power carried over to race relations in the American South. On March 4, 1897, William McKinley became president of the United States. No president of his time had more reason to fight for civil rights. A Republican, McKinley had served in the Civil War, championed civil rights in Congress, and dispatched troops to block lynchings while serving as governor of Ohio. Spanish outrages and atrocities against an oppressed people led McKinley into Cuba, he claimed. But as a candidate for president, and as president, McKinley wanted to erase sectional divisions, not aid oppressed Americans with military force. He remained largely and disappointingly silent on civil rights issues.[1] This, however, did not prevent black Americans from demanding justice.

127. *Moses Love & Co. to President William McKinley,*
December 4, 1899

Hon Pres & Sec of United States of America We the colored people of Yazoo County State of Miss. Do here call on you for a Separation in the State of Miss. We have no Pertection in this state it is Ruled by its Lynch law. & mob law Ever Week they is some colored man Lynch in this State and it have been so for a long time I believe if you care anything for the colored in this State you will he[a]r our cry We is Perishing in this State Please Separate us. The Govner of this State wont do anything for us. So we look to higher power. Please don't do like the V.P. I written to the V.P. & diden get any answer. I am asking for life Pertection you have herd of thoses Troubles in this State. I hope to he[a]r from you soon.

    Yours Truly

    Moses Love & Co.

SOURCE: Folder 4, box 1117A, 1898-17743, Department of Justice Year Files, 1887–1903, RG 60, National Archives, College Park, Maryland.

Three months later another African American citizen wrote McKinley, complaining about whites' vigilantism. James B. Moseley also begged for his race to be separated from whites. He had given up hope that barbaric whites could ever refrain from brutal violence.

128. *James B. Moseley to President William McKinley,* February 23, 1900

Kind sir please read all

To President McKinly Kind sir his exilency I regret very much to say there is a so called white caping here in the thirteenth and fourth districts in dyer county state of Tennessee white men going around sticking up notices on colored peoples gates ordering them to get out in ten days and if they are not out at that time the white men come together and go to the col peoples houses in the night well armed with Winchester shot guns two and three hundred in a gang and shoot in the houses cripple and kill some of them and drive them away from their homes burning and destroying their property and we have no where to go four families in a mile and half and one mile of dyersburg must get out by saturday night or take care what follow and this is hard I don't write for the Government to send soldiers here for a protection but I am in hopes that Congress will prepare a separate [state] from the white people and send us all to it and let us have a government of our own every time I pick up a paper to read I see where col men are lynched for rapeing white girls and white women and white men all south of the Ohio river say what they please and do what they want to Col girls and Col women and the Col men must not say anything and if the Col man does say any thing against the white man about his daughters wife and sisters the Col man is taken out after night and killed and you see mr president the Col people has no protection in the south I do say please separate us and put us in a country to our selves we have not privllage at all on the sixth day of march 1900 there be a primary election here for country officers and the office seekers have been all over the county asking the Col men to vote for them and they are all democrats and two thirds of the negroes will vote for them.

  I remain as ever respectfully

  James B. Moseley

SOURCE: Folder 5, box 1117A, 1898-17743, Department of Justice Year Files, 1887–1903, RG 60, National Archives, College Park, Maryland.

William McKinley did almost nothing to assist the desperate plight of his black constituents. To woo white southerners into the Republican Party, he instead championed sectional reconciliation. Like his Republican predecessors, however, he did try to placate black voters by appointing a few black men as postmasters. Black Republicans, after all, had backed his nomination in 1896, and he expected them to repeat the favor in 1900.[2] And so McKinley sent Frazier Baker to the Lake City, South Carolina, post office. As soon as Baker arrived, he encountered white hostility and violence.[3] When white racists killed Baker, the *Fairfield News and Herald* accused the dead man of having spoken "in a braggadocio manner."[4]

Federal authorities felt they could not ignore the murder of a postmaster. When the U.S. Attorney Abial Lathrop reported to the Attorney General shortly after the killings, he still hoped that the killers could be convicted in federal court.

129. *Abial Lathrop to Attorney General,* March 5, 1898

Immediately upon receipt of your telegram I communicated with the P. O. Inspectors at Lake City, and had a conference with them and with the Inspector in Charge, who came to Charleston for that purpose. We decided to make Florence, S. C. the base of our operations, that being the nearest point of sufficient size to enable us to work without too much publicity.

I have secured the services of a first class detective who will meet myself and the Inspectors at Florence on the 9th instant, and go to work at once. My investigations will be pursued in such a way as to supplement the work of the P. O. Inspectors, and we have arranged for such a plan of operations as will combine our efforts.

Of course it is too soon to expect any definite results, but I may say that we have already secured valuable information, and I believe that we shall be able to bring some, at least, of the guilty parties to trial.

There is, as you have no doubt seen, a satisfactory public expression of feeling throughout this state in regard to this case, and a general desire on the part of the people to have the guilty parties properly punished. But while this is true in a general way, we have already found that we cannot expect to receive any substantial assistance from the people of that immediate vicinity. Those who are not implicated themselves know that relatives and friends are likely to be, and this will deter them from acting in the premises, so that the only real advantage which we shall obtain from the public sentiment above referred to, will be in the probability of securing a jury that will be willing to render a proper verdict, but we shall have to depend upon our own efforts to procure the necessary evidence.

I will endeavor to keep you advised . . . but in this connection I would say that it would be unwise to enter fully into the details of evidence. The conspiracy which brought about this atrocious crime is far-reaching, and it is essential that the work of exposing it should be conducted with the utmost secrecy.

SOURCE: Box 1047A, Year Files, entry 72, Department of Justice Central files, Record Group 60, General Records of the Department of Justice, National Archives, College Park, Maryland.

Apparently unaware that the U.S. attorney Lathrop and government investigators had already begun to probe the conspiracy behind the crime, Ida B. Wells petitioned on behalf of Baker's widow. She asked how the government could fight Spanish oppression in Cuba but ignore American oppression in South Carolina.

130. *Ida B. Wells's Petition on Behalf of Frazier Baker's Widow and Children,* 1898

To His Excellency, William B. McKinley, President of the United States
    The citizens of Chicago, in Mass Meeting assembled, adopted a Memorial addressed to the President of the United States and Congress in which Memorial attention is called to the lynching of Frazier Baker, an honest capable law-abiding American citizen, at Lake City, South Carolina, February 24th, 1898. This victim of mob fury having been commissioned by you as

Postmaster, was killed because he was a colored man and refused to leave his post of duty. With him his infant child was killed and both were burned in the ruins of his home which had been set on fire by his assassins, only a few minutes before. While attempting to escape from the flames his wife and three children were made targets of white men whose proud boast is their chivalry towards womanhood. All were wounded, some of them maimed for life.

Your memorialists petition you to see that the assassins are apprehended and punished and ask that you recommend a national enactment to protect men, women and children from the awful epidemic of mob law.

We thus appeal to you in the assurance that we have a friend at court. The platform upon which you appealed to the country for support distinctly denounced mob rule, and you have as distinctly declared against lynching in your message to Congress. We now ask that intention manifest itself by action and that strong words interpret themselves in deeds.

For nearly two years the overwhelming sentiment of the American people has demanded that even at the risk of provoking war, this nation interfere with the political policy of a friendly nation. We defend ourselves by declaring against the barbarism of Spanish oppression. Strange that this sentiment so exercised over barbarism in Cuba should rest so complaisant over barbarism at home. During the past fifteen years more than 2,500 men, women and children have been put to death through lynchings, by hanging, shooting, drowning and burning alive. All this in our own land, under our own flag and yet our government has not taken the first step to stop the slaughter. Your Memorialists therefore respectfully suggest Justice like Charity begin at home.

Our faith in you inspires the belief that this appeal shall not be in vain. We command to you the case of the murdered Postmaster and ask that you show to his bereaved and cruelly wounded loved ones the same measure of justice which you would accord to an alien. You cannot bring back the husband and father, nor can you restore to the broken hearted mother the babe that was shot to death in her arms, but the nation owes that family the support and maintenance of which they were deprived by that brutal mob, in so far as money can requite their loss, these helpless ones should be indemnified.

SOURCE: Box 1047A, Year Files, entry 72, Department of Justice Central files, Record Group 60, General Records of the Department of Justice, National Archives, College Park, Maryland.

Even as Wells registered her complaint, federal officers pursued their investigation, running into a solid wall of opposition in Lake City. Even so, investigators learned that the lynchers had organized their killing, plotting to murder Baker almost as soon as he arrived in Lake City.

131. *Abial Lathrop to Attorney General,* April 18, 1898

While we have made some progress in the investigation of this case, we do not feel that we have sufficient testimony to justify us in causing warrants to be issued, and from the peculiar conditions of the case, it is probable that we shall not be able to identify the guilty persons with any degree of certainty until we can secure the testimony of some of the persons who are themselves to some extent connected with the crime. We have taken the statements of a large number of persons living at or in the vicinity of Lake City, and these statements show that those persons who, not being directly concerned, saw the fire of the burning building, or heard the guns on that occasion, were too much frightened to go out or make any effort to identify any of the persons engaged in the deed. We have some evidence of meetings held previous to the final tragedy, the purpose of the meetings being to devise means to remove postmaster Baker, and at which speeches were made by residents of the village advising extreme measures. Some of the persons who were present at these meetings have intimated that they are willing to give information, but only upon condition that they shall be protected, not only from prosecution but also from the other parties interested. I have not hesitated to offer immunity from prosecution, but in the matter of protection I have not felt authorized to make any expenditures for that purpose, and it seems clear from the statements of the Inspectors, and from my own observations, that some provision will have to be made in that behalf before we shall be able to get this testimony. The whole community is absolutely terrorized to such an extent that it is difficult to get anyone there to speak to a person supposed to be interested in the investigation, it being generally understood that to do so will place their lives in jeopardy. . . .

To be worth anything a witness must be removed from the vicinity of Lake City, and he must be assured that he will be kept away and protected from those who will certainly attempt to silence him.

SOURCE: Box 1047A, Year Files, entry 72, Department of Justice Central files, Record Group 60, General Records of the Department of Justice, National Archives, College Park, Maryland.

As federal officials investigated the Baker case, some South Carolina whites defended their state's rights, insisting that only the state could act against the lynchers.

132. Columbia Record, *State Sovereignty and Lynching*, 1898

The News and Courier's editorials favoring relinquishment of State sovereignty are receiving more attention from Northern papers than their importance warrants. Those utterances do not represent the sentiment of the people of South Carolina. They want the Lake City murderers tried and severely punished, but want the State Courts to deal with them. If the Federal Courts are allowed such an assumption of authority, as trial in them of the Lake City murderers would be, there is no telling how far they would then proceed to go in the direction of setting aside the powers and functions of the State Courts. It would be a short step from that to trial of political offenders, or alleged political offenders, in the Federal Courts. Is the News and Courier ready for that step?

SOURCE: *Columbia Record*, reprinted in *Charleston News and Courier*, March 5, 1878.

The *Charleston News and Courier*, the leading white newspaper in South Carolina, thought federal jurisdiction "unquestionable."

133. Charleston News and Courier, *Federal Jurisdiction*, 1898

Some of our contemporaries appear to be more solicitous about establishing the inconsistency of the News and Courier upon the principle of States' rights than they are about securing the punishment of the murderers of the negro postmaster at Lake City. Academic discussion may well wait upon the disposition of the more practical question of vindicating the law. The News and Courier is not ready for any step which is not authorized by the Constitution and the laws, and which will not subserve the ends of justice. We have not said one word "favoring relinquishment of State sovereignty," nor is the question of State sovereignty in any way involved in the present case. What we are after, and all that we are after, is the just and speedy punishment of the murderers of the postmaster at Lake City. We do not ask, and we should resist any "assumption of authority" by the Federal Courts, but we insist that the Federal Courts shall exercise the authority which is clearly and unmistakably conferred upon them by law. We insist that the members of the mob shall be tried in the United States Court for two reasons; first, because the United States Court has undoubted, and, we believe, exclusive jurisdiction in this case; and, second, because it would be impossible to convict them in the State Courts.

The jurisdiction of the United States in the Lake City case . . . is unquestionable. The law is clear upon this point. The issue has already been adjudicated by the United States Supreme Court. . . .

The lynching evil is a growing evil. It has not been punished anywhere, and practically no attempt has been made by the State authorities at any time to punish mob murders. The State is wholly inadequate in the present case, even if the State should or could claim jurisdiction. If the Lake City murderers are not caught and tried and punished by the United States authorities they will not be punished at all.

SOURCE: *Charleston News and Courier,* March 5, 1878.

On July 1 a U.S. Commissioner heard testimony from Lavinia Baker, her children, and certain members of the mob who had been convinced to testify against their fellows. After this testimony a grand jury agreed to indict thirteen men.

134. *Grand Jury Indictment in Frazier Baker Case,* 1898

The United States of America
District of South Carolina
In the United States Circuit Court.
Frazier B. Baker being then and there furthermore the duly appointed and commissioned Post Master at said Post Office of the United States at Lake City as aforesaid, and then and there furthermore duly acting as such Post Master as aforesaid; in the free exercise and enjoyment of a certain right and privilege secured to him the said Frazier B. Baker by the laws and Constitution of the United States, that is to say, the right and privilege to be and to act as the Post Master at and for the said Post Office of the United States. . . .

And the jurors aforesaid, upon their oaths aforesaid, do further present that Martin V. Ward [and the other defendants] . . . unlawfully willfully and maliciously did injure, deface and destroy certain mail matter. . . .

And the jurors aforesaid, upon their oaths aforesaid, do further present that

Martin V. Ward [and the other defendants] . . . unlawfully and feloniously did combine, conspire, confederate, and agree . . . to prevent, by force, intimidation, and threat, a certain person, to wit, one Frazier B. Baker . . . from accepting and holding a certain office, trust, and place of confidence under the United States, and from discharging the duties thereof, that is to say, the office of Post Master of the United States. . . .

And the jurors aforesaid, upon their oaths aforesaid, do further present that Martin V. Ward [and the other defendants] . . . unlawfully and feloniously did combine, conspire, confederate and agree, between and among themselves . . . to injure one Frazier B. Baker in his person, that is to say, by then . . . assaulting, beating, bruising, shooting, wounding, maltreating, killing, and murdering him the said Frazier B. Baker . . . on account of the said Frazier B. Baker's lawful discharge of the duties of the said office of Post Master of the United States.

SOURCE: *United States v. Martin V. Ward, etc.*, Docket Number 1897, Circuit Court of the United States, District of South Carolina, National Archives–Southeast Region.

After the grand jury returned its indictments, Lake City whites stepped up their campaign to intimidate the government's witnesses. The prosecutor noted that the threats caused "considerable anxiety and apprehension" among the witnesses and asked the U.S. marshall to increase his force of deputies at the trial.

The trial began in April. The government's prosecution allowed the victims an opportunity to speak. Frazier Baker's widow told a riveting story, one reprinted in white newspapers across South Carolina. Even the most recent scholarship sometimes denies that the federal government ever acted against the Lake City lynchers. This not only erases a serious federal effort against mob law but silences Lavinia Baker as well.[5]

135. *Lavinia Baker's Testimony,* 1899

Lavinia Baker was called. . . . The Baker woman drew every eye in the Court room as she stepped on the stand. The story she would have to tell had been anticipated. The spectators were looking for something thrilling and bloody. The witness was sworn. . . .

"On the night of February 21," said the witness, "we were aroused by the roaring of fire. My husband hurried up and threw two buckets of water on the flame. He called Rosa to run and help him put out the fire. This water helped to deaden the fire, but it caught at the top of the house when it was deadened below. The guns opened. My husband called to Lincoln to give the alarm. The boy said, 'I'm shot, I can't call any more.' Then Baker went to the door and gave the alarm. The flames advanced. Baker walked up and down and prayed. I was in the building with the baby in my arms. He saw that I could not move, and he grabbed me, saying, 'Come on, we might as well die running as standing.' At the door the baby was shot. The baby was shot out of my arms. I said, 'See, baby's dead.' Baker stepped back and saw his dead child. Then he opened the door and was shot. I followed. Baker fell over and died, leaning against my lap. I looked to see if the baby was breathing. It did not, and there was a wound on its right side. The wound looked like a bloody bruise. It was large, as if it was made by a slug. There was a large hole in the side and blood was flowing. The baby was Julia Baker, aged 1 year and 11 months. Baker was 42 years old. The blood was gushing from Baker's back when he fell. I held my head down to hear if he was breathing. He said nothing. I held up my left hand and I was shot above the wrist."

(The woman showed the jury the scarred mark on both sides of the arm.)

"I got the children," continued the woman, "and we ran as fast as we could. We ran across the road in front of the building. We went one hundred yards from the building and hid in a field until the fire was out and the shooting was over. Then we went to Duke Burgess's and remained until morning.

"When we left the building, in the light of the fire, I saw men on the north side, a few steps from the building. Did not notice what they had and could not see whether they were white or colored.

"I found one of my daughters at Burgess's when I got there, and the oldest child came in later. Rosa was shot in the right arm, Cora was shot in the right hand, and Lincoln was shot through the right arm and in the stomach.

"I remained all night at Burgess's, and then went to Lawrence Dove's, where I remained until March 24, when I was brought to Charleston and taken to the Colored Hospital, Dr. McClennan in charge. He attended us for a month, and we remained at the Hospital two months."...

Cross-Examined

Cross-examination by Mr. Legare: "I did not hear any horses before the shooting. The roaring of the fire awoke me. I stayed in the old field until the fire and the shooting were over. I was in the field about half an hour. Many shots were fired after I got in the field. None of us were shot outside the house.

"My husband had a gun in the house, but he did not use it. Yes, I wrote my brother next day that I did not know if the mob was white or colored."

Pressed by Mr. Legare, the witness said her husband was treasurer of the Colored Alliance at Effingham, but she did not know that he was accused of carrying off Alliance money. She did not remember that colored people were hunting her husband for carrying off money.

"We had only been in Lake City thirteen days. My husband went there some time before and sent for me."...

SOURCE: *Charleston News and Courier*, April 12, 1899.

Lavinia Baker could not identify one lyncher. But the government persuaded some members of the mob to testify, and they did.[6] After the government finished its case, the defendants made an alibi defense, claiming through perjured testimony that they had been miles away from the lynching.

In their arguments to the jury, the defense attorneys blamed the murder on President William McKinley, who had appointed Baker postmaster in the first place. Like Ida B. Wells, the accused lynchers' lawyer, George S. Legare, pointed out the contradiction between McKinley's war policies and his domestic agenda. In the Philippines, Legare claimed, the U.S. policy assumed that blacks could not govern themselves. But in South Carolina McKinley put blacks in charge of the mail. The implication, of course, was that McKinley was catering for black votes.

136. *George Legare, Argument for the Defense in the Frazier Baker Case, 1899*

Mr. Legare's Argument

At the afternoon session Mr. George S. Legare opened his argument for the defence. . . .

I shall purposely avoid appealing to your passions or prejudices in this case, for more reasons than one. I could not conscientiously ask you to condone the crime with which the prisoners at the bar stand charged. It is such an offence as would tend to shock the moral sensibilities of any civilized community, and I am glad to have learned from the testimony that the perpetrators of the offence had no intention of purposely injuring the wife and children of the deceased as is shown by the fact that not a single one of them are molested after leaving the building. But as great as is the crime, while we deprecate its commission, we maintain that the primary wrong can be traced to the very seat of the Government of the United States; that the responsibility rests with the President of this great Republic, and not with the quiet and unassuming inhabitants of the little town of Lake City. The President sits in Washington to-day, advocating the slaughter of thousands of negroes in the Philippine Islands because they are unable and unfit to govern themselves. You and I are taxed to assist in maintaining an army for the purpose of subduing these people, and many a poor soldier is ushered into the presence of his Maker in this attempt to govern people who are absolutely incapable of governing themselves. And yet he who is the advocate of all this at the same time proclaims that they are capable of governing the white people of the South. One of the principal issues involved in the war of secession was that of the South's maintaining control of the negro. Our people struggled for four long years for what they believed to be right, and were finally outnumbered and conquered. The war was over and our soldiers returned, weary and worn and broken-hearted, to their homes, to find the negroes not only citizens, and on an equal footing with themselves, but in control of the Government of the State. For twelve long years they wore the yoke of oppression, aye, until they could stand it no longer. Like the Phoenix, they arose from the ashes of the past, shook off the burden and proclaimed to the world in accents unmistakable that this was a white man's country. And when the President of the United States, regardless of past history, attempts to continue negro rule in the South the responsibility of the crime must rest with him. He made Baker a postmaster in a white community with the story of the killing of the negro postmaster at Hogansville still ringing in his ears.[7]

I have briefly alluded to these facts, Mr. Foreman and gentlemen, for the purpose of vividly bringing to your attention the reason for the strenuous effort the Government is making to secure the conviction of someone, whether innocent or guilty. Not satisfied with the ability of these capable and efficient United States attorneys, the

Government has employed the assistance of Mr. Bryan and of the distinguished ex-Attorney General of the State of South Carolina. Not satisfied with the work of one post office inspector, as is usual in matters of this kind, they have chosen three of the best, perhaps, they have in the service of the Government. Enormous rewards have been offered for the conviction of the parties who committed the deed. We find men arrested and brought to the City of Charleston under false charges and frightened or bribed into giving testimony. Witnesses are brought here and turned over to the tender mercies of Mr. Bell, who pays their board and their per diem for weeks and months. Confessions and statements are extorted from poor, ignorant and unscrupulous men by promises of protection and reward. And I deign to say that this has all emanated from the seat of the Government in Washington in its anxiety to uphold the hands of the President in his attempt to force upon the white people of the South this obnoxious negro rule. If the postmaster at Lake City had been a white man, and, through personal malice or otherwise, the people of that or any other community had seen fit to attack him as Baker was attacked, the Government of the United States would not have interfered. These unscrupulous and unheard-of efforts never would have been resorted to and the perpetrators of the deed, if discovered, would have been tried regularly in the Courts of the State of South Carolina. . . .

We have shown you by reliable witnesses the whereabouts of each and every defendant on the night that this offence was committed, and we have proved beyond a reasonable doubt that Newham, the Government's star witness, who claimed to be at Lake City on the day of the killing, was during the morning at Kingstree, and at the very time the offence was committed was two miles away.

SOURCE: *Charleston News and Courier,* April 20, 1899.

The jury could not agree on a verdict and the prosecution ended in a mistrial. It is a tribute to the government's effort that the jury refused to acquit the defendants outright. The Justice Department kept its file open until 1908, hoping for an opportunity to retry the killers of Frazier Baker.

Knowing the hopelessness of expecting protection from the state governments, African Americans beseeched the federal government to act against lynchers. Most whites believed that the Constitution would not permit federal lynching prosecutions. In 1902 Albert E. Pillsbury, the former attorney general of Massachusetts, spoke on behalf of black demands for justice. Pillsbury argued that Congress could constitutionally outlaw lynching.

137. Albert E. Pillsbury, "A Brief Inquiry into a Federal Remedy for Lynching," 1902

The progress of mob-law in many of the states invites, if it does not compel, a serious inquiry into the constitutional question of federal power to put an end to it. . . .

. . . it has generally been supposed that the federal government has no power to interfere. . . .

Inquiry into the constitutional grounds for the exercise of such a power by the United States may begin by taking an analogous case. The United States, by international law and by treaty obligations, owes to foreign governments a duty of protecting their subjects resident within the states. So highly is this duty regarded by the law of nations that breach of it may be *casus belli*. Within the last five years, to go back no farther, the United States has several times been called to account for the killing of foreign subjects by mobs within the states; although the practice of the state department has been, for prudential reasons, to disclaim any direct responsibility for these outrages.

Can it be doubted that the United States, having this duty of protection, and being answerable to the world for its performance, has power to perform it? There can be but one answer to this question. Whatever preconceived notions may have been, whatever the practice of the government may be, the powers of the United States are necessarily co-extensive with its lawful obligations. Where there is a recognized duty, there must be governmental power adequate to its discharge. Any other rule would make the government a name of reproach. . . .

The equality clause of the Fourteenth Amendment forbids the states to deny to any person within their jurisdiction the equal protection of the laws. This clause is judicially held to confer immunity from any discrimination, as a federal right. The protection which the state extends to one person must be extended to all. It does not forbid discrimination merely in the making of laws, but in the equal protection which the laws are designed to afford. Forbidding the state to deny equal protection is equivalent to requiring the state to provide it. Equal protection is withheld if a state fails to provide it, and the guaranteed immunity is infringed. The constitutional requirement may be violated by acts of omission, no less than by acts of commission. The omission of the proper officers of the state to furnish equal protection, in any case, is the omission of the state itself, since the state can act only by its officers. It would seem to follow that when a citizen or other person is put to death by a lawless mob, in default of the protection which the state is bound to provide for all alike, there is a denial of equal protection by the state, in the sense of the equality clause, which Congress may prevent or punish by legislation applying to any individuals who participate in or contribute to it, directly or indirectly.

The power to protect the lives of its citizens or subjects is an inherent power of every government. It was never doubted that the United States has this power, as a power necessarily implied, and may exercise it throughout the world outside the states. . . . The duty of a government to protect the lives of its citizens is correlative with the power. The citizen is entitled, as of right, to claim such protection. If the United States cannot exercise this power to its full extent within the states, it can be for no other reason than that it is reserved to the states, or to the people. . . .

The United States has, as all governments have, a political and legal interest in the lives of its citizens. If it has not full power to protect them in their lives, within the states as it has elsewhere, it can be, as already observed, only because that duty rests solely upon the states. If so, it is a duty owed to the United States, as well as to individual citizens. It would seem that open and notorious neglect or omission of this duty on the part of a state, by suffering lawless mobs to murder citizens for want of legal protection, may be declared an offence against the United States, and if so, that the United States may punish all persons who contribute to it.

... [I]f a state should omit to enact any legislation for the protection of a certain class of citizens against crimes of violence, forbidding and punishing such crimes only when committed against the other class or classes, it can hardly be doubted that Congress, under the enforcement clause, may supply the omission by direct legislation, or may perhaps annul the whole system of discriminating laws, leaving the state to provide others which will conform to the requirement of equality. The consequences of the failure of a state to enforce laws made for protection against violence are no less disastrous to the unprotected class than the failure of the state to make any such laws. It is difficult to perceive why the power and the duty of Congress to interfere, under the enforcement clause, are not as clear in the one case as in the other.

Apart from the Fourteenth Amendment, it may well be that the United States owes its citizens protection in their lives while not owing them a complete system of laws for the protection of all personal and property rights, and that its power is co-extensive with its duty, but extends no farther.

Without attempting an exhaustive inquiry into this delicate and difficult subject, it can safely be assumed that preconceived opinions are not conclusive of the question. In view of express constitutional provisions, and in the present state of judicial decision, the existence or non-existence of this power in the federal government can be determined only by submitting a statute to the test of judicial examination.

SOURCE: Albert E. Pillsbury, "A Brief Inquiry into a Federal Remedy for Lynching," *Harvard Law Review* 15 (March 1902): 707–713.

In September 1904 a mob set fire to the Huntsville, Alabama, jail to force out Horace Maples, accused of murder. The mob hanged Maples from a tree on the courthouse lawn. As it happened, federal prisoners were also present in the jail, prompting a U.S. government investigation. J. E. NeSmith, U.S. Marshall, identified members of the mob and criticized the sheriff for failing to protect Maples and other prisoners in the jail.

Judge Thomas Goode Jones heard the case. After his confrontation with Birmingham lynchers, and after a term as governor, President Theodore Roosevelt had appointed Jones U.S. District Court Judge in the Northern District of Alabama. Jones challenged mob law again. To do so, the former state officer had to convince a jury of Alabama white men that the federal government had the constitutional authority to act against a lynch mob of white men.

138. *Thomas Goode Jones, Charge to the Grand Jury,* October 11, 1904

Gentlemen of the Grand Jury: ... as the court knows from common knowledge, as well as from reports of its officers, a mob gathered in a stone's throw of this room, and in insolent defiance of the judges and laws of our states, and with studied insult and contempt for its civil and military power which sought to protect the Huntsville jail, assaulted the assembled forces of the law at their post of duty there. It broke down the doors of the jail, set it on fire, resisted efforts to put out the flames, and obstructed officers of the United States in their endeavors to remove United States prisoners from their cells to a place of safety.

This frenzied and savage work was done that Horace Maples, a negro, a citizen of Alabama and of the United States, who was there confined to be safely kept to answer the laws of the state of Alabama upon a charge of murder, should not be so kept and disposed of according to law, but instead, should be delivered to the mob and lawlessly put to death. From the same sources of information the court is advised that there were utterances of members of this mob, and speeches made to incite it to its crime, and other things done, which go to show that the mob, composed wholly of white men, was finally stirred to its purpose rather from prejudice against Maples' race than from indignation at the crime laid at his door, and that because of that race prejudice the mob did its murderous work to prevent Maples, who was accused of crime upon a white man, from enjoying the rights belonging to every freeman to be set free, if innocent, or to be condemned and punished if guilty, by the constituted tribunals of the land. . . .

Under the thirteenth amendment, Maples had the immunity as a citizen of the United States to be protected against lawless violence by the mob of whites, to prevent his enjoyment of the right to trial before the constituted tribunals as to his guilt or innocence of the crime of which he was accused, when such violence was directed towards him because he was a negro, with the intention to deprive him of that right. Was Maples taken from the officers of the state, and murdered because of indignation provoked by the crime laid at his door or other felonious motive, without reference to the race to which he belonged, and without any purpose on that account, to prevent his enjoyment of the common right of a trial in the court? His murder under such circumstances, would present the features of an ordinary murder which is a crime only against the laws of the state of Alabama, and in that event, you have nothing to do with it.

If, however, you find something more than a mere felonious purpose to avenge the crime imputed to him or general malevolence and that the mob was actuated by the bad spirit that a person of Maples' race when accused of crime should not have the right to be acquitted, if innocent, or condemned and punished by the court, if guilty, and that the mob hung him to prevent his enjoyment of that right because of his race, his murder by a mob or persons of a different race, constitutes a crime against the laws of the United States.

In that event it would be a conspiracy under that section to injure him in the free exercise or enjoyment of a right which was conferred upon him by the constitution not to be deprived, by lawless violence of a right of trial by the courts, because he was a negro. You may ask how you are to determine what motive induced the murder? The court can give you no more definite rule than to say, that the question must be determined by your common sense and consciences in the light of all the circumstances. The particular prejudice or motive which controls the conduct of men in any given case cannot be seen by the eye. We are all conscious of power which moves the winds and the waves, but we cannot see that power.

SOURCE: *Birmingham Age Herald*, October 12, 1904.

Jones's charge emphasized the Thirteenth Amendment. After the jurors indicted members of the lynch mob, the defendants complained that the federal government had no jurisdiction. In his opinion upholding the indictments, Jones shifted his focus to the Fourteenth Amendment.

139. *Judge Thomas Goode Jones, Opinion in* Ex parte Riggins, 1904

The vital purpose of the [Fourteenth] amendment in imposing the duty upon the state under this clause is not merely to secure formal recognition of the right in the Constitution and laws of the state, and provisions to enforce them, which, unless they are enforced, amount only to parchment due process of law, but that the duty should be so performed that it will result not merely in having proper laws and officers, but in the full enjoyment of the benefits of the operation of due process of law in individual cases. When a private individual takes a person charged with crime from the custody of the state authorities to prevent the state from affording him due process of law, and puts him to death to punish the crime and to prevent the enjoyment of such right, it is violent usurpation and exercise, in the particular case, of the very function which the Constitution of the United States itself, under this clause, directs the state to perform in the interest of the citizen. Such lawlessness differs from ordinary kidnapping and murder, in that the dominant intent and actual result is usurpation and exercise by private individuals of the sovereign functions of administering justice and punishing crime, in order to defeat the performance of duties required of the state by the supreme law of the land. The inevitable effect of such lawlessness is not merely to prevent the state from performing its duty, but to deprive the accused of all enjoyment, or opportunity of enjoyment, of rights which this clause of the Constitution intended to work out for him by the actual performance by the state of all the things included in affording due process of law, which enjoyment can be worked out in no other way in his individual case. Such lawlessness defeats the performance of the state's duty, and the opportunity of the citizen to have the benefit of it, quite as effectually and far more frequently than vicious laws, or the partiality or the inefficiency of state officers in the discharge of their constitutional duty. It is a great, notorious, and growing evil, which directly attacks the purpose which the Constitution of the United States had in view when it enjoined the duty upon the state. . . .

Certainly, if the legislative power to guaranty the performance of the duty is vested in Congress by the fourteenth amendment itself, Congress has power under section 8 of article 1 to pass all laws which shall be "necessary and proper" to carry into execution that guaranty. The legislative power to make good the guaranty involves the power to protect state officers when endeavoring to discharge the constitutional duty, and to punish private individuals who resist the execution of the laws, by whose enforcement alone the duty can be accomplished, and the rights, privileges, and immunities enjoyed, which the amendment intended to bestow, when it required the performance of the duty at the hands of the state. . . .

No one can deny that the fourteenth amendment conferred upon the citizen the right, privilege, or immunity to have his state afford him due process of law on accusation of crime against him, and that a right or privilege was thereby vested in the citizen, under the Constitution of the United States, to have the state perform this duty.

The very words of this clause, by their own unaided force, inevitably utter a command that the state shall afford due process to the citizen. It is therefore a right, privilege, or immunity of a citizen of the United States to have the state afford him due process of law. It is a universal rule of law, and common sense as well, that the grant of a right or privilege carries with it every right or privilege necessary to the enjoyment of the right granted, unless withheld by the terms of the grant. The grant here makes no such exception. The constitutional right of the citizen cannot bear fruit, or ripen into the enjoyment of due process at the hands of the state, if lawless outsiders prevent state officers from performing their duty concerning it. The right, privilege, or immunity of a citizen of the United States under this clause, which is to have his state give him the benefit of due process of law, therefore, necessarily carries with it and includes in it the right, privilege, or immunity to enjoy freedom, exemption, from lawless assault, which supervenes between the state and the performance of its duty, and by such violent interference prevents the citizen having, when the state is endeavoring to afford it, due process at the hands of the state. . . .

After anxious deliberation and careful examination of all the authorities, the court cannot resist the conclusion that Congress may protect the enjoyment of rights, privileges, or immunities given or secured by the fourteenth amendment, against impairment by lawless acts of private individuals, although neither state laws nor state officers are at fault, if such lawlessness takes the form of violence, directly preventing the state or its officers from affording due process to a prisoner, when the state is attempting to do so, provided such legislation does not go beyond prevention of that evil, and does not attempt to alter or interfere with state laws or the authority of its officers in executing them. The argument that Congress has no such power because the amendment is directed against denial of due process by the state, and that there is no denial by the state when neither its laws nor its officers are at fault, ignores the pregnant fact that the amendment creates a right, privilege, or immunity of a citizen of the United States to have enjoyment of the benefit of due process at the hands of the state, at least, when the citizen is in its custody and it is proceeding against him for infraction of its laws, and ignores the further equally important fact that such lawless violence of private individuals, by preventing the state's giving the benefit of due process of law when it is endeavoring to do so, directly and inevitably defeats the enjoyment of his right or privilege, created by the Constitution of the United States, to have enjoyment of the benefit of due process at the hands of the state, and thus fatally impairs enjoyment of the right, privilege, or immunity. It is the settled and unbroken doctrine of the Supreme Court of the United States that a right, "whether created by the Constitution of the United States, or only guaranteed by it, even without any express delegation of power, may be protected by Congress in such manner and form as Congress, in the legitimate exercise of its legislative discretion, shall provide." . . .

The only way to escape the application of this doctrine to this case is to show either that no right, privilege, or immunity is given by the fourteenth amendment to the citizen to enjoy due process at the hands of the state, when it is endeavoring to afford it, or that violence directed against its officers, which prevents them from doing so, does not deprive the citizen of the enjoyment of the benefits of the discharge of the duty by the state. The decisions of the Supreme Court put it beyond the pale of controversy that the prohibitions upon state power in the fourteenth amendment create rights, privileges, and immunities of citizens of the United States.

SOURCE: 134 F. 404; 1904 U.S. App.

The Supreme Court forced Jones to release his prisoners, and the killers of Horace Maples escaped justice. In *Hodges v. United States* (1906), David J. Brewer wrote that the Civil War amendments did "not an attempt to commit that race to the care of the Nation." Brewer insisted that only the states, and not the federal government, could prosecute lynchers.[8]

The states showed little capacity for prosecuting lynchers. In the years after Brewer's opinion, uncounted numbers of American citizens perished at the hands of mobs, mostly doing their work in obscure backcountry locales, away from inquiring outsiders. These neighborhood mobs enforced their colloquial justice seemingly unaware and unconcerned that Europe was girding for catastrophic war. On June 28, 1914, a Serbian assassinated Archduke Franz Ferdinand in the Bosnia-Herzegovinian city of Sarajevo, recently annexed by the Austrians. In a few weeks war engulfed Europe. On April 6, 1918, when continued German submarine attacks on American shipping convinced President Wilson to ask Congress for a declaration of war on Germany, mob law still ruled vast stretches of American soil.

World War I would touch every American citizen and reshape American life. What had been purely local now had international significance. Wilson created the Committee on Public Information to promote the war effort. Wilson's propagandists wanted to depict the United States as the champion of law pitted against the Germans' "lawless passion." Wilson recognized that Europeans and other foreigners scarcely found American propaganda credible when mobs continued to lynch persons. So Wilson asked state authorities to curb lynching for the good of the war effort against Germany. Wilson did not commit any federal resources to the battle against lynching or ask Congress to outlaw mob law. He merely asked the states to do more.

140. *Woodrow Wilson, "A Statement to the American People,"* July 26, 1918

My Fellow Countrymen: I take the liberty of addressing you upon a subject which so vitally affects the honor of the Nation and the very character and integrity of our institutions that I trust you will think me justified in speaking very plainly about it.

I allude to the mob spirit which has recently here and there very frequently shown its head amongst us, not in any single region, but in many and widely separated parts of the country. There have been many lynchings, and every one of them has been a blow at the heart of ordered law and humane justice. No man who loves America, no man who really cares for her fame and honor and character, or who is truly loyal to her institutions, can justify mob action while the courts of justice are open and the governments of the States and the Nation are ready and able to do their duty. We are at this very moment fighting lawless passion. Germany has outlawed herself among the nations because she has disregarded the sacred obligations of law and has made lynchers of her armies. Lynchers emulate her disgraceful example. I, for my part, am anxious to see every community in America rise above that level with pride and a fixed resolution which no man or set of men can afford to despise.

We proudly claim to be the champions of democracy. If we really are, in deed and in truth, let us see to it that we do not discredit our own. I say plainly that every American who takes part in the action of a mob or gives it any sort of countenance is no true son of this great Democracy, but its betrayer, and does more to discredit her by that single disloyalty to her standards of law and of right than the words of her statesmen or the sacrifices of her heroic boys in the trenches can do to make suffering peoples believe her to be their savior. How shall we commend democracy to the acceptance of other peoples, if we disgrace our own by proving that it is, after all, no protection to the weak? Every mob contributes to German lies about the United States what her most gifted liars cannot improve upon by the way of calumny. They can at least say that such things cannot happen in Germany except in times of revolution, when law is swept away!

I therefore very earnestly and solemnly beg that the governors of all the States, the law officers of every community, and, above all, the men and women of every community in the United States, all who revere America and wish to keep her name without stain or reproach, will cooperate—not passively merely, but actively and watchfully—to make an end of this disgraceful evil. It cannot live where the community does not countenance it.

I have called upon the Nation to put its great energy into this war and it has responded—responded with a spirit and a genius for action that has thrilled the world. I now call upon it, upon its men and women everywhere, to see to it that its laws are kept inviolate, its fame untarnished. Let us show our utter contempt for the things that have made this war hideous among the wars of history by showing how those who love liberty and right and justice and are willing to lay down their lives for them upon foreign fields stand ready also to illustrate to all mankind their loyalty to the things at home which they wish to see established everywhere as a blessing and protection to the peoples who have never known the privileges of liberty and self-government. I can never accept any man as a champion of liberty either for ourselves or for the world who does not reverence and obey the laws of our own beloved land, whose laws we ourselves have made. He has adopted the standards of the enemies of his country, whom he affects to despise.

Woodrow Wilson.

SOURCE: *Official Bulletin* 2 (July 26, 1918).

Despite Wilson's appeal, mobbing persisted, and African American citizens continued to plead for help from their president.

141. *J. E. Boyd to President Woodrow Wilson*, November 19, 1920

Please pardon me for taking your time to peruse this letter, *but*, because of the Perilousness of the times, I humbly bow at your feet and ask you to hear or read my plea.

A week or so ago, one colored woman was burned up alive in Florida, together with others.

Just yesterday, another colored woman was shot to death with others in Georgia. Now, I must beg you to pardon me for being a bit frank on this matter, please. Hasn't this gone far enough and too far?

You know by my very work of itself, that I am a friend to the South for what I am engaged in, means more to the Southland than it can mean to other sections of this country—preparing boys and girls of my race to render proficiency in those things they are needed, now, to do; which I feel is commonsense. I am paying no attention to the higher branches, simply preparing them for real proficient service.

Then, too, I can truthfully say before my God as my witness, that I voted for you for President of this country, each time you ran and would have voted for you had you run again for after having carefully studied the matters, & decided favorably to your policies. And, what is more, I have, in fact, great faith in you as a leader for this Nation. Your appointment of the colored colonels, the commissioned officers of colored men during those most trying days and many other reasons, make you rank high in the rank of liberal Executives of this nation. In fact, I regard you as second to none who have presided over the destinies of this nation. God knows I do and had you run again I had decided to offer my personal services on the platform for your re-election, even though it was or would have been departing from precedent.

Your Majesty, don't you abhor these horrifying occurrences? I know you do.

I don't condone crime among my people in the least, but since we have a law, shouldn't it be allowed to take its course? I know your answer at once. You need not reply for I am sure you oppose it.

You guided this nation safely and successfully through one of the most trying times that have ever come and now, as you are about to retire from office to rest for a while from your hard tasks, please do an act that will bring a halt to these awful and heart-rending atrocities as are occurring as above stated.

I believe that you can stop them and I don't feel that a Republican President can stop them. He may try, but most likely will add "fire to fury."

There are thousands and millions of Southern white people who oppose, absolutely, the commission of these dastardly acts and then, allow me to ask:

Doesn't God oppose such?

Now, I beg further to state that the awful race riots that occurred last year were heart rending to me and too, I was the first colored man in this country to plead for peace of my people. I wrote an article headed:

"Let Righteousness Rule. "Let God Fight our Battles."

This article caused me to be cursed by many of my race and I knew, in advance, that it would; but I felt that it was the thing to do. Too, after a careful consideration on the part of my people, they desisted in their hostilities toward me and

All quieted down.

However, I feel that God had you exalted to the Majestic position for His Glory and that He desires that you include this in your program:

Make lynching a federal crime.

It will be a blessing to the Southern White man as well as to the entire commonwealth and God knows it will.

This is one, if not the most progressive nation of the world and if lynching could be stopped *and it can*, the American white man will soon be enable to dictate the politics of the civilized world and God is making the Supreme effort for him to attain to this exalted position. He will reach it if he will simply fix it so that

The Law Will Be Honored.

When speaking with several different foreign statesmen at so many different times, I have heard them argue that the White man's lynching in this country scares the other Nations of American rule. Doesn't that seem reasonable?

Then, too, the crimes of this nation, so far as being committed by black people are due, most largely to ignorance for they are committed by ignorant colored people, 99 1/2 per cent of them. While, at times others are drawn into them as an aftermath, yet the origins accrue from the most illiterate classes.

A better school system in the rurals of colored communities would go far in ameliorating and almost obliterating the vicious acts or deeds of my people.

Can God get your services in this effort to *stop lynching*?

Please do not accept this letter as an effort to attempt to dictate to you, for it is not. God knows it is not. God has prompted me, an humble servant, to *humbly* plead to you for my people and others, for that matter, that

Law,

    Not mobs;

Take its Course.

What a halo of glory would bedeck your brow, in addition to what you already have, should you set in motion?

And, too, what a beautiful, heavenlike place this country be, when lynching shall have passed. What an influence over the peoples of this entire world would come to this country?

Lastly, but by no means, least; what a great and durable blessing would God bestow upon you and your posterity for the duration of eternity?

Humbly praying God to encourage you in this matter and to enable you to throw aside

"Every weight"

"that" would "beset you" and play the part of a Godly man, a humanitarian of the most royal,

And "cast the dye."

Saying nothing of the gallantry of our black boys over seas, which stands for itself, all things considered; simply to heighten this country in the estimation of the civilized world, God help you to heed the humble appeal from your humble and subservant servant

And Save This Country,

That God can have the opportunity of using it to lift the entire world

To a Higher, yes, to the Highest plane of civilization.

A word from you, followed up by constant importunities will start this matter to its final redemption, I do believe.

There are those who think they understand the South who are not of the South, but I fear they are simply mistaken and are losing time, almost as I see it in their advocacies, so far as the handling of racial conditions in the South Land.

You cannot be misunderstood and *will be understood* if you will dare do this God called for deed, far more than those of other sections, especially of the North.

Humbly praying, again, God to encourage you to

Be a Man for humanity,

And put forth your Herculean effort in this direction, I beg to remain for ever and for ever,

> Your humble and appreciative servant,
> J. E. Boyd
> Founder and Superintendent,
> Camps Normal Industrial Institute,
> Camps Gregg County, Texas
> Post Office Address
> Longview, Texas, Box 592

PS

"In as much as ye have done it unto the least of these, ye have done it unto Me."

Jesus Christ

As soon as this nation stops lynching, its Christianity will shine forth like unto a noonday sun and God will Bless it far more.

SOURCE: File 158260, box 1276, Straight Numerical Files, Central Files and Related Records, Record Group 60, Department of Justice, National Archives, College Park, Maryland.

J. E. Boyd, the writer of the letter quoted above, received the standard form letter federal officials always used when replying to such appeals. The assistant attorney general R. P. Stewart told Boyd that only the states could prosecute such crimes.[9]

When Warren G. Harding, a Republican, replaced Wilson, some African Americans dared hope that the party of Lincoln would do more than the Democrats had done. And, under Warren G. Harding, the Bureau of Investigation (later known as the Federal Bureau of Investigation) did investigate Ku Klux Klan activities. For example, the Bureau, cooperating with Army Intelligence, infiltrated the Boston Ku Klux Klan chapter.[10] The Bureau also took action after Ku Klux Klansmen kidnapped and whipped Theodore Schieflman, the Catholic mayor of Liberty, Kansas.[11]

In 1922, the same year the Bureau went to Kansas, Congress gave opponents of racial violence even more reason for hope. Since 1900 Congress had considered bills against lynching almost annually, usually banishing the proposed legislation to committee. In 1921, however, the House seriously considered a bill proposed by the St. Louis Republican Leonidas Dyer. On January 26, 1922, the House of Representative passed the Dyer Bill. All that remained was for the Senate to act. Some hoped that President Harding would call on the Senate to pass the bill.

142. *Ara Lee Settle of Armstrong Technical High School, Washington, D.C., to President Warren G. Harding, June 18, 1922*

I am taking the liberty of intruding this letter upon you, because I feel that the issues involved are as important as any questions that have ever been pressed upon you. It is to urge your support of the Dyer Bill.

Mr. President, lynching has been committed in the south for many years, but when the last presidential election took place, practically every colored boy and girl in America was for Warren G. Harding as president. Why did we want you? The answer was: He is a Republican and will stop that terrible crime—lynching. You were elected but now and then there could be heard of a few lynchings. Mr. President, why do they lynch the Negro? Has not he done his full share, or bit, in the making of this new land? When America was fighting for independence, was not Crispus Attucks, a negro, the first man killed? There are many other that could be named, but time and space will not permit me. When the trumpet was blown for civil strife, did not the Negro give his life as well as the Anglo-Saxon? During the world war, Negro boys also sacrificed their lives as well, and as bravely as the white man, that democracy might rule the earth. This reminds me of our glorious song "My Country tis of Thee, Sweet land of Liberty." Mr. President, you are aware of the fact that we have not our full liberty but still we sing the song by faith in the future.

I admit that there are some lawless Negroes in America, as well as whites, capable of committing horrible crimes. All people are not as good as others, but, Mr. president, what good does lynching do? One man may be lynched for a crime of which another has committed. It does not tend to make a nation better, it only brings race prejudice and hatred. What good or use is the law, if the lynchers are going to put the law in their own hands. Mr. President, imagine yourself about to be lynched for something of which you know nothing about. Men seize you from some place of refuge, carry you to the heart of the town, place a rope around you and burn you, while men, women and children are jeering amidst all your pain and agony. It is enough to make one ashamed not to use his full influence against this horrible crime.

A bill has been introduced in Congress by Representative Dyer (a Republican) to prevent lynching, or make it a criminal offense. Mr. President, it is incumbent upon you, the chief executive of all America to urge the passage of this bill. If lynching is permitted in the South, finally it will spread to the north, doing nothing but kindling the flames of racial and personal hatred, and sowing the seeds of internal strife. There are some courageous and conscientious senators who are in favor of the passage of the bill, but, Mr. President, we are looking to you to see it through. If this country had more men such as Mr. Dyer it would be "Sweet land of Liberty."

One might say, push the bill away until a more opportune time presents itself when they would be more able to debate on it. But as a well-known man has said, "Today is the only real day promised" Why not do that today and hurl lynching into a bottomless pit to remain forever. Mr. President, we are looking and pleading to you.

During the war the colored people were very patriotic, they bought Liberty Bonds, War Saving Stamps, Thrift Stamps, had meatless, sugarless, wheatless days, also they crocheted, knitted and embroidered for the boys over there while they were fighting for "dear old America," but mind you some of the same colored boys have since returned to America and have been lynched in a way that has been heretofore explained.

When lynching has been expunged, then we may all sing from our hearts with a true meaning

> "My Country 'tis of thee.
> Sweet land of Liberty,
> Of thee I Sing.
> Land where my fathers died,
> Land of the Pilgrims pride,
> From every mountain side,
> Let Freedom ring.

Once more, Mr. Harding, we are looking to you, to you, to you.
    Respectfully yours,
    Ara Lee Settle

SOURCE: File 158260.3 Straight Numerical Files, Department of Justice, Record Group 60, National Archives, College Park, Maryland.

Congress never passed a law against lynching. Even as it debated the Dyer Bill, however, the nature of the violence changed. In 1924 white racists hurled dynamite onto the roofs and porches of homes occupied by African Americans in Roanoke, Virginia.[12] Similar bombings occurred in Chicago, Kansas City, and Indianapolis. The *Norfolk Journal and Guide* condemned such bombings as "'Reds' tactics."[13] Plummer Bernard Young, editor of the *Journal and Guide*, intended to needle white racists by accusing them of acting like Communists at a time when those very same racists hated and feared communism.

NOTES

1. Xi Wang, *The Trial of Democracy: Black Suffrage and Northern Republicans, 1860–1910* (Athens: University of Georgia Press, 1997), 261–262; Richard B. Sherman, *The Republican Party and Black America: From McKinley to Hoover, 1896–1933* (Charlottesville: University Press of Virginia, 1973), 1–10.

2. Sherman, *The Republican Party and Black America*, 1–10.

3. *Columbia Register,* reprinted in *Fairfield News and Herald,* December 8, 1897.

4. *Fairfield News and Herald,* March 2, 1898.

5. David Blight, *Race and Reunion: The Civil War in American Memory* (Cambridge, Mass.: Harvard University Press, 2001), 349.

6. *Charleston News and Courier,* April 13, 1899.

7. McKinley appointed I. H. Loftin postmaster in Hogansville, Georgia. On September 15, 1897, someone shot Loftin, leaving him injured. The Georgia House of Representatives responded not by condemning the shooter but by censuring McKinley for making the appointment. Loftin recovered, but in February 1898 arsonists destroyed his post office. Loftin gave up and left Hogansville. See Sherman, *The Republican Party and Black America*, 10–11.

8. 203 U.S. 1.

9. R. P. Stewart, Assistant Attorney General to J. E. Boyd, December 7, 1920, file 158260, Straight Numerical Files, Central Files and Related Records, Department of Justice, Record Group 60, National Archives, College Park, Maryland.

10. John B. Hanrahan, to Director, Bureau of Investigation, October 7, 1921, 44–21, box 14, Federal Bureau of Investigation records, Department of Justice, RG 65, National Archives, College Park, Maryland; W. B. Poole, "Ku Klux Klan—in Boston—General Intelligence," September 24, 1921, ibid.

11. Harold McGugin to Harry M. Daugherty, October 16, 1922, 44–16, box 12, Federal Bureau of Investigation records, Department of Justice, RG 65, National Archives, College Park, Maryland; Charles William Sloan Jr., "Kansas Battles the Invisible Empire: The Legal Ouster of the KKK from Kansas, 1922–1927," *Kansas Historical Quarterly* 40 (fall 1974): 393–409.

12. *Norfolk Journal and Guide,* July 12, 1924.

13. Ibid., July 19, 1924.

11

The New Deal

Franklin Delano Roosevelt became president on March 4, 1933, pledging a new deal for the American people. FDR faced economic catastrophe, a Great Depression. But he also confronted perceptions that a massive crime wave had engulfed the country, organized lawlessness beyond the states' capabilities to control crime. Roosevelt energized the Federal Bureau of Investigation, launched a war on crime, and made FBI chief John Edgar Hoover into a national hero.

FDR's war on crime neglected lynching. In his memoir NAACP leader Roy Wilkins recalled feeling "outrage . . . over F.D.R.'s expedient cowardice on the issue." Wilkins vividly recalled that Roosevelt's attorney general called a national conference on crime in the fall of 1934. "It was a big affair," Wilkins recalled bitterly, but the official program contained not one word about lynching. "I couldn't believe it," Wilkins angrily wrote, a conference on crime sponsored by the Department of Justice and assembled under the president's leadership "that omitted from its agenda the most revolting crime of the day." When Wilkins protested, an assistant attorney general brushed him off.[1]

A wave of kidnappings, including the murder of the famed aviator Charles A. Lindberg's baby son, frightened white America a lot more than lynching did. Although unable to pass a law against lynching, Congress responded to the kidnapping threat by making kidnapping a federal crime. Members of Congress assumed that the Lindberg Law attacked a crime that threatened wealthy Americans only—white people. In 1934, however, Florida lynchers violated the Lindberg Law when they crossed into Alabama, kidnapped Claude Neal, an African American, and brought him back to Florida for a lynching.

The FBI did nothing, but the NAACP dispatched Howard Kester to investigate. Kester, a liberal white southerner, spent a week in Florida making inquiries.

143. *Howard Kester, "The Marianna, Florida, Lynching,"* November 20, 1934

On October 19th, 1934, Claude Neal, 23, of Greenwood, Florida, was arrested by Deputy Sheriff J. P. Couliette for the murder of Lola Cannidy, 20, also of Greenwood, Florida. Neal, when arrested, was working on a peanut farm belonging to Mr. John Green. He was taken in custody with another man whom investigating officers believed to be involved in the murder to the woods and questioned. It is alleged that a confession was wrung from Neal and that he assumed entire responsibility for the crime. Sheriff W. F. Chambliss, of Jackson county, who was at the Cannidy home at the time of the arrest was apparently aware of the lynching spirit which was beginning to rise throughout the little farming community, and ordered Neal to be taken, to

Chipley, Florida, for safekeeping, a distance of about 20 miles. With Neal were arrested his mother, Annie Smith, and his aunt, Sallie Smith.

The Mob Chases the Law

From the moment that Neal was arrested a blood-thirsty mob relentlessly pursued him. . . .

The angry mood of the crowd at Chipley caused the sheriff there to remove Neal to Panama City. From Panama City he was taken by boat to Pensacola. From Pensacola Neal was taken across the Florida line to Brewton, Alabama—a distance of 61 miles. Brewton is approximately 210 miles from Marianna, county-seat of Jackson county, Florida. . . .

An armed mob of approximately 100 men stormed the county jail at Brewton, Alabama, on the morning of October 26th. Neal was seized after Mike Shanholster, the jailor, unlocked his cell door, and was brought screaming and crying and placed in the front car in front of the county jail. The mob had triumphed. . . .

The Lynching of Claude Neal

According to a member of the mob with whom I talked, Claude Neal was lynched in a lonely spot about four miles from Greenwood, Florida, scene of the recent crime, and not in Alabama as it was first reported. After Neal was taken from the jail at Brewton, Alabama, he was driven approximately 200 miles over highway 231 leading into Marianna and from there to the woods near Greenwood where he was subjected to the most brutal and savage torture imaginable.

Neal was taken from the Brewton jail between one and two o'clock Friday morning, October 26. He was in the hands of the smaller lynching group composed of approximately 100 men—from then until he was left in the road in front of the Cannidy home late that same night. I was told by several people that Neal was tortured for ten or twelve hours. It is almost impossible to believe that a human being could stand such unspeakable torture for such a long period.

Due to the great excitement sweeping the entire northern section of Florida and southeastern Alabama and to the great number of people who wanted to participate in the lynching, the original mob which secured Neal from the jail at Brewton evidently decided that if all of the niceties of a modern Twentieth Century lynching were to be inflicted upon Neal that it would be unwise for a larger mob to handle the victim. They preferred that his last hours on earth be filled with the greatest possible humiliation and agony. However, the word was passed all over northeastern Florida and southeastern Alabama that there was to be a "lynching party to which all white people are invited," near the Cannidy home Friday night. It is also reported that the information was broadcast from the radio station at Dothan, Alabama. I talked to at least three persons who confirmed this statement.

A member of the lynching party with whom I talked described the lynching in all of its ghastliness, down to the minutest detail. After talking with him I went immediately to my room and tried to recall word for word all that he had told me. The story of the actual lynching as related to me and later corroborated by others is as follows:

"After taking the nigger to the woods about four miles from Greenwood, they cut off his penis. He was made to eat it. Then they cut off his testicles and made him eat them and say he liked it." (I gathered that this barbarous act consumed considerable time and that other means of torture were used from time to time on Neal.) "Then they sliced his sides and stomach with knives and every now and then somebody would cut off a finger or two. Red hot irons were used on the nigger to burn him from top to bottom." from time to time during the torture a rope would be tied around Neal's neck and he was pulled up over a limb and held there until he almost choked to death when he would be let down and the torture begin all over again. After several hours of this unspeakable torture, "they decided just to kill him."

Neal's body was tied to a rope on the rear of an automobile and dragged over the highway to the Cannidy home. Here a mob estimated to number somewhere between 3,000 and 7,000 from eleven southern states were excitedly waiting his arrival. When the car which was dragging Neal's body cane in front of the Cannidy home, a man who was riding the rear bumper cut the rope.

"A woman came out of the Cannidy house and drove a butcher knife through his heart. Then the crowd came by and kicked him and some drove their cars over him."

Men, women and children were numbered in the vast throng that came to witness the lynching. It is reported from reliable sources that the little children, some of them mere tots, who lived in the Greenwood neighborhood waited with sharpened sticks for the return of Neal's body and that when it rolled in the dust on the road that awful night these little children drove their weapons deep into the flesh of the dead man.

The body, which by this time, was horribly mutilated was taken by the mob to Marianna, a distance of ten or eleven miles, where it was hung to a tree on the northeast corner of the courthouse square. Pictures were taken of the mutilated form, and hundreds of photographs were sold for fifty cents each. Scores of citizens viewed the body as it hung in the square. The body was perfectly nude until the early morning when someone had the decency to hang a burlap sack over the middle of the body. The body was cut down about eight-thirty Saturday morning, October 27th, 1934.

Fingers and toes from Neal's body have been exhibited as souvenirs in Marianna where one man offered to divide the finger which he had with a friend as "a special favor." Another man has one of the fingers preserved in alcohol. . . .

Lack of Police Protection

During the rioting the city of Marianna was completely without police protection. I was told that members of the mob searched the town for members of the police force and threatened to beat them up if they were found. One observer said, "The United States army couldn't have stopped that crowd Saturday morning." When Mayor Burton realized what was going on and that the city was at the mercy of the mob he tried to locate the policemen but was unable to do so. He then tried personally to deputize some special officers but was unable to find anyone to serve. He later sent a friend out to find some men who would serve. This man finally returned and said that he could not find anyone who would serve.

National Guards

At this juncture the Mayor called Governor Sholtz[2] in Tallahassee. In response to the mayor's request a detachment of National Guards arrived from Apalachicola about 4:30 Saturday afternoon and gradually dispersed the mob. The guards patrolled the street of the town and particularly the Negro section. The mob retreated before the guards but left the parting warning that they would "be back Saturday to finish up what we started."

On the following Saturday the police force was increased by about twenty men. Several Negroes were attacked early Saturday morning by white men who were arrested and placed in jail. A drizzling rain began about 9 a.m., followed by a downpour about 11 a.m. which probably prevented another "day of terror and madness" in Marianna.

Source: Box 1279, file 158260, Straight Numerical Files, Central Files and Related Records, Record Group 60, Department of Justice, National Archives, College Park, Maryland.

The NAACP succeeded in persuading the largest and most important newspapers to publicize the incident. With so much news coverage of such a particularly gruesome killing, Walter White believed that the Neal lynching represented the NAACP's best chance to mobilize public opinion against lynching and persuade Congress to pass an anti-lynching law. In the 1930s kidnapping cases generally attracted emotional nationwide attention in a way that lynchings did not. White contrasted the FBI's energetic response to the Charles Mattson kidnapping with the government's refusal to investigate the lynching of Neal. Mattson, the ten-year-old son of a white Tacoma doctor, had been kidnapped on December 27, 1936, causing a national sensation. The *New York Times* carried the story of this local crime on its front page for six consecutive days. As White noted, the FBI quickly dispatched eight agents, but it soon dramatically augmented that force. Within four days of the boy's disappearance, the Associated Press counted forty-five FBI agents on the scene. Although Neal's killers definitely carried him across a state line in violation of the Lindberg Kidnapping Law, authorities recovered Mattson's body fifty miles from his home, meaning that no federal law had been violated since the kidnapper never crossed a state line. Nonetheless, even after this discovery, both J. Edgar Hoover and President Roosevelt pledged "all the facilities at the disposal of the Department of Justice" to the Mattson case.[3] White's entreaties left Cummings unmoved, and the white press did not object when the Justice Department listed the Mattson case as its "only" unsolved kidnapping, ignoring Neal altogether.

144. *Walter White to Attorney General Homer Cummings,* December 29, 1936

We commend the Department of Justice for its very prompt action in sending eight agents to take over the Mattson kidnapping case at Tacoma, Washington, as soon as the kidnapping was reporting to local police. However, the question arises as to what authority there is for the prompt action in this type of case where there is no evidence of the crossing of state lines and where the kidnapped person has not been kept for more than seven days.

There appears to be no evidence as yet that the kidnapped Mattson boy has been carried over the state line. In addition, Tacoma is geographically a considerable distance from the state border. It appears to be about 130 miles from the northern border, 140 miles from the southern border and almost 300 miles from the eastern border of Washington.

The "Lindbergh Law" provides "that the failure to release such person within *seven days* after he has been unlawfully seized . . . shall create a presumption that such person has been transported in interstate or foreign commerce, but such presumption shall not be conclusive" (underscoring ours). The Department of Justice entered the Mattson case immediately and before federal jurisdiction was established. It is obvious the strict letter of the law as to interstate transportation was not followed, as in your interpretation as to reward "or otherwise" of the Claude Neal case.

The enforcement of this law by the Bureau of Investigation has led the press of the country to conclude that although the kidnapping law applies only to kidnappers operating interstate, the Department of Justice generally assumes there has been a federal violation whenever an abduction is reported and the Bureau of Investigation immediately starts an investigation.

When you were requested to investigate the kidnapping and lynching of Claude Neal who was admittedly kidnapped and transported in interstate commerce, you decided that the Department of Justice could not act because the letter of the law was limited in its scope. You advised us that "the Department of Justice does not create the law. It seeks only to enforce it."

The Chief of the Bureau of Investigation, Mr. Hoover, in giving the record of the Department of Justice in kidnap cases, states that the Mattson kidnapping is the only unsolved kidnapping listed where the federal law has been violated. One should insert in Mr. Hoover's statement the word "white" kidnapping. The list does not include the cases of the Negroes, Claude Neal, kidnapped in Alabama and carried into Florida and lynched, and Ab Young, kidnapped in Tennessee and carried into Mississippi and lynched.

The Action of the Department of Justice in the Mattson case further substantiates the quite obvious conclusion that its agents act on administrative interpretation of the law in white cases and the strict letter of the law in Negro cases. The whole record of the Department of Justice in the enforcement of the kidnapping law indicates that it has established an administrative policy to the effect that the Federal kidnapping law applies only to the kidnapping of wealthy white citizens and white peace officers.

Mr. Attorney General, we again ask that the Department of Justice proceed against the kidnappers of Claude Neal.

SOURCE: File 158260.58, Straight Numerical Files, Central Files and Related Records, Department of Justice, Record Group 60, National Archives, College Park, Maryland.

Even three years after Neal's death, White continued to pepper the Justice Department with letters about the lynching.

145. *Walter White to Attorney General Homer Cummings,* January 5, 1937

We have read with interest the Associated Press dispatch of December 31 that you ordered the Bureau of Investigation of the Department of Justice to find a cloak which Mr. Campbell Prichett lost at a party given by you and Mrs. Cummings.

Has the Bureau found Mrs. Prichett's cloak yet? If so, may we inquire if it would not be possible for you to assign the operatives thus freed by the completion of that job to investigate the interstate kidnapping and subsequent lynching of Claude Neal in October, 1934, which, you may recall, we have been urging for more than two years?

SOURCE: File 158260.58, Straight Numerical Files, Central Files and Related Records, Department of Justice, Record Group 60, National Archives, College Park, Maryland.

Despite his frustrations, Walter White won unprecedented access to the Roosevelt White House through the First Lady, Eleanor Roosevelt. Mrs. Roosevelt felt frustrated that her husband's government could do so little to help the victims of European Nazism, so she devoted her energies to domestic oppression, especially lynching. She joined the NAACP herself and vouched for Walter White before FDR's advisers, including Steven Early. "Tommy" refers to another Roosevelt adviser, Thomas Corcoran.

146. *Eleanor Roosevelt to Steven Early,* August 8, 1935

Tommy gave me your memo in regard to Walter White.

I realize perfectly that he has an obsession on the lynching question and I do not doubt that he has been a great nuisance with his telegrams and letters, both now and in previous administrations. However, reading the papers in the last few weeks, does not give you the feeling that the filerbuster [*sic*] on the lynching bill did any good to the situation and if I were colored, I think I should have about the same obsession he has.

I do not think he means to be rude or insulting. It is the same complex with a great many people belonging to minority groups have, particularly martyrs. The type of thing which would make him get himself arrested in the Senate Restaurant is probably an inferiority complex which he tries to combat and which makes him far more aggressive than if he felt equality. It is worse with Walter White because he is almost white. If you ever talked to him, and knew him, I think you would feel as I do. He really is a very fine person with the sorrows of his people close to his heart.

SOURCE: Eleanor Roosevelt to Steve Early, August 8, 1935, file 1336, President's Personal File (Franklin D. Roosevelt Library, Hyde Park, New York). Reprinted by permission.

In 1937 Howard Kester investigated another lynching for the NAACP. The "Blow Torch Lynching" hit the newspapers just as the House of Representatives prepared to vote again on an NAACP-sponsored anti-lynching bill. With Washington newspapers carrying stories of blue flame torturing quivering human flesh, the representatives passed the bill. White racists ultimately defeated the proposed legislation by filibustering it to death in the Senate.

147. *Howard Kester, "Lynching by Blow Torch,"* April 13, 1937

On December 30, 1936, George Windham, who owned a small country store about ten miles from Duck Hill, Mississippi in the northeastern corner of Montgomery County was murdered by shots fired from a double barrelled shot-gun just as he was preparing to lock up his store for the night. No one seemed to have any very definite idea as to who committed the murder. Since the cash drawer had been locked and money taken from Windham's pocketbook it was assumed that robbery was the motive.

Prior to the murder a young Negro boy who bore the name of Roosevelt Townes had been in the vicinity and had lived with one "Bootjack" McDaniels of the Duck Hill community. . . . Shortly before the storekeeper was murdered it is alleged that Townes returned to Duck Hill and that immediately following the murder of Windham he disappeared. Certain that Townes' disappearance was positive proof of his guilt in connection with the murder, local officials forwarded a description of him to the Memphis police. He was subsequently arrested by the police of Memphis who allege that Townes made an open confession of having murdered the Montgomery County storekeeper. (The methods employed to obtain confessions from criminal suspects by Memphis police are known to be among the most brutal in the entire country and such confessions have no value whatever.) Following Townes' arrest he was sent to Jackson to await trial. Local officials arrested McDaniels upon the alleged confession of Roosevelt Townes.

Mob Violence Expected

On Tuesday, April 13 McDaniels and Townes were returned to Winona, county seat of Montgomery County, to stand trial. As is usual on such occasions a large number of people was gathered in the county seat for the trial. That mob violence was expected is evidenced by the fact that a court order was issued prohibiting the parking of automobiles or other vehicles about the court house. It is alleged that friends of the murdered storekeeper were notified of the probable time of the arrival of the prisoners from Jackson and of the exact nature and hour of the court's proceedings. It is furthermore alleged by citizens of Montgomery, Grenada, Chickasaw, Webster, and Calhoun counties that Sheriff Wright knew the mob.

Although a court order had been issued prohibiting the parking of automobiles around the court house, a Chevrolet school bus was parked in the prohibited zone. The school bus was particularly noticeable. Some thoughtful citizens of Winona inquired about the bus, sought to locate the driver, found that the key was missing but forgot that the bus could be easily rolled down the hill away from the prohibited area.

About noon Sheriff Wright, accompanied by two deputies, was proceeding with Townes and McDaniels from the court house to the jail where they had been arraigned and pleaded not guilty to the murder charges lodged against them when twelve men emerged from the crowd about the court house and seized the prisoners, who were not handcuffed.

One eye witness declared, "It was all very carefully planned and executed. There was no confusion. Apparently each man had a job to do and did it with dispatch." The two men were taken from the officers who offered no resistance and were thrown screaming into the waiting school bus which quickly drove away. (It is said by some observers that one deputy attempted to draw his gun but decided not to when two men threw guns into his stomach and back. It is also stated that the deputy was concerned for the Sheriff lest the latter get "mashed.")

"1,000 People Can Name Lynchers"

According to unimpeachable sources Sheriff Wright made no effort whatever to oppose the mob or to follow the departing school bus. About two hours after the mob had escaped with the prisoners Sheriff Wright was moved to call Governor White at Jackson to inform him that there had been a lynching. It is interesting to observe that although the Sheriff had not quitted the court house square he knew what had happened twenty miles away. The situation is further illuminated by the fact that while the sheriff could see what was going on at the scene of the lynching party some twenty miles away he was unable to recognize a single member of the mob, although completely surrounded by it. The apparent far-sightedness of the sheriff is attributed to the fact that he was raised in the northeastern section of Montgomery county where the lynching occurred, that the members of the mob were his personal friends and that they helped to elect him to his high office.

It is furthermore alleged that the district attorney, Clarence Morgan, who had been in public office for two decades, watched the proceedings from a window in the court house but did not see any of the members of the mob. And finally, it is alleged, that the Secretary of State of Mississippi, Walker Wood, viewed the scene from the door of his *Winona Times* and has been unable to recall any of the faces he saw. Despite these and other inexplicable happenings, an ex-mayor informed the writer: "There are a thousand people in Montgomery County who can name the lynchers."

Groceryman Windham ran his little store about ten miles in a northeasterly direction from Duck Hill. He was well known among the country people and his kinsmen were scattered in four counties. On the afternoon of April 13 the clan gathered to avenge in a bath of blood and fire the death of their relative. When the school bus arrived with its human sacrifice a crowd of three or four hundred men, women and children had gathered to observe the proceedings.

Chains and a Blow Torch

Two terror-stricken black men were dragged forth and with heavy chains tied securely to two lonely pine trees. One of the twelve white men produced a blow torch, applied a match and a flame of fire tore into the breast of McDaniels. The blue-white flame leaped into the soft skin and the odor of burnt flesh assailed the nostrils of Mississippi's first batch of 1937 lynchers. The piercing screams of the tortured men echoed among the hills and sent some of the wild-eyed children scurrying to their mother's sides. Mingled with the agonizing cries of the condemned men was the steady purr of the flaming death that issued from the blow torch. From the wracked body and crazed mind of the victim the mob wrung a confession of guilt. The torch was withdrawn and a volley of bullets brought welcome death to the tormented prisoner chained to a lonely pine tree.

Roosevelt Townes who had been accused of firing the fatal shot which killed Groceryman Windham had been forced to watch the mob's savage way with his former friend. Now he became the object of the mob's ferocity. The mob's appetite for brutality had now reached a high pitch and the masters of lynchings newest methods of torture determined to prolong the suffering of the next victim to the last possible moment. Again the hellish blow torch was lighted and driven into the quivering flesh of Roosevelt Townes. The flaming torch swept into the heaving breast of the terrorized man and was momentarily withdrawn as the mob watched him writhe in agony and pain. After a few minutes had passed the torch was applied to Townes' sweating back and the searing flame produced hideous holes wherever it touched. From breast to back and from back to breast the devilish machine accomplished its horrible task. Fingers and ears were seared from the writhing body. From head to foot the white fire ate livid holes into human flesh.

An Hour of Torture

Swaying and crying but held fast by heavy iron links, this truly strong man fed the mob's insatiable appetite for brutality and blood for one long hideous hour.

Nearby stood terrified Shorty Dorroh who had been produced by the mob following McDaniels alleged confession. Fearfully he watched the devastating flames devouring Townes and understood that he was to be the sacrifice in the mob's next gory assault. Growing weary of the groans of the stricken Townes a few members of the mob gathered wood and threw them down around his helpless feet. As five gallons of gasoline was thrown upon the heaving body, a match was lighted and Townes was covered instantly by a sheet of flaming fire.

Word came to the mob that Governor White at Jackson had ordered out the National Guard and being somewhat content with the day's proceedings they horsewhipped Dorroh and told him to leave the state.

Slowing the satiated mob left the horror-stricken scene for their respective homes. As black clouds settled over the horizon a desultory rain enveloped the woods in darkness and quenched the hot coals about the charred remains of Townes. . . .

Your investigator is convinced that mob action was anticipated; that the Sheriff of Montgomery County took no real precaution whatever to insure the accused a fair trial; that he made no effort to defend his prisoners against the mob; that he did not try to rescue the prisoners from the mob. Your investigator is reasonably convinced that the sheriff was in sympathy with the mob leaders and did not intend to permit the accused men to stand trial; and further that no effort will be made to identify the lynchers or prosecute the murderers of Townes and McDaniels; and finally that local officials are incompetent to cope with such occurrences and that only the Federal government can safely intervene in such matters on behalf of justice and fair play.

SOURCE: Howard Anderson Kester Papers, Southern Historical Collection, Wilson Library, University of North Carolina at Chapel Hill. Used by permission.

In 1939 Franklin Roosevelt appointed Frank Murphy, the former governor of Michigan, as Attorney General. Murphy promptly organized a Civil Liberties Unit within the Department of Justice and pledged to investigate all lynchings. Murphy changed federal policy toward mob violence and attempted to shift the course of American constitutionalism and federalism. Murphy proposed making the prosecution of lynchers a federal responsibility. Since the Congress had refused to pass a law against lynching, it must be said that Murphy attempted an end run around the legislative branch. He put his lawyers to work, poring over the United States Code, to find some existing law that could be used to do what the proposed anti-lynching law would have done, had Congress enacted such a law.

Department of Justice lawyers decided that the 1871 Ku Klux Klan Act could be converted into an anti-lynching law. The Klan Act had made it a crime for anyone acting "under color of law" to subject "any inhabitant of any state or territory . . . to the deprivation of any rights, privileges, or immunities secured or protected by the Constitution."

World War II made the department's work more urgent. Justice Department lawyers worried that Axis propagandists took advantage of American racial violence. African Americans called for "Double V," victory over enemies overseas but also against oppression at home. And, finally, the war accelerated mob violence. Returning veterans from minority groups attracted the attention of violent racists. In 1948 the Japanese-American Citizens League Antidiscrimination Committee reported that more than one hundred instances of arson, intimidation, and shootings of persons of Japanese ancestry took place in California between December 1944 and July 1946. "I think," Mike Masaoka said, "people are prone to forget that what happens to a Negro . . . can happen to them." He added that such "had been the experience of the Japanese-American society."[4]

The Civil Liberties Unit wanted to publicize its findings to build public support for the new policy. Victor Rotnem, a Department of Justice lawyer and leader of the department's new Civil Rights Section, explained that world war had made the policy change essential.

148. *Victor W. Rotnem, "The Federal Civil Right 'Not to Be Lynched,'"* February 1943

Prior to January 25, 1942, Cleo Wright, a Negro citizen of the State of Missouri and of the United States, had been arrested by the local police officers of Sikeston, Missouri, was being held under arrest in the local jail, and was facing charges of assault and attempted rape under the criminal laws of the State of Missouri. On January 25, 1942, in broad daylight, a mob broke into the jail, seized and removed Cleo Wright, tied his feet to the rear of an automobile, dragged him through the Negro section of the town, and then poured gasoline on his body and burned him to death.

Within forty-eight hours thereafter, the German and Japanese short wave radio broadcasters featured discussions of the "Sikeston Affair" in all its sordid details.

These broadcasts were relayed to the peoples of the Dutch East Indies and India at a time immediately preceding the fall of Java; and listeners were told, in effect:

"If the democracies win the War, here is what the colored races may expect of them!"

Thus the lynching at Sikeston, Missouri, became a matter of international importance and a subject of Axis propaganda.

On February 13, 1942, Assistant Attorney General Wendell Berge requested the Federal Bureau of Investigation to make a full inquiry into the lynching at Sikeston to determine whether there was any basis for prosecution by the federal government of the members of the mob, or other persons concerned. In authorizing the federal investigation, Attorney General Biddle indicated the significance of the incident to war morale, for he stated:

> With our country at war to defend our democratic way of life throughout the world a lynching has significance far beyond the community, or even the state, in which it occurs. It becomes a matter of national importance and thus properly the concern of the federal government.

Although it is a matter of national importance, yet, under our system of government, there must be found constitutional power for federal legislation before the federal government can concern itself through official action; and before an act can be made the basis for federal prosecution, even where there is constitutional power to legislate, applicable federal legislation must exist.

Attorney General Biddle directed that evidence on the lynching at Sikeston be presented to a federal grand jury. The session of the federal grand jury to hear this evidence began in St. Louis on May 13, 1942. On July 30, 1942, the United States Department of Justice made public the grand jury's report. The jury returned no indictments but made an advisory report to the United States District Court. This report recommended both state legislative and executive action, but it made no recommendation for a federal statute to make the lynching of a person *in custodia legis* of the state a federal crime. Nor did the jury find that a federal crime had been committed.

Describing the lynching as "a shameful outrage," and censuring the Sikeston police for having "failed completely to calm the situation," the federal grand jury report nevertheless eluded, "with great reluctance," that the facts disclosed constitute a federal crime under existing laws. Still, the jury report stated:

> In this instance a brutal criminal was denied *due process*. The next time the mob might lynch a person entirely innocent. But whether the victim be guilty or innocent, the blind passion of a mob cannot be substituted for *due process of law* if orderly government is to survive.

Since there is reason to suppose that the maintenance of due process of law within the states is a matter of federal concern under the Fourteenth Amendment of the Constitution of the United States, it is the purpose of this article to re-examine the question of whether, under already existing federal laws, lynching a person in the legal custody of a state may not now be a federal crime. No disrespect for the conclusions of the federal grand jury is intended. However, the determination of a grand jury that the facts disclosed do not constitute a federal crime under existing laws is not conclusive. A final determination of that question can be had only when an appeal presents to the United States Supreme Court the opportunity to hear and decide the issue.

. . . [I]t might be argued that the lynching of a person not yet accused of a crime or not yet taken into the legal custody of the state, is not a federal crime where no other relation to the federal government appears. But it is argued in many quarters that once a person has been accused of a state crime—and especially when he is in the legal custody of the state—because he has been accused or is under arrest for the commission of a crime—he has the right, under the Constitution of the United States, to a fair and impartial trial in the criminal courts of the state; that a mob in lynching him deprives him of this federally-secured right; that this deprivation of another's constitutional right is, in effect, an obstruction of federal justice. . . .

That lynching cannot be tolerated in a land engaged in carrying the Four Freedoms abroad is hardly arguable; and that state inaction exists, and will continue to exist, is scarcely subject to doubt. . . .

A person tried in the state courts has a theoretical right to have the state court's determinations reviewed in the light of the due process clause under the federal judicial power; and, if there is a denial of due process of law by the state, this right to review in the federal courts is very real and effective. To deprive a person of the opportunity for a reviewable trial, then, is to deprive him of a right that is not only secured to him by the Federal Constitution but enforceable and enforced in the federal courts, in brief, it is to interfere with the administration of federal justice, in this sense, itself.

In this view of the matter, there is not only federal "concern" when "our country is at war to defend our democratic way of life throughout the world" but there is both federal power to legislate and existing federal legislation implementing that power in peace as well as war. When the state itself denies due process of law in a criminal trial, the federal government grants relief to the injured person through its courts in review, without the aid of any statute—the Fourteenth Amendment. . . . When the functioning of due process of law in a state criminal action is prevented by private persons, is there not congressional power to make such interference with due process of law a federal crime? Or, is this the one area of federal constitutional government in which the individual is to be set above the state? Even to ask that question should startle American ears! . . .

Conclusion

A grand jury is not the final arbiter or even a persuasive voice of what comes within the purview of either the Constitution or the statutes of the United States. In view of the doubts shed upon the theory, if not the result, of the *Harris Case* in the *Hodges Case,* in view of the clear distinction between the facts of the *Hodges Case* and the *Powell* and Sikeston situations, in view of the unsatisfactory basis for the decision in the *Powell Case,* in view of the development of due process of law subsequent to all these cases, and in view of *United States v. Classic*—it would appear that the grand jury in the Sikeston matter should have overcome its "great reluctance," returned indictments, and left to the final arbiter in our constitutional system, the Supreme Court, the clarification of this important area of the law.

The evil of lynchings exists and doubt as to whether or not federal power now exists to remedy it can only adversely affect our national morale. Hence, it is highly desirable that whatever doubt that may exist be authoritatively resolved.

SOURCE: Victor W. Rotnem, "The Federal Civil Right 'Not to Be Lynched," *Washington University Law Quarterly* 28 (February 1943). Used by permission of Washington University School of Law.

Rotnem wrote his article after a Missouri grand jury refused to indict a gang of lynchers in 1942. A year later the Justice Department had better luck in Georgia, after a sheriff and two assistants beat a black man to death. Mack Claude Screws had become Baker County sheriff in 1936. He did not want to repeat the mistakes of Jack Griffin Sr., his predecessor whom he had ousted as sheriff. Many Baker County whites had accused Griffin of coddling black criminals when he blocked lynchings. Voters preferred Screws because he knew how to "handle" blacks, but his methods got him into trouble with the federal authority. In contrast to the Missouri jurors, a federal grand jury in Georgia indicted Screws and his cohorts and, even more remarkably, a trial jury proceeded to convict the trio.

Screws appealed his conviction to the U.S. Supreme Court. One faction of justices, led by Felix Frankfurter, wanted to declare the Enforcement Act unconstitutional as too vague. A majority rejected that argument but still overturned Screws's conviction.

William O. Douglas wrote the rule: The Department of Justice could prosecute lynchings, when a state officer participated, but government lawyers had to prove that the lynchers specifically intended to harm their victims' constitutional rights. They had to act "willfully." The United States finally had its anti-lynching law, albeit one requiring a nearly impossible standard of proof. After the *Screws* decision, FBI agents and government lawyers continued to investigate lynchings, hoping to bring additional prosecutions. But by 1955, when white Mississippians killed Emmett Till, the Justice Department had backed off and conducted no investigation.

149. *Justice William O. Douglas, Opinion of the U.S. Supreme Court, in Screws v. United States, 1945*

MR. JUSTICE DOUGLAS announced the judgment of the Court and delivered the following opinion, in which the CHIEF JUSTICE, MR. JUSTICE BLACK and MR. JUSTICE REED concur.

This case involves a shocking and revolting episode in law enforcement. Petitioner Screws was sheriff of Baker County, Georgia. He enlisted the assistance of petitioner Jones, a policeman, and petitioner Kelley, a special deputy, in arresting Robert Hall, a citizen of the United States and of Georgia. The arrest was made late at night at Hall's home on a warrant charging Hall with theft of a tire. Hall, a young negro about thirty years of age, was handcuffed and taken by car to the court house. As Hall alighted from the car at the court-house square, the three petitioners began beating him with their fists and with a solid-bar blackjack about eight inches long and weighing two pounds. They claimed Hall had reached for a gun and had used insulting language as he alighted from the car. But after Hall, still handcuffed, had been knocked to the ground they continued to beat him from fifteen to thirty minutes until he was unconscious. Hall was then dragged feet first through the court-house yard into the jail and thrown upon the floor dying. An ambulance was called and Hall was removed to a hospital where he died within the hour and without regaining consciousness. There was evidence that Screws held a grudge against Hall and had threatened to "get" him. . . .

An indictment was returned against petitioners—one count charging a violation of §20 of the Criminal Code, 18 U.S.C. §52 and another charging a conspiracy to violate §20 contrary to §37 of the Criminal Code, 18 U.S.C. §88. Sec. 20 provides:

> Whoever, under color of any law, statute, ordinance, regulation, or custom, willfully subjects, or causes to be subjected, any inhabitant of any State, Territory, or District to the deprivation of any rights, privileges, or immunities secured or protected by the Constitution and laws of the United States, or to different punishments, pains, or penalties, on account of such inhabitant being an alien, or by reason of his color, or race, than are prescribed for the punishment of citizens, shall be fined not more than $1,000, or imprisoned not more than one year, or both.

An analysis of the cases in which "willfully" has been held to connote more than an act which is voluntary or intentional would not prove helpful as each turns on its own peculiar facts. Those cases, however, make clear that if we construe "willfully" in §20 as connoting a purpose to deprive a person of a specific constitutional right, we would introduce no innovation. The Court, indeed, has recognized that the requirement of a specific intent to do a prohibited act may avoid those consequences to the accused which may otherwise render a vague or indefinite statute invalid. . . .

Moreover, the history of §20 affords some support for that narrower construction. . . . the word "willfully" was not added to the Act until 1909. Prior to that time it may be that Congress intended that he who deprived a person of any right protected by the Constitution should be liable without more. . . . We think the inference is permissible that its severity was to be lessened by making it applicable only where the requisite bad purpose was present. . . .

Once the section is given that construction, we think that the claim that the section lacks an ascertainable standard of guilt must fail. The constitutional requirement that a criminal statute be definite serves a high function. It gives a person acting with reference to the statute fair warning that his conduct is within its prohibition. This requirement is met when a statute prohibits only "willful" acts in the sense we have explained. One who does act with such specific intent is aware that what he does is precisely that which the statute forbids. He is under no necessity of guessing whether the statute applies to him for he either knows or acts in reckless disregard of its prohibition of the deprivation of a defined constitutional or other federal right. Nor is such an act beyond the understanding and comprehension of juries summoned to pass on them. The Act would then not become a trap for law enforcement agencies acting in good faith. "A mind intent upon willful evasion is inconsistent with surprised innocence."

It is said, however, that this construction of the Act will not save it from the infirmity of vagueness since neither a law enforcement official nor a trial judge can know with sufficient definiteness the range of rights that are constitutional. But that criticism is wide of the mark. For the specific intent required by the Act is an intent to deprive a person of a right which has been made specific either by the express terms of the Constitution or laws of the United States or by decisions interpreting them. . . .

The difficulty here is that this question of intent was not submitted to the jury with the proper instructions. The court charged that petitioners acted illegally if they applied more force than was necessary to make the arrest effectual or to protect themselves from the prisoner's alleged assault. But in view of our construction of the word "willfully" the jury should have been further instructed that it was not sufficient that petitioners had a generally bad purpose. To convict it was necessary for them to find that petitioners had the purpose to deprive the prisoner of a constitutional right, e.g. the right to be tried by a court rather than by ordeal. And in determining whether that requisite bad purpose was present the jury would be entitled to consider all the attendant circumstances—the malice of petitioners, the weapons used in the assault, its character and duration, the provocation, if any, and the like. . . .

Since there must be a new trial, the judgment below is *Reversed*.

SOURCE: 325 U.S. 91.

At his second trial, the jury acquitted Screws. He served as sheriff of Baker County for twenty years and then went on to the Georgia legislature. He died February 12, 1965, and is buried in Mt. Carmel Church Cemetery, Baker County.

Despite the *Screws* setback, Department of Justice officers continued to investigate and prosecute lynching cases for several years.

Sometimes these cases involved returning black servicemen. In Georgia, whites killed two black men and their wives, on July 25, 1946. An FBI investigation failed to produce evidence that the Department of Justice could take to trial. These killings remain unsolved, although in 2001 the governor of Georgia offered a new reward for information leading to the capture of the lynchers.[5] Even as the FBI's New Orleans office dispatched investigators to Georgia, it learned that it had work to do in Louisiana. On August 8, 1946, a Louisiana mob attacked a black army veteran named John C. Jones and his young cousin, Albert Harris. Jones died but Harris survived and made an affidavit describing his ordeal. Either Harris or the transcriber of his statement recorded the name of one lyncher incorrectly. "Sam Mettrick" was actually Sam Maddry.

150. *Albert Harris Jr., Affidavit,* August 29, 1946

I am 17 years old and was born and have lived all my life in Cotton Valley, Louisiana. On the 31st of July, 1946 at 6 or 6:30 at night Sam Mettrick, O. H. Haynes, Jr., Deputy Sheriff of Minden, a man named Perry, and Charlie Edwards, Deputy Sheriff of Cotton Valley and Spring Hill, came to my house and arrested me. They then drove me in a car to Dennis' store where they stopped and accused me and Jones of going in a white man's yard and said Jones attempted to rape Sam Mettrick's son's wife and that I was watching for him. Then they drove me to Spring Hill to see Sam Mettrick's son, Sammy, where he was working at the International Paper Company. They asked Sammy if I was the boy and he said, "Yes, he's the one named Sonnyman."

After we left Spring Hill, Haynes and Perry took me past my house and then to Minden to the jail house. That is where they kept me from that Wednesday evening until Friday evening. They did not question me at all then. Sheriff Haynes took me out of jail where the mob could get me at Dixie End. He said he was going to Shreveport and would ride me part way home. We drove along the highway to Shreveport until he came to Highway 90 at Dixie End, 18 miles from my home. Highway 90 goes in back of my house. When we got to Highway 90 he told me that was as far as he was going. I saw a car there. It was a blue Buick about 1938 or 1939. I saw the car before I got out of the sheriff's car, but I did not know it was the mob, so I got out of the sheriff's car and made about a 50-yard dash down the road, and they came after me and put guns on me. They put me in the car and took me past Charlie Johnson's place. They accused me of peeping for Jones and asked me about Jones and threatened to kill me if I did not tell them that Jones did it. They took me out by Charlie Johnson's café, tied me to an oil well, and that is where they beat me. Jones was not with me then. They were trying to make me tell that Jones was the one who went in the yard. They beat me with straps, sticks. After they beat me about two hours, they told me if I did not tell it they were going to kill me. So I told them that Jones was the one, to keep them from killing me. Then they let me go. They took me about half a mile above my house in an automobile and put me out. I do not know whose automobile it was, and did not know the driver. I only know Sam Mettrick and Slim Perkins of the ones who were beating me. They were not connected with the law at all as I know of. When they were beating me there were five of them and I only know those two.

After I got home, my mother and father took me to Henderson, Texas. I got there that Saturday morning at 5 o'clock and stayed there all day Saturday until Sunday morning at 5. My father carried me back to Minden and had me at the sheriff's office at 12:30 P.M. that Sunday. My father left me there. They told him they were going to keep me two days, and after my father left, he said several days. Haynes asked me did Jones go in this man's yard, and I told him no, and he told me that I was lying, so he took me and put me in jail. I stayed in jail from Sunday until Thursday night. They did not beat me in jail. That is when they came and got me again. All this time I had not seen Jones, but he was in jail. He was on one side of the corridor and I was on the other side. I could not see him, but I know he was there because I could talk to him, and I did talk to him. The sheriff told me that Sunday evening that he had Jones. The sheriff told me that I told the mob crowd that Jones was the one who did it. I told him they beat me and made me tell them.

Thursday night the sheriff told me he was going to turn us loose, and we hadn't done anything, the lady didn't have any charges on us. This was about 8:30. He opened the door and said he was going to turn us loose. Jones went out first, I was next, and Haynes was behind me. Jones did not say anything to the sheriff. He did not push us out. We walked right out.

They were on the outside of the jail standing behind the post so we could not see them. I did not know anyone but Mettrick in the crowd. There were about 10 of them. Five got Jones and five got me. Jones started hollering soon as the crowd grabbed him. I did not say anything when they grabbed me. They hit him on the head trying to make him stop. Mettrick was in the group that grabbed me. When Jones hollered Haynes was behind me. Haynes saw them take us. He had a gun. After they hit Jones, Haynes helped them put Jones in the car. Three men had me. I was looking at every bit of it. Mettrick had me in the belt, and two other guys had me on each arm. Haynes was the only one in the jail at that time.

They put me in a car. There were two different cars. I did not know whether Sheriff Haynes was in the car with Jones. They took us about 15 miles below Minden, and that is where they beat me again and killed Jones. They had nearly killed him before they put him in the car. From the time the cars left and we were beaten, I did not see the sheriff again. In the last mob, the only one I recognized was Mettrick.

They took Jones on one side of the creek. I do not know what they did to him. They took me to the other side. They tied my hands and feet. They put their feet on my head and my feet so I could not move. Some stepped on my head and some stepped on the rest of my body. Then they beat me again with a strap. Mettrick was in the crowd that was beating me. After they beat me, they told me to leave Cotton Valley and not be caught back there anymore. That is when they hit me with a big gun over my eye and knocked me out.

After I came to, they were gone. I heard Jones groaning. They had cut the ropes from my hands and feet. I went over to see about Jones. He was in a bad condition. He was bleeding about the head and about the body too. He was not dead, but he was dying. He could speak. He told me to get him a drink of water. About 15 minutes after that I felt his pulse and decided he had died. I was there when he died. I did not ask him who the people were who beat him and he did not tell me. He did not talk much.

Then I left there and went to Minden to my uncle's. I stayed up there all night and all the next day until the next night. My cousin from Shreveport came over and got a taxi and we went in the taxi to Cotton Valley where my mother was.

When I left Jones he was not burned. After I got on the road, they were coming back. I saw the cars, so I got in the woods. I am quite sure it was the mob coming back. I saw the car they had brought me in. It was brown, a '39 Chevrolet. When they brought us there the car I was in was leading. Mettrick was not driving the car. I did not see the other car no more than coming out of the jail and I just glanced at it then. Every time I saw the car after I had left Jones I went in the woods.

I got into town and could not get out of the way of one car, and was walking down the street. The city police stopped me and asked me where was the other boy. I told them he was in the woods. He asked me where. I said I did not know exactly because I did not know the woods so well. They asked me did I know any of the mob. I told them no because if I had said yes they would have done something to me.

SOURCE: Albert Harris Jr., affidavit, August 29, 1946, section 1, 144-33-24, box 794, Civil Rights Division, Department of Justice, RG 60, National Archives, College Park, Maryland.

The lynchers beat and tortured John C. Jones with a blowtorch. Walter White of the NAACP called the Department of Justice, asking for an FBI investigation. The department obliged, but it was the NAACP that located Albert Harris, hiding in Michigan.[6] A federal grand jury indicted deputy sheriff Oscar Henry Haynes Jr., Samuel Clinton Maddry Sr., Charles Melvin Edwards, Harry Edward Perry, Willie Drayton Perkins, and Benjamin Geary Gantt, the Minden chief of police. FBI investigators believed that Gantt played no role in the lynching, and authorities dropped those charges directed at him. The other defendants went to trial, prosecuted by the U.S. attorney Malcolm Lefargue.

151. *Theron L. Caudle to Malcolm Lefargue,* March 5, 1947

Your courtesy in advising me so promptly as to the verdict of acquittal in the *O. H. Haynes, Jr.,* case which was concluded on March 1, 1947, is very much appreciated. I share with you the keen regret felt over losing the case, but I want you to know that the Department has full confidence in your efforts to fairly and vigorously present the case.

At your earliest convenience will you kindly forward me a transcript of the evidence. I would like to review the evidence as it developed in the course of the trial in order to be in a position to answer inquiries made to the Civil Rights Section by the President's Committee on Civil Rights which was recently appointed. In this connection I will greatly appreciate your frank comments along the following lines.

What were the determining factors in your opinion which influenced the jury in acquitting the defendants. For example, (1) Was the Government's evidence insufficient? (2) Did our witnesses break down upon cross-examination or otherwise look weak in general appearances before the jury? (3) Did the inflammatory statements made by the defendant's counsel before the jury as reported in the press have any material bearing on the outcome? (4) Do you believe that any racial prejudice entertained by the jury materially effected the result? (5) Did you get any impression that the jury was loathe to convict in a Federal Court on a civil rights charge when the primary crime, if any, was murder? (6) Finally, I am particularly interested in your opinion as to the effect upon the jury of the charge that in order to convict it must believe the acts in question were committed by the defendants for the specific purpose of depriving the victims of the Federal right in issue.

SOURCE: Theron Caudle to Malcolm Lafargue, March 5, 1947, section 2, 144-33-24, box 794, Civil Rights Division, Department of Justice, RG 60, National Archives, College Park, Maryland.

152. *Malcolm Lefargue to Theron L. Caudle,* March 11, 1947

In reply to Paragraph Three of your letter, I will answer your questions categorically, as asked:
(1) No;
(2) Our witnesses did not break down. However, the greater part of them had criminal records and were confined in the Webster Parish Jail at the time Harris and Jones were taken by the mob. This, of course, was to be expected, since the acts of the mob were committed on the jail premises;

(3) No;

(4) Yes. As a matter of fact, it is my opinion that the case was decided wholly on this point;

(5) No. I feel that if this case had involved whites altogether the jury may have voted a conviction;

(6) It is my opinion that the Judge's charge, as given, on the question of specific intent did not have any material effect on the jury. I believe that, if the case had been one in which there had been no racial prejudice, the question of the defendants' guilty [sic] or innocence would have been determined strictly on the facts, without too much regard to the technical legal questions as contained in the Court's charge.

The Judge's charge on the specific intent was a verbatim recital of our charge, as prepared by the Civil Rights Section, and the facts as presented by the Government in the trial of the case, all things being equal, would have been sufficient under the charge to support a conviction.

SOURCE: Malcolm Lefargue to Theron L. Caudle, March 11, 1947, section 2, 144-33-24, box 794, Civil Rights Division, Department of Justice, RG 60, National Archives, College Park, Maryland.

153. *Turner L. Smith Memorandum to Theron L. Caudle*, March 17, 1947

You will note that the entire transcript will run around $350. I doubt that it will be worth this much to us. Apparently our "clients" think that we did everything we could in the case. . . .

SOURCE: Turner L. Smith memorandum to Theron L. Caudle, March 17, 1947, section 2, 144-33-24, box 794, Civil Rights Division, Department of Justice, RG 60, National Archives, College Park, Maryland.

Smith's reference to "our clients" means the NAACP. And Smith was correct. Walter White wrote in his autobiography that "the Department of Justice had utilized every possible section of the ineffective federal statutes which were then in effect."[7] White, of course, had spent decades trying to persuade Congress to pass a law against lynching on the theory that existing law did not adequately outlaw mob violence. In fact, the prosecutor did not think the statutes so ineffective at all. According to Lafargue, the prosecution tripped on race alone, not the law. Nonetheless, in the 1950s, the Department of Justice stopped automatically investigating every lynching complaint filed. FBI agents did not begin searching for the killers of Emmett Till, for example, until 2004.

NOTES

1. Roy Wilkins, with Tom Mathews, *Standing Fast: The Autobiography of Roy Wilkins* (New York: Viking, 1982), 132.

2. David Sholtz served as Florida's governor from January 4, 1933, until January 5, 1937.

3. *New York Times,* December 28, 29, 20, 31, 1936; January 1, 4, 12, 13, 1937.

4. Statement of Mike Masaoka, *Hearings before Subcommittee No. 4 of the Committee on the Judiciary, House of Representatives,* 80th Congress, 2d sess., February 4, 1948, 68–72.

5. Laura Wexler, *Fire in a Canebrake: The Last Mass Lynching in America* (New York: Scribner, 2003).

6. Walter White, *A Man Called White: The Autobiography of Walter White* (New York: Viking, 1948), 323–325.

7. Ibid., 325.

12

High-Tech Lynchings

In October 1991 Clarence Thomas, named to serve on the Supreme Court by President George H. W. Bush, ran into trouble as the Senate considered whether to confirm his nomination or not. The Thomas nomination already troubled Democratic senators. Thomas was a conservative, the kind of nominee Democrats usually opposed, but he was also African American and Democrats hesitated to deny a seat to the Supreme Court to a member of a minority group so seldom represented on the Court. Charges that he had sexually harassed a female subordinate surfaced and senators confronted him with the allegations. Thomas fired back, accusing Senate Democrats of trying to "lynch" him. Thomas compared his confirmation hearings to "a circus" which he blasted as "a national disgrace." He then said, "From my standpoint as a black American, as far as I'm concerned, it is a high-tech lynching for uppity blacks who in any way deign to think for themselves, to do for themselves, to have different ideas." Thomas charged that the senators intended to frighten all black Americans, saying, in effect, that, "unless you kowtow to an old order, this is what will happen to you. You will be lynched, destroyed, caricatured by a committee of the U.S. Senate rather than hung from a tree."[1]

Thomas thought his lynching "high-tech" because the news media had spread the charges against him by television, computer, and satellite. Modern news dissemination is a high-tech operation. In fact, the spread of information about every lynching reflected the technology of its times in the sense that news organizations reported neighborhood lynchings to the world through an increasingly sophisticated machinery. Technology attacked and broke down the neighborhood isolation that once shielded lynchers from widespread scrutiny.

By 1947, when a crowd of South Carolina taxi drivers killed Willie Earle, a national market for news about lynching flourished. South Carolina's energetic young governor, a D-Day veteran named Strom Thurmond, impressed northern journalists by appointing a special prosecutor and dispatching state police officers to investigate. Thurmond even welcomed FBI help and the federal agents joined South Carolina officers to identify thirty-one lynchers. *Time, Life, Newsweek,* and the *New Republic* all sent reporters to cover the trial which the *New York Times* hailed as the biggest lynching trial in history.

FBI agents vigorously and effectively investigated the lynching, persuading twenty-six of the lynchers to confess their crimes. The agents learned that the cab drivers believed that Willie Earle had murdered cab driver Thomas W. Brown. Brown's fellow drivers decided to exact their revenge by taking Earle from jail and killing him. The following confession is typical of the statements the lynchers made as a result of FBI interrogation.

154. *Jessie Lee Sammons Statement, Greenville, S.C.,* February 19, 1947

I, Jessie Lee Sammons, make the following voluntary statement to Edwin R. Groves & Richard Wood who have identified themselves to me as Special Agents of the Federal

Bureau of Investigation and James Bigham who has identified himself to me as a Detective with the Greenville Police Department. I have been told that I do not have to make any statement and that anything I say or any statement I give may be used against me in a court of law. No threats or promises have been made to me and no force has been used to cause me to give this statement.

I was born August 3, 1917 at Greenville, S.C., and live with my wife, Martha, and children at 112 W. Broad Street, Greenville, S.C. I am a taxi driver with the American Cab Co. in Greenville, S.C. and have been with them since this cab company started.

On Monday, Feb. 17, 1947, between 2:00 and 3:00 A.M. I came out of the Southern Cafe at the Southern Railroad Depot on W. Washington Street. I saw Hendrix Rector, Paul F. Griggs, Jr., Marvin Henry Fleming, Johnny F. Willimon and they were walking over toward the cafe from the place where they had parked their cabs. Perry Murrell came out of the cafe behind me. Rector said to me, "Are you going with us?" I said, "Where are you going?" He said, "Over to get the negro at Pickens." I told him I had not thought about it and he said, "Well, we're going." Everybody then told one another to meet at 4:00 A.M. at the Saluda River bridge about halfway between Greenville & Easley. We were to meet at the tourist camp just across the bridge, I heard the drivers tell each other.

I then drove alone to the American Cab Co. office. Rector was there at the office in a yellow cab when I got there. I went in and checked my sheets with Mr. Norris & O. C. Berry. I then went outside & saw two yellow cabs. One was driven by Rector and one by Marvin H. Fleming. There was one Blue Bird cab. Rector came out of the office & showed the ten or fifteen drivers what cabs to get into. He told me to get in his cab. I sat on the back seat beside Walt Crawford and Ernest Stokes. In the front seat with Rector were Johnny Willimon and Perry Murrell. He then went out to Bramlett Road, turned right on to Parker Road and turned to the right to the first street to the right which was Reedy Street. We went to the first house on the right on the first curve of Reedy Street. Rector got out and then went into a white bungalow house. He came right back out and when he got to the car he said he got some shells. He turned around & we went back the way we came. We went on county roads & came out on the Easley highway near Noah Smith's junkyard. We then went to the tourist camp just across the Saluda River bridge: There were four or five cars there when we arrived. We got there about 4:00 A.M. and waited there for about 30 minutes. There were between ten and fifteen cars there by 4:30 A.M. All were cabs except one which was a 1942 Ford four door, black. It was shiny and had a nickle-plated spotlight on the drivers side. The majority of the cabs were yellow cabs. Some of the men bought some liquor and there was one-fifth of liquor passed around in Rector's cab.

The lead car, a yellow cab, came by and the man on the right side of the front seat said to Rector, "Let's all keep together." The man who said that was the leader. The driver of this lead cab wore a mustache, had black hair, dark complected and was fleshy; his face was full looking. I know that Claude Carter's brother, Hubert Carter, was sitting on the right side of the rear seat of this lead cab.

When we started off Red Fleming was following the lead cab and we were behind Fleming. We had a flat tire at the stockade near Pickens. All the cars stopped at the stockade. We left the cab and Murrell, Rector, & I got in the cab of Red Fleming. When we left the stockade we went about one mile and passed Paul F. Griggs' cab on the side of the road with a flat tire. He told us later about having the flat tire & catching a ride with another cab.

We arrived at the Pickens County jail at about 5:00 A.M. Fleming parked just behind the lead cab on the side of the jail. The car that was not a cab pulled in front of the jail & turned its spotlight on the front door. About half the cabs parked on the street in front of the jail & about half on the side of the jail. The leader and one man with a shotgun went to the door first. The leader called the jailer "Ed" but I do not know what was said. The jailer opened the door and the leader said, "We've come to get the negro who killed Mr. Brown." The jailer said, "I guess you boys know what you're doing, don't you?" The leader said, "I guess we do or we wouldn't be here." I was standing in the yard at that time. The leader, the man with the shotgun & several others then went in. Then Rector, Murrell, Willimon & I went in together. When we got in the jailer was in the first room on the left dressing. The leader & the man with the shotgun were in his room just inside the door. Either the leader or man with the shotgun said to the jailer, "You know me. I've been over here before. No one's going to hurt you."

"After the jailer got dressed about forty men followed him to get the keys & then up to the cells. I did not go up to the place where the negro was.

"As soon as the crowd left to go up for the negro I went over to the telephone on the hall table and started to pick up the phone. Either Griggs or Rector came over to me & asked me what I was doing. I said I was going to fix it so no call could be made on it. He said there was no use in that & when I took my hand off he wiped the phone with his handkerchief. He told me to be careful & not leave my fingerprints on it. Later I again put my hand on the phone but did not tamper with it. When I took my hand off I used my handkerchief to wipe off any fingerprints.

"A man with a single barrel shotgun was guarding the stairway from the hall. This stairway led to bedrooms on the second floor, I went upstairs & went into the bedroom that faced the stairway. Someone was in bed asleep. While I was up there a woman came out of the other bedroom. I asked her if there was a phone up there & she said there was none up there. I then went back downstairs. I started out the front door. Hubert Carter was coming into the hall holding the negro by the arm & shoving him along. He shoved the negro against me which put the negro on my left side. I did not take hold of him. Rector came up right behind me. Carter, Rector, & I walked with the negro to the leader's car.

When we got to the lead car Carter shoved the negro into the rear seat. Carter sat on the right side of the rear seat beside the negro. He had held to the negro as he got him into the rear seat & climbed over him to sit on the other side of him. I sat next to the negro just behind the driver and Paul Griggs, Jr. sat in my lap. The same driver drove the lead cab who had driven it to the jail. There were two men beside the driver. The man in the center had the gun. "We then went out the Easley Highway. We turned to the left after we passed Easley. We stopped near the Saluda River dam.

While we were riding along after we passed Easley the negro said he did stab the old man but was not the only one involved. He did not mention any name of anyone who was with him. The negro had not been questioned. When we started from the jail the man on the right front seat turned to the negro & said, "I guess you know what we got you for?" The negro said, "I guess I do know what you got me for. For stabbing and cutting Mr. Brown." When we passed Easley the negro told all about stabbing Mr. Brown. I recall he said he did it & that the man in the front seat with the shotgun turned & asked him some questions. The man with the shotgun was drinking heavy. I don't recall any more of the conversation with him.

We next stopped at the place near the Saluda dam. I got out & did not ride with the negro any more. A crowd gathered around the car where the negro was and they asked questions. The negro was talking about Mr. Brown. We were there ten or fifteen minutes. I don't know which car I got in. I saw a car that was not a cab & was watching it.   I was upset because I thought it was not one of the crowd. Then I was told it was with us & was the only car not a cab.

We then went to the place where the negro was killed. This was on Bramlett Road at the slaughter pen. I saw the negro pulled out of the car. I got out & walked up the road past the scene by 30 or 40 feet from where the negro was killed. I saw Rector with a knife, a small pocket knife. I know he and Paul Griggs were there with the negro. I did not actually see anyone cut the negro. He was cut before he was shot. I could hear the cutting of clothing and flesh, I heard no noise made by the negro. A fleshy man who was drunk shot one time at the negro with the single barrel gun. He then begged for more shells but no one gave him more shells. I heard three shots. I think this man was Garvin Roberson but am not sure. I know that more than one man fired shots at the negro.

Rector got in the same car with me. He was holding the wood piece that fits under the barrel in front of the trigger guard. He said, "that son-of-a-bitch broke my gun." I did not see who had either of the shotguns.

The cab I got into was a Yellow painted black. I recall the driver was fat. He was wearing glasses. He looked like John Clifton Joy. I do not know who else was in the cab: I got out at the Southern Depot & went in the Southern Cafe. I got a cup of coffee. The man, George, a Greek, behind the counter said, "did you get him?" he said, "you know." I said, "I don't know what you're talking about."

Either that night or that morning I was sitting at the corner of Coffee & N. Main talking in my cab with Johnny J. Willimon. He said, "I got blood on my knife & on my pants." He said he got it off. I think this conversation took place Feb. 17, 1947 at about 9:00 or 10:00 P.M. . . .

I have had read to me all the above statement and it is true to the best of my knowledge and belief.

Witness;

Edwin R. Groves, FBI J. D. Bigham

Richard E. Wood, FBI

/s/ Jessie Lee Sammons

SOURCE: James W. Cannon, "Willie Eugene Bishop . . ." FBI Report, February 28, 1947, in file 144-68-21, Civil Rights Division, Litigation Case files, Classified Subject Files, Record Group 60, General Records of the Department of Justice, National Archives, College Park, Maryland.

The cab driver's confession, actually transcribed by the FBI agents from an oral statement, seems stilted at best, disingenuous at worst. At critical points the driver cannot remember names or recognize faces. He lapses into the passive voice and uncertainty when "the negro was killed."

A different narrative appeared in the *New Yorker*. That magazine sent the English writer Cicily Isabel Fairfield, pen name "Rebecca West," down for the cab drivers' trial. Rebecca West had already sharpened her court reporting skills on postwar trials of Nazi leaders and English traitors. Her writing revealed an uncanny eye for the telling detail, which she used to skewer the Nazis. In South Carolina, where she had to be more restrained, she gently reported that she liked the townspeople, her hotel, the defendants, the jurors, and even the jailer who yielded Willie Earle to the mob without a fight. In her own way, West believed she had to be as guarded in what she said as the confessing lynchers. Like the drivers, West could not really empathize with Greenville's black population, who seemed like ciphers in her account. More consciously, West and her *New Yorker* editor tried to avoid offending white southerners by not giving the lynchers the same treatment she had given the Nazis. By her account, the not guilty verdict seemed an entirely sensible and logical result.

155. *Rebecca West, "Opera in Greenville," 1947*

On February 15, 1947, an incident occurred that drew the taxi-drivers of Greenville very close together. A driver named Brown picked up a Negro fare, a boy of twenty-four called Willie Earle, who asked him to drive to his mother's home in Pickens County, about eighteen miles from Greenville. . . .

Willie Earle reached his home that night on foot. Brown was found bleeding from deep knife wounds beside his taxi a mile or two away and was taken to a hospital, where he sank rapidly. Willie was arrested, and put in Pickens County Jail. Late on the night of February 16th, the melancholy and passionate Mr. Roosevelt Carlos Hurd was, it was said, about certain business. Later, the jailer of the Pickens County Jail telephoned to the sheriff's office in Greenville to say that a mob of about fifty men had come to the jail in taxi-cabs and forced him to give Willie Earle over to them. A little later still, somebody telephoned to the Negro undertaker in the town of Pickens to tell him that there was a dead nigger in need of his offices by the slaughter-pen in a by-road off the main road from Greenville to Pickens. He then telephoned the coroner of Greenville County, whose men found Willie Earle's mutilated body lying at that place. He had been beaten and stabbed and shot in the body and the head. The bushes around him were splashed with his brain tissue. His own people sorrowed over his death with a grief that was the converse of the grief Brown's friends felt for him. They mourned Brown because he had looked after them; Willie Earle's friends mourned him because they had looked after him. He had made a number of respectable friends before he became morose and intractable.

Attorney General Tom C. Clark sent in a number of F.B.I. men to look hard for the murderers of Willie Earle. This step evoked, of course, the automatic resentment against federal action which is characteristic of the South; but it should have been remembered that the murderers were believed to number about fifty, and Greenville had nothing like a big enough police staff to cope with such an extensive search. The sensitivity based on a concern for States' rights was inflamed by a rumor that Attorney General Clark had sent in the F.B.I. men without consulting, or even informing, the Governor of South Carolina. Whether this rumor was true or false, it was believed and it accounted for much hostility to the trial which had nothing to do with approval of lynching. Very soon the F.B.I. had taken statements from twenty-six men, who, along with five others whom they had mentioned in their statements, were arrested and charged with committing murder, being accessories before or after the fact of murder, and conspiring to murder. . . .

It cannot be said . . . that the prosecution had put together a valid argument for a conviction. Timid muddling by someone or some people who were not only muddlers but had an eye on the political weather had drawn most of its claws. As the case was handled, the jury cannot be blamed for returning an acquittal. If it had convicted on any of the indictments, even on the least, which related to conspiracy, either the verdict would have been reversed by a superior court or a very dangerous precedent would have been established. The trial had not the pleasing pattern, the agreeable harmony and counterpoint, of good legal process, however much the Judge tried to redeem it. But whether the jury returned their verdict of not guilty because they recognized the weakness of the State's case, it was hard to guess. It was the habit of certain people connected with the case to refer to the jury with deep contempt, as a parcel of boobs who could be seduced into swallowing anything by anybody who knew how to tickle them up by the right mixture of brutish prejudice and corny sentimentality; and it was odd to notice that the people who most despised the jury were those who most despised the Negroes. To me, the jurymen looked well built and well groomed; and they stayed awake, which is the first and most difficult task of a juror, although they, like the attorneys, kept their coats on when the heat was a damp, embracing fever. I marveled at nothing about this jury except its constitution. As Greenville is a town with, it is said, twenty-five millionaires and a large number of prosperous and well-educated people, it may have seemed peculiar that the jury should consist of two salesmen, a farmer, a mechanic, a truck driver, and seven textile workers. Some of the prosperous citizens had indeed appeared on the list of the veniremen from which the jurors were selected, but they had been singularly fortunate in being challenged by the attorneys. The unpopular task of deciding a lynching case therefore fell to an unfavored group who had not the money to hire a bodyguard or to leave the town. They would, let us remember, have been in a most difficult position if they had returned a verdict of guilty. . . . It is one of the mysteries of this case that the trial was not shifted to another town.

SOURCE: "Opera in Greenville," by Rebecca West (Copyright © Estate of Rebecca West 1947), first appeared in the *New Yorker* 23 (June 14, 1947): 31ff., and is reproduced here by permission of PFD (www.pfd.co.uk) on behalf of the Estate of Rebecca West. It was reprinted in *Antilynching Hearings before Subcommittee No. 4 of the Committee on the Judiciary House of Representatives*, 80th Congress, 2d sess., February 4, 1948. Serial No. 14.

In 1954, just seven years after Willie Earle perished alongside a South Carolina highway, the Supreme Court shocked the South when it ruled school segregation unconstitutional in *Brown*

v. Board of Education. White southern politicians like Mississippi's senator James O. Eastland decried the Supreme Court's decision as unconstitutional and vowed never to bow before such judicial legislation. A year after the Supreme Court handed down its decision, a Chicago teenager named Emmett Till journeyed into the Mississippi Delta to spend the summer with his uncle and aunt.

In August, Till entered a little grocery store in Money, Mississippi, where he encountered Carolyn Bryant. Bryant recalled later that Till, "a Negro man," had entered the store asking for candy. When she held out her hand, her customer grabbed it in a strong grip and said, "How about a date, baby?" When she tried to turn away, Till grabbed her waist with both hands and said, "What's the matter baby, can't you take it?" She claimed later that Till used "unprintable" language and bragged that he had been "with white women before." According to Bryant, the whistle came later, when she went out to the car to get a pistol. Till, still enjoying his prank, remained on the porch.[2]

Bryant may have tailored her story to excuse her husband's conduct. In 1974 David Shostak interviewed Crosby Smith, brother-in-law to Moses Wright, still living in the same Mississippi Delta where Emmett Till had perished. Smith believed that Till had innocently said to Bryant, "Gee, you look like a movie star," and nothing more. Smith also added that Maurice Wright, Till's cousin, not Carolyn Bryant, related the incident to Roy Bryant. And Maurice Wright had resented Emmett Till, wearing Chicago clothes with a little money in his pocket. "I don't think Maurice liked Emmett much, but I don't guess he figured what was going to happen to him, either." So, when Maurice spoke to Roy Bryant, "he also added a whole lot more to it than there actually was."[3] The danger for Bryant's husband seemed stark as he listened to the grinning black youth telling him about Emmett Till's alleged sexual harassment of his wife. He might become the butt of black people's jokes if he did nothing. Roy Bryant recruited his half-brother and went to Moses Wright's house in the middle of the night to demand "that boy who done that talk at Money."[4] The white men took Till and disappeared into the Mississippi darkness.

Carolyn Bryant described her encounter with Till at the trial of her husband and his half-brother for the kidnapping and murder of Till. The trial was for show, put on for the large number of northern journalists. After the all-white jury swiftly acquitted the defendants, John William Milam and Roy Bryant, the two told their story to the journalist William Bradford Huie. Milam did most of the talking, seeking to justify the killing through Huie. According to Milam, they originally intended to frighten Till, not kill him. But Till refused to be frightened. In his interview with Huie, Milam tried to position Till as the representative of everything that threatened the white South in 1955.

To this day rumors persist that others beyond Milam and Bryant participated in the lynching of Till. In 2004 the Justice Department announced it would investigate the murder, working with state officials.

156. *William Bradford Huie, "The Shocking Story of Approved Killing in Mississippi,"* January 24, 1956

Milam: "Well, what else could we do? He was hopeless. I'm no bully; I never hurt a nigger in my life. I like niggers—in their place—I know how to work 'em. But I just decided it was time a few people got put on notice. As long as I live and can do anything about it, niggers are gonna stay in their place. Niggers ain't gonna vote where I live. If they did, they'd control the government. They ain't gonna go to school with my kids. And when a nigger even gets close to mentioning sex with a white woman, he's tired o' livin'. I'm likely to kill him. Me and my folks fought for this country, and we've got some rights. I stood there in that shed and listened to that nigger throw that poison at me, and I just made up my mind. 'Chicago boy,' I said, 'I'm tired of 'em sending your kind down here to stir up trouble. Goddamn you, I'm going to make an example of you—just so everybody can know how me and my folks stand.'"

So big Milam decided to act. He needed a weight. He tried to think where he could get an anvil. Then he remembered a gin which had installed new equipment. He had seen two men lifting a discarded fan, a metal fan three feet high and circular, used in ginning cotton.

Bobo wasn't bleeding much. Pistol-whipping bruises more than it cuts. They ordered him back in the truck and headed west again. They passed through Doddsville, went to the Progressive Ginning Company. This gin is 3.4 miles east of Boyle; Boyle is two miles south of Cleveland. The road to this gin turns left of U.S. 61, after you cross the bayou bridge south of Boule.

Milam: "When we got to that gin, it was daylight, and I was worried for the first time. Somebody might see us and accuse us of stealing the fan."

Bryant and Big Milam stood aside while Bobo loaded the fan. Weight: 74 pounds. The youth still thought they were bluffing.

They drove back to Glendora, then north toward Swan Lake and crossed the "new bridge" over the Tallahatchie. At the east end of this bridge, they turned right, along a dirt road which parallels the river. After about two miles, they crossed the property of L. W. Boyce, passing near his house.

About 1.5 miles southeast of the Boyce home is a lonely spot where Big Milam has hunted squirrels. The river bank is steep. The truck stopped 30 yards from the water.

Big Milam ordered Bobo to pick up the fan.

He staggered under its weight . . . carried it to the river bank. They stood silently . . . just hating one another.

Milam: "Take off your clothes."

Slowly, Bobo sat down, pulled off his shoes, his socks. He stood up, unbuttoned his shirt, dropped his pants, his shorts.

He stood there naked.

It was Sunday morning, a little before 7.

Milam: "You still as good as I am?"

Bobo: "Yeah."

Milam: "You've still 'had' white women?"

Bobo: "Yeah."

That big .45 jumped in Big Milam's hand. The youth turned to catch that big, expanding bullet at his right ear. He dropped.

They barb-wired the gin fan to his neck, rolled him into 20 feet of water.

For three hours that morning, there was a fire in Big Milam's back yard: Bobo's crepe-soled shoes were hard to burn.

Seventy-two hours later—eight miles downstream—boys were fishing. They saw feet sticking out of the water. Bobo.

The majority—by no means *all*, but the *majority*—of the white people in Mississippi 1) either approve Big Milam's action or else 2) they don't disapprove enough to risk giving their "enemies" the satisfaction of a conviction.

Source: William Bradford Huie, "The Shocking Story of Approved Killing in Mississippi," *Look* 20 (January 24, 1956): 50.

At the bottom of Mississippi, below Hattiesburg, Highway 11 runs from Poplarville to Lumberton. On the night of February 23, 1959, a black man raped June Walters as she sat in her husband's car, which had broken down along the road. When Walters reported that she had been raped, Mississippi and Louisiana highway patrol officers arrested about thirty black men, herding them into Lumberton for a lineup. Tips led police to the home of Mack Charles Parker. Officers dragged Parker out of his house and beat him in the woods; his screams could be heard several houses away. When the officers took Parker back to the small jail in Lumberton, June Walters identified him as the man who had raped her. A Mississippi highway patrol officer promptly unsnapped his holster and offered his service revolver to Walters' husband. "Son, you got a gun or do you want mine?" he asked.[5]

Jimmy Walters declined the offer, and Mack Charles Parker entered Mississippi's criminal justice system. J. P. Walker, an ex-deputy and candidate for sheriff, organized the lynch mob that went to the Pearl River County Courthouse. Older members of the community carried out the lynching, seeing it as an artifact of an old vigilante tradition. When journalists and FBI agents arrived, however, the town rallied behind the lynchers. National hostility inspired local unity.[6]

On May 25 the Justice Department announced that the FBI's extensive investigation had failed to unearth a violation of federal law. The Bureau turned its evidence over to the state. The state grand jury did not meet until November. When it did, grand jurors refused to return any indictments connected to the lynching. The Justice Department's initial decision not to prosecute now inspired fresh protest. Arthur J. Freund of the American Bar Association wrote Attorney General William P. Rogers to suggest "you are in legal error" and to urge Rogers to read Victor Rotnem's 1943 article.[7] Members of Congress demanded an explanation.[8] When news reached Washington that the Mississippi grand jury had done nothing, Acting Attorney General Lawrence Walsh promptly announced that a federal grand jury would investigate. The department dispatched two top trial lawyers, Ben Brooks and William Kehoe, to Mississippi to assist in prosecuting the case. In December, Justice Department lawyers debated whether federal law really covered the lynching. St. John Barrett reviewed the history of federal efforts against lynching, including Judge Thomas Goode Jones's efforts in Alabama more than fifty years earlier.

157. *St. John Barrett to Brooks and Kehoe,* December 21, 1959

I want to give you my thoughts on possible use of 18 U.S.C. 241 in this case. . . .

Facts

As I understand them, the facts with regard to Parker's exercise and enjoyment of his right to due process of law at the hands of the State of Mississippi, are these:

Parker was arrested at 9:45 a.m. in Lumberton, Mississippi, by City Marshal Hammond Slade, for investigation of the charge of rape under Mississippi law. The offense for which he was arrested had been committed in Pearl River County earlier the same day. At 10:00 a.m., while still in custody, he was identified by the rape victim, Mrs. June Virginia Walters, as her assailant. Parker was thereupon transported in custody to the Hinds County Jail in Jackson, Mississippi, to undergo lie detector tests. . . .

While Parker was in the Hinds County Jail he engaged, or his family engaged for him, Attorney R. Jess Brown, of the Mississippi bar. Brown visited and interviewed Parker in the Hinds County Jail and undertook to represent him.

After he had undertaken to represent Parker[,] Brown telephoned Pearl River County District Attorney Stewart to request a preliminary hearing on the charges against Parker. In the conversations Stewart advised against bringing Parker back to Pearl River County for a hearing because, as Stewart said, local feeling was such that Parker's safety would be in jeopardy. On March 17 Brown wrote Stewart withdrawing his request for a preliminary hearing. Brown followed this letter up by another on March 18, stating that the reasons for withdrawing his request for a preliminary hearing were the statements made by Stewart regarding the danger of bringing Parker back to Pearl River County. . . .

During this period there was discussion among members of the community that any conviction of Parker would be reversed by the federal courts on the grounds that Negroes had been excluded from the jury. There were also reports that some members of the community objected to Parker's being represented by a Negro attorney inasmuch as the attorney would necessarily cross examine the alleged victim of the rape and kidnapping, who was a white woman. None of these expressions of feeling, however, have been directly connected with the persons who later participated in Parker's lynching.

At around midnight of April 24, a group of men wearing hoods and masks entered the Pearl River County Court House, forcibly removed Parker from his cell in the jail portion of the building, drove him away in a car, and killed him. At the time of the abduction Parker was technically in the custody of Sheriff Moody, who had responsibility for the jail. However, there were no jail attendants on duty then. Jailer Jewel Alford admits that he provided the lynchers with the keys with which to enter the jail. One witness had identified Alford as being one of the men who removed Parker from his cell. . . .

The only formidable barrier to the use of 18 U.S.C. 241 to punish conspiracies to injure or oppress a citizen in the free exercise and enjoyment of his rights to procedural due process while he is being prosecuted by a state for violation of state law, is the decision of the Court in *United States* v. *Powell,* 212 U.S. 564. Powell and his co-defendant Riggins were prosecuted under R.S. 5508 (the predecessor of 18 U.S.S. 241) for conspiring to lynch a Negro who was in the custody of the Sheriff of Madison County, Alabama, awaiting trial on a charge of murder. The trial court denied a petition for habeas corpus filed by Riggins and seeking release on the ground the indictment failed to charge any offense against the laws of the United States. 134 Fed. 404. Judge Jones, in his opinion, was of the view that although Fourteenth Amendment rights can be *denied* only by the state, Congress had "the power to protect state officers when endeavoring to discharge the official duty, and to punish private individuals who resist the execution of the laws, by whose enforcement alone the duty can be accomplished." 134 Fed. 411. The Supreme Court affirmed on the narrow ground that habeas corpus was not the proper remedy. 199 U.S. 547. Powell, Riggins' co-defendant, demurred to the indictment. In the meantime, since Judge Jones' ruling on Riggins' petition for habeas corpus, the Supreme Court had decided *Hodges* v. *United States,* 203 U.S. 1 (1905). In *Hodges* the Court, although having before it a situation which did not relate in any way to state action, had made the general observation: ". . . [T]hat the Fourteenth and Fifteenth Amendments do not justify the legislation is also beyond dispute, for they, as repeatedly held, are restrictions upon state action, and no action on the part of the State is complained of." 203 U.S. 14. In ruling on Powell's demurrer Judge Jones, though still expressing belief that his views in *Ex Parte Riggins* had been correct, felt bound by the Supreme Court's language in *Hodges* and sustained the demurrer. The Supreme Court, in a *per curiam* opinion citing only Hodges as authority, affirmed the ruling of Judge Jones. . . .

It is clear that the *Hodges* case, strictly speaking, was no authority for the ruling in *Powell.* However, at the time of deciding *Hodges* the Supreme Court had recently before had the Powell situation before it in *Ex Parte Riggins,* 199 U.S. 547. Judge Jones relied on *Hodges* in reversing himself and hence the Supreme Court's affirmance on the basis of its language in *Hodges* would seem to have been a carefully considered decision even though the Court rendered it without written opinion. Nonetheless, the *per curiam* nature of the *Powell* case might be used to minimize its authority.

The text of the indictment against Powell is reported at 151 Fed. 649. It would appear difficult to frame an indictment in the Parker case which we could contend was significantly different from the indictment of Powell. There are, however, some points that could be urged. The indictment of Powell does not specify the particular rights, such as right to counsel, to cross examine witnesses, etc., in the exercise of which he was injured and oppressed. Furthermore, it does not appear that the nature of the injury and oppression is set forth, i.e., the abduction and killing. From the opinions, however, we can presume that these facts were set forth in other counts as the appellate courts were well aware of the events involved. Perhaps the principal feature which might be incorporated into a Parker indictment which was not in the Powell indictment is a detailed allegation of specific intent. Although these devices should be used to their fullest, it seems to be that the Court's decision in *Powell* must, in substance, be overruled before a similar prosecution in the Parker case can be sustained.

Non-Color-of-law Conspiracy to Injure and Oppress Mississippi Authorities

In *Brewer* v. *Hoxie School District No. 46,* 238 F.2d 91 (1956), the Court of Appeals for the Eighth Circuit affirmed the order of the District Court enjoining interference with the school authorities of Hoxie, Arkansas, in their efforts to desegregate the Hoxie Schools. Although there was no specific statutory authority for the school board to bring such an action, the court held that the school board had an implied right under the United States Constitution to be free from the harassing tactics of the individual defendants and that such right was enforceable through injunction proceedings. After noting that the school board, under the doctrine enunciated in *Brown* v. *Board of Education,* had a general duty to desegregate its schools, the court said:

> The plaintiffs . . . have a right, which is a federal right, to be free from direct interference in the performance of that duty. [238 F.2d 99]

The basis . . . of the Hoxie holding is compelled as a matter of logic. A person must necessarily have the *right* to do that which the law says he *must* do as a matter of duty. A duty necessarily implies a right. In *Hoxie* the court went further and held that the right could be enforced in a court of equity even though Congress had not explicitly defined a cause of action in the holder of the right.

Just as the school authorities in Hoxie had a duty to accord equal protection of the laws to the Negro students, so the Sheriff, Prosecutor and Judge in Pearl River County had the duty to accord Parker due process of law. If the Hoxie school authorities had a federal right to be free from interference in performance of their duty, it would seem that the Pearl River County authorities were equally entitled to be free from interference. . . .

The implied right of state officials to be free from interference in performing their constitutional duties is not a Fourteenth Amendment right in the usual sense. It is not a right to be free from state action. Rather, it is a right of the state to be free from certain private action. The right arises from the relationship of the state official to the federal government, which government has imposed upon him certain duties under the Fourteenth Amendment.

SOURCE: File 144-41-304, Civil Rights Division, Litigation Case files, Classified Subject Files, Record Group 60, General Records of the Department of Justice, National Archives, College Park, Maryland.

In January Federal Judge Sidney Mize convened a grand jury to investigate the Parker lynching. The federal jurors also refused to return any indictments, in part because Mize, a strong supporter of Mississippi's segregationist system, discouraged them.

After Parker's death, racial violence heated up. White southerners relied on racial violence to block civil rights advances. This violence ranged from minor pushing and shoving to murder. On June 12, 1963, Byron De La Beckwith assassinated Medgar Evers.[9] Ku Klux Klan dynamiters tried to blow up Martin Luther King and did kill four children at Birmingham's Sixteenth Street Baptist Church. Race rioting followed: every summer from 1964 through 1968 saw rioting in the North, Midwest, and West. Assassins killed Martin Luther King, Robert Kennedy, and Malcolm X. So much violence marked the 1960s that some Americans feared their country was coming unglued.

In this environment the historian Richard Maxwell Brown emerged as the nation's leading expert on vigilantism. His first book, *The South Carolina Regulators,* appeared in 1963 and looked at a colonial vigilante episode. Brown appraised these vigilantes positively, even though subsequent historians argued that the colonial regulators made the South safe for slavery.[10] Thereafter Brown worked to distinguish the "good" vigilantes from the "bad" variety. Brown argued that "good" vigilantes enjoyed the backing of their communities. The problem with this is that lynchers characteristically imagine that their communities support their violence. Brown's formulation privileges lynchers cruel enough to overawe potential opponents. White racists, for example, believed "good" blacks sided with them against "bad" black "criminals." The meaning of community is also quite elastic, allowing for the inclusion or exclusion of particular groups as needed. Interestingly, although Brown wrote in a time of increasing racial violence, he still believed that the "good" vigilantes outnumbered the "bad." Brown essentially repeated Hubert Howe Bancroft's 1887 argument approving of some mobs, those populated with the better class of people.

158. Richard Maxwell Brown, "The Ideology of Vigilantism," 1969

The Two Models of Vigilantism

Two "models" of vigilante movements developed. One was the "good" or socially constructive model in which the vigilante movement dealt with a problem of disorder straightforwardly and then disbanded. The result was an increase in the social stability of the locality; the movement was, thus, socially constructive. The other model was the "bad" or socially destructive one in which a vigilante movement encountered such strong opposition that the result was an anarchic and socially destructive vigilante war. Some movements, hence, behaved according to the ideal theory of vigilantism while others did not. Some were socially successful; others were not.

THE SOCIALLY CONSTRUCTIVE MODEL

The socially constructive movement occurred where the vigilantes represented a genuine community consensus. Here a decided majority of the people either participated in the movement or approved of it. Vigilantism of this sort simply mobilized the community and overwhelmed the unruly outlaws and lower people. The community was left in a more orderly and stable condition, and the social functions of vigilantism were served: the problem of community order was solved by the consolidation of the three-level social structure and solidification of the supporting community values.

Although the methods used were often harsh and arbitrary, most vigilante movements—large and small—conformed to the socially constructive model. One of the best examples was the northern Illinois Regulator movement of 1841. The northern Illinois movement confronted a classic threat to community order: an agglomeration of outlaw gangs was nearing control of the area. With the regular government virtually powerless, the respectable leading men (the community upper level) took the law into their own hands with the help of the middle level farmers.

Since 1835 the situation in the Rock Valley of northern Illinois had gone from bad to worse. Several gangs of horse thieves and counterfeiters found the Rock River country a convenient corridor for illicit operations in Wisconsin, Illinois, Iowa, and Missouri. The Driscoll and Brodie gangs had made Ogle and De Kalb Counties a virtual fief. The Oliver gang dominated Winnebago County. The Bliss-Dewey-West ring waxed strong in Lee County, while the Birch gang of horse thieves ranged in all quarters. By 1840 the desperadoes were numerous enough to control elections in Ogle

County and similarly threaten other counties. One summer the outlaws even went so far as to burn down the newly constructed courthouse at Oregon, Illinois.

Finally, in April 1841, 15 "representative men" of Ogle County formed the first Regulator company. In no time at all the counties were dotted with Regulator squads, but the most vigorous were those of Ogle. The Regulators embodied the social, economic, and political prestige of Ogle County: John Phelps was the county's oldest and wealthiest settler and the founder of the county seat, Oregon. Peter Smith combined a bank presidency with the ownership of 1,600 acres of land. The farmers who made up the bulk of the movement were substantial property holders; they had taken up Government land claims ranging from 240 to 600 acres. These solid citizens brooked no opposition. They burned the Rockford *Star* to the ground soon after it published an anti-Regulator editorial. But on the whole, the local elite kept the movement well under control. Having accomplished their purpose in a campaign of whipping, hanging, and firing squads, the Regulator companies disbanded. Socially they left the Rock Valley in a better state than before they organized.

The northern Illinois Regulator movement exhibited the major characteristics of the successful frontier vigilante movement. It was organized in a rational way. Mass participation of respectable men was the mode, but the movement was dominated, clearly, by the social and economic elite of the area. The Regulators were implacable in their war on the outlaws and unrelenting in the face of opposition. Although the Rockford *Star* opposed the Regulators, no anti-Regulator coalition, as a whole, developed. The outlaw gangs were isolated and broken up. The vigilante leaders desired the assurance of their position at the upper level of their communities but were not power mad. With the outlaw threat put down, peace and order reigned.

THE SOCIALLY DESTRUCTIVE MODEL

In the socially destructive model, anarchy was the result of the vigilante movement. Because there was no community consensus behind the vigilante movement, strong opposition appeared, and civil conflict flared. In the socially constructive model, opposition to the vigilantes was narrowly restricted to outlaws and lower people who could gain no support from the remainder of the community. For the vigilantes to be stymied a broad antivigilante coalition was necessary. The formation of an antivigilante coalition almost inevitably condemned the community to a chaotic internecine struggle between the vigilantes and their opponents.

Respectable men did not join the antivigilante coalition because of any great sympathy for the outlaws and lower people. They were impelled into opposition by things the vigilantes did or stood for. Sometimes two or three powerful local families would join the antivigilante movement. In some cases, these families had been carrying on a feud of sorts with leading vigilante families. Sometimes a local political party or faction went into the antivigilante movement, because the vigilantes were dominated by the rival party or faction. If the leading Democrats of a community, for example, were found among the vigilantes, the antivigilante coalition would probably attract the local Whigs. Political rivalries were often linked to vigilante strife, for in many instances vigilante leaders harbored political ambitions and were not above using the movement to promote their personal goals. Economic rivalries among community leading men also were a factor in pro and con vigilante alignments; acute mercantile competition sometimes caused a leading storekeeper to go into the opposition if his rival was a vigilante. Thus, personal, family, political, and economic antagonisms accounted for a readymade vigilante opposition in some communities.

At other times vigilante extremism drew into opposition decent men who otherwise probably would not have opposed them. The best vigilante movements usually attracted a fringe of sadists and naturally violent types. Often these men had criminal tendencies and were glad to use the vigilante movement as an occasion for giving free reign to their unsavory passions. It was always a problem for vigilante leaders to keep these elements under control, and sometimes a movement was taken over or seriously skewed by these social misfits. Sadistic punishment and torture, arbitrary and unnecessary killings, and mob tyranny marked vigilante movements that had truly gone bad. When this happened, many sound and conservative men felt they must oppose the vigilantes with whose original objectives they had probably felt no quarrel.

Examples of the socially destructive model did not occur as often as the constructive model, but when they did extremely violent conflicts tended to appear. Among the leading instances were the East Texas Regulators (versus the Moderators), 1840–44; the Southwest Missouri Slickers (versus the Anti-Slickers), 1842–44; and the Southern Illinois Regulators (versus the Flatheads), 1846–50. Sometimes an antivigilante coalition arose which although unable to match vigilante strength, possessed the potential of calling in outside help and, hence, could define the limits of vigilante power. The antivigilante Law and Order faction in San Francisco, 1856, played this role. The vigilantes there would have liked to have hanged Judge David S. Terry but did not dare do so, for the Law and Order faction would have almost certainly obtained Federal action against the vigilantes. Similarly, the Moderators in the South Carolina back country, 1769, were not strong enough to overturn Regulator domination, but they did check the movement and bring its excesses to an end.

As the career of the socially destructive model proceeded, the moral standing of the vigilantes and the opposing coalition tended to be increasingly compromised. As the struggle became more violent, the respectable men of the antivigilante coalition put a higher premium on the violent talents of the outlaw element with which they otherwise had nothing in common. So, too, did the original vigilantes themselves recruit and acquire a criminal fringe which they put to mercenary use. With the community descending bloodily into chaos, wise and prudent men left if they could. The opposing movements tended to fall more and more into the control of the worst and most extreme of their adherents. About this time the desperate neutral residents would beseech State authorities for the intervention of the militia, and the "war" would subside fitfully in the presence of the state troops.

The Regulator-Moderator war of east Texas (1840–44) was representative of the degenerate, socially destructive vigilante situation. The scene was the redland and piney wood country of east Texas in the days of the Lone State Republic. The center of the conflict was in Shelby County. Fronting on the Sabine River where it formed the boundary between Louisiana and Texas, Shelby County lay in an old border area that had never been known for peace and calm. In 1840 the Regulator movement arose as a quite honest and straightforward attack on a ring of corrupt county officials who specialized in fraudulent land transactions. The rise of the Regulators was probably inevitable in any case, for the county had long wilted under the plague of counterfeiting, horse thievery, Negro stealing, and common murder and mayhem. However, the Regulators overplayed their hand, especially after their original leader, Charles W. Jackson, was killed and replaced by the nefarious adventurer, Watt Moorman. Bad elements infiltrated both the regulators and their opponents, the Moderators, but by comparison the latter seemed to become less obnoxious. Although some honorable and level-headed citizens like John W. Middleton stayed with the Regulators to the end, an attitude of wild vengefulness came to be characteristic of the band. The early ne'er-do-well group among the Moderators dwindled. As more and more citizens were forced to take sides, many joined the Moderators in reaction to the sadism and vindictiveness of the swashbuckling Watt Moorman who affected a military uniform and blew great blasts on a hunting horn to summon his henchmen.

The original reasons for the founding of the Regulator movement were all but forgotten. The war became a thing in itself, a complexity of personal and family feuds that was consuming the area in blood lust. Several attempts to restore peace failed. Complete anarchy was the situation in 1844 when an all-out battle between two armies of several hundred men each was only forestalled by the dramatic intervention of Sam Houston and the militia. After 4 years, 18 men had been killed and many more wounded. A stream in the vicinity was called "Widow's Creek." The killing of so many leaders and the exhaustion of the survivors probably explain why the war was not revived after Sam Houston and the militia withdrew. Ex-Regulators and ex-Moderators warily fought side by side in separate companies in the Mexican War, but for 50 years east Texans were reluctant to discuss the episode lest old enmities be rekindled. . . .

An Evaluation of American Vigilantism

In shortrun practical terms, the vigilante movement was a positive facet of the American experience. Many a new frontier community gained order and stability as the result of vigilantism which reconstructed the community structure and values of the old settled areas while dealing effectively with a problem of crime and disorder.

From a longer perspective, the negative aspects of vigilantism appear. Although the era of classic vigilantism came to an end in the 1890's, the tradition lived on. In fact, it was extended into areas of American life where it was wholly inappropriate. Thus arose the latter day phenomenon of neovigilantism.

Neovigilantism grew mainly after the Civil War and was largely a response to the problems of an emerging urban, industrial, racially and ethnically diverse America. The transition from the old to the new vigilantism was heralded by the San Francisco Vigilance Committee of 1856. The latter represented a blending of the methods of the old vigilantism with the victims of the new. Virtually all the features of neovigilantism were present in the San Francisco movement of 1856. Neovigilantism was to be frequently urban rather than rural, and that was the case in San Francisco. The old vigilantism had been directed mainly at horsethieves, counterfeiters, outlaws, bad men, and lower people. Neovigilantism found its chief victims among Catholics, Jews, immigrants, Negroes, laboring men and labor leaders, political radicals, and proponents of civil liberties. The actions and overtones of the San Francisco movement were strongly imbued with the passions and prejudices that came to feature in the neovigilantism.

The San Francisco vigilantes were ethnically biased; their ire focused on one group: the Irish. The vigilantes were anti-Catholic; their hero and martyr was the anti-Romanist editor, James King of William, and most of their victims in 1856 were Catholics. Although their ranks included laborers and mechanics, there was a distinct class tinge to the 1856 movement: middle and upper class merchants were aligned against the lower class adherents of the San Francisco Democratic machine. Last but not least was a disregard for civil liberties. Angered by the arguments of John Nugent of the San Francisco *Herald* in favor of regular justice, the merchant vigilantes of (56 quickly organized an advertising boycott that transformed the *Herald* overnight from the strongest to the weakest of the city's major dailies.

Source: Richard Maxwell Brown, "The American Vigilante Tradition," in Hugh Davis Graham and Ted Robert Gurr, eds., *Violence in America: Historical and Comparative Perspective* (Washington: U.S. Government Printing Office, 1969), 1:143–146, 152.

As late as 1971 Brown still saw no difference between "vigilantism" and "lynching," terms he used interchangeably. In 1975, in *Strain of Violence,* Brown continued his campaign to distinguish good mobbing from the bad by claiming that "the term lynch mob refers to an organized, spontaneous, ephemeral mob" while vigilantes pursued "a systematic" program.[11] Making a distinction between lynchers and vigilantes served to advance the more important distinction Brown advocated, the one that saved the helpful from confusion with the "socially destructive." Even here Brown follows Bancroft, who had recognized in 1887 that the word "lynching" was in such bad odor that it could not be applied to "good" mobs.

159. Richard Maxwell Brown, "Legal and Behavioral Perspectives on American Vigilantism," 1971

The late nineteenth-century rampages of Western vigilantes, Southern lynch mobs, and Northern and Eastern white caps seemed to challenge the stability of American life. Was America threatened by this upsurge of violence, or was the violence itself an understandable—and not really harmful, indeed helpful—response to problems that were not being met by the regular system of law and order? Many leading members of the legal profession, and other prominent Americans, answered the question by their actions; they participated in vigilante movements and lynch law action. The legal illuminati answered the question in their writings. Their conclusion, on the whole, was that vigilants and lynch mobs acted in response to an unsatisfactory American legal system. To a qualified approval of vigilantism and lynch law, the legal illuminati added suggestions for the improvement of the legal system which would have moved it in the direction of lynch law. . . .

[A] more realistic, behavioral way of viewing American vigilantism is to see it in the context of a continuum of American justice that ranges between the poles of *due process of law* and the *control of crime.* Viewed in this way vigilantism is not the opposite of legal justice, but rather, possesses an affinity to the order of legal justice that emphasizes crime control rather than due process. The legal approach stressing crime control occupies a middle position between legal due process and extralegal vigilantism. The key point is that both extralegal vigilantism and legal crime control share the same overriding value emphasis: the repression of criminal conduct. The crucial distinction, then, is not legal versus extralegal action but extralegal and crime control versus due process of law.

It has been common for well-meaning opponents of vigilantism and lynch law to make the case that if the vigilantes had "expended in the discharge of their duties as citizens the same energy and public spirit they displayed as vigilantes, officers could have been elected who would fearlessly and faithfully have performed their duty." The sentiment is a laudable one, but it misses the point. The reality is that during the nineteenth century and on into the twentieth Americans supported a dual system of legal and extralegal justice by adherence to the primary value of repression of crime with little regard for procedural safeguards. Thus, Americans did not feel themselves any less public spirited when they participated in lynch law. Instead they saw vigilante participation as an act of public spirit as important in its own way as the election of upright officials. Americans felt that there were certain functions in preserving public order that the legal authorities would not, could not, or should not be expected to perform. Those functions the people themselves assumed as vigilantes.

Vigilantism and lynch law comprised the main stream of violent American extralegal justice from the late colonial period to the early decades of the twentieth century. (In this treatment "vigilantism" will be used as a general term for extralegal violence in support of community order as well as the more specific sense of organized volunteer committees of citizens which take the law into their own hands. "Lynch law," referring to the act or practice of inflicting extralegal punishment, will be used interchangeably with vigilantism. . . .) Flourishing most frequently in frontier areas but by no means confined to them, vigilantism first appeared as a large scale organized movement in the "regulator" organization of the South Carolina back country in 1767–1769. Ten years later, in 1779–1780, "lynch law" was first executed against frontier Tories and outlaws in Revolutionary Virginia under the direction of Colonel Charles Lynch.

SOURCE: Richard Maxwell Brown, "Legal and Behavioral Perspectives on American Vigilantism," in Donald Fleming and Bernard Bailyn, eds., *Perspectives in American History* 5 (1971): 95–96, 98, 100–101. Reprinted with permission.

On March 21, 1981, two Alabama members of the Ku Klux Klan cruised the streets of Mobile, Alabama, looking for a black man to kill. Henry Francis Hays and James "Tiger" Knowles said later that they wanted revenge because a jury had just acquitted a black man accused of killing a white police officer. They also wanted a trophy to show Henry's father, Benny Jack Hays, an Alabama Ku Klux Klan leader.

When Hays and Knowles found Michael Donald, they forced him into their car, drove to Baldwin County, and beat him with a stick more than one hundred times before cutting his throat. The two Klansmen hanged Donald's body from a tree limb across the street from Benny

Hays's house. Alabama had not executed a white man for killing a black man since 1913. In this case, however, prosecutors convinced Knowles to testify against Hays and won a death sentence. The Supreme Court of Alabama upheld this sentence in a *per curiam* opinion, meaning all members of the majority claim the opinion rather than a single judge. In 1997 Alabama authorities executed Henry Hays.

160. *Supreme Court of Alabama, Opinion in* Henry F. Hays v. State of Alabama, 1985

The trial court's order sentencing the appellant to death contains a fair recitation of the facts as follows:

"The Court finds the facts to be that from the evidence and beyond a reasonable doubt that the defendant and James "Tiger" Knowles, both members of the Ku Klux Klan, on the day of March 20, 1981, went to the home of Hays' brother-in-law, Frank Cox, and secured a rope. Knowles tied the rope into a hangman's noose. Later on in the evening of the same day, the defendant, Knowles and others were playing cards and watching television at the defendant's apartment. During the 10 p.m. news, the defendant and Knowles learned that a Mobile County Circuit Court jury, having heard the case involving the slaying of a white Birmingham police officer by a black man, could not reach a verdict and a mistrial had been declared. The events of this trial and previous trials of this particular case had been discussed by the defendant, Knowles and others at a Klan meeting.

"After the news, the defendant and Knowles left the apartment and drove around looking for a black man to hang. Neither the defendant nor Knowles knew the victim, Michael Donald, and he was abducted by the defendant and Knowles simply because he was a black man who was alone.

"The defendant and Knowles took Michael Donald to a location off Highway 225 in Baldwin County, Alabama, tied a rope around his neck, robbed him and proceeded to choke and beat him until he was unconscious. The defendant, stating that he wanted to make sure the victim was dead, cut Donald's throat three times with a knife. The two then placed Donald's body back into the vehicle and returned to Herndon Avenue in Mobile County, Alabama. Later, the defendant and Knowles took the body across the street on Herndon Avenue and hung it from a tree. The Court finds from the evidence beyond a reasonable doubt that these activities of the defendant and Knowles were performed in conjunction with the burning of a cross on the grounds of the Mobile County Courthouse on the night of March 20, 1981, by other Klan members. The defendant is a leader in the Klan, known as the Exalted Cyclops."

We do, however, think it is necessary to add the following facts. After having obtained the rope that was eventually used to hang the victim, and prior to returning to the apartment, the appellant and Knowles obtained a .22-caliber pistol from another Ku Klux Klansman. After hearing the news of the mistrial, the appellant and Knowles left the apartment "for the purpose to go hang someone." After driving around for approximately 45 minutes, they found what they were looking for, a lone black man walking along the street; Knowles testified "He was by himself so he seemed like a good victim at that time because he was by himself and in a secluded area." The appellant pulled his car over to the curb, and Mr. Knowles leaned out the window and asked Mr. Donald for directions to a certain nightclub. As Mr. Donald approached the car in order to aid the apparently lost drivers, Mr. Knowles pulled out the .22-caliber pistol and forced Mr. Donald into the back seat of the car. Mr. Knowles got into the back seat of the car with Mr. Donald and forced the latter to empty his pockets, including his wallet, which was laid on the floor of the appellant's car. While driving to Baldwin County, the victim stated, according to Knowles, "'Oh, God, I can't believe this is happening. Do anything you want to just . . . just let me go.'" Knowles continued: "And the defendant asked him if he had heard about the Atlanta killings at that time. . . . And Donald said, 'Yes.' And he [appellant] said, 'You know you could wind up like that.' And then he [Donald] said 'Oh, God,' he said, 'Please you can do anything you want to me. Beat me or anything, just don't kill me.'"

SOURCE: *Henry. F. Hays v. State,* 518 So.2d 749 (1985).

On July 1, 1991, President George Bush nominated Clarence Thomas to serve on the U.S. Supreme Court. Liberal members of the Senate agonized over how to oppose a black conservative candidate for the Court. A former employee of Thomas then stepped forward, testifying that Thomas had sexually harassed her, making explicit references to pornographic movies he had seen. Given a chance to rebut Anita Hill's allegations, Thomas very effectively introduced lynching as a metaphor for his own experience.

161. *Clarence Thomas, Further Testimony of Hon. Clarence Thomas, of Georgia, to Be Associate Justice of the U.S. Supreme Court,"* 1991

The CHAIRMAN. Do you have anything you would like to say?

Judge THOMAS. Senator, I would like to start by saying unequivocally, uncategorically that I deny each and every single allegation against me today that suggested in any way that I had conversations of a sexual nature or about pornographic material with Anita Hill, that I ever attempted to date her, that I ever had any personal sexual interest in her, or that I in any way ever harassed her.

Second, and I think a more important point, I think that this today is a travesty. I think that it is disgusting. I think that this hearing should never occur in America. This is a case in which this sleaze, this dirt was searched for by staffers of members of this committee, was then leaked to the media, and this committee and this body validated it and displayed it in prime time over our entire nation.

How would any member on this committee or any person in this room or any person in this country would like sleaze said about him or her in this fashion or this dirt dredged up and this gossip and these lies displayed in this manner? How would any person like it?

The Supreme Court is not worth it. No job is worth it. I am not here for that. I am here for my name, my family, my life and my integrity. I think something is dreadfully wrong with this country, when any person, any person in this free country would be subjected to this. This is not a closed room.

There was an FBI investigation. This is not an opportunity to talk about difficult matters privately or in a closed environment. This is a circus. It is a national disgrace. And from my standpoint, as a black American, as far as I am concerned, it is a high-tech lynching for uppity-blacks who in any way deign to think for themselves, to do for themselves, to have different ideas, and it is a message that, unless you kow-tow to an old order, this is what will happen to you, you will be lynched, destroyed, caricatured by a committee of the U.S. Senate, rather than hung from a tree....

Senator HATCH. ... Now, I want to ask you about this intriguing thing you just said. You said some of this language is stereotype language? What does that mean, I don't understand.

Judge THOMAS. Senator, the language throughout the history of this country, and certainly throughout my life, language about the sexual prowess of black men, language about the sex organs, of black men, and the sizes, et cetera, that kind of language has been used about black men as long as I have been on the face of this Earth. These are charges that play into racist, bigoted stereotypes and these are the kind of charges that are impossible to wash off. And these are the kinds of stereotypes that I have, in my tenure in Government, and the conduct of my affairs, attempted to move away from and to convince people that we should conduct ourselves in a way that defies these stereotypes. But when you play into a stereotype it is as though you are skiing downhill, there's no way to stop it.

And this plays into the most bigoted, racist stereotypes that any black man will face.

Senator HATCH. Well, I saw—I didn't understand the television program, there were two black men—I may have it wrong, but as I recall—there were two black men talking about this matter and one of them said, she is trying to demonize us. I didn't understand it at the time. Do you understand that?

Judge THOMAS. Well, I understand it and any black man in this country—Senator, in the 1970's I became very interested in the issue of lynching. And if you want to track through this country, in the 19th and 20th centuries, the lynchings of black men, you will see that there is invariably or in many instances a relationship with sex—an accusation that that person cannot shake off. That is the point that I am trying to make. And that is the point that I was making last night that this is high-tech lynching. I cannot shake off these accusations because they play to the worst stereotypes we have about black men in this country.

Senator HATCH. Well, this bothers me, Judge Thomas. It bothers me.

Judge THOMAS. It bothers me.

Senator HATCH. I can see why. Let me, I hate to do this, but let me ask you some tough questions. You have talked about stereotypes used against black males in this society. In the first statement of Anita Hill she alleges that he told her about his experiences and preferences and would ask her what she liked or if she had ever done the same thing? Is that a black stereotype?

Judge THOMAS. No.

SOURCE: Nomination of Judge Clarence Thomas to be Associate Justice of the Supreme Court of the United States, Hearings Before the Committee on the Judiciary, U.S. Senate, 102d Congress, 1st sess., part 4 of four parts, 156–158, 202.

NOTES

1. *St. Louis Post-Dispatch,* October 12, 1991.

2. Christopher Metress, ed., *The Lynching of Emmett Till: A Documentary Narrative* (Charlottesville: University of Virginia Press, 2002), 90–91.

3. David A. Shostak, "Crosby Smith: Forgotten Witness to a Mississippi Nightmare," *Negro History Bulletin* 38 (December 1974–January 1975): 320–325.

4. Metress, *The Lynching of Emmett Till,* 69.

5. Howard Smead, *Blood Justice: The Lynching of Mack Charles Parker* (New York: Oxford University Press, 1986), 3–13.

6. Smead, *Blood Justice,* 72–73.

7. Arthur J. Freund to William P. Rogers, May 26, 1959, file 144-41-304, Civil Rights Division, Litigation Case files, Classified Subject Files, Record Group 60, General Records of the Department of Justice, National Archives, College Park, Maryland.

8. Malcolm R. Wilkey to W. Wilson White, June 15, 1959, file 144-41-304, Civil Rights Division, Litigation Case files, Classified Subject Files, Record Group 60, General Records of the Department of Justice, National Archives, College Park, Maryland.

9. Reed Massengill, *Portrait of a Racist: The Man Who Killed Medgar Evers?* (New York: St. Martin's, 1994); Adam Nossiter, *Of Long Memory: Mississippi and the Murder of Medgar Evers* (Reading: Addison Wesley, 1994); Maryanne Vollers, *Ghosts of Mississippi: The Murder of Medgar Evers, the Trials of Byron De La Beckwith, and the Haunting of the New South* (Boston: Little, Brown, 1995); Bobby Delaughter, *Never Too Late: A Prosecutor's Story of Justice in the Medgar Evers Case* (New York: Scribner, 2001).

10. Rachel N. Klein, in *Unification of a Slave State: The Rise of the Planter Class in the South Carolina Backcountry, 1760–1808* (Chapel Hill: University of North Carolina Press, 1990), 49, describes the regulators as "the vanguard of the planter class."

11. Richard Maxwell Brown, *Strain of Violence: Historical Studies of American Violence and Vigilantism* (New York: Oxford University Press, 1975), 21.

Index

Dempsey, E. H., 200

Devereaux, Nancy, 35

Diaz, Porfirio, 175–176, 178

Dickinson, Frank, 100

Dimsdale, Thomas J., 91

Dinnerstein, Leonard, xvi, 3, 193

Dolby, William, 140

Dollard, John, 2, 13–14

Donald, Michael, lynching victim, 266–268

Donnelly, Joseph G., 168–175

Donovan, A. L., 66

Dorroh, Shorty, 237

Dorsey, Hugh, 198–199

Douglas, William O., 241–243

Douglass, Frederick, 5

Dove, Lawrence, 214

Doyle, Edmund, 42

Du Bois, W. E. B., xvii, 115, 203

Duck Hill, Mississippi, lynching, 234–238

Duke, Henry, 96

Dyer, Leonidas, author of Dyer Bill, 226, 228

Dyer, Thomas G., 61

Earle, John, 67

Earle, William, 67

Earle, Willie, lynching victim, 249–255

Early, Steven, 234

East Point, Georgia, whipping affair, 116

Eastland, James O., 255

Eastland, James S., 187–189, 205n6

Eaton, L. B., U. S. Marshal, 111

Edgerton, Sidney, 91

Edmiston, William, 31, 33

Edwards, Charles Melvin, 243, 246

Eglan, Nathaniel, 96

Elaine, Arkansas, 199–202

Ellicott, Andrew, 29–30

Emmons, Halmer Hull, 112

Evers, Medgar, 260

Fairfield News and Herald, 208

Falluja, Iraq, 189

Fanning, A. C. W., 43

Fayette County, Ohio, 140

Federal Bureau of Investigation, 226; New Deal, 229, 241; Willie Earle lynching investigation, 249–254; Mack Charles Parker investigation, 257–260; Clarence Thomas investigation, 269

Felton, Rebecca Latimer, 142–144

Ferdinand, Archduke Franz, 222

Feudal influence on South, 9–11

Fifteenth Amendment of U.S. Constitution, 5–6

Filmore, Millard, 71

Fitz-Stephen, James Lynch, 26–28

Fleming, J. L., 131

Fleming, Marvin Henry, 250–251

Foote, Henry Stuart, 71, 72–73

Forbes, Pearl, 126

Fortune, Timothy Thomas, 115–116; influence, 128, 130–131, 203

Fourteenth Amendment of U.S. Constitution, 104–105, 111–112, 217–218, 220–221, 260

Frank, Leo, lynching victim, xvi, 190–193, 198

Frankfurter, Felix, 241

Freedmen's Bureau, 96–97, 102

Freeman, A. D., 149

Freud, Sigmund, 13

Freund, Arthur J., 257

Fuller, Melville, 154–155

Gaines, E. P., 42

Galway, Ireland, 26–28

Gantt, Benjamin Geary, 246

Gardner, Mills, 141

Garland, A. B., Jr., 136

Garrison, William Lloyd, 74

Garza, Agistin S., 177

Gender and lynching, 3, 6–9, 10–11, 15–16, 20–22, 76–77, 78–79, 107, 140–151, 196, 198–199, 268–269

George, James Zachariah, 138, 158n4

Gihon, John H., 87

Gilje, Paul, xv

Gordon, Oscar, 155–156

Gordon, Oscar, Jr., 155–156

Goss, Zachariah, lynching victim, 33

Graham, E. A., 136

Graham, Stephen, 197–198

Grant, Anthony, lynching victim, 1

Grant, Silas, lynching victim, 1

Grant, Ulysses S., reports on lynching, 96–97, 99

Gray, J. M., 122

Greeley, Horace, 75–76

Green, John, 229

Greenville, South Carolina, 249–254

About the Editor

Christopher Waldrep is Jamie and Phyllis Pasker Professor of History at San Francisco State University. He is the author of *Roots of Disorder: Race and Criminal Justice in the American South, 1817–1880* and *The Many Faces of Judge Lynch: Extralegal Violence and Punishment in America,* among others. He lives in Martinez, California, with his wife, Pamela, and their two daughters, Janelle and Andrea.

CPSIA information can be obtained
at www.ICGtesting.com
Printed in the USA
LVHW010418050921
696998LV00007B/592